Adaptive

THE FIRST AND ONLY **ADAPTIVE READING EXPERIENCE** DESIGNED TO TRANSFORM THE WAY STUDENTS READ

> More students earn **A's** and **B's** when they use McGraw-Hill Education **Adaptive** products.

SmartBook®

Proven to help students improve grades and study more efficiently, SmartBook contains the same content within the print book, but actively tailors that content to the needs of the individual. SmartBook's adaptive technology provides precise, personalized instruction on what the student should do next, guiding the student to master and remember key concepts, targeting gaps in knowledge and offering customized feedback, driving the student toward comprehension and retention of the subject matter. Available on smartphones and tablets, SmartBook puts learning at the student's fingertips—anywhere, anytime.

> Over **4 billion questions** have been answered, making McGraw-Hill Education products more intelligent, reliable, and precise.

STUDENTS WANT

Mc Graw Hill Education **SMARTBOOK®**

95% of students reported **SmartBook** to be a more effective way of reading material

100% of students want to use the Practice Quiz feature available within **SmartBook** to help them study

100% of students reported having reliable access to off-campus wifi

90% of students say they would purchase **SmartBook** over print alone

95% reported that **SmartBook** would impact their study skills in a positive way

Mc Graw Hill Education

*Findings based on a 2015 focus group survey at Pellissippi State Community College administered by McGraw-Hill Education

POWER Learning

Foundations of Student Success

SECOND EDITION

Robert S. Feldman
University of Massachusetts Amherst

P.O.W.E.R. LEARNING: FOUNDATIONS OF STUDENT SUCCESS, SECOND EDITION

1 2 3 4 5 6 7 8 9 0 RMN/RMN 1 0 9 8 7 6

ISBN 978-0-07-784214-7 (student edition)
MHID 0-07-784214-6 (student edition)
ISBN 978-1-259-69913-9 (annotated instructor's edition)
MHID 1-259-69913-7 (annotated instructor's edition)

Senior Vice President, Products & Markets: *Kurt L. Strand*
Vice President, General Manager, Products & Markets: *Michael Ryan*
Vice President, Content Design & Delivery: *Kimberly Meriwether David*
Director: *Scott Davidson*
Director, Product Development: *Meghan Campbell*
Executive Director of Development: *Ann Torbert*
Executive Marketing Manager: *Keari Green*
Product Developer: *David Ploskonka*
Digital Product Developer: *Kevin White*
Digital Product Analyst: *Thuan Vinh*
Senior Director, Content Design & Delivery: *Terri Schiesl*
Executive Program Manager: *Mary Conzachi*
Senior Content Project Manager: *Danielle Clement*
Senior Buyer: *Sandy Ludovissy*
Senior Designer: *Debra Kubiak*
Senior Content Licensing Specialist (Image): *Shawntel Schmitt*
Content Licensing Specialist (Text): *Lori Slattery*
Cover Image: © *Paul Bradbury/Getty Images*
Typeface: *11/13 STIX Mathjax Main*
Compositor: *SPi Global*
Printer: *R. R. Donnelley*

Library of Congress Cataloging-in-Publication Data
Names: Feldman, Robert S. (Robert Stephen), 1947- author.
Title: P.O.W.E.R. learning : foundations of student success / Robert S.
    Feldman.
Other titles: POWER learning
Description: Second edition. | New York, NY : McGraw-Hill Education, [2017]
Identifiers: LCCN 2015047126 | ISBN 9780077842147 (alk. paper)
Subjects: LCSH: College student orientation. | Study skills. | Life skills. |
    Success.
Classification: LCC LB2343.3 .F439 2017 | DDC 378.1/98—dc23
LC record available at http://lccn.loc.gov/2015047126

Dedication

To my students, who make teaching a joy.

ROBERT S. FELDMAN

Bob Feldman still remembers those moments of being overwhelmed when he started college at Wesleyan University. "I wondered whether I was up to the challenges that faced me," he recalls, "and—although I never would have admitted it at the time—I really had no idea what it took to be successful at college."

That experience, along with his encounters with many students during his own teaching career, led to a life-long interest in helping students navigate the critical transition that they face at the start of their own college careers. Professor Feldman, who went on to receive a doctorate in psychology from the University of Wisconsin–Madison, is now Deputy Chancellor and Professor of Psychological and Brain Sciences at the University of Massachusetts Amherst. He is founding director of *POWER Up for Student Success,* the first-year experience course for incoming students.

Professor Feldman's proudest professional accomplishment is winning the College Outstanding Teaching Award at UMass. He also has been named a Hewlett Teaching Fellow and was Senior Online Instruction Fellow. He has taught courses at Mount Holyoke College, Wesleyan University, and Virginia Commonwealth University.

Professor Feldman is a Fellow of the American Psychological Association, the Association for Psychological Science, and the American Association for the Advancement of Science. He is a winner of a Fulbright Senior Research Scholar and Lecturer award and has written over 200 scientific articles, book chapters, and books. His books, some of which have been translated into Spanish, French, Portuguese, Dutch, Japanese, and Chinese, include *Improving the First Year of College: Research and Practice; Understanding Psychology,* 12/e; and *Development Across the Life Span,* 7/e. His research interests encompass the study of honesty and truthfulness in everyday life, development of nonverbal behavior in children, and the social psychology of education. His research has been supported by grants from the National Institute of Mental Health and the National Institute on Disabilities and Rehabilitation Research.

With the last of his three children completing college, Professor Feldman occupies his spare time with pretty decent cooking and earnest, but admittedly unpolished, piano playing. He also loves to travel. He lives with his wife, who is an educational psychologist, in a home overlooking the Holyoke mountain range in western Massachusetts.

Brief Table of Contents

Table of Contents

3 Taking Notes   58

4 Taking Tests   81

5 Reading and Remembering

109

6 Choosing Your Courses and Academic Program

136

8 Transfer Strategies: Making the Leap from Community College to a Four-Year School

9 Diversity and Relationships

12 Careers

In the first edition of *P.O.W.E.R. Learning*—the book on which this text is based—I wrote about Mark Johnson, a student whom I encountered early in my teaching career. Smart, articulate, and likable, he certainly wanted to succeed in college, and he seemed every bit as capable as those students who were doing quite well. Yet Mark was a marginal student, someone who allowed multiple opportunities to succeed to pass him by. Although he clearly had the talent necessary to be successful in college—and ultimately in life—he lacked the skills to make use of his talents.

Over the years, I encountered other students like Mark. I began to wonder: Was there a way to teach *every* student how to succeed, both academically and beyond the classroom? *P.O.W.E.R. Learning: Foundations of Student Success* embodies the answer to this question.

Written for instructors who wanted a briefer text and one that would work particularly well at colleges with shorter programs of study, *P.O.W.E.R. Learning: Foundations of Student Success* is based on the conviction that *good students are made, not born*. The central message is that students can be successful in college and later in their careers if they follow the basic principles and strategies presented in this book.

This text is designed to be used by students in courses that promote student success. For many students, the first-year experience course is a literal lifeline. It provides the means to learn what it takes to achieve academic success and to make a positive social adjustment to the campus community.

I wrote *P.O.W.E.R. Learning: Foundations of Student Success* because no existing text provided a systematic framework that could be applied in a variety of topical areas and that would help students to develop learning and problem-solving strategies that would work effectively both in and out of the classroom. The book is an outgrowth of my experience as a college instructor, most of it involving first-year students, combined with my research on the factors that influence learning.

Judging from the response to the earlier versions of this book—now in use at hundreds of colleges and universities around the world, and translated into languages ranging from Chinese to Spanish—the approach embodied in the book resonates with the philosophy and experience of many educators. Specifically, the text provides a framework that students can begin to use immediately to become more effective students. That framework is designed to be

▶ Clear, easy to grasp, logical, and compelling, so that students can readily see its merits.

▶ Effective for a variety of student learning styles—as well as a variety of teaching styles.

▶ Workable within a variety of course formats and for supplemental instruction.

▶ Valuable for use in learning communities.

▶ Transferable to settings ranging from the classroom to the dorm room to the board room.

▶ Effective in addressing both the mind *and* the spirit, presenting cognitive strategies and skills, while engaging the natural enthusiasm, motivation, and inclination to succeed that students carry within them.

Based on comprehensive, detailed feedback obtained from both instructors and students, *P.O.W.E.R. Learning: Foundations of Student Success* meets these aims. The book will help students confront and master the numerous challenges of the college experience through use of the P.O.W.E.R. learning approach, embodied in the five steps of the acronym *P.O.W.E.R.* (*P*repare, *O*rganize, *W*ork, *E*valuate, and *R*ethink). Using simple—yet effective—principles, *P.O.W.E.R. Learning: Foundations of Student Success* teaches the skills needed to succeed in college and careers beyond.

The Goals of *P.O.W.E.R. Learning: Foundations of Student Success, 2e*

P.O.W.E.R Learning addresses five major goals:

▶ **To provide a systematic framework for organizing the strategies that lead to success in the classroom and careers:** First and foremost, the book provides a systematic, balanced presentation of the skills required to achieve student and career success. Using the *P.O.W.E.R.* framework and relying on proven strategies, *P.O.W.E.R. Learning: Foundations of Student Success* provides specific, hands-on techniques for achieving success as a student.

▶ **To offer a wide range of skill-building opportunities:** *P.O.W.E.R. Learning: Foundations of Student Success* provides a wealth of specific exercises, diagnostic questionnaires, case studies, and journal writing activities to help students to develop and master the skills and techniques they need to become effective learners and problem solvers. *Readers learn by doing.*

▶ **To demonstrate the connection between academic success and career success:** Stressing the importance of *self-reliance* and *self-accountability,* the book demonstrates that the skills required to be a successful student are tied to career and personal success as well.

▶ **To develop critical thinking skills:** Whether to evaluate the quality of information found on the Internet or in other types of media, or to judge the merits of a position taken by a friend, colleague, or politician, the ability to think critically is more important than ever in this age of information. Through frequent questionnaires, exercises, journal activities, and guided group work, *P.O.W.E.R. Learning: Foundations of Student Success* helps students to develop their capacity to think critically.

▶ **To provide an engaging, accessible, and meaningful presentation:** The fifth goal of this book underlies the first four: to write a student-friendly book that is relevant to the needs and interests of its readers and that will promote enthusiasm and interest in the process of becoming a successful student. Learning the strategies needed to become a more effective student should be a stimulating and fulfilling experience. Realizing that these strategies are valuable outside the classroom as well will provide students with an added incentive to master them.

In short, *P.O.W.E.R. Learning: Foundations of Student Success* gives students a sense of mastery and success as they read the book and work through its exercises. It is meant to engage and nurture students' minds and spirits, stimulating their intellectual curiosity about the world and planting a seed that will grow throughout their lifetime.

Changes That Make a Difference: New to the Second Edition

The valuable input we have received from **P.O.W.E.R. Learning**'s reviewers, along with the feedback from the tens of thousands of students and the hundreds of instructors who used the prior editions, and classroom testing, have resulted in the addition of new and updated information, reflecting advances in our understanding of what makes students successful and changes in college instruction. The following sample of new and revised topics provides a good indication of the book's currency:

CHAPTER 1—P.O.W.E.R. LEARNING: BECOMING AN EXPERT STUDENT
- ▶ New material on "Growth Mindset"
- ▶ Activities optimized for Connect

CHAPTER 2—MAKING THE MOST OF YOUR TIME
- ▶ Material reorganized to balance section length
- ▶ Revised material on procrastination and balancing school and life, including childcare demands and eldercare demands

CHAPTER 3—TAKING NOTES
- ▶ Material reorganized to balance section length
- ▶ New material on Strategies for Using Your Notes

CHAPTER 4—TAKING TESTS
- ▶ Material reorganized to balance section length and increase clarity
- ▶ New material covering digital study groups and online classes
- ▶ Activities optimized for Connect

CHAPTER 5—READING AND REMEMBERING
- ▶ Content on Reading and Memory combined into a single chapter and updated, strengthening coverage of both topics
- ▶ Activities optimized for Connect

CHAPTER 6—CHOOSING YOUR COURSES AND ACADEMIC PROGRAM
- ▶ Material reorganized to balance section length
- ▶ Activities optimized for Connect
- ▶ Updates to factor in new job market data and school options

CHAPTER 7—TECHNOLOGY AND INFORMATION COMPETENCY
- ▶ Material reorganized to balance section length and clarity
- ▶ Section expanded on Evaluating the Information You Find on the Web

- ▸ New and revised material on Distance Learning and Online Classes
- ▸ New material on Social Media Etiquette and Personal Brand Management
- ▸ Updates for current technology and security

CHAPTER 8—TRANSFER STRATEGIES

- ▸ Updates to data pertaining to degrees and job salaries

CHAPTER 9—DIVERSITY AND RELATIONSHIPS

- ▸ Material reorganized to balance section length and clarity
- ▸ Material on Diversity expanded

CHAPTER 10—MONEY MATTERS

- ▸ Reorganized to prioritize Building a Financial Philosophy
- ▸ Content on Credit Cards updated
- ▸ Activities optimized for Connect
- ▸ College funding information updated

CHAPTER 11—JUGGLING: STRESS, FAMILY, AND WORK

- ▸ Reorganized to create sections on Physical Health and Mental Health
- ▸ Activities optimized for Connect
- ▸ Material in Keeping Well expanded

CHAPTER 12—CAREERS

- ▸ Data on occupations updated
- ▸ Coverage of Resumes and Cover Letters updated

More than ever before, the concept of "student" is changing. The idea that a student encompasses a cross-section of 18-year-olds attending a four-year university no longer applies as universally as it once did.

Students are also

Employees
Employers
Co-workers
Parents
Friends
Siblings
Little League coaches
Taxi drivers
Overworked
Overcommitted
Overwhelmed

The list can probably go on from there. What else are you?

The purpose of this text is to take the P.O.W.E.R. framework, which has been proven effective, and apply it to a different type of student. While understanding your own study habits is important, how to study in a dorm is not information that every student needs. Just as our ideas of students are evolving, so can the texts that serve them.

We want all students to understand what it takes to be successful in school, life, and career. By providing a context that applies to students in a variety of educational models, we can better foster connections between the classroom and the professional arena. The educational conversation this text facilitates should speak to students who are more than just . . . students.

Succeed Now

School + Career + Life

Text Features: Achieving P.O.W.E.R. the Goals of Learning

P.O.W.E.R. Learning provides a systematic framework for organizing the strategies that lead to success

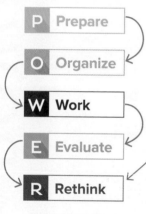

P.O.W.E.R. Plan
- **P** Prepare
- **O** Organize
- **W** Work
- **E** Evaluate
- **R** Rethink

Each chapter utilizes the principles of the **P.O.W.E.R. system (Prepare, Organize, Work, Evaluate, and Rethink),** so students can clearly see how easy it is to incorporate this effective process into their everyday routine. The P.O.W.E.R. Plan illustration highlights the key steps for the corresponding chapter material.

The goals of *P.O.W.E.R. Learning: Foundations of Student Success* are achieved through a consistent, carefully devised set of features common to every chapter. Students and faculty endorsed each of these elements.

Handy, updated **reference charts** appear throughout the text for quickly accessing and organizing important material.

Weekly Timetable

Week of: _____ Week #: _____

	Mon	Tues	Wed	Thurs	Fri	Sat	Sun
6–7 a.m.							
7–8 a.m.							
8–9 a.m.							
9–10 a.m.							
10–11 a.m.							
11–12 (noon)							
12 (noon)–1 p.m.							
1–2 p.m.							
2–3 p.m.							
3–4 p.m.							
4–5 p.m.							
5–6 p.m.							
6–7 p.m.							
7–8 p.m.							
8–9 p.m.							
9–10 p.m.							
10–11 p.m.							
11 p.m.–12 (midnight)							
12 (midnight)–1 a.m.							
1–2 a.m.							
2–3 a.m.							
3–4 a.m.							
4–5 a.m.							
5–6 a.m.							

figure 2.3
Weekly Timetable
Make a single copy of this blank timetable. Then fill in your regular, predictable time commitments. Next, make as many copies as you need to cover each week of the term. Then, for each week, fill in the date on the left and the number of the week in the term on the right, and add in your irregular commitments.

But every minute you invest now in organizing your time will pay off in hours that you will save in the future.
Follow these steps in completing your schedule:

▶ **Start with the master calendar, which shows all the weeks of the term on one page.** Work on the master calendar every class assignment you have for the entire term, noting it on the date that it is due. Also include major events at work, such as days when you might need to work overtime. In addition, include important activities from your personal life, drawn from your list of priorities. For instance, if your spouse or child has a performance or sporting event you want to attend, be sure to mark it down.

---

table 4.3   Action Words for Essays

These words are commonly used in essay questions. Learning the distinctions among them will help you answer essay questions effectively.

Analyze: Examine and break into component parts.

Clarify: Explain with significant detail.

Compare: Describe and explain similarities.

Compare and contrast: Describe and explain similarities and differences.

Contrast: Describe and explain differences.

Critique: Judge and analyze, explaining what is wrong—and right—about a concept.

Define: Provide the meaning.

Discuss: Explain, review, and consider.

Enumerate: Provide a listing of ideas, concepts, reasons, items, etc.

Evaluate: Provide pros and cons of something; provide an opinion and justify it.

Explain: Give reasons why or how; clarify, justify, and illustrate.

Illustrate: Provide examples; show instances.

Interpret: Explain the meaning of something.

Justify: Explain why a concept can be supported, typically by using examples and other types of support.

Outline: Provide an overarching framework or explanation—usually in narrative form—of a concept, idea, event, or phenomenon.

Prove: Using evidence and arguments, convince the reader of a particular point.

Relate: Show how things fit together; provide analogies.

Review: Describe or summarize, often with an evaluation.

State: Assert or explain.

Summarize: Provide a condensed, precise list or narrative.

Trace: Track or sketch out how events or circumstances have evolved; provide a history or timeline.

which are more free-form and may have several possible answers, short-answer and fill-in questions are usually quite specific, requiring only one answer.
Use both the instructions for the questions and the questions themselves to determine the level of specificity that is needed in an answer. Try not to provide too much or too little information. Usually, brevity is best.

▶ **Multiple-choice questions.** If you've ever looked at a multiple-choice question and said to yourself, "But every choice seems right," you understand what can be tricky about this type of question. However, there are some simple strategies that can help you deal with multiple-choice questions.

P.O.W.E.R. Learning offers a wide range of skill-building opportunities

Every chapter offers numerous Try It! activities for gaining hands-on experience with the material covered in the chapter. These include questionnaires, self-assessments, and group exercises to do with classmates.

---

1 | Try It! P O W E R

Determine the Diversity of Your Community

Try to assess the degree of diversity that exists in your community. *Community* can be a loosely defined term, but for this Try It! think of it as the group of people you encounter and interact with on a regular basis. When thinking of diversity, remember to include the many different ways in which people can be different from one another, including race, ethnicity, culture, sexual orientation, physical challenges, and so on.

1. List all of the groups in your community. Overall, how diverse would you say your community is?

2. Are there organizations in your community that promote diversity or work to raise the visibility and understanding of particular groups?

3. How diverse is your college's student body in terms of different racial, ethnic, or cultural groups? (You may be able to find statistics for this on your college's website.)

4. Is your college community more or less diverse than your community at large? Why do you think this might be?

5. How does the diversity in your community compare to the following statistics for the United States (as of the 2010 census)? White, 72 percent; Hispanic or Latino, 16 percent; black or African American, 13 percent; Asian, 5 percent; two or more races, 3 percent; American Indian and Alaska Native, .9 percent; Native Hawaiian and other Pacific Islander, .2 percent; other race, 6 percent. (Note: These percentages add up to more than 100 percent because Hispanics may be of any race and are therefore counted under more than one category.)

Every chapter includes an updated list of the three types of **resources** that are useful in finding and utilizing information relevant to the chapter: on-campus resources, books, and websites. This material helps students study and retain important concepts presented in the chapter, as well as guides future inquiry.

[RESOURCES]

AT SCHOOL

Anyone who feels he or she is facing discrimination based on race, gender, ethnic status, sexual orientation, or national origin should contact a college official *immediately*. Sometimes there is a specific office that handles such complaints. If you don't know which campus official to contact, speak to your academic advisor or someone in the dean's office and you'll be directed to the appropriate person. The important thing is to act and not to suffer in silence. Discrimination not only is immoral, but is against the law.

Course Connections

Staying Alert in Class

If you're having trouble staying alert and—even worse—staying awake in class, the best solution is to get more sleep. Short of that, there are several strategies you can try to help you stay awake:

- Throw yourself into the class. Pay close attention, take notes, ask questions, and generally be fully engaged in the class. You should do this anyway, but making a special effort when you're exhausted can get you through a period of fatigue.
- Sit up straight. Pinch yourself. Stretch the muscles in different parts of your body. Fidget. Any activity will help you thwart fatigue and feel more alert.
- Eat or drink something cold in class (if your school and instructor permit it). The mere activity of eating a snack or drinking can help you stay awake.
- Avoid heavy meals before class. Your body's natural reaction to a full stomach is to call for a nap—the opposite of what you want to achieve.
- Stay cool. Take off your coat or jacket and sit by an open window. If it's warm, ask your instructor if there's a way to make the classroom cooler.
- Take off *one* shoe. This creates a temperature difference, which can be helpful in keeping you awake.

Every chapter includes a **Course Connections** box that shows students how to use the chapter's content to maximize their success in particular classes.

The goals of *P.O.W.E.R. Learning: Foundations of Student Success* are achieved through a consistent, carefully devised set of features common to every chapter. Students and faculty endorsed each of these elements.

P.O.W.E.R. *Learning* demonstrates the connection between academic success and success beyond the classroom

The **Career Connections** feature links the material in the chapter to the world of work, demonstrating how the strategies discussed in the chapter are related to career choices and success in the workplace.

Career Connections

Choosing a Job That's Right for You

It's a question no family member can resist asking, and one that you've probably asked yourself: What kind of work are you going to do when you graduate?

Happily, it's a question you don't have to answer, at least not yet. Although some students know from their first day in college what they want to do (and actually choose their college on that basis), many—perhaps most—don't decide on a career path until late in their academic career.

And that's fine. After all, one of the reasons you are in college is to expose yourself to the universe of knowledge. In one sense, keeping your options open is a wise course. You don't want to prematurely narrow your options and discard possibilities too early. And even if you're quite sure in your choice of careers, it doesn't hurt to explore new possibilities.

In the Career Connections features in previous chapters, we've discussed various strategies for exploring future professions. Here, in summary, are some steps to take to identify a career:

1. **Clarify the goal of your search.** There's no single perfect career choice. Some people search for the ideal career, assuming that they need to identify the one and only career for which they have been destined. The reality is that there are many careers they could choose that would make them equally happy and satisfied.

   Start with what you already know about yourself. You've already done a lot of mental work toward narrowing down a profession. Do you hate the sight of blood? Then you're probably well aware you're not cut out to be a nurse or veterinary assistant. Does the sight of a column of numbers bring an immediate yawn? Count out accounting and statistics.

   Awareness of your likes and dislikes already puts you on the road to identifying a future career. Knowing what you don't want to do helps identify what you do want to do and narrows down the kinds of occupations for which you're more suited.

2. **Gather information.** The more you know about potential careers, the better. Examine career-planning materials, read industry profiles, and visit relevant websites (such as the excellent Department of Labor site at **www.bls.gov/oco/**). Talk with career counselors. Discuss your options with people who work in professions in which you're interested. Find out how they chose their career, how they got their current job, and what advice they have for you.

   In addition, consider participating in an internship in a profession that you think might be attractive. *Internships* are off-campus, temporary work situations that permit you to obtain experience in a particular field. They are not always paid, but in many cases they can substitute for a course. For example, you might be able to receive three college credits for spending 10 hours a week at a work site during the course of a term.

   Internships are an excellent way to learn about a profession, up close and personal. Working as an intern will let you know the kinds of things employees do on a day-to-day basis and the responsibilities and duties of the profession you're interested in. You can gain experiences that you would not be able to get on campus.

3. **Narrow down your choices.** Once you've gathered enough information to give yourself a reasonable comfort level, narrow down the choices. If it's early in your college career, you don't need to make up your mind. If it's late and you feel the pressure to choose, then make the decision. Just do it. Remember, there's no single, absolutely correct decision; there are many right decisions.

   Whatever it is you ultimately choose as a career, think of it only as a first step. As the average life span continues to lengthen due to advances in medical technology, most people will pass through several careers during the course of their lives. By periodically taking stock of where you are and considering your goals, you'll be in a position to make career changes that bring you closer to your ideal.

Speaking *of* Success

Source: Courtesy of C'Ardiss Gardner

NAME:	**C'Ardiss Gardner**
SCHOOL:	**South Seattle Community College**
HOME:	**Seattle, Washington**

When C'Ardiss Gardner began college, she was already familiar with challenge. She became a mother at age 16 and chose to finish high school while working two jobs to support her infant.

Despite the challenges, Gardner not only finished her high school requirements early but also had enough credits to start at the local community college. When she started at South Seattle Community College, not only was she taking classes, but she was working two part-time jobs. But eventually, she was forced to delay her college plans to take a third job to support herself. For three years she juggled work and child rearing.

But Gardner also had plans. She got married and reenrolled at South Seattle. After graduating with her associate's degree, she was accepted to four-year colleges around the country. She decided to move her family to the East Coast to attend Yale University. Gardner graduated from Yale with a B.A. in African-American Studies. She and her family returned to Seattle, where she now is raising three children, working as the registrar of a prep school, and studying for a master's degree in education at Seattle University.

"Attending school as an African-American student with a small child was very challenging. I did not come from a community that supported or encouraged kids like me to go to college," said Gardner.

"Even something as simple as writing was enough to set me apart from the other students, who had spent years learning how to write at a college level. I had to learn those things, and it was very difficult," she noted. "One of the most important things I learned was to access as many resources as I could to help learn skills I was lacking. Professors offered help by reading my drafts before I turned essays or papers in. By accepting help, I was able to improve my writing skills and improve my grades."

The skills Gardner developed while at South Seattle Community College laid the groundwork for her future academic success and became the foundation upon which she has been able to build the rest of her life. Not only has she been able to continue her education, but she plans to use her skills to help pave the way for other students to access education.

[RETHINK]
- How do you think Gardner's reading skills helped her achieve her academic successes?
- What types of resources do you think Gardner accessed to help her develop learning skills?

Many new **Speaking of Success** articles have been added that profile real-life success stories. Some of these people are well-known individuals, whereas others are current students or recent graduates who have overcome academic difficulties to achieve success. In addition, **critical thinking questions** end each **Speaking of Success** profile.

From the Perspective of . . . This feature highlights how the lessons learned in this course impact you both now and in your future career. Created to show the correlation between academic and professional life, these features answer the question of why this course matters and how it will impact student growth long after graduation.

From the perspective of . . .

A STUDENT Time logs can be helpful tools when determining how you spend your time; they can also help you find more time for the activities you enjoy doing. What areas of your life do you wish you had more time to spend on?

≫LO2-2 Set Your Priorities

By this point you should have a good idea of what's taking up your time. But you may not know what you should be doing instead.

To figure out the best use of your time, you need to determine your priorities. **Priorities** are the tasks and activities you need and want to do, rank-ordered from most important to least important. There are no right or wrong priorities; you have to decide for yourself what you wish to accomplish. Maybe spending time on your studies is most important to you, or working to earn more money, or maybe your top priority is spending time with your family. Only you can decide. Furthermore, what's

priorities
The tasks and activities that one needs and wants to do, rank-ordered from most important to least important.

Source: © Richard Drury/ Photodisc/Getty Images

P.O.W.E.R. Learning helps you develop critical thinking skills

The growing number of military veterans entering college is reflected in the text. Emphasis on their unique situation and transition into academic life is highlighted.

posttraumatic stress disorder (PTSD)
A psychological disorder in which a highly stressful event has long-lasting consequences that may include reexperiencing the event in vivid flashbacks or dreams.

Multitask. Don't draw strict limits regarding what you do and when. If you have a free 20 minutes at your job, use the time to catch up on reading for classes. When your children are napping, see if there is work for your job you can accomplish at home. You don't want to fill every spare minute with work, but you want to take advantage of the gaps in your hectic day.

Posttraumatic Stress Disorder (PTSD)

Some students who have been exposed to severe personal stressors experience **posttraumatic stress disorder**, or **PTSD**, in which a highly stressful event has

Journal Reflections

My Reading Preferences

Think about what you like and don't like to read by answering these questions.

1. Do you read for pleasure? If so, what do you read (e.g., magazines, newspapers, novels, humor, short stories, nonfiction, illustrated books)?

2. What makes a book enjoyable? Have you ever read a book that you "couldn't put down"? If so, what made it so good?

3. What is the most difficult book you are reading this semester? Why is it difficult? Are you enjoying it?

4. Think about when you read for pleasure compared with when you read material for a class. How does the way you read differ between the two types of material?

5. How well do you remember the last book or magazine you read for pleasure? Do you remember it better than your last college reading assignment? Why do you think this might be?

The **Journal Reflections** feature provides students with the opportunity to keep an ongoing journal, making entries relevant to the chapter content. Students are asked to reflect and think critically about related prior experiences. These conclude with questions designed to elicit critical thinking and exploration.

The Case of . . .
The Way He Studies

Roger Chen is working on his degree in criminal justice. He always begins a reading assignment by looking over the learning objectives for that day's chapter, something his professor stresses. Then he begins reading, using a highlighter to underline the important stuff, usually about every third sentence. He studies with headphones on because he read somewhere that music improves your concentration. And he usually has a basketball game on his laptop—no sound—which he checks every time he finishes reading a page or two. He likes to draw arrows from tables and charts to the material they represent. In fact, he likes to doodle. His margins are filled with definitions of key terms and lots of pictures of dragons. Roger is not big on note cards or writing notes outside the book. "Keep it simple" is his motto. Right before a test, he skims through the highlighted material and looks over the charts and tables. He sometimes gives himself a short quiz aloud on the key words of the chapter. Roger does okay. He never fails a test, but he never gets more than a low B either.

1. What study techniques is Roger using that can help him understand and retain the material? How would you advise him to make the most of the techniques he's using?

2. What should Roger change to make his study habits more effective and efficient?

3. What new study techniques would you suggest to Roger to improve his performance in his courses?

4. What techniques might Roger use to memorize long lists or other key material from his reading?

5. How might Roger effectively use writing as a way to stay focused on his reading?

Each chapter ends with a **case study (The Case of . . .)** to which the principles described in the chapter can be applied. Case studies are based on situations that students might themselves encounter. Each case provides a series of questions that encourage students to consider what they've learned and to use critical thinking skills in responding to these questions.

P.O.W.E.R. Learning provides an engaging, accessible, and meaningful presentation

An appealing design and visual presentation highlight large, clear photos carefully selected to show the diversity of students as well as the latest in technological aids and devices.

Chapter-opening scenarios describe an individual grappling with a situation that is relevant to the subject matter of the chapter. Readers will be able to relate to these vignettes, which feature students running behind schedule, figuring out a way to keep up with reading assignments, or facing a long list of vocabulary words to memorize.

Key terms appear in boldface in the text and are defined in a hyperlink to the glossary. In addition, they are listed in a **Key Terms and Concepts** section at the end of the chapter.

Learning Outcomes

By the time you finish this chapter you will be able to

» LO 4-1   Identify the kinds of tests you will encounter in college.

» LO 4-2   Explain the best ways to prepare for and take various kinds of tests.

» LO 4-3   Analyze the best strategies for answering specific kinds of test questions.

CHAPTER **4**

Taking Tests

Source © Blend Images - Hill Street Studios/Brand X Pictures/Getty Images

Looking Ahead

Although many tests are not as critical as Chandra Farris's algebra final, tests do play a significant role in everyone's academic life. Students typically experience more anxiety over tests than over anything else in their college careers. If you're returning to college after a long break, or perhaps struggled with tests earlier in your academic career, you may find the prospect of taking a test especially intimidating.

But tests don't have to be so anxiety producing. There are strategies and techniques you can learn to reduce your fear of test taking. In fact, learning how to take tests is in some ways as important as learning the content that they cover. Taking tests effectively does not just involve mastering information; it also requires mastering specific test-taking skills.

One of the most important goals of this chapter is to take the mystery out of the whole process of taking tests. To do that, you'll learn about the different types of tests and strategies you can start using even before you take a test. You'll gain insight into how different kinds of tests work and how best to approach them, and you'll also learn about the various types of test questions and strategies for responding most effectively to each type.

This chapter also explores two aspects of test taking that may affect your performance: test anxiety and cramming. You will learn ways to deal with your anxiety and keep cramming to a minimum—but you will also learn how to make the most of cramming, if you do have to resort to it.

The chapter ends with suggestions for evaluating your performance toward the end of a test and for using what you learn to improve your performance the next time around.

» LO 4-1   Getting Ready

Tests may be the most unpopular part of college life. Students hate them because they produce fear, anxiety, apprehension about being evaluated, and a focus on grades instead of learning for learning's sake. Instructors often don't like them very much either, because they produce fear, anxiety, apprehension about being evaluated, and a focus on grades instead of learning for learning's sake. That's right: Students and instructors dislike tests for the very same reasons.

But tests are also valuable. A well-constructed test identifies what you know and what you still need to learn. Tests help you see how your performance compares with that of others. And knowing that you'll be tested on a body of material is certainly likely to motivate you to learn that material more thoroughly.

[**KEY TERMS AND CONCEPTS**]

Academic honesty (p. 99)	Educated guessing (p. 98)	Study groups (p. 90)
Cramming (p. 91)	Plagiarism (p. 99)	Test anxiety (p. 87)

All of these reviewed and tested features are designed not only to help students understand, practice, and master the core concepts presented in this text, but also to collectively support the main goals and vision of this text, as demonstrated here:

The P.O.W.E.R. Resources

The same philosophy and goals that guided the writing of *P.O.W.E.R. Learning: Foundations of Student Success* led to the development of a comprehensive teaching package. Through a series of focus groups, questionnaires, and surveys, we asked instructors what they needed to optimize their courses. We also analyzed what other publishers provided to make sure that the ancillary materials accompanying *P.O.W.E.R. Learning: Foundations of Student Success* would surpass the level of support to which instructors are accustomed. As a result of the extensive research that went into devising the teaching resources, we are confident that whether you are an instructor with years of experience or are teaching the course for the first time, this book's instructional package will enhance classroom instruction and provide guidance as you prepare for and teach the course.

Print Resources

ANNOTATED INSTRUCTOR'S EDITION

The Annotated Instructor's Edition (AIE), prepared by Joni Webb Petschauer and Cindy Wallace of Appalachian State University, contains the full text of the student edition of the book with the addition of notes that provide a rich variety of teaching strategies, discussion prompts, and helpful cross-references to the Instructor's Resource Manual. The AIE has been completely redesigned in an effort to provide more frontline teaching assistance.

INSTRUCTOR'S RESOURCE MANUAL

Written by Joni Webb Petschauer and Cindy Wallace of Appalachian State University with additional contributions from experienced instructors across the country, this manual provides specific suggestions for teaching each topic, tips on implementing a first-year experience program, handouts to generate creative classroom activities, audiovisual resources, sample syllabi, and tips on incorporating the Internet into the course.

CUSTOMIZE YOUR TEXT

P.O.W.E.R. Learning: Foundations of Student Success can be customized to suit your needs. The text can be abbreviated for shorter courses and can be expanded to include semester schedules, campus maps, additional essays, activities, or exercises, along with other materials specific to your curriculum or situation. Chapters designed for student athletes, transferring students, and career preparation are also available.

Human Resources

WORKSHOPS WITH AUTHOR AND AUTHOR TEAM

Are you faced with the challenge of launching a first-year experience course on your campus? Would you like to invigorate your college success program, incorporating the most recent pedagogical and technological innovations? Is faculty recruitment an obstacle to the success of your program? Are you interested in learning more about the P.O.W.E.R. system?

Workshops are available on these and many other subjects for anyone conducting or even just considering a first-year experience program. Led by author Robert

Feldman; *P.O.W.E.R. Learning: Foundations of Student Success* Instructor's Resource Manual authors Joni Webb Petschauer and Cindy Wallace; or one of the McGraw-Hill P.O.W.E.R. Learning consultants, each workshop is tailored to the needs of individual campuses or programs. For more information, contact your local representative, or e-mail us at student.success@mheducation.com.

Digital Resources

LASSI: LEARNING AND STUDY STRATEGIES INVENTORY

The LASSI is a 10-scale, 80-item assessment of students' awareness about and use of learning and study strategies related to skill, will, and self-regulation components of strategic learning. The focus is on both covert and overt thoughts, behaviors, attitudes, and beliefs that relate to successful learning and that can be altered through educational interventions. Research has repeatedly demonstrated that these factors contribute significantly to success in college and that they can be learned or enhanced through educational interventions.

The LASSI is available in print or online at **www.hhpublishing.com**. Ask your McGraw-Hill sales representative for more details.

IMPLEMENTING A STUDENT SUCCESS COURSE

This innovative web content assists you in developing and sustaining your Student Success course. Features include a "how to" guide for designing and proposing a new course, with easy-to-use templates for determining budget needs and resources. Examples of model programs are provided from two-year, four-year, and career schools. The site explores course goals, such as orientation and retention, and provides research data to support your proposal. Also included are materials to help sustain your course, such as faculty development programs and online resources.

MCGRAW-HILL *CONNECT*®

CONNECT® offers a number of powerful tools and features to make managing assignments easier, so faculty can spend more time teaching. With *Connect,* students can engage with their coursework anytime and anywhere, making the learning process more accessible and efficient.

LEARNSMART

LearnSmart is an adaptive study tool proven to strengthen memory recall, increase class retention, and boost grades. Students are able to study more efficiently because they are made aware of what they know and don't know. Real-time reports quickly identify the concepts that require more attention from individual students—or the entire class.

SMARTBOOK

SmartBook is the first and only adaptive reading experience designed to change the way students read and learn. It creates a personalized reading experience by highlighting the most impactful concepts a student needs to learn at that moment in time. As a student engages with SmartBook, the reading experience continuously adapts by highlighting content based on what the student knows and doesn't know. This ensures that the focus is on the content he or she needs to learn, while simultaneously promoting long-term retention of material. Use SmartBook's real-time reports to quickly identify the concepts that require more attention from individual students—or the entire class. The end result? Students are more engaged with course content, can better prioritize their time, and come to class ready to participate.

MCGRAW-HILL CAMPUS™

McGraw-Hill Campus™ is a new one-stop teaching and learning experience available to users of any learning management system. This institutional service allows faculty and students to enjoy single-sign-on (SSO) access to all McGraw-Hill Higher Education materials, including the award-winning McGraw-Hill *Connect* platform, from directly within the institution's website. McGraw-Hill Campus provides faculty with instant access to teaching materials (e.g., eTextbooks, test banks, PowerPoint slides, animations, and learning objectives), allowing them to browse, search, and use any ancillary content in our vast library. Students enjoy SSO access to a variety of free products (e.g., quizzes, flash cards, narrated presentations) and subscription-based products (e.g., McGraw-Hill *Connect*). With McGraw-Hill Campus, faculty and students will never need to create another account to access McGraw-Hill products.

The POWER to Succeed!

The POWER of Support!

Let the McGraw-Hill Student Success Team support your course with our workshop program.

▶ Planning to develop a first-year experience course from scratch?

▶ Reenergizing your first-year experience course?

▶ Trying to integrate technology in your class?

▶ Exploring the concept of learning communities?

We offer a range of author- and consultant-led workshops that can be tailored to meet the needs of your institution.

Our team of experts, led by *P.O.W.E.R. Learning: Foundations of Student Success* author Robert Feldman, can address issues of course management, assessment, organization, and implementation. How do you get students to commit to your program? How do you achieve support from your institution? How can you evaluate and demonstrate the effectiveness of your first-year experience course? These are questions that every program faces. Let us help you to find an answer that works for you.

Other workshop topics may include

▶ Classroom Strategies for Enhancing Cultural Competence: The P.O.W.E.R. of Diversity

▶ Using Learning Styles in the Classroom

▶ Creating Student Success Courses Online

▶ Motivating Your Students

To schedule a workshop, please contact your local McGraw-Hill representative. Alternately, contact us directly at student.success@mheducation.com to begin the process of bringing a P.O.W.E.R. Learning workshop to you.

The POWER to Create Your Own Text!

Do you want to

▶ Cover only select chapters?

▶ Personalize your book with campus information (maps, schedules, registration materials, etc.)?

▶ Add your own materials, including exercises or assignments?

▶ Address specific student populations, such as student athletes and transferring students?

P.O.W.E.R. Learning: Foundations of Student Success can be customized to suit your needs.*

* Orders must meet our minimum sales unit requirements.

WHY CUSTOMIZE?

Perhaps your course focuses on study skills and you prefer that your text not cover life issues such as money matters, health and wellness, or information on choosing a major. Whatever the reason, we can make it happen, easily. McGraw-Hill Custom Publishing can deliver a book that perfectly meets your needs.

WHAT WILL MY CUSTOM BOOK LOOK LIKE?

Any chapters from the *P.O.W.E.R. Learning: Foundations of Student Success* book that you include will be in full color. Additional materials can be added between chapters or at the beginning or end of the book in black and white. Binding (paperback, three-hole punch, you name it) is up to you. You can even add your own custom cover to reflect your school image.

WHAT CAN I ADD?

Anything! Here are some ideas to get you started:

▶ **Campus map** or anything specific to your school: academic regulations or requirements, syllabi, important phone numbers or dates, library hours.

▶ **Calendars** for the school year, for local theater groups, for a concert series.

▶ **Interviews** with local businesspeople or your school's graduates in which they describe their own challenges and successes.

▶ **Your course syllabus or homework assignments** so your students have everything they need for your course under one cover and you don't have to make copies to hand out.

SPECIAL CHAPTERS DESIGNED FOR THE UNIQUE NEEDS OF YOUR STUDENTS!

Several additional chapters are available for your customized text and have been designed to address the needs of specific student populations.

▶ *Strategies for Success for Student Athletes.* This chapter discusses the unique challenges of student athletes, such as managing school and team pressures, using resources and understanding eligibility, and knowing when and how to ask for help. It also addresses special concerns such as burnout, dealing with injury, and hazing.

▶ *Making Good Decisions.* This chapter focuses on strategies for improving decisions and effective problem solving. In addition, it discusses how to recognize and correct problems that affect critical thinking.

HOW DO I CREATE A CUSTOM BOOK?

The secret to custom publishing is this: Custom Publishing Is Simple!

HERE ARE THE BASIC STEPS:

▶ You select the chapters you would like to use from *P.O.W.E.R. Learning: Foundations of Student Success* with your McGraw-Hill sales representative.

▶ Together, we discuss your preferences for the binding, the cover, etc., and provide you with information on costs.

▶ We assign your customized text an ISBN and your project goes into production. A custom text will typically publish within 6–8 weeks of the order.

▶ Your book is manufactured and it is put into inventory in the McGraw-Hill distribution center.

▶ You are sent a free desk copy of your custom publication.

▶ Your bookstore calls McGraw-Hill's customer service department and orders the text.

You select what you want—we handle the details!

Contact us:

Canada: 1-905-430-5034
United States: 1-800-446-8979
E-mail: student.success@mheducation.com

I am indebted to the many reviewers of *P.O.W.E.R. Learning* who provided input at every step of development of the book and the ancillary package. These dedicated instructors and administrators provided thoughtful, detailed advice, and I am very grateful for their help and insight. They include the following:

Judith Lynch, Kansas State University; Dr. G. Warlock Vance, Randolph Community College; Leah Graham, Broward College; Sara Henson, Central Oregon Community College; Jamie Jensen, Boise State University; Barbara West, Central Georgia Technical College; Pauline Nugent, Missouri State University; Rob Bertram, Bradley University; Anne Knop, Manor College; Ashley Stark, Dickinson State University; Christie Carr, Austin Community College; Andrea Smith, Florida Gateway College; Dale S. Haralson, Hinds Community College; Donna Burton, NC State University; Norman Smith, Eckerd College; Sam Mulberry, Bethel University; Diane Fox, Saint Mary's College; Amy Hassenpflug, Liberty University; Mary Beth Willett, University of Maine; Jennifer Clevenger, Virginia Tech; Heidi Zenie, Three Rivers Community College; Jeffrey Hall, Ashford University; Jennifer Scalzi-Pesola, American River College, Sierra; Jarlene DeCay, Cedar Valley College; Beverly Dile, Elizabethtown Community and Technical College; Linda Girouard, Brescia University; Malinda Mansfield, Ivy Tech Community College; Karline Prophete, Palm Beach State College; Kelley Butler Heartfield, Ivy Tech Community College; Stephen Coates-White, South Seattle College; Erin Wood, Catawba College; Cari Kenner, St. Cloud State University; Amanda Bond, Georgia Military College–Columbus; Alex E. Collins, Miami Dade College; Erik Christensen, South Florida State College; J. Andrew Monahan, Suffolk County Community College; Chad Brooks, Austin Peay State University; Cindy Stewart, Blue Ridge CTC; Sherri Stepp, Marshall University; Amy Colon, SUNY Sullivan; Darla Rocha, San Jacinto College; Suzanne F. Pearl, Miami Dade College, Wolfson Campus; Kalpana Swamy, Santa Fe College; Rebecca Samberg, Housatonic Community College; Jeannette McClendon, Napa Valley College; Jeri O'Bryan-Losee, Morrisville State College; Donna Ragauckas, Santa Fe College; Professor Terry Rae Gamble, Palm Beach State College; Barbara Putman, Southwestern Community College; Nikita Anderson, University of Baltimore; Maria Christian, Oklahoma State University Institute of Technology; Alexandra Lis, Miami Dade College, Kendall Campus; Kim Cobb, West Virginia State University; Kim Thomas, Polk State College; Michael Turner, Northern Virginia Community College; Candace Weddle, The South Carolina School of the Arts at Anderson University; Elizabeth Kennedy, Florida Atlantic University; Ronda Jacobs, College of Southern Maryland; Kim Crockett, West Georgia Technical College; Melissa Woods, Hinds Community College; Joe French, Columbia Southern University and Waldorf College; Faye Hamrac, Reid State Technical College; Jyrece McClendon, Palm Beach State College; Aubrey Moncrieffe, Jr., Housatonic Community College; Karen Jones, Zane State College; Peggy Whaley, Murray State University; Marilyn Olson, Chicago State U; Joyce McMahon, Kansas City, Kansas Community College; Kaye Young, Jamestown Community College; Diana Ivankovic, Anderson University; Joseph, Ivy Tech Community College; Matt Kelly,

Murray State University; Ronda Dively, Southern Illinois University–Carbondale; Dr. Julia Cote, Houston Community College; Beverly Russell, College of Southern Maryland; Donna Hanley, Kentucky Wesleyan College; Shane Williamson, Lindenwood University; Cheyanne Lewis, Blue Ridge Community and Technical College; Linda Randall, Georgia Southwestern State University; Linda Gannon, College of Southern Nevada (CSN); Ronnie Peacock, Edgecombe Community College; Deborah Vance, Ivy Tech Community College; Melinda Berry, Trinity Valley Community College; Sandy Lory-Snyder, Farmingdale State College; Melody Hays, South College–Asheville; Dwedor Ford, Central State University; Kim Smokowski, Bergen Community College; Dr. Brenda Tuberville, Rogers State University; Professor Jeannie Gonzalez, Miami Dade College, Kendall Campus; Joyce Kevetos, Palm Beach State College; Kelly S. Moor, Idaho State University; Brad Broschinsky, Idaho State University; Debbie Gilmore, Temple College; Miriam Chiza, North Hennepin Community College; Paul Hibbitts, Jr., Central Georgia Technical College; Mark Hendrix, Palm Beach State College; Laurie Sherman, Community College of Rhode Island; Pamela Moss, Midwestern State University; Alison Collman, Palm Beach State College; Julie Hernandez, Rock Valley College; Nina M. Scaringello, Suffolk County Community College–Grant Campus; Dr. J. Brown, Temple College, Temple, Texas; Stephen Phelps, Temple College; Yvonne Mitkos, Southern Illinois University Edwardsville; Annette Fields, University of Arkansas at Pine Bluff; Christopher L. Lau, Hutchinson Community College; Mary Davis, Angelina College; Pat Wall, Isothermal Community College; Winifred Ferguson Adams, Angelina College; Barbara A. Sherry, Northeastern Illinois University; Jose L. Saldivar, The University of Texas–Pan American; Dr. Michael J. Alicea, Miami Dade College; Karen Nelson, Craven Community College; Jennifer Boyle, Davidson County Community College; Dianna Stankiewicz, Anderson University; Brent Via, Virginia Western Community College; Brent Jackson, Central Carolina Technical College; Professor Lottie T. McMillan, Miami Dade College, North Campus; John Pigg, Tennessee Technical University; Andrea Serna, National American University; Mirjana M. Brockett, Georgia Institute of Technology; Linda McCuen, Anderson University; Charlene Latimer, Daytona State College; Eleanor Paterson, Erie Community College; Keri Keckley, Crowder College; June DeBoer, Calvin College; Chareane Wimbley-Gouveia, Linn-Benton Community College; Ross Bandics, Northampton Community College; Gloria Alexander, Bowie State University; Bickerstaff, Holmes; Scott H. O'Daniel, Ivy Tech Community College; Lourdes Delgado, Miami Dade College; Julie Bennett, Central Methodist University; Miriam McMullen-Pastrick, Penn State Erie; Kay Flowers, Idaho State University; Joseph Kornoski, Montgomery County Community College; Jacqui Slinger, Bluffton University; Mark A. Dowell, Randolph Community College; Eva Menefee, Lansing Community College; Shari Waldrop, Navarro College; Liese A. Hull, University of Michigan; Jenny Beaver, Rowan-Cabarrus Community College; Kenneth Christensen, University of Southern Mississippi; Susan Bossa, Quincy College; Daniel Thompson, CSU Long Beach; Betty Stack, Rowan Cabarrrus Community College; Kristin Asinger, University of Pittsburgh-Bradford; Carmalita M. Kemayo, EdD, University of Illinois Springfield; MaryJo Slater, Community College of Beaver County; Jeannette Sullivan, Palm Beach State College; Michael Corriston, Southeast Kentucky Community and Technical College.

The students in my own First-Year Experience courses (some of whom are shown here) provided thoughtful and wise advice. I thank them for their enthusiasm and eager willingness to provide constructive feedback.

Professors Cindy Wallace and Joni Webb Petschauer of Appalachian State University wrote the Instructor's Resource Manual and provided notes and tips for the Annotated Instructor's Edition. I thank both of them for their enthusiasm, good ideas, dedication, and friendship.

Edward Murphy, Ed.D., an educational testing expert, helped develop the exercises in the book, and I'm grateful for his excellent work.

John Graiff was a great help on every level in putting this book together, and I thank him for his willingness to go the extra mile.

I am proud to be part of an extraordinary McGraw-Hill editorial, marketing, and sales team. My publisher, Scott Davidson, has brought enthusiasm and intelligence to the project, and I welcome his good work, support, and friendship. I am also grateful to David Ploskonka, product developer who worked on the project, whose keen editorial eyes, creativity, and wealth of good ideas have improved this book significantly. I would also like to thank team members Danielle Clement, senior content project manager; Debra Kubiak, senior designer; and Kevin White, digital product developer, who helped modify and create the P.O.W.E.R. series digital content.

P.O.W.E.R. Learning author Bob Feldman and some of his First-Year Experience program participants.

There are several folks who, while no longer officially working on the project, still patiently answer my queries and offer their advice, for which I am extremely grateful. Andy Watts made superb contributions in extending the reach of *P.O.W.E.R. Learning,* and I'm very grateful for his work and even more for his friendship. Phil Butcher, Thalia Dorwick, David Patterson, Allison McNamara, and Alexis Walker were part of the team that developed the book, and I'm ever thankful for their efforts. Above all, I'm grateful to Rhona Robbin, the first development editor on the project, and sponsoring editor Sarah Touborg, who provided the impetus for the book. Certainly, the pages of *P.O.W.E.R. Learning* continue to reflect their many contributions.

Without a doubt, there is no better publishing group in the business than the one that worked on *P.O.W.E.R. Learning.* I count myself extremely lucky not only to have found myself a part of this world-class team, but to count each of them as friends.

In the end, I am eternally indebted to my family, both extended and immediate. Sarah, Jeff, and Lilia; Josh, Julie, and Naomi; Jon, Leigh, Alex, Miles; and of course Kathy, thank you for everything.

Robert S. Feldman

Congratulations! You are at the beginning of an academic journey that will impact your future in ways you can only imagine. This text and this course are designed to help make that journey as meaningful and enriching as possible. As you begin this chapter of your life, remember that you are not alone.

Every first-year student (like many returning students) encounters challenges. Whether it be juggling family, work, and school or preparing for a test, the challenges you face are daunting.

This is where *P.O.W.E.R. Learning: Foundations of Student Success* comes in. It is designed to help you to master the challenges you'll face in school as well as in life after graduation. The P.O.W.E.R. Learning system—which is based on five key steps embodied in the word P.O.W.E.R. (Prepare, Organize, Work, Evaluate, and Rethink)—teaches strategies that will help you become a more successful student and that will give you an edge in attaining what you want to accomplish in life.

But it's up to you to make use of the book. Familiarize yourself with the features of the book (described above) and use the built-in learning aids within the book, on the accompanying website, and in Connect. By doing so, you'll maximize the book's usefulness and get the most out of it.

Finally, I welcome your comments and suggestions about *P.O.W.E.R. Learning: Foundations of Student Success,* as well as about the website that accompanies the book. You can write me at the Chancellor's Office at the University of Massachusetts, Amherst, Massachusetts 01003. Even easier, send me an e-mail message at feldman@chancellor.umass.edu. I will write back!

P.O.W.E.R. Learning: Foundations of Student Success presents the tools that can maximize your chances for academic and life success. But remember that they're only tools, and their effectiveness depends on the way in which they are used. Ultimately, you are the one who is in charge of your future. Make the journey a rewarding, exciting, and enlightening one!

Robert S. Feldman

CHAPTER 1

Learning Outcomes

By the time you finish this chapter you will be able to

» LO **1-1**   Explain the benefits of a college education.

» LO **1-2**   Identify the basic principles of P.O.W.E.R. Learning.

» LO **1-3**   Identify your learning styles and how they affect your academic success.

P.O.W.E.R. Learning: Becoming an Expert Student

Source: © Monkey Business Images/Getty Images

It is 4:00 p.m. Bonnie Rojas wakes up her husband, Theo, by tugging on his sock. Although he only got into bed at noon, he rises and puts on his uniform as Bonnie changes clothes herself. She is just coming in from her job as a part-time legal assistant, and he is dressing for class, before he starts his night shift as a trainee corrections officer.

Before leaving for school and work, he helps Bonnie prepare dinner and does some homework. He is taking evening courses at a community college in the hope of attaining a degree in criminology. Tonight he has to deal with two classes: Sociology and Legal Principles in Corrections, both of which require a lot of memorization and quizzes. He plans to do some cramming on the bus to school.

Bonnie also is a student. She is working toward an associate's degree in paralegal studies. Every semester, Bonnie and Theo coordinate their work and class schedules carefully.

As Theo heads out the door, he worries about the frantic pace of their lives, calculating how little time he and Bonnie actually spend together. Although he never admits it to Bonnie, he wonders if he can really succeed as a student and if he will ever find a real job in corrections. Closing the door, he says to himself, "I just have to do this, though I'm not really sure how or if I'm going to make it."

Looking Ahead

Whether academic pursuits are a struggle or come easily to you . . . whether you are returning to college or attending for the first time . . . whether you are gaining new skills for your current job or are starting on a whole new career path—college is a challenge. Every one of us has concerns about our capabilities and motivation, and new situations—like starting college—make us wonder how we'll succeed.

That's where this book comes in. It is designed to help you learn the best ways to approach the challenges you'll face, not just in college but in your career and life too. It will teach you practical strategies, hints, and tips that can lead to success, all centered on an approach to achieving classroom and career success: P.O.W.E.R. Learning.

This book is designed to be useful in a way that is different from other college texts. It presents information in a hands-on format. It's meant to be used, not just read. Write on it, underline words and sentences, use a highlighter, circle key points, and complete the questionnaires right in the book. The more exercises you do, the more you'll benefit from the book. Remember, this is a book of practical tools to help you not only during college but throughout your career and in your everyday life, so it's a good idea to invest your time here and now. If the learning techniques you master here become second nature, the payoff will be enormous.

This first chapter lays out the basics of P.O.W.E.R. Learning. It will also help you figure out the way you learn best and how you can use your personal learning style to study more effectively.

» LO 1-1 Why Go to College?

Congratulations. You're in college.

But why? Although it seems that it should be easy to answer this question, for most people it's not. The reasons people go to college vary from the practical ("I need new skills for my job"), to the lofty ("I want to build a better life for my family"), to the vague ("Why not?—I don't have anything better to do"). Consider your own reasons for attending college, as you complete **Try It! 1**.

It's likely that one of your top reasons for attending college is to further your career. In fact, surveys of first-year college students at all types of institutions

Why Am I Going to College?

Place 1, 2, and 3 by the three most important reasons that you have for attending college:

____ I want to get a good job when I graduate.

____ I want to make my family proud.

____ I couldn't find a decent job.

____ I want to try something different.

____ I want to get ahead at my current job.

____ I want to pursue my dream job.

____ I want to improve my reading and thinking skills.

____ I want to become a more cultured person.

____ I want to meet new people from different backgrounds.

____ I want to make more money.

____ I want to learn more about things that interest me.

____ A mentor or role model encouraged me to go.

____ I want to prove to others that I can succeed.

Now consider the following:

- What do your answers tell you about yourself?
- What reasons besides these did you think about when you were applying to college?
- How do you think your reasons compare with those of other students who are starting college with you?

show that the vast majority say they want to learn about things that interest them, get training for a specific career, land a better job, and make more money (see **Figure 1.1**). Statistics clearly demonstrate that a college education helps people find better jobs. On average, college graduates earn about 75 percent more than high school graduates over their working lifetime. That difference adds up: Over the course of their working lifetimes, college graduates earn close to a million dollars more than those with only a high school degree. Furthermore, as jobs become increasingly complex and technologically sophisticated, college will become more and more of a necessity.

But even if you feel the only reason you're in college is to help your career prospects, remember that the value of college extends far beyond dollars and cents. Consider these added reasons for pursuing a college education:

▶ **You'll learn to think critically and communicate better.** Here's what one student said about his college experience after he graduated: "It's not about what you major in or which classes you take. . . . It's really about learning to think and to communicate. Wherever you end up, you'll need to be able to analyze and solve problems—to figure out what needs to be done and do it."[1]

Education improves your ability to see situations and think about them more clearly. It helps you understand the world—understand it as it is now, and prepare to understand it as it will be.

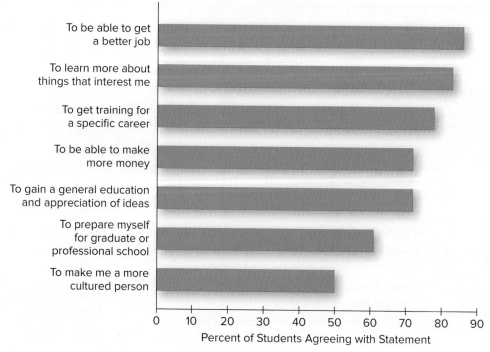

figure 1.1
Choosing College
These are the reasons that first-year college students most often gave for why they enrolled in college, when asked in a national survey.

Source: The American Freshman: National Norms for 2012," published by American Council on Education and University of California at Los Angeles Higher Education Research Institute.

▶ **You'll be able to better deal with advances in knowledge and technology that are changing the world.** Genetic engineering . . . drugs to reduce forgetfulness . . . increased use of robots . . . computers that respond to our thoughts. No one knows what the future will hold, but you can prepare for it through a college education. Education can provide you with intellectual tools that you can apply regardless of the specific situation in which you find yourself.

▶ **You'll acquire skills and perspectives that will shape how you deal with new situations and challenges.** The only certainty about how your life will unfold is that you will be surprised at what is in store for you. College prepares you to deal with the unexpected that characterizes all our lives.

▶ **You'll be better prepared to live in a world of diversity.** The racial and ethnic composition of the United States is changing rapidly. Whatever your ethnicity, chances are you'll be working and living with people whose backgrounds, lifestyles, and ways of thinking may be entirely different from your own.

You won't be prepared for the future unless you understand others and their cultural backgrounds—as well as how your own cultural background affects you.

▶ **You'll make learning a lifelong habit.** College isn't the end of your education. There's no job you'll have that won't change over time, and you'll be required to learn new skills. College starts you down the path to lifelong learning.

To help you attain these benefits, it's time to introduce you to a process that will help you achieve success, both in college and in later life: P.O.W.E.R. Learning.

Journal Reflections

My School Experiences

Throughout this book, you will be given opportunities to write out your thoughts. These opportunities—called Journal Reflections—offer a chance to think critically about the chapter topics and record your personal reactions to them. As you create your reflections, be honest—to yourself and to your instructor.

Completing these Journal Reflections provides a variety of benefits. Not only will you be able to mull over your past and present academic experiences, you'll also begin to see patterns in the kind of difficulties—and successes!—you encounter. You'll be able to apply solutions that worked in one situation to others. And one added benefit: You'll get practice in writing.

If you save these entries and return to them later, you may be surprised at the changes they record over the course of the term. You can write them out.

1. Think of one of the successful experiences you've had during your previous years in school or on the job. What was it?

2. What made the experience successful? What did you learn from your success?

3. Think of an experience you had in school that did not go as you had hoped, and briefly describe it. Why did it occur?

4. What could you have done differently? What did you learn from it?

5. Based on these experiences of success and failure, what general lessons did you learn that could help you to be more successful in the future, both in the classroom and in your career?

» LO 1-2 P.O.W.E.R. Learning:
The Five Key Steps to Achieving Success

P.O.W.E.R. Learning itself is merely an acronym—a word formed from the first letters of a series of steps—that will help you take in, process, and make use of the information you'll acquire in college. It will help you to achieve your goals, both while you are in college and later, after you graduate.

Prepare, **O**rganize, **W**ork, **E**valuate, and **R**ethink. That's it. It's a simple but effective framework. By using the P.O.W.E.R. Learning framework (illustrated in the P.O.W.E.R. Plan diagram), you will increase your chances of success at any

P.O.W.E.R. Learning
A system designed to help people achieve their goals, based on five steps: Prepare, Organize, Work, Evaluate, and Rethink.

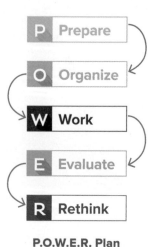

P.O.W.E.R. Plan

task, from writing a college paper to buying weekly groceries to filling out a purchase order.

Keep this in mind: P.O.W.E.R. Learning isn't a product that you can simply pull down off the bookshelf and use without thinking. P.O.W.E.R. Learning is a process, and you are the only one who can make it succeed. Without your personal investment in the process, P.O.W.E.R. Learning consists of just words on paper.

Relax, though. You already know each of the elements of P.O.W.E.R. Learning, and you may discover that you are already putting this process, or parts of it, to work for you. You've applied and been accepted into college. You may also have held down a job, started a family, and paid your monthly bills. Each of these accomplishments required the use of the P.O.W.E.R. Learning methods. What you'll be doing throughout this book is becoming more aware of these methods and how you can use them to help you in situations you will face in college and your career.

P Prepare

Chinese philosopher Lao Tzu said that travelers taking a long journey must begin with a single step.

But before they even take that first step, travelers need to know several things: what their destination is, how they're going to get there, how they'll know when they reach the destination, and what they'll do if they have trouble along the way.

Everyone goes to school for their own reasons. Gwen recently visited a friend in the hospital and was struck by how much she wanted to be a part of the health-care community. John has survived several rounds of layoffs at his job and wants to make himself more marketable.

Sources: © Commercial Eye/The Image Bank/Getty Images; Nick White/Digital Vision/Getty Images

In the same way, you need to know where you're headed as you embark on the academic journeys involved in college. Whether it be a major, long-term task, such as landing a new and better job, or a more limited activity, such as getting ready to complete a paper due in the near future, you'll need to prepare for the journey.

Setting Goals

Before we seek to accomplish any task, all of us do some form of planning. The trouble is that usually we make our plans without conscious thought, as if we were on autopilot. However, the key to success is to make sure that planning is systematic.

The best way to plan systematically is to use goal-setting strategies. In many cases, goals are clear and direct. It's obvious that our goal in washing dishes is to have the dishes end up clean. We know that our goal at the gas station is to put gas in the car's tank. We go to the post office to buy stamps and mail letters.

Other goals are not so clear-cut. In fact, often the more important the task—such as going to college—the more complicated our goals may be.

From the perspective of . . .

A STUDENT What goals did you set when you decided to go school? What can you do to ensure that you meet these goals?

Source: © Cathy Yeulet/Hemera/Getty Images Plus/Getty Images

What's the best way to set appropriate goals? Here are some guidelines:

▶ **Set both long-term and short-term goals. Long-term goals** are aims relating to major accomplishments that take some time to achieve. **Short-term goals** are relatively limited steps on the road to accomplishing your long-term goals. For example, one of the primary reasons you're in college is to achieve the long-term goal of helping your career. But to reach that goal, you have to accomplish a series of short-term goals, such as completing a set of required courses and earning your degree. Even these short-term goals can be broken down into shorter-term goals. In order to complete a required course, for instance, you have to accomplish short-term goals such as completing a paper, taking several tests, and so on.

▶ **Make goals realistic and attainable.** Someone once said, "A goal without a plan is but a dream." We'd all like to win gold medals at the Olympics or become CEO of Nike or write best-selling novels. Few of us are likely to achieve such goals.

Be honest with yourself. There is nothing wrong with having big dreams. But it is important to be realistically aware of all that it takes to achieve them. If our long-term goals are unrealistic and we don't achieve them, the big danger is that we may reason—incorrectly—that we are inept

long-term goals
Aims relating to major accomplishments that take some time to achieve.

short-term goals
Relatively limited steps toward the accomplishment of long-term goals.

> "Goal setting, as far as I can see it, is simply a state of mind, a way of thinking about things. A goal setter makes sure he accomplishes what he needs to accomplish."
> Gottesman, G. (1994). *College Survival.* New York: Macmillan. P. 70.

Setting Measurable Objectives

Try your hand at turning the following broad goals into *measurable* achievement objectives. To give you an example, the first one is filled in.

Broad Goal	Measurable Objectives
1. I want to quit smoking.	1. By 6 months from now, I will reduce my cigarette smoking from 2 packs a day to ½ pack a day, and by 12 months, I will be down to zero.
2. I need to stop wasting time on the Internet when I'm supposed to be working.	
3. I wish I had time to read more and be better informed.	
4. I'm feeling out of touch with my family and friends. I have to do something about it.	
5. I used to have hobbies. Now I don't do anything for fun.	

and lack ability and use this as an excuse for giving up. If goals are realistic, we can develop a plan to attain them, spurring us on to attain more.

▶ **State goals in terms of behavior that can be measured against current accomplishments.** Goals should represent some measurable change from a current set of circumstances. We want our behavior to change in some way that can usually be expressed in terms of numbers—to show an increase ("raise my grade point average 10 percent") or a decrease ("reduce wasted time by two hours each week"); or to be maintained ("keep in touch with my out-of-town friends by sending four e-mail messages each month"), developed ("participate in one workshop on job interview skills"), or restricted ("reduce my cell phone expenses 10 percent by texting less").

Try It! 2 and **Try It! 3** are designed to help you create a workable framework for goal achievement in your everyday life and your college life. Try It! 2 focuses on restating the broad, vague everyday goals we all set in our minds as measurable achievement objectives. Try It! 3 focuses on your school-related goals, guiding you in setting manageable short-term goals that will help you reach long-term goals.

▶ **Goals should involve behavior over which you have control.** We all want world peace and an end to poverty. Few of us have the resources or capabilities to bring either about. On the other hand, it is realistic to want to work in small ways to help others, such as by volunteering at a local food bank.

▶ **Identify how your short-term goals fit with your long-term goals.** Your goals should not be independent of one another. Instead, they should fit together into a larger dream of who you want to be. Every once in a while, step back and consider how what you're doing today relates to the kind of career that you would ultimately want to have.

What Are Your Goals?

Before you begin any journey, you need to know where you are going. To plan your academic journey—and your later career—you first need to set goals. *Short-term goals* are relatively limited objectives that bring you closer to your ultimate goal. *Long-term goals* are aims relating to major accomplishments that take more time to achieve.

In this Try It!, think about your short- and long-term academic and career goals for a few minutes, and then list them. Because short-term goals are based on what you want to accomplish in the long term, first identify your long-term goals. Then list the short-term goals that will help you reach your long-term goals. An example is provided for each kind of goal:

Long-Term Goal #1: Get a college degree _____
   Related Short-Term Goals:

- Complete four courses with a grade of B or above each term
- _____
- _____
- _____
- _____

Long-Term Goal #2: _____
   Related Short-Term Goals:

- _____
- _____
- _____
- _____
- _____

Long-Term Goal # 3: _____
   Related Short-Term Goals:

- _____
- _____
- _____
- _____
- _____

Long-Term Goal #4: _____
   Related Short-Term Goals:

- _____
- _____
- _____
- _____
- _____

Long-Term Goal #5: _____
   Related Short-Term Goals:

- _____
- _____
- _____
- _____
- _____

After you complete the chart, consider how easy or difficult it was to identify your long-term goals. How many of your long-term goals relate to college, and how many to your future career? Do any of your short-term goals relate to more than one long-term goal?

By determining where you want to go and expressing your goals in terms that can be measured, you have already made a lot of progress. But there's another step you must take on the road to success.

The second step in P.O.W.E.R. Learning is to organize the tools you'll need to accomplish your goals. Building on the goal-setting work you've undertaken in the preparation stage, it's time to determine the best way to accomplish the goals you've identified.

How do you do this? Suppose you've decided to paint a room in your house. Let's say that you've already determined the color you want and the kind of paint you need (the preparation step in P.O.W.E.R. Learning). The next stage involves buying the paint and brushes and preparing the room for being painted—all aspects of organizing for the task.

Similarly, your academic success will hinge to a large degree on the thoroughness of your organization for each academic task that you face. In fact, one of the biggest mistakes that students make in college is plunging into an academic project—studying for a test, writing a paper, completing an in-class assignment— without being organized.

The Two Kinds of Organization: Physical and Mental

On a basic level is *physical organization,* involving the mechanical aspects of task completion. For instance, you need to ask yourself if you have the appropriate tools, such as pens, paper, and a calculator. If you're using a computer, do you have access to a printer? Do you have a way to back up your files? Do you have the books and other materials (including Internet sites and resources) you'll need to complete the assignment? Will the campus bookstore be open if you need anything else? Will the library be open when you need it? Do you have a comfortable place to work?

Mental organization is even more critical. Mental organization is accomplished by considering and reviewing the academic skills that you'll need to successfully complete the task at hand. You are an academic general in command of considerable forces; you will need to make sure your forces—the basic skills you have at your command—are at their peak of readiness.

For example, if you're working on a math assignment, you'll want to consider the basic math skills that you'll need and brush up on them. Just actively thinking about this will help you organize mentally. Similarly, you'd want to mentally review your knowledge of engine parts before beginning repair work (either in class or on the side of the road!). Why does mental organization matter? The answer is that it provides a context for when you actually begin to work. Organizing paves the way for better performance later.

Too often students or workers on the job are in a hurry to meet a deadline and figure they had better just dive in and get it done. Organizing can actually *save* you time, because you're less likely to be anxious and end up losing your way as you work to complete your task.

Much of this book is devoted to strategies for determining—*before* you begin work on a task—how to develop the mental tools for completing an assignment. However, as you'll see, all of these strategies share a common theme: that success

Looking at the Big Picture

It's natural to view college as a series of small tasks—classes to attend, a certain number of pages to read each week, a few papers due during the term, quizzes and final exams to study for, and so on.

But such a perspective may lead you to miss what college, as a whole, is all about. Using the P.O.W.E.R. Learning framework can help you take the long view of your education, considering how it helps you achieve your long- and short-term goals for your professional and personal life (the *Prepare* step) and what you'll need to do to maximize your success (the *Organize* step). By preparing and organizing even before you step foot in the classroom for the first time, you'll be able to consider what it is that you want to get out of college and how it fits into your life as a whole.

comes not from a trial-and-error approach, but from following a systematic plan for achievement. Of course, this does not mean that there will be no surprises along the way, nor that simple luck is never a factor in great accomplishments. But it does mean that we often can make our own luck through careful preparation and organization.

W | Work

You're ready. The preliminaries are out of the way. You've prepared and you've organized. Now it's time to get started actually doing the work.

In some ways work is the easy part, because—if you conscientiously carried out the preparation and organization stage—you should know exactly where you're headed and what you need to do to get there.

It's not quite so easy, of course. How effectively you'll get down to the business at hand depends on many factors. Some may be out of your control. There may be a power outage that closes down the library or a massive traffic jam that delays your getting to work. But most factors are—or should be—under your control. Instead of getting down to work, you may find yourself thinking up "useful" things to do—like finally cleaning underneath the couch—or simply sitting captive in front of the TV. This kind of obstacle to work relates to motivation.

Developing a Growth Mindset

Do you think some people are born smart and are destined to be high achievers, while others—maybe even yourself—don't have enough intelligence to ever do really well in school?

If you believe this, you need to think again. Intelligence is something that is not fixed. Instead, it is fluid and flexible, and through hard work and effort, people can do better than they ever thought possible. In fact, the brain is like any muscle: the more you use it, the stronger it becomes.

Students who hold a **growth mindset** believe that people can increase their abilities and do better through hard work. They challenge themselves to try to

growth mindset
Belief that people can increase their abilities and do better through hard work.

increase their success, even if at first they fail. They are more persistent in the face of obstacles, and they try harder.

Can you develop a growth mindset? The answer is yes. By telling yourself that success is the result of effort, not how smart you are, you are more likely to do better on tasks in the future. Remember, success is about analyzing the causes of your performance, and thinking about how you might do things differently to bring about a better outcome. It's a matter of motivation.

Finding the Motivation to Work

"If only I could get more motivated, I'd do so much better with my ___" (insert *schoolwork, job, diet, exercising,* or the like—you fill in the blank).

All of us have said something like this at one time or another. We use the concept of **motivation**—or its lack—to explain why we just don't work hard at a task. But when we do that, we're fooling ourselves. We all have some motivation, that inner power and psychological energy that directs and fuels our behavior. Without any motivation, we'd never get out of bed in the morning.

We've also seen evidence of how strong our motivation can be. Perhaps you love to work out at the gym. Or maybe your love of music helped you learn to play the guitar, making practicing for hours a pleasure rather than a chore. Or perhaps you're a single parent, juggling work, school, and family, and you get up early every morning to make breakfast for your kids before they go off to school.

All of us are motivated. The key to success in the classroom and on the job is to tap into, harness, and direct that motivation.

If we assume that we already have all the motivation we need, P.O.W.E.R. Learning becomes a matter of turning the skills we already possess into a habit. It becomes a matter of redirecting our psychological energies toward the work we wish to accomplish.

In a sense, everything you'll encounter in this book can help you to improve your use of the motivation that you already have. But there's a key concept that underlies the control of motivation—viewing success as a consequence of effort:

Effort ⟶ Success

Suppose, for example, you've gotten a good performance review from your new supervisor. The boss beams at you as she discusses your results. How do you feel?

You will undoubtedly be pleased, of course. But at the same time you might think to yourself, "Don't get cocky. It was just luck." Or perhaps you explain your success by thinking, "The new boss just doesn't know me very well."

If you often think this way, you're cheating yourself. Using this kind of reasoning when you succeed, instead of patting yourself on the back and thinking with satisfaction, "All my hard work really paid off," is sure to undermine your future success.

A great deal of psychological research has shown that thinking you have no control over what happens to you sends a powerful and damaging message to your self-esteem—that you are powerless to change things. Just think of how different it feels to say to yourself, "Wow, I worked at it and did it," as compared with "I lucked out" or "It was so easy that anybody could have done it."

In the same way, we can delude ourselves when we try to explain our failures. People who see themselves as the victims of circumstance may tell themselves, "I'm just not smart enough,"

---

motivation

The inner power and psychological energy that directs and fuels behavior.

"The function of the university is not simply to teach bread-winning, or to furnish teachers for the public schools or to be a center of polite society: it is, above all, to be the organ of that fine adjustment between real life and the growing knowledge of life, an adjustment which forms the secret of civilization."

W. E. B. DuBois, *The Souls of Black Folk,* **1903.**

when they don't do well on an academic task. Or they might say, "My co-workers don't have children to take care of."

The way in which we view the causes of success and failure is, in fact, directly related to our success. Students who generally see effort and hard work as the reason behind their performance usually do better in college. Workers who see their job performance in this way usually do better in their careers. It's not hard to see why: When such individuals are working on a task, they feel that the greater the effort they put forth, the greater their chances of success. So they work harder. They believe that they have control over their success, and if they fail, they believe they can do better in the future.

Here are some tips for keeping your motivation alive, so you can work with your full energy behind you:

▶ **Take responsibility for your failures—and successes.** When you do poorly on a test, don't blame the teacher, the textbook, or a job that kept you from studying. When you miss a work deadline, don't blame your boss or your incompetent co-workers. Analyze the situation, and see how you could have changed what you did to be more successful in the future. At the same time, when you're successful, think of the things you did to bring about that success.

▶ **Think positively.** Assume that the strengths that you have will allow you to succeed and that, if you have difficulty, you can figure out what to do, or get the help you need to eventually succeed.

▶ **Accept that you can't control everything.** Seek to understand which things can be changed and which cannot. You might be able to get an extension on a paper due date, but you are probably not going to be excused from a college-wide requirement.

To further explore the causes of academic success, consider the questions in **Try It! 4**, then discuss them with your classmates.

E Evaluate

"Great, I'm done with the work. Now I can move on."

It's natural to feel relief when you've finished the work necessary to fulfill the basic requirements of a task. After all, if you've written the five double-spaced pages required for an assignment or completed a difficult task at work, why shouldn't you heave a sigh of relief and just hand in your work?

The answer is that if you stop at this point, you'll almost be guaranteed a mediocre result. Do you think Shakespeare dashed off the first draft of *Hamlet* and, without another glance, sent it to the Globe Theater for production? Do professional athletes just put in the bare minimum of practice to get ready for a big game? Think of one of your favorite songs. Do you think the composer wrote it in one sitting and then performed it in a concert?

In every case, the answer is no. Even the greatest creation does not emerge in perfect form, immediately meeting all the goals of its producer. Consequently, the fourth step in the P.O.W.E.R. process is **evaluation**, which consists of determining how well the product or activity we have created matches our goals for it. Let's consider some steps to follow in evaluating what you've accomplished:

evaluation
An assessment of the match between a product or activity and the goals it was intended to meet.

▶ **Take a moment to congratulate yourself and feel some satisfaction.** Whether it's been studying for a test, writing a paper, completing a report,

Examining the Causes of Success and Failure

Complete this Try It! while working in a group. First, consider the following situations:

1. Although he checked and rechecked his work, Charles is told by his boss Martha that the numbers in his draft quarterly report were not accurate enough for distribution. Martha tells him she had to have Beth correct the numbers and produce a final product. Charles is disgusted with himself and angry at his boss and at Beth. He tells himself, "I'll never be good enough to make it as an accountant—and certainly not here where things are stacked against me because I'm not in the in-group. I'd better just give up and go back to the basic clerical work I did before I went for the promotion."

2. Shauna works all through the weekend to produce an interim profit-and-loss (P&L) statement, which is well received at the Monday afternoon executive committee meeting. She is happy, but when her boss comments that interim P&L statements are never looked at as closely as quarterly and annual statements, she decides she succeeded only because her work wasn't judged against a very high standard.

3. Nasir was told in his evaluation that he needs to work faster to keep up with the pace of the accounting department. He makes up his mind to work more quickly and efficiently, even taking work home to boost his output. However, he still can't produce the dozens of financial analyses that his co-workers routinely turn out every week. Distressed, he considers quitting his job because he thinks that he'll never be successful in corporate accounting.

Now consider the following questions about each of the situations:

1. What did each employee conclude was the main cause of his or her performance?
2. What effect does this conclusion seem to have on the employee?
3. Taking an outsider's point of view, what do *you* think was probably the main cause of the employees' performance?
4. What advice would you give each person?

Now consider these broader questions:

1. What are the most important reasons some people are more professionally successful than others?
2. How much does ability determine success? How much does luck determine success? How much do circumstances determine success?
3. If someone performs poorly at a job, what are the possible reasons for his or her performance? If someone performs well, what are the possible reasons for his or her performance? Is it harder to find reasons for good performance than for poor performance? Why?

or finishing a hard task at work, you've done something important. You've moved from ground zero to a spot that's closer to your goal.

▶ **Compare what you've accomplished with the goals you're seeking to achieve.** Think back to the goals, both short-term and long-term, that you're seeking to achieve. How closely does what you've done match what you're aiming to do? For instance, if your short-term goal is to complete a math problem set with no errors, you'll need to check over the work carefully to make sure you've made no mistakes.

▶ **Have an out-of-body experience: Evaluate your accomplishments as if you were a respected mentor from your past.** If you've written a paper, reread it from the perspective of a favorite teacher. If you've prepared a report, imagine you're presenting it to a boss who taught you a lot. Think about the comments you'd give if you were this person.

▶ **Evaluate what you've done as if you were your current instructor or supervisor.** Now exchange bodies and minds again. This time, consider what you're doing from the perspective of the person who gave you the assignment. How would he or she react to what you've done? Have you followed the assignment to the letter? Is there anything you've missed?

▶ **Based on your evaluation, revise your work.** If you're honest with yourself, it's unlikely that your first work will satisfy you. So go back to *Work* and revise what you've done. But don't think of it as a step back: Revisions you make as a consequence of your evaluation bring you closer to your final goal. This is a case where going back moves you forward.

There are always things we can use as excuses for our own failures. Can you think of a time when you shifted blame away from yourself for a failure? Was it a reasonable course of action? Why or why not?
Source: © Digital Vision/Getty Images

R | Rethink

They thought they had it perfect. But they were wrong.

In fact, it was a $1.5 billion mistake—a blunder on a grand scale. The finely ground mirror of the Hubble space telescope, designed to provide an unprecedented glimpse into the vast reaches of the universe, was not so finely ground after all.

Despite an elaborate system of evaluation designed to catch any flaws, there was a tiny blemish in the mirror that was not detected until the telescope had been launched into space and started to send back blurry photographs. By then, it seemed too late to fix the mirror.

Or was it? NASA engineers rethought the problem for months, devising and then discarding one potential fix after another. Finally, after bringing a fresh eye to the situation, they formulated a daring solution that involved sending a team of astronauts into space. Once there, a space-walking Mr. Goodwrench would install several new mirrors in the telescope, which could refocus the light and compensate for the original flawed mirror.

Although the engineers could not be certain that the $629 million plan would work, it seemed like a good solution, at least on paper. It was not until the first photos were beamed back to Earth, though, that NASA knew their solution was A-OK. These photos were spectacular.

It took months of reconsideration before NASA scientists could figure out what went wrong and devise a solution to the problem they faced. Their approach exemplifies—on a grand scale—the final step in P.O.W.E.R. Learning: rethinking.

To *rethink* what you've accomplished earlier means bringing a fresh—and clear—eye to what you've done. It involves using **critical thinking**, thinking that involves reanalyzing, questioning, and challenging our underlying assumptions. Whereas evaluation means considering how well what we have done matches our initial goals, rethinking means reconsidering not only the outcome of our efforts, but also our goals and the ideas and the process we've used to reach them. Critically rethinking what you've done involves analyzing and synthesizing ideas, and seeing the connections between different concepts.

We'll be considering critical thinking throughout this book, examining specific strategies in every chapter. For the moment, the following steps provide a general framework for using critical thinking to rethink what you've accomplished:

▶ **Review how you've accomplished the task.** Consider the approach and strategies you've used. What seemed to work best? Does your review suggest any alternatives that might work better the next time?

▶ **Question the outcome.** Take a "big picture" look at what you have accomplished. Are you pleased and satisfied? Is there something you've somehow missed?

▶ **Identify your underlying assumptions; then challenge them.** Consider the assumptions you made in initially approaching the task. As you look back, are these underlying assumptions still reasonable? If you had used different assumptions, would the result have been similar or different?

▶ **Consider alternatives rejected earlier.** You probably discarded possible strategies and approaches before completing your task. Now's the time to think about those approaches once more and determine if they might have been more appropriate than the road you did follow.

▶ **Ask yourself: What would you do differently if you had the opportunity to try things again?** It's not too late to change course.

▶ **Finally, reconsider your initial goals.** Are they achievable and realistic? Do your goals, and the strategies you used to attain them, need to be modified? Critically rethinking the objectives and goals that underlie your efforts is often the most effective route to success.

Completing the Process

The rethinking step of P.O.W.E.R. Learning is meant to help you understand your process of work and to improve the final product if necessary. But mostly it is meant to help you grow, to become better at whatever it is you've been doing. Like a painter looking at his or her finished work, you may see a spot here or there to touch up, but don't destroy the canvas. Perfectionism can be as paralyzing as laziness. Keep in mind these key points:

▶ **Know that there's always another day.** Your future success does not depend on any single assignment, paper, or test. Don't fall victim to self-defeating thoughts such as "If I don't do well on this test, I'll never graduate" or "Everything is riding on this one project." Nonsense. In school, on the job, and in life, there is almost always an opportunity to recover from a failure.

P.O.W.E.R. Learning and the World of Work

As we've discussed, the P.O.W.E.R. Learning process has applications both in the classroom and on the job. In Career Connections boxes, we'll highlight ways in which the principles we're discussing can help you excel in the workplace. Take a look at these "help wanted" advertisements and online postings. They illustrate the importance of the components of P.O.W.E.R. Learning in a wide variety of fields.

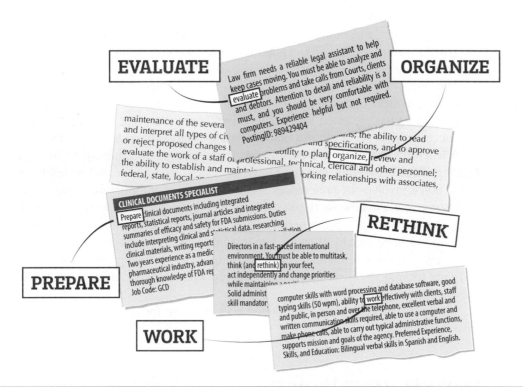

EVALUATE

ORGANIZE

Law firm needs a reliable legal assistant to help keep cases moving. You must be able to analyze and evaluate problems and take calls from Courts, clients and debtors. Attention to detail and reliability is a must, and you should be very comfortable with computers. Experience helpful but not required. PostingID: 989429404

maintenance of the severa... and interpret all types of civ... or reject proposed changes t... evaluate the work of a staff of professional, technical, clerical and other personnel; the ability to establish and maintai... federal, state, local a...

...rs; the ability to read ...and specifications, and to approve ...ability to plan, organize, review and ...orking relationships with associates,

CLINICAL DOCUMENTS SPECIALIST
Prepare clinical documents including integrated reports, statistical reports, journal articles and integrated summaries of efficacy and safety for FDA submissions. Duties include interpreting clinical and statistical data, researching clinical materials, writing reports...
Two years experience as a medic... pharmaceutical industry, advan... thorough knowledge of FDA re... Job Code: GCD

RETHINK

Directors in a fast-paced international environment. You must be able to multitask, think (and rethink) on your feet, act independently and change priorities while maintaining a posit... Solid administ... skill mandatory...

PREPARE

computer skills with word processing and database software, good typing skills (50 wpm), ability to work effectively with clients, staff and public, in person and over the telephone, excellent verbal and written communication skills required, able to use a computer and make phone calls, able to carry out typical administrative functions, supports mission and goals of the agency. Preferred Experience, Skills, and Education: Bilingual verbal skills in Spanish and English.

WORK

▶ **Realize that deciding when to stop work is often as hard as getting started.** Knowing when you have put in enough time studying for a test, or have revised a paper sufficiently, or have reviewed your figures adequately on a math problem set, is as much a key to success as properly preparing. If you've carefully evaluated what you've done and seen that there's a close fit between your goals and your work, it's time to stop work and move on.

▶ **Use the strategies that already work for you.** Although the P.O.W.E.R. Learning framework provides a proven approach to attaining success, employing it does not mean that you should abandon strategies that have brought you success in the past. Using multiple approaches, and personalizing them, is the surest road to success.

As much as anything else, doing well in college and on the job depends on an awareness *of yourself*. What are your strengths? What are your weaknesses? What do you do better than most people, and what are your areas for improvement? If you can answer such questions, you'll be able to harness the best of your talents and anticipate any challenges you might face. The next section will aid you in understanding yourself better by helping you identify your personal learning styles.

»LO1-3 Discovering Your Learning Styles

Members of the Trukese people, a small group of islanders in the South Pacific, often sail hundreds of miles on the open sea. They manage this feat with none of the navigational equipment used by Western sailors. No compass. No chronometer. No sextant. They don't even sail in a straight line. Instead, they zigzag back and forth. Yet they almost always reach their destination with precision.

Trukese sailors can't really explain how they learned to navigate or the processes that they use, but clearly they are successful sailors.

The case of Trukese sailors vividly illustrates how there are different ways to learn and to achieve our goals.

Each of us has preferred ways of learning, approaches that work best for us. Our success is dependent not just on how well we learn, but on *how* we learn.

A **learning style** reflects a person's preferred manner of acquiring, using, and thinking about knowledge. We don't have just one learning style, but a variety of styles. Some involve our preferences regarding the way information is presented to us, some relate to how we think and learn most readily, and some relate to how our personality traits affect our performance. An awareness of your learning styles will help you in college by allowing you to study and learn course materials more effectively. On the job, knowing your learning styles will help you master new skills and techniques, ensuring you can keep up with changing office practices or an evolving industry.

We'll start by considering the preferences we have for how we initially perceive information.

learning style
One's preferred manner of acquiring, using, and thinking about knowledge.

What Is Your Preferred Receptive Learning Style?

One of the most basic aspects of learning styles concerns the way in which we initially receive information from our sense organs—our **receptive learning style**. People differ in how they most effectively process information and which of their senses they prefer to use in learning. Specifically, there are four different types of receptive learning styles:

receptive learning style
The way in which we initially receive information.

read/write learning style
A style that involves a preference for written material, favoring reading over hearing and touching.

▶ **Read/write learning style.** If you have a **read/write learning style**, you prefer information that is presented visually in a written format. You feel most comfortable reading, and you may recall the spelling of a word by thinking of how the word looks. You probably learn best when you have the opportunity to read about a concept rather than listening to a teacher explain it.

visual/graphic learning style
A style that favors material presented visually in a diagram or picture.

▶ **Visual/graphic learning style.** Those with a **visual/graphic learning style** learn most effectively when material is presented visually in a diagram or picture. You might recall the structure of an engine or a part of the human body by reviewing a picture in your mind, and you benefit from instructors who make frequent use of visual aids in class, such as videos, maps, and models. Students with visual learning styles find it easier to see things in their mind's eye—to visualize a task or concept—than to be lectured about them.

▶ **Auditory/verbal learning style.** Have you ever asked a friend to help you put something together by having her read the directions to you while you worked?

If you did, you may have an auditory/verbal learning style. People with **auditory/verbal learning styles** prefer listening to explanations rather than reading them. They love class lectures and discussions, because they can easily take in the information that is being talked about.

▶ **Tactile/kinesthetic learning style.** Those with a **tactile/kinesthetic learning style** prefer to learn by doing—touching, manipulating objects, and doing things. For instance, some people enjoy the act of writing because of the feel of a pencil or a computer keyboard—the tactile equivalent of thinking out loud. Or they may find that making a three-dimensional model helps them understand a new idea.

To get a sense of your own receptive learning style, complete **Try It! 5**. But remember, having a particular receptive learning style simply means that it will be easier to learn material that is presented in that style. It does not mean you cannot learn any other way!

Receptive learning styles have implications for effective studying in class or learning new skills on the job:

If you have a read/write style, consider writing out summaries of information, highlighting and underlining written material, and using flash cards. Transform diagrams and math formulas into words.

If you have a visual/graphic style, devise diagrams and charts. Translate words into symbols and figures.

If you have an auditory/verbal style, recite material out loud when trying to learn it. Work with others in a group, talking through the material, and consider recording lectures.

If you have a tactile/kinesthetic style, incorporate movement into your study. Trace diagrams, build models, arrange flash cards and move them around. Keep yourself active when learning, taking notes, drawing charts, and jotting down key concepts.

Source: © Jack hollingsworth/Photodisc/Getty Images

Steven Spielberg is a self-admitted visual learner. How can you use your own learning style to influence your career decisions?
Source: © James Devaney/WireImage/Getty Images

auditory/verbal learning styles
A style that favors listening as the best approach to learning.

tactile/kinesthetic learning style
A style that involves learning by touching, manipulating objects, and doing things.

From the perspective of . . .

A MEDICAL ASSISTANT You shouldn't see your learning style as a limitation. Repeating instructions aloud as a nursing assistant is one way for auditory learners to ensure they are comprehending instructions. How can you adapt your learning style in multiple career settings?

What's Your Receptive Learning Style?

Read each of the following statements and rank them in terms of their usefulness to you as learning approaches. Base your ratings on your personal experiences and preferences, using the following scale:

1 = Not at all useful

2 = Not very useful

3 = Neutral

4 = Somewhat useful

5 = Very useful

	1	2	3	4	5
1. Studying alone					
2. Studying pictures and diagrams to understand complex ideas					
3. Listening to class lectures					
4. Performing a process myself rather than reading or hearing about it					
5. Learning a complex procedure by reading written directions					
6. Watching and listening to film, computer, or video presentations					
7. Listening to a book or lecture on a CD or on computer					
8. Doing lab work					
9. Studying teachers' handouts and lecture notes					
10. Studying in a quiet room					
11. Taking part in group discussions					
12. Taking part in hands-on demonstrations					
13. Taking notes and studying them later					
14. Creating flash cards and using them as a study and review tool					

Multiple Intelligences: Showing Strength in Different Domains

Do you feel much more comfortable walking through the woods than navigating city streets? Are you an especially talented musician? Is reading and using a complicated map second nature to you?

If so, in each case you may be demonstrating a special and specific kind of intelligence. According to psychologist Howard Gardner, rather than asking "How smart are you?" we should be asking a different question: "How are you smart?" To answer the latter question, Gardner has developed a *theory of multiple*

15. Memorizing and recalling how words are spelled by spelling them "out loud" in my head					
16. Writing down key facts and important points as a tool for remembering them					
17. Recalling how to spell a word by seeing it in my head					
18. Underlining or highlighting important facts or passages in my reading					
19. Saying things out loud when I'm studying					
20. Recalling how to spell a word by "writing" it invisibly in the air or on a surface					
21. Learning new information by reading about it in a book					
22. Using a map to find an unknown place					
23. Working in a study group					
24. Finding a place I've been to once by just going there without directions					

Scoring: The statements cycle through the four receptive learning styles in this order: (1) read/write; (2) visual/graphic; (3) auditory/verbal; and (4) tactile/kinesthetic.

To find your primary learning style, disregard your 1, 2, and 3 ratings. Add up your 4 and 5 ratings for each learning style (i.e., a "4" equals 4 points and a "5" equals 5 points). Use the following chart to link the statements to the learning styles and to write down your summed ratings:

Learning Style	Statements	Total (Sum) of Rating Points
Read/write	1, 5, 9, 13, 17, and 21	
Visual/graphic	2, 6, 10, 14, 18, and 22	
Auditory/verbal	3, 7, 11, 15, 19, and 23	
Tactile/kinesthetic	4, 8, 12, 16, 20, and 24	

The total of your rating points for any given style will range from a low of 0 to a high of 30. The highest total indicates your main receptive learning style. Don't be surprised if you have a mixed style, in which two or more styles receive similar ratings.

intelligences that offers a unique approach to understanding learning styles and preferences.

The multiple intelligences view says that we have eight different forms of intelligence, each relatively independent of the others and linked to a specific kind of information processing in our brains:

▶ *Spatial intelligence* relates to skills involving spatial configurations, such as those used by artists and architects.

▶ *Interpersonal intelligence* is found in learners with particularly strong skills involving interacting with others, such as sensitivity to the moods, temperaments, motivations, and intentions of others.

In any given day, graphic designers must be able to create amazing visuals and also do the requisite paperwork to accompany their projects. Which types of intelligence would be most important to succeed in this career?
Source: © Rawpixel Ltd/iStock/Getty Images Plus/Getty Images

▶ *Intrapersonal intelligence* relates to a particularly strong understanding of the internal aspects of oneself and having access to one's own feelings and emotions.

▶ *Musical intelligence* involves skills relating to music.

▶ *Bodily kinesthetic intelligence* relates to skills in using the whole body or portions of it in the solution of problems or in the construction of products or displays, exemplified by dancers, athletes, actors, and surgeons.

▶ *Naturalist intelligence* involves exceptional abilities in identifying and classifying patterns in nature.

All of us have the same eight kinds of intelligence, although in different degrees, and they form the core of our learning styles and preferences. These separate intelligences do not operate in isolation. Instead, any activity involves several kinds of intelligence working together. And, as Gardner points out, these eight intelligences may be only scratching the surface of what our capabilities are. He suggests there may be even more intelligences that shape how we interact with the world. For example, there may be an "existential intelligence," which involves indentifying and thinking about the fundamental questions of human existence.

Personality Styles

Our learning styles are also influenced by our personality. Are you likely to perform at an open mic night at a café? Or is the idea of getting on a stage totally lacking in appeal (if not completely terrifying)? Do you relate to the world around you primarily through careful planning or by spontaneously reacting?

According to the rationale of the *Myers-Briggs Type Indicator,* a questionnaire frequently used in business and organizational settings to place people in 1 of 16 categories, personality type plays a key role in determining how we react to different situations. Specifically, we work best in situations in which others—students, instructors, or co-workers—share our preferences and in which our personality is most suited to the particular task on which we are working. Four major personality dimensions are critical. Although we'll describe the extremes of each dimension, keep in mind that most of us fall somewhere between the end points of each dimension.

▶ **Introverts versus extraverts.** A key difference between introverts and extraverts is whether they enjoy working with others. Independence is a key characteristic of introverted learners. They enjoy working alone and they are less affected by how others think and behave. In contrast, extraverts are outgoing and more affected by the behavior and thinking of others. They enjoy working with others, and they are energized by having other people around.

▶ **Intuitors versus sensors.** Intuitors enjoy solving problems and being creative. They get impatient with details, preferring to make leaps of judgment, and they enjoy the challenge of solving problems and taking a big-picture approach. People categorized as sensors, on the other hand, prefer a concrete, logical approach in which they can carefully analyze the facts of the situation. Although they are good with details, they sometimes miss the big picture.

- **Thinkers versus feelers.** Thinkers prefer logic over emotion. They reach decisions and solve problems by systematically analyzing a situation. In contrast, feeling types rely more on their emotional responses. They are aware of others and their feelings, and they are influenced by their personal values and attachments to others.

- **Perceivers versus judgers.** Before drawing a conclusion, perceivers attempt to gather as much information as they can. Because they are open to multiple perspectives and appreciate all sides of an issue, they sometimes have difficulty completing a task. Judgers, in comparison, are quick and decisive. They like to set goals, accomplish them, and then move on to the next task.

The Origins of Our Learning Styles

For many of us, our learning style preferences result from the kind of processing our brain "specializes" in. **Left-brain processing** concentrates more on tasks requiring verbal competence, such as speaking, reading, thinking, and reasoning. Information is processed sequentially, one bit at a time.

On the other hand, **right-brain processing** tends to concentrate more on the processing of information in nonverbal domains, such as the understanding of spatial relationships, recognition of patterns and drawings, music, and emotional expression. Furthermore, the right hemisphere tends to process information globally, considering it as a whole. Consequently, people who naturally tend toward right-brain processing might prefer visual/graphic learning styles.

Here are some key facts to remember about learning, personality, and processing styles:

- **You have a variety of styles.** As you can see in the summary of different categories of styles in **Table 1.1**, there are several types of styles. For any given task or challenge, some types of styles may be more relevant than others. Furthermore, success is possible even when there is a mismatch between what you need to accomplish and your own pattern of preferred styles. It may take more work, but learning to deal with situations that require you to use less preferred styles is important for college and your career.

- **Your style reflects your preferences regarding which abilities you like to use—not the abilities themselves.** Styles are related to our preferences and the mental approaches we like to use. You may prefer to learn tactilely, but that in itself doesn't guarantee that the products that you create tactilely will be good. You still have to put in work!

- **Your style will change over the course of your life.** You can learn new styles and expand the range of learning experiences in which you feel perfectly comfortable. In fact, you can conceive of this book as one long lesson in learning styles because it provides you with strategies for learning more effectively in a variety of ways.

- **You should work on improving your less preferred styles.** Although it may be tempting, don't always make choices that increase your exposure to preferred styles and decrease your practice with less preferred styles. The more you use approaches for which you have less of a preference, the better you'll be at developing the skills associated with those styles.

- **Work cooperatively with others who have different styles.** If your instructor or supervisor asks you to work cooperatively, seek out classmates or co-workers who have styles that are different from yours. Not only will working with people with differing styles help you achieve collective success, but you can also learn from observing others' approaches to tackling tasks.

left-brain processing
Information processing primarily performed by the left hemisphere of the brain, focusing on tasks requiring verbal competence, such as speaking, reading, thinking, and reasoning; information is processed sequentially, one bit at a time.

right-brain processing
Information processing primarily performed by the right hemisphere of the brain, focusing on information in nonverbal domains, such as the understanding of spatial relationships and recognition of patterns and drawings, music, and emotional expression.

table 1.1   Learning, Personality, and Processing Styles

All of us have particular learning, personality, and processing styles that we tend to rely on. At the same time, we also have capabilities in less preferred styles. So, for example, although you may be primarily a read/write learner, you have the capacity to use auditory/verbal and tactile/kinesthetic approaches. Note in particular that the four categories of personality styles are considered independent of one another. For instance, you may be an extravert and at the same time a sensor, a feeler, and a judger. Furthermore, although the "Using the Style" column suggests ways that those with a particular style can make the most of that style, you should also try strategies that work for styles different from your own.

Category	Type	Description	Using the Style[3]
Receptive Learning Styles	Read/write	A style that involves a preference for material in a written format, favoring reading over hearing and touching.	Read and rewrite material; take notes and rewrite them; organize material into tables; transform diagrams and math formulas into words.
	Visual/graphic	A style that favors material presented visually in a diagram or picture.	Use figures and drawings; replay classes and discussions in your mind's eye; visualize material; translate words into symbols and figures.
	Auditory/ verbal	A style in which the learner favors listening as the best approach.	Recite material out loud; consider how words sound; study different languages; record lectures or training sessions; work with others, talking through the material.
	Tactile/ kinesthetic	A style that involves learning by touching, manipulating objects, and doing things.	Incorporate movement into studying; trace figures and drawings with your finger; create models; make flash cards and move them around; keep active during class and meetings, taking notes, drawing charts, jotting down key concepts.
Multiple Intelligences	Logical- mathematical	Strengths in problem solving and scientific thinking.	Express information mathematically or in formulas.
	Linguistic	Strengths in the production and use of language.	Write out notes and summarize information in words; construct stories about material.
	Spatial	Strengths involving spatial configurations, such as those used by artists and architects.	Build charts, graphs, and flowcharts.
	Interpersonal	Found in learners with particularly strong skills involving interacting with others, such as sensitivity to the moods, temperaments, motivations, and intentions of others.	Work with others in groups.
	Intrapersonal	Strengths in understanding the internal aspects of oneself and having access to one's own feelings and emotions.	Build on your prior experiences and feelings about the world; use your originality.

[3] Adapted from D. Lazear, *The Intelligent Curriculum: Using MI to Develop Your Students' Full Potential* (Tucson, AZ: Zephyr Press, 1999).

Category	Type	Description	Using the Style[3]
	Musical	Strengths relating to music.	Write a song or lyrics to help remember material.
	Bodily kinesthetic	Strengths in using the whole body or portions of it in the solution of problems or in the construction of products or displays, exemplified by dancers, athletes, actors, and surgeons.	Use movement in studying; build models.
	Naturalist	Exceptional strengths in identifying and classifying patterns in nature.	Use analogies based on nature.
Personality Styles	Introvert versus extravert	Independence is a key characteristic of introverted learners, who enjoy working alone and are less affected by how others think and behave. In contrast, extraverts are outgoing and more affected by the behavior and thinking of others. They enjoy working with others.	Experiment with studying or working in groups compared with by yourself; consider your performance collaborating compared with working on your own.
	Intuitor versus sensor	Intuitive people enjoy solving problems and being creative, often taking a big-picture approach. Sensors, on the other hand, prefer a concrete, logical approach in which they can carefully analyze the facts of the situation.	For intuitors, reflect on the personal meaning of material and seek out tasks that involve creativity. For sensors, seek out concrete tasks that involve the application of logical principles.
	Thinker versus feeler	Thinkers prefer logic over emotion, reaching decisions through rational analysis. In contrast, feelers rely more on their emotions and are influenced by their personal values and attachments to others.	Thinkers should seek to systematically analyze situations, attempting to identify patterns. Feelers should use emotional responses to reflect on material.
	Perceiver versus judger	Before drawing a conclusion, perceivers attempt to gather as much information as they can and are open to multiple perspectives. Judgers, in comparison, are quick and decisive, enjoying setting goals and accomplishing them.	Perceivers organize material sequentially and into component parts; for judgers, goal setting facilitates learning.
Brain Processing Styles	Left-brain processing	Information processing that focuses on tasks requiring verbal competence, such as speaking, reading, thinking, and reasoning; information is processed sequentially, one bit at a time.	Organize material logically; identify patterns; make tables of key information; break material into component parts.
	Right-brain processing	Information processing that focuses on information in nonverbal domains, such as the understanding of spatial relationships, recognition of patterns and drawings, music, and emotional expression.	Identify patterns; use graphs and drawings; read aloud; create models.

Learning about Learning: The Theories That Explain How You Learn

Learning styles reflect how each of us prefers to study and approach new information that we encounter in our classes. But all of us are affected by some basic processes that underlie learning.

Researchers have developed a number of **learning theories**, which are broad explanations about how we learn. Each of these theories takes a different approach and looks at somewhat different factors that help us to learn. Understanding the theories behind learning will help you study, remember information, and ultimately be a better learner. We'll consider the three main approaches.

learning theory

A broad explanation about how one learns.

Operant Conditioning Approaches: The Reinforcement behind Learning

Very good . . . What a clever idea . . . Fantastic . . . I agree . . . Excellent . . . Super . . . Great point . . . This is the best paper you've ever written . . . You are really getting the hang of it . . . I'm impressed . . . A+

Did you ever wonder why we love to be praised? It turns out that positive affirmations of this sort underlie a type of learning known as operant conditioning, which is the basis for many of the most important kinds of learning.

Operant conditioning is learning in which a behavior is made more or less likely to recur regularly because of the presence of a reinforcer. **Reinforcers** are things that increase the probability that a behavior will occur again. If you study hard for a test and are rewarded with a high grade, the high grade serves as a reinforcer. Operant conditioning theory tells us that you are more like to study hard in the future because of the reward you received. On the other hand, if you party hard the night before a test and receive a low grade, operant conditioning theory suggests that in the future you will avoid partying before a test.

operant conditioning

Learning in which behavior is modified by the presence of a reinforcer.

reinforcer

A thing that increases the probability that a behavior will occur again.

Cognitive Approaches: The Thoughts Behind Learning

Some learning theorists focus on the thought processes that underlie learning. According to cognitive approaches to learning, our cognitions (or thoughts) shape the way we learn. In particular, they look at the importance of observational learning, in which we learn by watching, and imitating, the behavior of other people.

Observational learning takes place in four steps:

1. Paying attention and perceiving the most critical features of another person's behavior

2. Remembering the behavior

3. Reproducing the action

4. Being motivated to learn and carry out the behavior

Not all behavior that we witness is learned or carried out. Whether we later imitate someone else depends, in part, on what eventually happens to that person as a result of the behavior.

If we observe a friend who studies more frequently than we do and notice that she receives higher grades, we are more apt to model her behavior than if her studying leads to nothing more than a sharp decline in her social life and an increase in fatigue. Models who are seen receiving reinforcement for their actions are more likely to be mimicked than those who are observed receiving punishment.

Classical Conditioning Approaches: Does the Name Pavlov Ring a Bell?

Ivan Pavlov was a Russian scientist who discovered, quite accidentally, one of the basic kinds of learning, called classical conditioning. In studying salivation in dogs, he found that sometimes the mere sight of the person who normally brought the dog's food, or even the sound of that person's footsteps, was enough to produce salivation in the dogs.

Pavlov's genius lay in his ability to recognize the implications of this discovery. He saw that the dogs were responding not only on the basis of a biological need (hunger) but also as a result of learning—or, as it came to be called, classical conditioning. **Classical conditioning** is a type of learning in which a neutral stimulus (such as someone's footsteps) comes to elicit a response after being paired with a different stimulus (such as food) that naturally brings about that response.

To demonstrate classical conditioning, Pavlov (1927) attached a tube to the salivary gland of a dog, allowing him to measure precisely the dog's salivation. He then rang a bell and, just a few seconds later, presented the dog with meat. This pairing occurred repeatedly and was carefully planned so that each time exactly the same amount of time elapsed between the presentation of the bell and the meat. At first the dog would salivate only when the meat was presented, but soon it began to salivate at the sound of the bell. In fact, even when Pavlov stopped presenting the meat, the dog still salivated after hearing the sound. The dog had been classically conditioned to salivate to the bell.

But what about humans? In fact, Pavlov's discovery of classical conditioning has some very practical implications for how we come to associate various stimuli with responses. For example, you may not go to a dentist as often as you should because of previous associations of dentists with pain. Similarly, we may come to associate academic tests with negative emotions and anxiety, which can hinder our performance.

classical conditioning
A type of learning in which a neutral stimulus elicits a response after being paired with a natural stimulus.

Why Learning Theories Matter

Although the basics of the three main learning theories are somewhat abstract, each has important practical implications for helping you to learn better. For example, operant conditioning suggests that rewarding yourself while you study with periodic breaks will make your study sessions more productive, because the breaks act as a reinforcer. Similarly, using cognitive approaches to learning, you might watch the behavior of other students who have been successful and try to imitate their study habits. Finally, classical conditioning, which focuses on learning through associations, suggests that studying in the room where you'll later be taking a test will help you to perform better on the test, because it will help trigger memories of the material you studied earlier—an idea that research has proven correct.

If you are wondering which of the theories is "best," you're asking the wrong question. Each of the theories takes a different approach and focuses on different aspects of learning, in much the same way that we can take multiple routes on a map to the same location. Understanding each of the learning theories, along with knowledge of your preferred learning styles, will help you develop your own personal learning system that can help you become a more successful student.

Speaking *of* Success

Source: Courtesy of Albertina Abouchar

NAME: **Albertina Abouchar**

SCHOOL: **Mesa Community College, Mesa, Arizona**

MAJOR: **Psychology**

Like many older students returning to school, Albertina Abouchar wasn't quite sure she would be able to take on the demands of a college curriculum. But with the support of a friend who had obtained her degree as an older student, Abouchar settled on a two-year community college and launched her pursuit of a college degree.

"I chose Mesa Community College because it didn't feel intimidating, offered a lot of flexibility, and was affordable," she noted. "Also, it had small class sizes and direct interaction with professors, as well as location, because I did not want to waste time commuting."

Finding the right school turned out to be the easy part.

"The first challenge was self-doubt, letting go of the thought that I was too old or not good enough for college," she said. "The best advice I gave myself was to get started despite the doubts and to take one step at a time. I started with Psychology 101, a subject that interested me. Getting an A in that class gave me the confidence to continue."

Once Abouchar settled in she was able to develop a number of approaches to dealing with the challenges of being a first-time college student, and managing a family as well.

"Being a mother with lots of family responsibilities, time management was always a challenge. I set up time for attending classes and time for homework," she explained. "During those assigned times during the week, school came first, no matter how big the pile of laundry. I committed to what I felt I could do, and I didn't take on more responsibility than I could handle."

"Another challenge was to read textbooks without losing concentration. If I couldn't get past a few pages in a textbook, I found other sources of the same information (teacher's slides, online videos, visual aids, etc.)," she added. "Then, I went back to the book, and I didn't find it so hard to follow."

Studying is a matter of finding your own style and making sure to ask for help when you need it, according to Abouchar, who plans to continue her education at a four-year college and major in psychology.

[RETHINK]

- Why do you think it was important to Abouchar to have the support of a friend who had successfully completed college as an older student?

- Abouchar suggests the importance of taking one step at a time. How might you apply that advice to your own academic life?

Looking Back

LO 1-1 Explain the benefits of a college education.

▶ The reason first-year college students most often cite for attending college is to get a better job, and college graduates earn more on average than nongraduates.

▶ College also provides many other benefits. These include becoming well educated, learning to think critically and communicate effectively, and understanding the interconnections among different areas of knowledge, our place in history and the world, and diversity.

LO 1-2 Identify the basic principles of P.O.W.E.R. Learning.

▶ P.O.W.E.R. Learning is a systematic approach people can easily learn, using abilities they already possess, to acquire successful habits for learning and achieving personal goals.

▶ P.O.W.E.R. Learning involves **P**reparation, **O**rganization, **W**ork, **E**valuation, and **R**ethinking.

▶ To *prepare,* learners set both long-term and short-term goals, making sure that their goals are realistic, measurable, and under their control—and will lead to their final destination.

▶ They *organize* the tools they will need to accomplish those goals.

▶ They get down to *work* on the task at hand. Using their goals as motivation, expert learners also understand that success depends on effort.

▶ They *evaluate* the work they've done, considering what they have accomplished in comparison with the goals they set for themselves during the preparation stage.

▶ Finally, they *rethink,* reflecting on the process they've used, taking a fresh look at what they have done, and critically rethinking their goals.

LO 1-3 Identify your learning styles and how they affect your academic success.

▶ People have patterns of diverse learning styles—characteristic ways of acquiring and using knowledge.

▶ Learning styles include read/write, visual/graphic, auditory/verbal, and tactile/kinesthetic styles (the receptive learning styles).

▶ The multiple intelligences view says that we have eight different forms of intelligence, each relatively independent of the others.

▶ Personality styles that influence learning are classified along dimensions of introversion/extraversion, intuition/sensing, thinking/feeling, and perceiving/judging.

▶ Knowing your learning styles can help you identify the specific techniques that will allow you to master material in class and on the job most effectively.

▶ Learning theories explain the ways in which we learn. The three main perspectives are operant conditioning, cognitive approaches, and classical conditioning approaches.

[KEY TERMS AND CONCEPTS]

Auditory/verbal learning style (p. 19)
Classical conditioning (p. 27)
Critical thinking (p. 16)
Evaluation (p. 13)

Growth mindset (p. 11)
Learning style (p. 18)
Learning theory (p. 26)
Left-brain processing (p. 23)

Long-term goals (p. 7)
Motivation (p. 12)
Operant conditioning (p. 26)
P.O.W.E.R. Learning (p. 5)

[R E S O U R C E S]

ON CAMPUS

Every college provides a significant number of resources to help its students succeed and thrive, ranging from the activities coordination office to a multicultural center to writing labs to career centers. You can check them out on your college's website, catalog, or phone directory to see which of the following resources are available to you.

For example, here's a list of some typical campus resources, many of which we'll be discussing in future chapters:

- Activities/clubs office
- Adult and reentry center
- Advising center
- Alumni office
- Art gallery
- Bookstore
- Career center
- Chaplain/religious services
- Child care center
- Cinema/theater
- Computing center/computer labs
- Continuing education
- Disability center (learning or physical disabilities)
- Financial aid office

- Fitness center/gymnasium
- Health center
- Honors program
- Housing center
- Information center
- Intramural sports
- Language lab
- Lost and found
- Math lab
- Multicultural center
- Museum
- Online Education (distance learning) office
- Off-campus housing and services
- Ombudsman/conflict resolution

- Photography lab
- Police/campus security
- Post office
- Printing center
- Registration office
- Residential Life office
- School newspaper
- Student Government office
- Student Affairs office
- Study abroad/exchange programs
- Testing center
- Volunteer services
- Work-study center
- Writing lab

If you are commuting to school, your first "official" encounters on campus are likely to be with representatives of the college's Student Affairs office or its equivalent. The Student Affairs office has the goal of maintaining the quality of student life, helping ensure that students receive the help they need. Student Affairs personnel often are in charge of student orientation programs that help new students familiarize themselves with their new institution.

Whatever college representatives you deal with during your first days of college, remember that their job is to help you. Don't be shy about asking questions about what you may expect, how to find things, and what you should be doing.

Above all, if you are experiencing any difficulties, be certain to make use of your college's resources. College success does not come easily for anyone, particularly when it demands juggling responsibilities of work and family. You should make use of whatever support your college offers.

IN PRINT

For a variety of views of what it takes to be a successful college student, read *How to Survive Your Freshman Year: By Hundreds of College Sophomores, Juniors, and Seniors Who Did,* 5th edition, published by Hundreds of Heads Books (2013).

To learn more about who your first-year classmates are across the United States, take a look at Kevin Eagan and colleagues' *The American Freshman: National Norms for Fall 2014* (Higher Education Research Institute, 2014). The book provides a comprehensive look at the attitudes and opinions of first-year college students, based on the results of a national survey.

Finally, Thomas Armstrong and Sue Teele's *Rainbows of Intelligence: Exploring How Students Learn* (2015) provides an introduction to learning styles, offering tips and suggestions for making use of the ways that people learn.

ON THE WEB

The following sites on the web provide opportunities to extend your learning about the material in this chapter.

▶ The University of Buffalo (**http://ub-counseling.buffalo.edu/adjusting.php**) Counseling Services offers a site on adjusting to campus life that includes links to relationships, health, and study skills.

▶ The Learn More Resource Center, sponsored by the state of Indiana (**www.learnmoreindiana.org**), provides information on a variety of useful topics regarding adjustment to college life, including comments by students on their experiences. It covers such topics as where to live, how to select classes, how to study and learn, and much more.

▶ **EducationPlanner.org**, a public service of the Pennsylvania Higher Education Assistance Agency, offers an interactive set of questions that can help you find out what kind of student you are, what your learning style is, and which study habits you can improve. **http://www.educationplanner.org/students/self-assessments/kind-of-student.shtml**

The Case of . . .

College Daydreams

Danny Lipovak was having second thoughts about his decision to enroll in a Vehicle Maintenance and Repair program at a local community college. First of all, his English was shaky, even after nine months in the United States. His job at a local service station gave him plenty of speaking practice, but he was still far from fluent, and his reading and writing skills were lacking.

Second, he was no genius at school even in his native Croatia. He had no proof that he could actually succeed in an American college. None of his relatives had gone to college, and neither had any of his co-workers at the service station. When he told his uncle Roman of his plans, he had been greeted with a burst of laughter. "You kidding?"

Roman had said. "You, a college boy? You sure have big ideas!" His co-workers were no more encouraging, calling him a dreamer and making fun of his college plans.

He was forced to question whether college was really worth the time and money. He was learning auto mechanics on the job already, and his boss assured him he could continue to work at the station as long as he liked. Every day he was given new tasks to try out, and he was always picking up new skills.

Maybe everyone was right. Maybe he *was* only daydreaming. Who was he to go for a college degree?

And yet, getting an education had always been one of his secret ambitions. . . .

1. What arguments could you provide Danny about the value of a college education?

2. Do you think that Danny's doubts are common?

3. What might Danny do to help deal with his doubts about the value of college? Is there anyone he should talk to aside from his relatives and co-workers?

4. How much weight should Danny place on the opinions and joking of relatives and friends? Can you explain their reactions? Do you think Danny's situation is rare or normal, given his background?

5. How would you respond to Danny's worries about his fitness for college work?

6. Do you share any of Danny's concerns about the value of a college education? Do you have additional ones?

CHAPTER 2

Learning Outcomes

By the time you finish this chapter you will be able to

» LO **2-1**   Discuss strategies to manage your time effectively.

» LO **2-2**   Explain ways to balance competing priorities.

» LO **2-3**   Identify ways to deal with surprises and distractions.

Making the Most of Your Time

Source: © BFG Images/Getty Images

Joe Davies groaned as the alarm rang. He'd done it again. Fallen asleep when he should have been studying. And he had a test in accounting today. As he rushed to make his first class, Joe despaired of ever getting his life under control. It had seemed so easy when he'd planned it a year ago. He'd take classes in the morning, study in the afternoon, go to work in the evening. But his plans had fallen apart right from the get-go. The way classes were scheduled made it impossible to take a full load and have his afternoons free for study. So he'd dropped two classes. Then, his shift from 10:00 p.m. to 4:00 a.m. at the supermarket didn't really give him enough time to sleep before his first class. He started sleeping in the afternoons and studying after work. Except most nights turned out like this last one. He'd arrive home, exhausted, and lie down "for just a few minutes." The next thing he knew it was morning and he was running late, completely unprepared. Joe felt hopelessly trapped by the limits of time.

Looking Ahead

Does Joe's story sound familiar? Do you feel that the faster you race to get everything done, the farther behind you fall? Do you feel, as Joe does, trapped by the limits of time?

You're not alone. Most of us wish we had more time to accomplish the things we need to do. However, some people are a lot better at juggling their time than others. What's their secret?

There is no secret. No one has more than 24 hours a day and 168 hours a week. The key to success lies in figuring out our priorities and better using the time we do have.

Time management is like juggling a bunch of tennis balls. For most of us, juggling doesn't come naturally, but it is a skill that can be learned. Not all of us will end up perfect jugglers (of tennis balls or time), but with practice, we can become a lot better at it.

This chapter will give you strategies for improving your time management skills. After helping you analyze the ways you currently use—and misuse—time, it gives you strategies for planning your time, including ways to deal with the inevitable interruptions and personal habits that can undermine your best intentions. It will give you skills that are important for success in every area: college, career, and personal life.

Because juggling the priorities of college and work with other aspects of life (such as parenthood or hobbies) presents special challenges, we also consider ways to deal with competing goals.

» LO 2-1 Time for Success

Without looking up from the page, answer this question: What time is it?

Most people are pretty accurate in their answer. And if you aren't sure, it's very likely that you can find out. Your cell phone may display the time; you may be wearing a wristwatch; or there may be a clock on the wall, desk, or computer screen.

Even if you don't have a timepiece of some sort nearby, your body keeps its own beat. Humans have an internal clock that regulates the beating of our heart, the pace of our breathing, the discharge of chemicals within our bloodstream, and many other bodily functions.

We can't escape time. Even if we ignore it, it's still going by, ticking away, minute by minute, hour by hour. So the main issue in using your time well is, "Who's in charge?" We can allow time to slip by and let it be our enemy. Or we can take control of it and make it our ally.

By taking control of your time, you'll increase your chances of success, both in college and in your career. Perhaps more important, the better you are at managing the time you devote to your studies and your job, the more time you will have to spend on your outside interests. (You can get a sense of your own personal time

Find Your Time Style

For each pair of statements, check the one that best describes you.

- ☐ 1a. I set an alarm and get up when it rings, allowing enough time to prepare for the morning.
- ☐ 1b. I hit the snooze button several times and often wake up later than I should.
- ☐ 2a. I usually arrive a few minutes early for classes and appointments.
- ☐ 2b. I am always rushing to get places and usually end up being late.
- ☐ 3a. I like to start major projects and class assignments well ahead of when they're due.
- ☐ 3b. I put off big tasks and studying for tests until the last minute.
- ☐ 4a. When working on a major project, I schedule several short breaks so that my focus remains sharp.
- ☐ 4b. I give myself breaks whenever a task gets confusing or starts to feel like work.
- ☐ 5a. I try to work away from distractions and remain focused until a task is done.
- ☐ 5b. I am easily interrupted, putting aside what I'm doing for something new.
- ☐ 6a. I keep a list of things I need to buy and bundle all my errands into one weekly trip.
- ☐ 6b. I run out whenever I need something, even if I've made several trips that day.
- ☐ 7a. I keep all my appointments on a pocket calendar or smartphone, and I check it daily.
- ☐ 7b. I often forget appointments and have to reschedule them.
- ☐ 8a. I break big projects into a series of steps so I can tackle the first task right away.
- ☐ 8b. When faced with a big task, I feel overwhelmed and turn my mind away from it until later.
- ☐ 9a. I keep a list of all the tasks I've completed each day, so I know where to start tomorrow.
- ☐ 9b. At the end of the day, I have no idea where the time went.

Count up your *b* responses. Two *b*s or less? You manage your day pretty efficiently. Three or four *b*s? You could be more efficient. Look to the *a* statements for clues to help you. More than four *b*s? You need to adopt a new set of strategies to control your time. Right now, it controls you.

---

style by completing **Try It! 1**.) *The goal of time management is not to schedule every moment of the day so we become hostages to a rigid timetable. Instead, the goal is to make informed choices about how we use our time.* The time management strategies we'll discuss can help you better harness time for your own ends, rather than letting the day slip by, without thought. In short, time management doesn't control us. Rather, it frees us to do the things we want and need to do.

 **P Prepare**

Learning Where Time Is Going and Where It Should Go

Before you get somewhere, you need to know where you're starting from and where you want to go. So the first step in improving your time management skills is figuring out how you're managing your time now.

Create a Time Log

"Where did the day go?" If you've ever said this to yourself, one way of figuring out where you've spent your time is to create a time log. A time log is the most essential tool for improving your use of time.

P Prepare
Learn where time is going

O Organize
Use a master calender, weekly timetable, and daily to-do list

W Work
Follow the schedules you've put together

E Evaluate
Keep track of your short-term and long-term accomplishments

R Rethink
Reflect on your personal style of time management

P.O.W.E.R. Plan

Create a Time Log

Keep track of the way you spend your time across seven days on time logs. Insert the amount of time you spend on each activity during each one-hour period for a single day. Do the same thing for every day of the week on separate time logs. *Be sure to make copies of this log before you fill it in for the first day.*

Analyze your log: After you complete your log for a week, analyze how you spend your time according to the major categories on the log. Add up the amount of time you've spent on each category. You can also create other broad categories that eat up significant amounts of time.

Now consider the following:

1. What do you spend most of your time on?

2. Are you satisfied with the way that you are using your time? Are there any areas that seem to use up excessive amounts of time?

3. Do you see some simple fixes that will allow you to use time more effectively?

 WORKING IN A GROUP

Compare your use of time during an average week with the time use of your classmates. What are the major differences and similarities in the use of time?

time log

A record of how one spends one's time.

A **time log** is simply a record of how you actually have spent your time—including interruptions. It doesn't have to be a second-by-second record of every waking moment. But it should account for blocks of time in increments as short as 15 minutes.

Look at the blank time log in **Try It! 2**. As you fill out the log, be specific, indicating not only what you were doing at a given time (for example, "studying for economics quiz") but also the interruptions that occurred (such as "answered cell phone twice" or "switched to Internet for 10 minutes").

Time Log

Day: _____   Date:_____

	personal care	food	classes	studies	work	recreation	sleep	other
6–7 a.m.								
7–8 a.m.								
8–9 a.m.								
9–10 a.m.								
10–11 a.m.								
11–12 (noon)								
12 (noon)–1 p.m.								
1–2 p.m.								
2–3 p.m.								
3–4 p.m.								
4–5 p.m.								
5–6 p.m.								
6–7 p.m.								
7–8 p.m.								
8–9 p.m.								
9–10 p.m.								
10–11 p.m.								
11 p.m.–12 (midnight)								
12 (midnight)–1 a.m.								
1–2 a.m.								
2–3 a.m.								
3–4 a.m.								
4–5 a.m.								
5–6 a.m.								

By looking at how much time you spend doing various activities, you now know where your time goes. How does it match with your perceptions of how you spend your time? Be prepared to be surprised, because most people find that they're spending time on a lot of activities that just don't matter very much.

> "You may delay, but time will not."
> **Benjamin Franklin**

From the perspective of . . .

A STUDENT Time logs can be helpful tools when determining how you spend your time; they can also help you find more time for the activities you enjoy doing. What areas of your life do you wish you had more time to spend on?

» LO 2-2 Set Your Priorities

priorities

The tasks and activities that one needs and wants to do, rank-ordered from most important to least important.

By this point you should have a good idea of what's taking up your time. But you may not know what you should be doing instead.

To figure out the best use of your time, you need to determine your priorities. **Priorities** are the tasks and activities you need and want to do, rank-ordered from most important to least important. There are no right or wrong priorities; you have to decide for yourself what you wish to accomplish. Maybe spending time on your studies is most important to you, or working to earn more money, or maybe your top priority is spending time with your family. Only you can decide. Furthermore, what's important to you at this moment may be less of a priority to you next month, next year, or five years from now.

Source: © Richard Drury/ Photodisc/Getty Images

For the purpose of effective time management in college, the best procedure is to start off by identifying priorities for an entire term. What do you need to accomplish? Don't just choose obvious, general goals, such as "passing all my classes." Instead, think about your priorities in terms of specific, measurable activities, such as "studying five hours before each exam"—*not* "studying harder," which is too vague. (Look at the example of a priority list in **Figure 2.1** and also at the **Course Connections** feature.)

Priority	Ranking
Study for each class at least 30 minutes/day	1
Start each major paper 2 weeks in advance of due date	2
Hand in each paper on time	1
Review for test starting a week before test date	2
Be on time for job	1
Work out 3x/week	3

figure 2.1
Sample List of Priorities

Study Time: How Much Is Enough?

What would you guess is the average number of hours instructors think you should be studying each week? In the view of instructors queried in surveys, students should spend, on average, 6 hours per week preparing for *each* class in which they're enrolled. And if they're taking courses in the sciences and engineering, instructors expect their students to put in even more hours.[1]

Keep in mind that study time does not include actual class time. If you add that in, someone taking four classes would need 24 hours of outside class preparation and would be in class for 16 hours—for a total of 40 hours, or the equivalent of full-time employment.

If you've underestimated the amount of time instructors believe is necessary to devote to class preparation, you may need to rethink the amount of time you'll need to allocate to studying. You might also speak to your individual instructors to see what they believe is an appropriate amount of preparation. Although they may not be able to give exact figures, their estimates will help you prioritize what you need to do to be a successful student.

Write your priorities on the chart in **Try It! 3** (on page 42). After you've filled out the chart, organize it by giving each priority a ranking from 1 to 3.

A "1" represents a priority that absolutely must be done; without it you'll suffer a major setback. For instance, showing up for work should receive a priority ranking of "1"; carving out time to take those guitar lessons you always wanted to take might be ranked "3" in terms of priority. The important point is to rank-order your priorities to reveal what is and is not important to accomplish during the term.

Setting priorities will help you determine how to make the best use of your time. No one has enough time to complete everything; prioritizing will help you make informed decisions about what you can do to maximize your success.

O Organize | Mastering the Moment

You now know where you've lost time in the past, and your priority list is telling you where you need to head in the future.

Now for the present. You've reached the point where you can organize yourself to take control of your time. Here's what you'll need:

▶ A **master calendar** that shows all the weeks of the term on one page. You don't need to buy one; you can make it easily enough yourself. It need not be great art; a rough version will do. The important point is that it must include every week of the term and seven days per week. (See an example of a master calendar in **Figure 2.2**.)

▶ A weekly timetable. The **weekly timetable** is a master grid with the days of the week across the top and the hours along the side. This will permit you to write in all your regularly scheduled activities, as well as one-time appointments when they arise. (A blank weekly timetable is provided in **Figure 2.3**.)

master calendar
A schedule showing the weeks of a longer time period, such as a college term, with all assignments and important activities noted on it.

weekly timetable
A schedule showing all regular, prescheduled activities due to occur in the week, together with one-time events and commitments.

figure 2.2
Master Calendar Sample

Writing

M	T	W	TH	F	SA	S
Sept. 7	8	9 Classes Start	10	11	12 Camping →	13
14	Add/drop 15 ends	16	English 17 short paper due	18	19	20
21	Work 22	23	English 24 short paper due	Work 25	26	27
28	29	30 Math exam	OCT 1 English short paper due	Legal 2 Studies quiz	3	4
5	Legal Studies 6 paper due	7	English 8 short paper due	Work 9	10	11
12	Work 13	14	English short 15 paper due	Legal 16 Studies quiz	17	18
First-yr 19 seminar journal due	20	Math 21 exam	English 22 short paper due Dad's bd-call	Work 23	Bartending 24 job	25
Work 26	English 27 midterm exam	28	Eng-short 29 paper due	Legal Studies 30 quiz	31	NOV 1
2	3	4	English 5 short paper due	Work 6	7	Darcey's 8 Wedding!
9	Work 10	Holiday- 11 Veteran's Day	Eng-short 12 paper due	Legal 13 Studies quiz Math exam	14	15
First-yr 16 seminar group project due	17	Preregistration 18 for next semester	English 19 short paper due	20	21	22
23	Work 24	25	Thanksgiving 26	No Classes! 27	28	29
30	DEC 1 Legal Studies paper due	2	English 3 short paper due	Work 4	5	6
First-yr 7 seminar final journal due	Work 8	9	Legal 10 studies quiz	Math exam 11 Last day of class!!	12	13
English 14 final exam	Legal 15 Studies final exam	16	Math 17 final exam	Legal 18 Studies exam MY birthday!	19	20
21	22	23	24	25 Xmas	26	27

daily to-do list

A schedule showing the tasks, activities, and appointments due to occur during the day.

► A daily to-do list. Finally, you'll need a **daily to-do list.** The daily to-do list can be written on a small, portable calendar that includes a separate page for each day of the week. Or you can keep it virtually in a smartphone or iPad. Whatever form your daily to-do list takes, make sure you can keep it with you all the time.

The basic organizational task you face is filling in these three schedules. You'll need at least an hour to do this, so set the time aside. In addition, there will be some repetition across the three schedules, and the task may seem a bit tedious.

Weekly Timetable

Week of: _____   **Week #** _____

	Mon	Tues	Wed	Thurs	Fri	Sat	Sun
6–7 a.m.							
7–8 a.m.							
8–9 a.m.							
9–10 a.m.							
10–11 a.m.							
11–12 (noon)							
12 (noon)–1 p.m.							
1–2 p.m.							
2–3 p.m.							
3–4 p.m.							
4–5 p.m.							
5–6 p.m.							
6–7 p.m.							
7–8 p.m.							
8–9 p.m.							
9–10 p.m.							
10–11 p.m.							
11 p.m.–12 (midnight)							
12 (midnight)–1 a.m.							
1–2 a.m.							
2–3 a.m.							
3–4 a.m.							
4–5 a.m.							
5–6 a.m.							

figure 2.3
Weekly Timetable
Make a single copy of this blank timetable. Then fill in your regular, predictable time commitments. Next, make as many copies as you need to cover each week of the term. Then, for each week, fill in the date on the left and the number of the week in the term on the right, and add in your irregular commitments.

But every minute you invest now in organizing your time will pay off in hours that you will save in the future.
Follow these steps in completing your schedule:

▶ **Start with the master calendar, which shows all the weeks of the term on one page.** Write on the master calendar every class assignment you have for the entire term, noting it on the date that it is due. Also include major events at work, such as days when you might need to work overtime. In addition, include important activities from your personal life, drawn from your list of priorities. For instance, if your spouse or child has a performance or sporting event you want to attend, be sure to mark it down.

Set Priorities

Set your priorities for the term. They may include getting to class on time, finishing papers and assignments by their due dates, devoting a certain number of hours to your job, or spending time with your family. To get started, list priorities in any order. Be sure to consider priorities relating to your classes, work, family, social obligations, and health. After you list them, assign a number to each one indicating its level—giving a "1" to the highest-priority items, a "2" to medium-priority items, and a "3" to the items with the lowest priority.

List of Priorities	
Priority	Priority Index

Now redo your list, putting your number 1s first, followed by as many of your number 2s and 3s as you feel you can reasonably commit yourself to.

Finally, schedule some free time—time when you promise yourself you will do something that is just plain fun. Consider these days to be written in stone, and promise yourself that you won't use them for anything else, except for something enjoyable. Just knowing that you have some downtime planned will help you to throw yourself into more demanding tasks. In addition, getting into the habit of allowing yourself time to relax and reflect on your life is as important as any other time management skill you may learn.

You now have a good idea of what the next few weeks have in store for you. You can identify just by looking at your master calendar the periods when you are going to be especially busy. You can also note the periods when you will have less to do.

Use the off-peak periods to get a head start on future assignments!

Final List of Priorities
Priority
1.
2.
3.
4.
5.
6.
7.
8.
9.
10.
11.
12.

Now consider the following:

- What does this list tell you about your greatest priorities? Are they centered around school, your current work schedule, friends and family, or some other aspect of your life?
- Do you have so many "1" priorities that they will be difficult or impossible to accomplish successfully? How could you go back to your list and trim it down even more?
- What does this listing of priorities suggest about how successful you'll be during the upcoming term?

In this way, your master schedule can help you head off disaster before it occurs.

▶ **Now move to the weekly timetable provided in Figure 2.3**. Fill in the times of all your fixed, prescheduled activities—the times that your classes meet, when you have to be at work, the times you have to pick up your child at day care, and any other recurring appointments.

Once you've filled in the weekly timetable, you'll have a bare-bones picture of the average week. You will still need to take into account the specific activities that are required to complete the assignments on the master calendar.

To move from your "average" week to specific weeks, make photocopies of the weekly timetable that now contains your fixed appointments. Make

Journal Reflections

Where Does My Time Go?

1. When would you prefer to wake up if you did not have the obligations and responsibilities you currently have?

2. When do you typically go to bed on a typical weekday night? When would you prefer to go to bed if you did not have the obligations and responsibilities you currently have?

3. Would you characterize yourself as a "morning person," who accomplishes the most in the early morning, or more as a "night person," who is most comfortable doing work in the evenings? What implications does this have for your scheduling of classes and work shifts?

4. Generally speaking, how would you characterize your time management skills? What would be the benefit to you personally if you could manage time more effectively? What goals might you accomplish if you had more time at your disposal?

enough copies for every week of the term. On each copy write the week number of the term and the specific dates it covers. (See a sample in **Figure 2.4**.)

Using your master calendar, add assignment due dates, tests, and any other activities on the appropriate days of the week. Then pencil in blocks of time necessary to prepare for those events.

How much time should you allocate for schoolwork? One very rough rule of thumb holds that every one hour that you spend in class requires, on average, two hours of study outside of class to earn a B and three hours of study outside of class to earn an A. Do the arithmetic: If you are taking 15 credits (with each credit equivalent to an hour of class per week), you'll need to plan for 30 hours of studying each week to earn a B average—an intimidating amount of time. Of course, the amount of time you must allocate to a specific class will vary from week to week, depending on what is happening in the class.

For example, if you estimate that you'll need five hours of study for a midterm exam in a certain class, pencil in those hours. Don't set up a single block of five hours. People remember best when their studying is spread out over shorter periods rather than attempted in one long block of time. Besides, it will probably be hard to find a block of five straight hours on your weekly calendar.

Keep in mind that estimates are just that: estimates. Don't think of them as set in stone. Mark them on your weekly calendar in pencil, not pen, so you can adjust them if necessary.

But remember: It's also crucial not to overschedule yourself. You'll still need time to eat, to talk with your friends, to spend time with your family, and to enjoy yourself in general. If you find that your life is completely filled with things that you feel you must do to survive and that there is no room for fun, then take a step back and cut out something to make some time for yourself in your daily schedule. Finding time for yourself is as important as carving out time for what others want you to do. Besides, if you are overworked, you're likely to "find" the time by guiltily goofing off without really setting aside the time and enjoying it.

▶ **If you've taken each of the previous steps, you're now in a position to work on the final step of organization for successful time management: completing your daily to-do list.** Unlike the master calendar and weekly timetable—both of which you develop weeks or even months in advance—complete your daily to-do list just one day ahead of time, preferably at the end of the day.

List all the things that you intend to do during the next day, and their priority. Start with the things you know you *must* do and which have fixed times,

Short- and long-term priorities may not always match. What would you do if a class you needed to graduate conflicted with your daughter's weekly soccer game?
Source: © SW Productions/Brand X Pictures/Punchstock

such as classes, work schedules, and appointments. These are your first priority items. Then add in the other things that you *should* accomplish, such as an hour of study for an upcoming test or a trip to the garage to have your oil changed. Finally, list things that are lower in priority but enjoyable, setting aside time for a run or a walk, for example.

Don't schedule every single minute of the day. That would be counterproductive, and you'd end up feeling like you'd failed if you deviated from your schedule. Instead, think of your daily to-do list as a path through a forest. If you were hiking, you would allow yourself to deviate from the path,

Sometimes it is okay (and even necessary) to simply relax. Make sure that you make time to unwind!
Source: © KidStock/Blend Images/Brand X Pictures/Getty Images

figure 2.4
A Sample Weekly Timetable

Source: © Brand X Pictures/PunchStock

Weekly Timetable

Week of: 9/28   Week # 3

	Mon	Tues	Wed	Thurs	Fri	Sat	Sun
6–7 a.m.							
7–8 a.m.							
8–9 a.m.							
9–10 a.m.	9.05 Math	9.05 Legal Studies	9.05 Math	9.05 Math	9.05 Legal Studies		
10–11 a.m.		↓		↓			
11–12 (noon)		11.15 Writing I		11.15 Writing I			
12 (noon)–1 p.m.	12.20 First Year Seminar	↓		↓			
1–2 p.m.	↓	Work	Work	Work	Work		
2–3 p.m.							
3–4 p.m.							
4–5 p.m.							
5–6 p.m.		↓	↓	↓	↓		
6–7 p.m.							
7–8 p.m.							
8–9 p.m.							
9–10 p.m.							
10–11 p.m.							
11 p.m.–12 (midnight)							
12 (midnight)–1 a.m.							
1–2 a.m.							
2–3 a.m.							
3–4 a.m.							
4–5 a.m.							
5–6 a.m.							

occasionally venturing onto side tracks when they looked interesting. But you'd also be keeping tabs on your direction so you ended up where you needed to be and not miles away from your car or home.

Like the sample daily to-do list in **Figure 2.5,** yours should include a column to check or cross off after you've completed an activity. There's something very satisfying in acknowledging what you have accomplished.

>> LO 2-3   W Work

Controlling Time

You're in luck: There is no work to time management—or at least not much more than you've already done. The work of time management is to follow the schedules that you've prepared and organized. But that doesn't mean it will be easy. Our

figure 2.5
Sample Daily To-Do List

To-Do List for _____ (date)		
Item Item	Priority	Completed
Call Chris to get anatomy notes	1	✓
Meet with Dr. Hernandez about paper	1	✓
Work on outline for legal studies paper	2	✓
Return books to library	2	
Pick up Nettie at school	1	✓
Call Deena about Saturday	2	
Do laundry	3	

lives are filled with surprises: Things take longer than we've planned. A friend we haven't spoken to in a while calls to chat, and it seems rude to say that we don't have time to talk. A crisis occurs; buses are late; computers break down; kids get sick.

The difference between effective time management and time management that doesn't work lies in how well you deal with the inevitable surprises.

There are several ways to take control of your days and permit yourself to follow your intended schedule:

▶ **Just say no.** You don't have to agree to every request and every favor that others ask of you. You're not a bad person if you refuse to do something that will eat up your time and prevent you from accomplishing your goals. And if you do decide to do someone else a time-consuming favor, try to come up with the most efficient way of accomplishing it. Don't let all your time get taken up by the priorities of others.

From the perspective of . . .

A WORKING PARENT The balancing act between work and family can be a challenge. How can a weekly timetable help you ensure all areas of your life are getting the attention they deserve?

Source: © Rubberball/Getty Images

▶ **Get away from it all.** Go to the library. Lock yourself into your bedroom. Find a quiet, out-of-the-way coffee shop. Any of these places can serve to isolate you from everyday distractions and thereby permit you to work on the tasks that you wish to complete. Try to adopt a particular spot as your own, such as a nook in the library or a local café. If you use it enough, your body and mind will automatically get into study mode as soon as you seat yourself there.

▶ **Enjoy the sounds of silence.** Although many people insist they accomplish most while a television, radio, or CD is playing, scientific studies suggest otherwise: We are able to concentrate most when our environment is silent. So even if you're sure you work best with a soundtrack playing, experiment and work in silence for a few days. You may find that you get more done in less time than you would in a more distracting environment.

▶ **Take an e-break.** Text messages, phone calls, Facebook status updates, instant messages, e-mail. Who doesn't love to hear from others?

We may not control when communications arrive, but we can make the message wait until we are ready to receive it. Take an e-break, then shut down your communication sources for a period of time. (To identify more time busters that steal hours from your day, see **Try It! 4**.)

▶ **Expect the unexpected.** Interruptions and crises, minor and major, can't be eliminated. However, they can be prepared for.

How is it possible to plan for surprises? Though it may still be too early in the term to get a clear picture of what sorts of unanticipated events you'll encounter, you should keep an eye out for patterns. Perhaps one instructor routinely gives surprise assignments. Maybe you're frequently asked to work extra hours on the weekends when another employee doesn't show up.

You'll never be able to escape from unexpected interruptions and surprises that require your attention. But by trying to anticipate them in advance, and thinking about how you'll react to them, you'll be positioning yourself to react more effectively when they do occur.

▶ **Combat procrastination. Procrastination**, the habit of putting off and delaying tasks that need to be accomplished, is like a microscopic parasite. It is invisible to the naked eye, but it eats up your time nonetheless.

procrastination
The habit of putting off and delaying tasks that need to be accomplished.

Procrastination

You can't control interruptions and crises that are imposed upon you by others. But even when no one else is throwing interruptions at us, we make up our own. Procrastination is a problem that almost all of us face, but you can combat it.

If you find yourself procrastinating, several steps can help you:

Break large tasks into small ones. People often procrastinate because a task they're seeking to accomplish appears overwhelming. If writing a 15-page paper seems nearly impossible, think about writing a series of five 3-page papers. If reading a 400-page book seems impossible, think of it as reading two 200-page books.

Start with the easiest and simplest parts of a task, and then do the harder parts. Succeeding initially on the easy parts can make the harder parts of a task less daunting—and make you less apt to procrastinate in completing the task.

Get the hard parts of a task out of the way first. In contrast to the previous strategy for avoiding procrastination, it sometimes helps to tackle the hardest part of a task first. Getting the hard parts out of the way will make it a lot easier to complete the remaining parts of what you are trying to accomplish.

Just begin! Sometimes the hardest part of an activity is simply getting started. So take the leap and begin the task, and the rest may follow more easily.

Identify Your Time Busters

Time busters are everywhere and they steal precious hours each day. Place a check mark before each time buster that's robbing you.

_____ I check e-mail throughout the day and read text messages the moment they arrive.

_____ I run out for things as I need them or do an errand when it occurs to me.

_____ I do several things at the same time, jumping from one task to another without completing any of them.

_____ It's hard to find what I need because my workspace is cluttered with coffee cups, magazines, and papers.

_____ I visit social networking sites and/or web surf several times a day.

_____ I take frequent breaks to grab a cup of coffee or play a video game.

_____ I watch a lot of TV.

_____ I rarely get a good night's sleep, so I feel tired most of the time.

_____ I don't make lists of what needs to be done or prioritize projects.

_____ When faced with a major task, I'm likely to do a load of laundry or text a friend.

Scoring: If you checked two or fewer items, you're well organized and rarely waste time. If you checked three or four items, you've got a time leak that needs fixing. Review and apply the time management strategies we've discussed. More than four checks? You're sinking under all those lost hours. Time for an overhaul.

Now, consider the following:

- If you often waste time, why do you think you do so?
- Are there particular kinds of assignments that make wasting time seem especially attractive as you try to avoid them?
- Does lack of organization play a role in the amount of time you choose to waste? Is there something that you can do right now to better organize your time, your tasks, or your workspace? How might you get started on it?

 WORKING IN A GROUP

Think about the ways you wasted time in the past several days. Describe what you were doing and estimate how much time was lost in each instance. Was there something else you should have been doing during this time? What was the task? Was there a reason you were avoiding it? Ask others what strategies they might suggest for minimizing time busters.

Work with others. Just being in the same physical location with others can motivate you sufficiently to accomplish tasks that you consider unpleasant and on which you might be tempted to procrastinate. For instance, filling out tedious order forms can be made easier if you collaborate with co-workers. Beware, though—if you spend too much time socializing, you lower the likelihood of success.

Understand that false starts are part of the learning process. Accept that sometimes you will go in the wrong direction when working on a project. Don't let the fear of making mistakes hold you back. Such false starts are part of how we learn.

Keep the costs of procrastination in mind. Procrastination doesn't just result in delay; it may also make the task harder than it would have been if you hadn't procrastinated. Not only will you ultimately have less time to complete the task, but you may have to do it so quickly that its quality may be diminished. In the worst scenario, you won't be able to finish it at all.

Balance School and Work Obligations with Family Demands

If you have a job and are a student and also have caregiver responsibilities for children or other family members such as aging parents, time management is especially challenging. Not only does your family demand—and deserve—substantial quantities of time, but juggling school and work and family obligations can prove exhausting. However, there are some specific strategies that can help.

Dealing with Childcare Demands

Provide activities for your children. Kids enjoy doing things on their own for part of the day. Plan activities that will keep them happily occupied while you're doing work.

Make spending time with your children a priority. Carve out "free play" time for your kids. Even 20 minutes of good time devoted to your children will give all of you a lift. No matter how busy you are, you owe it to your children—and yourself—to spend time as a family.

Source: © George Doyle and Ciaran Griffin/ Stockbyte/Getty Images

Enlist your child's help. Children love to play adult; if they're old enough, ask them to help you study. Maybe they can help you clear a space to study. Perhaps you can give them "assignments" that they can work on while you're working on your assignments.

Encourage your child to invite friends over to play. Some children can remain occupied for hours if they have a playmate.

Use television appropriately. Television viewing is not all bad, and some shows and DVDs can be not just engaging, but educational. The trick is to pick and choose what your children watch.

Find the best child care or babysitters available. The better the care your children are getting, the better you'll be able to concentrate on your classes or your job. You may still feel guilty that you're not with your children as much as you'd like, but accept that guilt. Remember, your attendance in college and good performance at work builds a better future for your children.

Use your children's "downtime" effectively. If your children are young, use their nap time as a chance to catch up on work or chores. Or consider getting up early, before your children wake up, for a period in which you will have fewer interruptions than later in the day.

> "I had a friend who was taking classes to become a paralegal. He always complained about how he didn't have enough time between taking classes and holding down his job. But he was always inviting me and his other friends out to movies, insisting we stay at the bar for one more round. It wasn't a surprise when he eventually dropped out of school. It wasn't that he didn't have enough time. It was that he spent it on all the wrong things."
>
> **Bell Hansom, restaurant manager**

Dealing with Eldercare Demands

Encourage as much independence as possible on the part of older adults for whom you are responsible. Not only will it take some of the pressure off you, but it will be helpful to the older adult.

Ask for support from your siblings and other family members. Caring for an ill or aging parent should be a family affair, not a burden that falls on any one individual.

On-the-Job Time Management

In the business world, schedules are unpredictable. Crises occur, perhaps due to manufacturing problems or client demands, which require sudden flurries of work. For employees with a demanding boss who may, without warning, give them an urgent assignment due the next morning, time is always at a premium. In some jobs, you may be forced to drop everything you normally work on and pitch in on a sudden new task. As a result, your plans to complete your everyday work may be disrupted completely.

Simply put, time management is an essential survival skill when developing your career. Learning the basic principles of time management now will help you well beyond your years in college, and throughout your later career. You'll also want to learn new time-management strategies specific to the working world. For instance, if you supervise other employees, it may be possible to delegate some work to them, allowing them to help you complete assignments on time. Or sometimes it may be possible to deflect assignments brought to you by a boss to some other unit or department. Always keep in mind what it is possible for you to do alone—and what is impossible without the aid of co-workers. Don't be afraid to ask for help. In the working world, the end result is what counts above all.

Determine what community resources are available. Local centers for aging may provide assistance not only to the elderly but also to their caregivers.

Respect your own needs. Remember that your own priorities are important. Elders for whom you are responsible will understand that you will sometimes need to put yourself first.

Balancing School and Work Demands

Juggling school and a job can be a real challenge. Not only must you manage your time to complete your schoolwork, but in many cases you'll also face time management demands while you are on the job. Here are some tips to help you keep everything in balance:

▶ *If you have slack time on the job, get some studying done.* Try to keep at least some of your textbooks, class notes, or notecards always with you so you can refer to them. Of course, you should never do schoolwork without your employer's prior agreement. If you don't get permission, you may jeopardize your job.

▶ *Use your lunch or dinner hour effectively.* Although it's important to eat nutritious meals and not to wolf down your food, you may be able to use some of the time allotted to you for meals to fit in some studying.

▶ *Ask your employer about flextime.* If your job allows it, you may be able to set your own hours, within reason, as long as the work gets done. If this is an option for you, use it. Although it may create more time management challenges for you than would a job with set hours, it also provides you with more flexibility.

▶ *Accept new responsibilities carefully.* If you've barely been keeping up with the demands of work and school, don't automatically accept new job responsibilities without carefully evaluating how they fit with your long-term priorities. If your job is temporary and you're not planning to stay, you might want to respectfully decline substantial new duties or an increase in the number of hours you work. On the other hand, if you plan to continue in the job once you're done with school, then accepting new responsibilities may be more reasonable.

(handwritten: Not impress your emp ⑤)

Checking Your Time

Evaluating how you use your time is pretty straightforward: You either accomplished what you intended to do in a given period, or you didn't. Did you check off all the items on your daily to-do list? If you go over your list at the end of every day, not only will you know how successful your time management efforts have been, but you will be able to incorporate any activities you missed into the next day's to-do list.

The checkoff is important because it provides an objective record of what you have accomplished on a given day. Just as important, it provides you with concrete reinforcement for completing the task. As we have noted, there are few things more satisfying than gazing at a to-do list with a significant number of check marks.

Of course, you won't always accomplish every item on your to-do list. That's not surprising, or even particularly bad, especially if you've included some second- and third-level priorities that you don't absolutely have to accomplish and that you may not really have expected you'd have time for anyway.

Give yourself a virtual pat on the back for completing the things that you've accomplished. Successful time management is not easy, and if you've improved at all, you deserve to feel some personal satisfaction.

R Rethink # Reflecting on Your Personal Style of Time Management

At the end of the day, after you've evaluated how well you've followed your time management plan and how much you've accomplished, it's time to rethink where you are. Maybe you've accomplished everything you set out to do, and every task for the day is completed, and every item on your to-do list has a check mark next to it.

Or maybe you have the opposite result. Your day has been a mess, and you feel as if nothing has been accomplished. Because of a constant series of interruptions and chance events, you've been unable to make headway on your list.

Or—most likely—you find yourself somewhere in between these two extremes. Some tasks got done, while others are still hanging over you. Now is the time to rethink in a broad sense how you manage your time by doing the following:

▶ **Reassess your priorities.** Are your long- and short-term goals appropriate? Are you expecting too much of yourself, given the constraints in your life? Reassess your priorities to be sure you're attempting to do what is most important to you.

▶ **Reconsider your personal style of time management.** We've outlined one method of time management. Although it works well for most people, it isn't for everyone. Some people just can't bring themselves to be so structured and scheduled. They feel hemmed in by to-do lists.

If you're one of those people, fine. You don't need to follow the suggestions presented in this chapter exactly. In fact, if you go to any bookstore or office supply store, you'll find lots of other aids to managing your time. Publishing companies produce elaborate planners, such as DayTimers. In addition, software companies produce computerized time management software, such as Microsoft's Outlook or Apple's Calendar, that reside on a computer and wireless handheld devices such as an Android smartphone or iPhone. Many cell phones contain a calendar system and alarm, and they can be set to provide periodic reminders.

However you choose to manage your time, the important thing is to do so consistently. And remember that whatever approach to time management you take, it will work best if it is compatible with your own personal values and strengths. Keep experimenting until you find an approach that works for you.

▶ **Consider doing less.** If you keep falling behind, do less. There are only 24 hours in the day, and we need to sleep for about a third of the time. In the remaining hours, it may be nearly impossible to carry a full load of classes and work full-time and care for a child and still have some time left to have a normal life.

Consequently, if you consistently fall behind in your work, it may be that you are just doing too much. Reassess your goals and your priorities, and make choices. Determine what is most important to you. It's better to accomplish less, if it is accomplished well, than to accomplish more, but poorly.

▶ **Do more.** Although it is a problem that many of us would envy, some people have too much time on their hands. Their classes may not be too demanding, or work demands may suddenly slacken off. If this happens to you, take advantage of your time. For example, you might use the extra time to simply relax and enjoy your more unhurried existence. There is a good bit to be said for having time to let your thoughts wander. We need to take time out to enjoy our friends, admire the flowers in the park, exercise, consider the spiritual side of our lives, and the like. On the other hand, if you consistently have more time than you know what to do with, reflect on what you want to accomplish and add some activities that help you reach your goals. For example, consider becoming involved in a service learning activity. Volunteer your time to the community. Talk to your academic advisor about taking an extra course during the next term.

But whatever you decide to do, make a real decision. Don't let the time slip away. Once it's gone, it's gone forever.

> "Our costliest expenditure is time."
> **Theophrastus, quoted in Diogenes Laertius's** *Lives and Opinions of Eminent Philosophers*, **tr. R. D. Hicks (Loeb Classical Library, 1925).**

Speaking *of* Success

Source: Courtesy of Chuong Dang

NAME: **Chuong Dang**

HOME: **San Diego, California**

SCHOOL: **San Diego Mesa College, San Diego; University of California at San Diego**

Many English-speaking students choose a foreign language as part of their curriculum or to complement their major. However, some students, like Chuong Dang, have to learn English as a second language.

A biology major at the University of California at San Diego, Dang noted his struggles to adapt to his new language while studying at San Diego Mesa College.

"My first encounter with English was in Vietnam but we learned mostly through listening and it wasn't a good way," he explained. "When I arrived here I wasn't able to understand very well at all."

While at Hoover High School Dang was able to refine his skills in English, but he suffered a setback once he entered San Diego Mesa College.

"I found it quite difficult to attend English 101 even though I had a push from high school," he said. "I had to withdraw after the first class because I could not meet the requirements."

Dang explained that part of the problem was finding the right teacher, one who would take into consideration the challenges he faced in learning a new language.

"I took another class where the teacher understood writing from an immigrant's perspective as opposed to that of a native English speaker," he explained. "Through rewriting essays and guidance from the teacher I was able to improve my ability to speak and write in English."

One approach Dang began using and still uses to this day is his school's writing workshop. It was there that he was able to refine both his writing and his speaking skills.

"The writing workshop at Mesa was a big help. They would go over my essays and help me to format my ideas in English and help me to rephrase what I was trying to say," he said.

"Every time I would go to the workshop there would be a different person and because of that I would learn different things each time," he added.

Hoping to continue on to graduate school, Dang wants to do cancer research. He also stresses the importance of reading and meeting new people as a way to learn about not only the language, but the culture as well.

"I would suggest to other students that they read and read," Dang suggests. "Read newspapers and books about recent events and history as well as a variety of things about the United States. It was one of the ways that I was able to learn about American culture."

[RETHINK]

- How reasonable was Dang's strategy of seeking out a sympathetic teacher when he faced problems with English?

- Why do you think Dang suggests that students "read and read"? Do you think his advice applies only to non-native English speakers?

Looking Back

LO 2-1 Discuss strategies to manage your time effectively.

▶ Decide to take control of your time.

▶ Become aware of the way you use your time now.

▶ Set clear priorities.

▶ Use time management tools such as a master calendar, a weekly timetable, and a daily to-do list.

LO 2-2 Explain ways to balance competing priorities.

▶ Deal with surprises by saying no, getting away from it all, working in silence, taking control of communications, and leaving slack in your schedule to accommodate the unexpected.

▶ Avoid procrastination by breaking large tasks into smaller ones, starting with the easiest parts of a task first; working with other people; and calculating the true costs of procrastination. Identify your time busters and minimize them.

LO 2-3 Identify ways to deal with surprises and distractions.

▶ Consider how your competing priorities relate to one another.

▶ Manage work time carefully, use slack time on the job to perform school assignments, use flextime, accept new responsibilities thoughtfully, and assign the proper priority to work.

[KEY TERMS AND CONCEPTS]

Daily to-do list (p. 40)   Priorities (p. 38)   Time log (p. 36)

Master calendar (p. 39)   Procrastination (p. 48)   Weekly timetable (p. 39)

[RESOURCES]

ON CAMPUS

The college official who determines when classes meet is known as the registrar. If you are having difficulty in scheduling your classes, the registrar's office may be helpful. In addition, your academic advisor can help you work out problems in enrolling in the classes you want.

For help with such issues as planning a study schedule for the upcoming term, dealing with multiple assignments and obligations on the same date, or dealing with competing academic and work demands, consult with your campus learning center. The staff can help you sort out the various options you may have.

IN PRINT

Stephen Covey's *The Seven Habits of Highly Successful People* (Simon & Schuster, 2013) and Laura Stack's *What to Do When There's Too Much to Do* (Berrett-Koehler Publishers, 2012) offer practical, hands-on guides to time management.

Microsoft Outlook 2013 Step by Step (Microsoft Press), by Joan Lambert and Joyce Cox, provides a quick, hands-on introduction to Microsoft's Outlook software, a popular time management program that is part of the Microsoft Office Suite.

Finally, Andrew Smart's *Autopilot: The Art and Science of Doing Nothing* (OR Books, 2013) is an antidote to the impulse to schedule every minute of our days. The book celebrates taking time out and devoting it to oneself, using scientific findings to explain the importance of doing nothing.

ON THE WEB

The *P.O.W.E.R. Learning* Connect Library provides online versions of all the time management forms presented in this chapter. You can complete the forms online or download them and print out as many copies as you need.

▶ Penn State University offers helpful advice on time management at **http://pennstatelearning.psu.edu/time-management.**

▶ Useful tips for managing your time and prioritizing (and re-prioritizing) tasks can be found at the California Polytech website at **http://sas.calpoly.edu/asc/ssl/ timemgmt-strategies.html.**

Images in this chapter: *Pencil on stack of notebooks:* © C Squared Studios/Photodisc/Getty Images; *Four students:* © Purestock/Getty images; *Apples:* © Isabelle Rozenbaum/PhotoAlto/Getty Images; *Group of happy business people:* © Yuri/iStock/Getty Images.

The Case of . . .

The Vanishing Hours

Amanda Jordan stared at the clock. Two in the morning, and she'd just finished the first of three final papers due tomorrow. Make that today. She knew she should have been working on the research and rough drafts over the past two weeks, but she was so far behind on her reading, she had no clue about any of the topics her professors had assigned.

On paper, her schedule looked great. Three classes, starting at 9:00, with an hour break between each. Her plan had been to do the reading between classes while each subject was fresh in her mind. She'd do her late afternoon shift at the student center cafeteria, be home by 8:00 p.m., and have the whole evening to hang out with friends, do her laundry, or put in extra class prep—exactly what she should have been doing for her final papers.

The trouble was, the hour between classes always seemed to shrink. She had to move from one building to another, check her text messages, grab a cup of coffee. The hour just . . . went. After work, she often had to dash to the local mini-mart or wait for take-out. The apartment she shared was usually full of people. It was nice to see her friends, but it was noisy. By the time the last person left, she was dead tired and in no mood to study.

Amanda looked at the clock: 2:30 a.m. She'd just lost another half-hour, reflecting on her troubles.

1. How could Amanda have used time management tools to avoid falling so far behind in her reading and preparing her final papers?

2. Is there anything Amanda could have done to make better use of the hour she had between each of her classes? What specific advice would you give her to reduce the time "shrinkage" she experiences?

3. What strategies would you advise Amanda to use to make more effective use of her evening hours?

4. What advice could you give Amanda to try to prevent problems in time management in her next term?

Source: © Dirk Lindner/Image Source

Taking Notes

Learning Outcomes

By the time you finish this chapter you will be able to

» **LO 3-1**   Describe techniques for taking notes in class.

» **LO 3-2**   Apply techniques for taking notes from written materials.

» **LO 3-3**   Explain methods for effective notetaking.

Nan Jackson frowned. Her professor was going way too fast. She couldn't write down everything he was saying. In fact, she wasn't getting even one-third of it. She wished her professor hadn't banned laptops from the classroom—she could type faster than she could write—but he said too many students were web surfing or watching YouTube.

"Underline that concept. It will be on the test."

Nan's heart skipped a beat. What concept? She was still writing down what he'd said several minutes ago.

My notes are useless, Nan thought. *They're an unreadable scribble because I'm rushing to get every word down, and they're full of holes because I always miss something.*

Later, Nan mentioned her frustration to a friend over coffee. Her friend advised her to check out one of the notetaking workshops the college offered. She'd learn lots of strategies for effective, efficient notetaking.

Nan had only one question: "Where do I sign up?"

Looking Ahead

Nan Jackson's recognition of her poor notetaking skills and her willingness to do something about it are important steps in improving her academic performance, and they will likely contribute to her career success later.

In this chapter we discuss effective strategies for taking notes during class lectures and other kinds of oral presentations, as well as from written sources such as textbooks. There's a lot more to good notetaking than you probably think—or maybe a lot less, if you view notetaking as "getting everything down on paper." As we explore the ins and outs of notetaking, we'll pause along the way to discuss the tools of the notetaking trade, how to be an active learner, how to think your way to good notes, and how to deal with disorganized instructors.

≫ LO 3-1 Taking Notes in Class

Perhaps you know a student who desperately tries to write down everything the instructor says, resulting in a set of notes that are virtually a transcript of everything spoken in class. And maybe you believe that if only you took such comprehensive notes, you'd be a much better student.

However, contrary to what you may think, good notetaking does not mean writing down every word that an instructor utters. With notetaking, less is often more. We'll see why as we consider the basic steps in P.O.W.E.R. notetaking.

 Prepare   ## Considering Your Goals

As with other academic activities, preparation is a critical component of notetaking. The following steps will prepare you for action:

▶ **Identify the instructor's—and your—goals for the course.** On the first day of class, most instructors talk about their objectives, what they hope you'll get out of the class, and what you'll know when it's over. Most restate the information on the class syllabus, the written document that explains the assignments

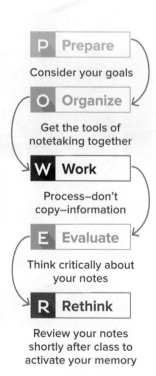

P Prepare
Consider your goals

O Organize
Get the tools of notetaking together

W Work
Process–don't copy–information

E Evaluate
Think critically about your notes

R Rethink
Review your notes shortly after class to activate your memory

P.O.W.E.R. Plan

for the term. For example, they may say that they want you to "develop an appreciation for the ways that statistics are used in everyday life."

The information you get during that first session and through the syllabus is critical. If the instructor's goals aren't stated explicitly, you should attempt to figure them out. In addition to those "external" goals, you should have your own goals. What is it you want to learn from the course? How will the information from the course help you enhance your knowledge, improve your career prospects, and achieve your dreams?

▶ **Complete assignments before coming to class.** Always go to class prepared. Complete all of your reading and other assignments beforehand. Instructors assume that their students have done what they've assigned, and their lectures are based on that assumption. It's virtually impossible to catch on to the gist of a lecture if you haven't completed the assignments.

▶ **Accept the instructor, despite his or her limitations.** Not every instructor is a superb lecturer. Accept the fact that just as there are differences in skills among students, some instructors are better at lecturing than others. Ultimately, it's your responsibility to overcome a lecturer's flaws. A challenging lecturer is not an excuse to do poorly or to give up. Don't let a poor lecture style—or the fact that the instructor has a bad haircut or a mouth that droops to one side or wrinkled clothing—get in the way of your education. You're going to notice these things, but don't let them interfere with your goals. Good notetaking requires being prepared to listen to the material.

▶ **Perform a preclass warm-up.** No, this doesn't mean doing stretches just before each class. As you head to class or settle into your seat, skim your notes from the previous lecture, looking over what the instructor said and where that lecture left off. You should also briefly review the main headings or summary section of any reading you've been assigned.

The warm-up doesn't have to be long. The goal is simply to refresh yourself, to get yourself into the right frame of mind for the class.

> "The highest result of education is tolerance."
>
> **Helen Keller, author**

Sometimes distracting seats have less to do with location and more to do with the person sitting next to you. Don't be afraid to put some physical distance between yourself and a distracting neighbor.

Source: © Purestock/Getty Images

▶ **Choose a seat that will promote good notetaking.** You should certainly choose a seat that permits you to see and hear clearly, but there's more to your choice than that. Picking the right seat in a classroom can make a big difference.

Where is the best place to sit? Usually it's front and center. Instructors make more eye contact with the people near them, and they sometimes believe that the best, most engaged students sit closest.

Furthermore, sitting in the back of the class may make you feel disengaged and out of touch with what is happening at the front of the room. In turn, this seating choice may make it easier for your mind to wander.

Journal Reflections

How Do I Take Notes?

1. Describe your typical notetaking techniques in a few sentences. Do you try to write down as much of what the instructor says as possible? Do you tend to take only a few notes? Do you often find you need more time to get things down?

2. Overall, how effective would you say your notetaking techniques are?

3. In which classes do your techniques work best? Worst? Why?

4. Do your notes ever have "holes" in them—due to lapses of attention or times when you couldn't get down everything you wanted to? When do you usually discover these holes? What do you do about them?

 **Organize**

Getting the Tools of Notetaking Together

Do you have a favorite pen? A preferred type of notebook?

Most of us have distinct tastes in the types of tools we use for various tasks: a favorite screwdriver, a preferred style of mouse, a brand of running shoes we find most comfortable. You should determine your preferred classroom "tools," too. Taking your favorite kind of notebook and pen to class can give you the confidence and focus you need to take effective notes.

There are several things to consider as you prepare for class:

▶ **Choose the appropriate writing utensil.** Generally, using a pen is better than using a pencil. Ink is less likely to smudge, and what you produce with ink is usually brighter and clearer—and therefore easier to use when studying. However, for math and accounting classes, where you may be copying down or even working through formulas in class, a pencil might be better, because it's easier to erase if you make a mistake when copying detailed, complex information.

Sometimes you may want to use a combination of pen and pencil. And in some cases you might use several different colors. One color—such as red—might signify important information that the instructor mentions will be on the test. Another color might be reserved for definitions or material that is copied from the board. And a third might be used for general notes on the lecture.

► **Choose a notebook that assists in notetaking.** Loose-leaf notebooks are particularly good for taking notes because they permit you to go back later and change the order of the pages or add additional material in the appropriate spot. But whatever kind of notebook you use, *use only one side of the page for writing: keep one side free of notes.* There may be times when you're studying when you'll want to spread your notes in front of you, and it's much easier if no material is written on the backs of pages.

► **Consider the benefits of taking your textbook to class.** It's generally a good idea to take your textbook to class, unless your instructor advises you otherwise. Sometimes instructors will refer to information contained in it, and sometimes it's useful to have it handy to clarify information that is being discussed. You can also use it to look up key terms that may momentarily escape you. But don't, under any circumstances, use class time as an opportunity to read the textbook!

► **Consider the pros and cons of using a laptop computer to take notes in class.** There are several advantages: Legibility problems are avoided, and it's easy to go back and revise or add material after you've taken the notes.

There are also potential pitfalls. You may end up keyboarding more and thinking less. Or you may succumb to the temptation to check your e-mail or watch a YouTube video, rather than listening to your instructor.

Because of these drawbacks, some instructors have strong feelings against the use of laptops in their class. Consequently, be sure to ask for permission before using your laptop to take notes.

From the perspective of . . .

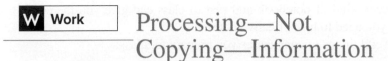

A STUDENT Using a laptop is advantageous for students who type faster than they write. What are some of the advantages of taking handwritten notes?

Source: © BJI/Blue Jean Images/Getty Images

W	Work

Processing—Not Copying—Information

With pen poised, you're ready to begin the work of notetaking. The instructor begins to speak and you start to write as quickly as you can, taking down as many of the instructor's words as possible.

Stop! You've made your first mistake. The central act in taking notes is not writing; listening and thinking are far more important. The key to effective notetaking is to write down the right amount of information—not too much and not too little.

Successful notetaking involves not just *hearing* what is said, but *listening actively.* **Hearing** is the involuntary act of sensing sounds. The annoying drip of a faucet or the grating sound of a co-worker's voice speaking on the phone in the next cubicle

hearing
The involuntary act of sensing sounds.

Determine Your Listening Style

☐ 1a. When I'm listening in class, I lean back and get as comfortable as possible.

☐ 1b. When I'm listening in class, I sit upright and even lean forward a little.

☐ 2a. I let the instructor's words wash over me, generally going with the flow of the lecture.

☐ 2b. I try to guess in advance what the instructor is going to say and what direction the lecture is taking.

☐ 3a. I regard each lecture as a separate event, not necessarily related to what the instructor has said before or will say the next time.

☐ 3b. As I listen, I regularly ask myself how this relates to what was said in previous classes.

☐ 4a. When I take notes, I try to reproduce the instructor's words as closely as possible.

☐ 4b. When I take notes, I try to interpret and summarize the ideas behind the instructor's words.

☐ 5a. I don't usually question the importance of what the instructor is saying or why it's the topic of a lecture or discussion.

☐ 5b. I often ask why the content of the lecture is important enough for the instructor to be speaking about it.

☐ 6a. I rarely question the accuracy or logic of a presentation, assuming that the instructor knows the topic better than I do.

☐ 6b. I often ask myself how the instructor knows something and find myself wondering how it could be proved.

☐ 7a. I just about never make eye contact with the instructor.

☐ 7b. I often make eye contact with the instructor.

If you tended to prefer the "a" statements in most pairs, you have a more passive listening style. If you preferred the "b" statements, you have a more active listening style. Based on your responses, consider ways that you can become a more active listener.

are two examples of how hearing is both involuntary and often meaningless. In contrast, **active listening** is the voluntary act of focusing on what is being said, making sense of it, and thinking about it in a way that permits it to be recalled accurately. Listening involves concentration. And it requires shutting out competing thoughts, such as what we need to pick up at the grocery store or why our date last night went so badly wrong. (To get a sense of your own listening skills, complete **Try It! 1.**)

Keeping the importance of active listening in mind, consider the following recommendations for taking notes in class:

> **Listen for the key ideas.** Not every sentence in a lecture is equally important, and one of the most useful skills you can develop is separating the key ideas from supporting information. Good lecturers strive to make just a few main points. The rest of what they say consists of explanation, examples, and other supportive material that expands on the key ideas.

> Your job, then, is to distinguish the key ideas from their support. To do this, you need to be alert and always searching for your instructor's **meta-message**—that is, the underlying main ideas that a speaker is seeking to convey, or the meaning behind the overt message you hear.

> How can you discern the meta-message? One way is to *listen for key-words*. Instructors know what's important in their lecture; your job is to figure it out, not just from what they say but from how they say it.

active listening
The voluntary act of focusing on what is being said, making sense of it, and thinking about it in a way that permits it to be recalled accurately.

meta-message
The underlying main ideas that a speaker is seeking to convey; the meaning behind the overt message.

For instance, listen for clues about the importance of material. Phrases like "don't forget . . . ," "be sure to remember that . . . ," "you need to know . . . ," "the most important thing that must be considered . . . ," "there are four problems with this approach . . . ," and—a big one—"this will be on the test . . ." should cause you to sit up and take notice. Another good sign of importance is repetition. If an instructor says the same thing in several ways, it's a clear sign that the material being discussed is important.

Be on the lookout for nonverbal signals too. Does an instructor get excited about a particular topic? Does he or she seem unenthusiastic when talking about something? Use nonverbal cues to gauge the importance of a particular part of a message relative to other things being said.

Finally, listen for what is not being said. Sometimes silence is not just golden, but informative as well. By noting what topics are not being covered in class, or are presented only minimally, you can gauge the relative importance of ideas in comparison with one another.

This is where preliminary preparation and organization come in. The only way to know what's left out of a lecture is to have done the assigned readings in advance. Also, don't be fooled into thinking that if a topic is not covered in class, it's unimportant: Most instructors believe students are responsible for all material that is assigned, whether or not it's explicitly covered in class.

▶ **Use short, abbreviated phrases—not full sentences—when taking notes.** Forget everything you've ever heard about always writing in full sentences. If you try to write notes in complete sentences, you'll soon become bogged down, paying more attention to your notes than to your instructor. In fact, if you use full sentences, you'll be tempted to try transcribing every word the instructor utters, which, as you now know, is not a good idea at all.

Instead, write in phrases, using only key words or terms. Save full sentences for definitions or quotations that your instructor clearly wants you to know word for word. For example, consider the following excerpt from a lecture:

There are two kinds of job analyses used by human resource experts: First, there are job- or task-oriented analyses, and second, there are worker- or employee-oriented analyses. Job analyses just describe the tasks that need to be accomplished by a worker. For example, heart surgeons need to be able to operate on patients in order to carry out their jobs. In contrast, employee-oriented job descriptions need to describe knowledge, skills, and abilities the employee must have to get the job done. For example, surgeons need to understand the different types of blood vessels in the heart in order to be successful. Most job analyses include elements of both job-oriented and employee-oriented types.

If you were taking notes, you might produce the following:

2 kinds job analyses:
  1. Job-oriented (= task-oriented): tasks needed to get job done. Ex: heart surgeon operates
  2. Worker-oriented (= employee-oriented): knowledge, skills, abilities, etc. necessary to do job.
     Ex: surgeon knows blood vessels
     Most j.a. a combination

Note how the lecturer used almost 120 words, while the notes used only around 35 words—less than one-third of the lecture.

- **Use abbreviations.** One way to speed up the notetaking process is through the use of abbreviations. Among the most common:

and	*& or +*	with	*w/*	without	*w/o*
care of	*c/o*	leads to; resulting in	→	as a result of	←
percent	*%*	change	D	number	*#*
that is	*i.e.*	for example	*e.g.*	and so forth	*etc.*
no good	*n.g.*	question	*?*	compared with	*c/w*
page	*p.*	important!	*!!*	less than	*<*
more than	*>*	equals, same as	*=*	versus	*vs.*

- **Take notes in outline form.** It's often useful to take notes in the form of an outline. An outline summarizes ideas in short phrases and indicates the relationship among concepts through the use of indentations.

  When outlining, it's best to be formal about it, using roman numerals, regular numbers, and capital and small letters (see the example in **Figure 3.1**). Or, if you prefer, you can also simply use outlining indentations without assigning numbers and letters.

From the perspective of . . .

A MEDICAL ASSISTANT Learning abbreviations is an important aspect of life in a medical office. How can taking notes with abbreviations while in school help you learn important notations for your medical career?

  Outlining serves a number of functions. It forces you to try to determine the structure of the lecture. Organizing the key points and noting the connections among them helps you remember the material better because you have processed it more. The effort involved in outlining also keeps your mind from drifting away from the lecture. Use **Try It! 2**, "Outline a Lecture," to practice your outlining skills.

- **Copy key information written on the board or projected from PowerPoint slides or overheads.** If your instructor provides a definition, quotation, or formula, you probably should add it to your notes. In fact, such prominently displayed material has "test item" written all over it. You might want to highlight such material in some way in your notes.

- **Take advantage of PowerPoint slides provided online by your instructor.** Some instructors will post their PowerPoint slides before class. If they do, print them out and bring them to class. (To save paper, you can usually print them as an outline, rather than with each slide on a separate page.)

  You can use the printout of the slides as the basis for your notes, filling in the details provided during the lecture on the printout. Even if your instructor doesn't post the slides until after class, it's still a good idea to print them out

figure 3.1
A Sample Outline

I. Difficulties faced by students seeking affordable child care

   A. Students subject to high costs of private child care

      1. Sometimes need to find alternative care

      2. Forced to take on part-time work to pay for child care

      3. Hard to find high-quality care

   B. Need to drop or reschedule classes due to child care limitations

II. Possible solutions

   A. College offers subsidized child care

      1. Advantage: Lower costs, convenience

      2. Potential problems

         a. Care may not be available for night classes

         b. School uses funds for child care instead of investing in education

   B. Using friends and family

      1. Advantage: Lower cost

      2. Disadvantages

         a. Availability may be inconsistent

         b. Care may not be available when needed

         c. Child may not be as secure if left with friends

III. Summary

   A. Advantages and disadvantages to both solutions

   B. May need new, creative solutions

and keep them with the notes you create in class. The combination of your notes and the PowerPoints will be invaluable when reviewing and studying the material.

▶ **Pay particular attention to the points raised by instructors at the end of classes.** Instructors often provide a summary of the discussion, which is worthy of inclusion in your notes.

▶ **Ask questions.** One of the most important things you can do during a class is to ask questions. Raising questions will help you evaluate, clarify, and ultimately better understand what your instructor is saying. Even beyond these critical goals, questions serve several other purposes.

For one thing, raising questions will help you to personalize the material being covered, permitting you to draw it more closely into your own framework and perspective. Furthermore, when you ask a question and it is answered, you become personally engaged in what the instructor is saying. In very large classes, asking questions may be the only way that an instructor can get a sense of you as an individual.

Questioning also increases your involvement in the class as a whole. If you sit back and never raise questions in class, you are much less likely to feel a real part of the class. Becoming an active questioner will rightly make you feel like you have contributed something to the class. Remember, if you are unclear about some point, it is likely that others share your lack of clarity.

Outline a Lecture

Working with others in the group, take turns slowly reading sections of the following lecture to each other.* As the paragraph is being read, outline the main arguments in the space below.

In 1985 Joseph Farman, a British earth scientist working in Antarctica, made an alarming discovery. Scanning the Antarctic sky, he found less ozone than should be there—not a slight depletion but a 30% drop from a reading recorded 5 years earlier in the Antarctic!

At first the scientist thought that this "ozone hole" was an as-yet-unexplained weather phenomenon. Evidence soon mounted, however, pointing to synthetic chemicals as the culprit. Detailed analyses of chemicals in the Antarctic atmosphere revealed a surprisingly high concentration of chlorine, a chemical known to destroy ozone. The source of the chlorine was a class of chemicals called chlorofluorocarbons (CFCs). CFCs have been manufactured in large amounts since they were invented in the 1920s, largely for use as coolants in air conditioners, propellants in aerosols, and foaming agents in making Styrofoam. CFCs were widely regarded as harmless because they were chemically unreactive under normal conditions. But in the thin atmosphere over Antarctica, CFCs condense onto tiny ice crystals; warmed by the sun in the spring, they attack and destroy ozone without being used up.

The thinning of the ozone layer in the upper atmosphere 25 to 40 kilometers above the surface of the earth is a serious matter. The ozone layer protects life from the harmful ultraviolet (UV) rays from the sun that bombard the earth continuously. Like invisible sunglasses, the ozone layer filters out these dangerous rays. When UV rays damage the DNA in skin cells, it can lead to skin cancer. Every 1% drop in the atmospheric ozone concentration is estimated to lead to a 6% increase in skin cancers. The drop of approximately 3% that has already occurred worldwide therefore is estimated to have led to as much as a 20% increase in skin cancers.

The world currently produces about 1 million tons of CFCs annually, three-fourths of it in the United States and Europe. As scientific observations have become widely known, governments have rushed to correct the situation. By 1990, worldwide agreements to phase out production of CFCs by the end of the century had been signed. Nonetheless, most of the CFCs manufactured since they were invented are still in use in air conditioners and aerosols and have not yet reached the atmosphere. As these CFCs, as well as CFCs still being manufactured, move slowly upward through the atmosphere, the problem can be expected to grow worse. Ozone depletion has now been reported over the North Pole as well, and there is serious concern that the Arctic ozone hole will soon extend over densely populated Europe and the northeastern United States.

Write your outline here.

After you have outlined the passage, compare your outline with that of others who took notes on the same passage.

- Did you all agree on the main ideas of each passage?
- How do your notes differ from others', and what are the similarities?
- How might you improve your notes to better capture the main points?
- Would a different topic produce greater or fewer difficulties—for example, Database Design & Application?

Collectively, produce what you believe is the ideal outline, then compare it with those produced by other groups.

*This exercise is adapted from G. Johnson, *The Living World,* 2nd ed. (New York: McGraw-Hill, 2000).

Finally, by asking questions in class, you serve as a role model for other students. Your questions may help break the ice in a class, making it easier for others to raise issues that they have about the material. And ultimately the answers that the instructor provides to others' questions may help you to better understand and/or evaluate your understanding of the material.

» LO 3-2 Strategies for Using Your Notes

The key to effective notetaking is to keep a balance between too many and too few notes.

Keep a Balance between Too Many Notes and Too Few Notes

The best way to achieve this balance is by paying close attention in class. By being alert, engaged, and involved in class, you'll be able to make the most of the techniques we've discussed. The result: notes that capture the most important points raised in class and that will optimize your recall and mastery of the course subject matter (see a sample of two students' notes in **Figure 3.2**).

Use Special Techniques for "Problem Instructors"

He talks too fast . . . she mumbles . . . he puts down people when they ask a question . . . she rambles and goes off on boring tangents . . . she explains things in a way that doesn't make much sense.

figure 3.2
Notes on a Lecture

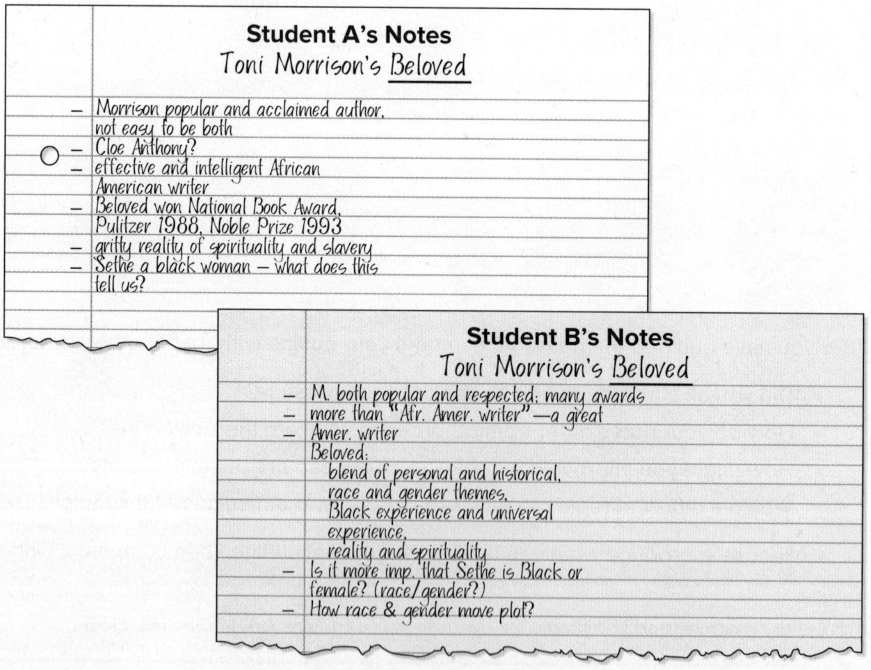

Student A's Notes
Toni Morrison's Beloved

- Morrison popular and acclaimed author, not easy to be both
- Cloe Anthony?
- effective and intelligent African American writer
- Beloved won National Book Award, Pulitzer 1988, Noble Prize 1993
- gritty reality of spirituality and slavery
- Sethe a black woman – what does this tell us?

Student B's Notes
Toni Morrison's Beloved

- M. both popular and respected; many awards
- more than "Afr. Amer. writer" – a great
- Amer. writer
- Beloved:
  blend of personal and historical,
  race and gender themes,
  Black experience and universal
  experience,
  reality and spirituality
- Is it more imp. that Sethe is Black or female? (race/gender?)
- How race & gender move plot?

Not every instructor comes to class with a clear, compelling lecture and then presents it beautifully. All of us have suffered through lectures that are deficient in one or more ways. What should you do when you find yourself in such a situation?

1. *Ask questions about the material.* Even if you have no idea what is going on in class—or especially if you have no idea—ask questions. You probably are not the only one struggling with the instructor's shortcomings. You will be doing everyone in the class a favor if you admit you're not following what an instructor is saying and respectfully ask for clarification.

2. *Ask—privately and politely—for the instructor to alter the way material is presented.* It is not bad classroom etiquette to ask an instructor to speak a little more slowly. Instructors sometimes get carried away with enthusiasm and begin speaking faster and faster without even being aware of it. Very often a reality check from a student will be welcome. But don't couch your comment in a way that makes the instructor feel inept ("Could you slow down? You're going too fast and losing me"). Instead, keep the comment neutral, without placing blame. For instance, you might simply say, "I'm having trouble keeping up with you; would it be possible for you to speak a little more slowly?"

3. *Pool your resources.* Get together with other students in the class and work out a strategy for dealing with the situation. If an instructor speaks too fast and you just can't keep up with the flow of information, meet with your fellow students and compare what you've gleaned from the class. They may have understood or noted material that you missed, and vice versa. Together, you may be able to put the pieces of the puzzle together and get a fuller understanding of the material.

4. *Listen to the lecture again.* You might bring a digital recorder to class (but request the instructor's permission first!). Then, after class, you can play back the recording at your leisure. If you record it in a digital format, you could store it on your computer for a review before a test. In fact, in some cases instructors may use "lecture capture" software that uploads what they say in class to a website. Such software allows you to review the lecture, sometimes with the PowerPoint slides that were projected while the instructor was teaching.

5. *Talk with the instructor after class.* If you feel totally lost after a lecture, or even if you've missed only a few points, speak with the instructor after class. Ask for clarification and get him or her to re-explain points that you missed. Such a dialogue will help you understand the material better.

6. *Remember that this too shall pass.* Finally, keep in mind that this is a temporary condition; your experience usually won't last more than one term. Most instructors are conscientious and well prepared, and unless you have enormously bad luck, the unpleasant experience you're having now will not be routine.

If you've ever been totally lost following a lecture, you may have discovered that speaking with your instructor immediately after class was helpful. Most instructors are very happy to go over and clarify key points that they've covered during class. They also appreciate your initiative and interest.
Source: © MachineHeadz/E-plus/Getty Images

Thinking Critically About Your Notes

Toward the end of class, take a moment to look over your notes. Now's the time—before the class has ended—to evaluate what you've written.

After being sure you can answer yes to the most basic question—can I read what I've written?—ask yourself these questions:

▶ Do my notes do a good job of representing what was covered in class?

▶ Do they reflect the emphases of the instructor?

▶ Are there any key points that are not entirely clear?

▶ Do I need help clarifying any of the points my instructor made?

Evaluating your notes is a critical part of the notetaking process. You can get a sense of how effective your notetaking has been while you still have a chance to ask your instructor to clarify anything that is not clear.

Perhaps, for example, you've left out a keyword in a definition. Maybe you don't understand a concept fully, even though you've written about it in your notes. Possibly you've left out the third step in a list of six steps necessary to accomplish something.

If you look over your notes while you're still in class, you have time to ask your instructor for clarification. Or you can wait until the end of class and raise your question privately. Most instructors will be happy to answer questions from students who have obviously been actively listening. Just make sure that you add what they tell you to your notes so you'll be able to refer to them later. (To practice evaluating your notes, complete **Try It! 3.**)

R | Rethink ## Activating Your Memory

The lecture has ended and class is over. You put the top on your pen, close your notebook, stash everything in your bag, and head out for a cup of coffee before your next class or before going to work.

Wait! Before you close up your notebook, finish the P.O.W.E.R. process. Rethink what you've heard. Spending 5 or 10 minutes reconsidering what you've written right now can save you *hours* of work later. The reason: Rethinking promotes the transfer of information into long-term memory (something discussed more in Chapter 5). As you link the new information you've taken down to what you already know and then integrate it, you essentially plug this information into your memory in a much more meaningful way, which means you can remember it better and more easily.

If you looked over your notes to clarify and evaluate the information in them in class, you've already begun the process. But once class is over, you need to review the material more formally. Here's how to do it:

▶ **Rethink as soon as possible.** Time is of the essence! The rethinking phase of notetaking doesn't have to take long; 5 to 10 minutes are usually sufficient. The more critical issue is *when* you do it. The longer you wait before reviewing your notes, the less effective the process will be.

> "I'd think to myself 'I don't need to write that down, I'll remember it.' A few days later, it was like, '*What* did he say . . .?' "
>
> Student, Duke University, in S. Tyler, *Been There, Should've Done That* (Haslett, MI: Front Porch Press, 1997), p. 114.

Evaluate Your Class Notes

Take a set of notes you made recently during one of your classes and evaluate it on the following criteria.

Statement	Not Even Slightly	Slightly	Moderately	Pretty Well	Very Well
1. I can read my notes (i.e., they are legible).					
2. Someone else can read my notes.					
3. My notes represent the key points that were covered in class.					
4. My notes reflect the instructor's emphases.					
5. There are no gaps in my notes where I missed a point, definition, or formula.					
6. I used abbreviations effectively in my notes.					
7. The notes contain no extraneous material.					
8. I could turn my notes into a coherent outline.					
9. I understand the class content the notes reflect.					
10. Using only the notes, I will be able to reconstruct the essential content of the class 3 months from now.					

WORKING IN A GROUP

What do your answers tell you about the effectiveness of your notetaking skills? What might you do differently the next time you take notes?

Evaluate and compare the notes you took during the previous 20 minutes of the class you are in now. How do your notes compare with those of the other members of your group?

There's no doubt that the best approach is to review the material just after the class has ended. As everyone else is leaving, just stay seated and go over your notes. This works fine for classes late in the day, when no other class is scheduled in the room. But what if you must vacate the room immediately after class? The next best thing is to find a quiet space somewhere nearby and do your rethinking there.

In any case, don't let the day end without examining your notes. In fact, reconsidering material just before you go to sleep can be particularly effective.

▶ **Make rethinking an active process.** Some people feel the notes they take in class are akin to historical documents in a museum, with Do Not Touch! signs hanging on them. On the contrary, think of your notes as a construction project and yourself as the person in charge of the project.

When you review your notes, do so with an eye to improving them. If any information is not entirely clear, change the wording in your notes, adding to or amending what's there. If certain words are hard to read, fix them; it won't be any easier to read them the night before a test—in fact, chances are that you'll have even more trouble.

If, after rethinking the material, you don't understand something, ask your instructor or a friend to clarify it. And when you receive an explanation, add it to your notes so you won't forget it. (You might want to use a different colored pen for additions to your notes, so you'll know they came later.)

▶ **Think critically about the material in your notes.** As you review the information, think about the material from a critical point of view. Go beyond the facts and pieces of information, integrating and evaluating the material.

In addition, as you rethink your notes, don't think of them only in terms of a single lecture or a single class. Instead, take a longer view. Ask yourself how they fit into the broader themes of the class and the goals that you and the instructor have for the term. How will the information be useful to you? Why did the instructor emphasize a particular point?

▶ **Create concept maps. Concept mapping** (sometimes called "mind mapping") is a method of structuring written material by graphically grouping and connecting key ideas and themes. In contrast with an outline, a concept map visually illustrates how related ideas fit together. The pictorial summary gives you another handle to store the information in memory, and it focuses your thinking on the key ideas from the lecture.

In a concept map, each key idea is placed in a different part of the map, and related ideas are placed near it—above, below, or beside it. What emerges does not have the rigid structure of an outline. Instead, a "finished" concept map looks something like a map of the solar system, with the largest and most central idea in the center (the "sun" position), and related ideas surrounding it at various distances. It has also been compared to a large tree, with numerous branches and subbranches radiating out from a central trunk. (**Figure 3.3** presents a sample concept map.)

Building a concept map has several advantages. It forces you to rethink the material in your notes in a new style—particularly important if you used traditional outlining while taking the notes. In addition, it helps you tie together the material for a given class session. Finally, it will help you build a master concept map later, when you're studying the material for a final exam.

concept mapping

A method of structuring written material by graphically grouping and connecting key ideas and themes.

»LO3-3 Taking Notes as You Study

Weighing as much as five pounds, bulky and awkward, and filled with more information than you think anyone could ever need to know, it's the meat and potatoes of college work: your course textbook. You might feel intimidated by its size; you might think you'll never be able to read it, let alone understand, learn, and recall the material in it. How will you manage?

The answer involves taking **study notes**, notes taken for the purpose of reviewing material. They are the kind of notes that you take now to study from later.

study notes

Notes taken for the purpose of reviewing material.

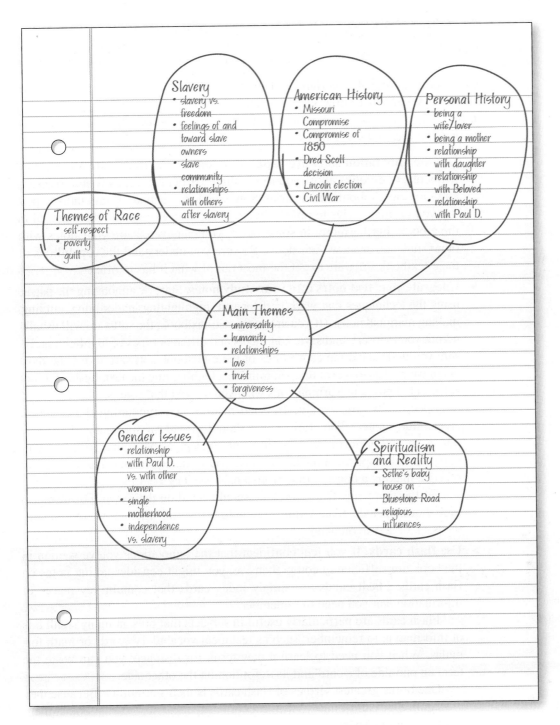

figure 3.3
A Concept Map of Toni Morrison's *Beloved*.

(We'll consider research notes, notes that you take to write a paper or prepare a report when we discuss writing papers.)

Several strategies are useful for taking study notes from written material such as magazines, books, journals, and websites. The approach that works best depends on whether you're able to write on the material you wish to take notes on.

Taking Notes on Material You Can Write On or Annotate Digitally

Some forms of digital materials, such as the typical online textbook, have built-in software systems that allow you to create notes or to highlight the text. For such virtual material, as well as hard-copy materials that you own, here are some suggestions for creating study notes:

▶ **Use the annotation software capabilities on virtual material.** Most online textbooks or e-books allow you to highlight particular passages and to insert, and save, notes about the material. Some devices, such as certain tablets, permit you to use a stylus to physically write (and save) notes on the material in the e-book. Furthermore, in some cases, you can even share your notes with other students, or view their notes. Be sure you understand the capabilities of the e-textbook software to get the most out of what it has to offer.

▶ **Integrate your text notes into your study notes.** Start by annotating the pages, using the techniques that work best for you: highlighting, underlining, circling, making marginal notes. (If you are using an e-textbook, the software will usually permit you to insert, and save, comments and different types of highlighting. Be sure you understand the capabilities of the e-textbook software to get the most out of what it has to offer.) Keep in mind that highlighting the text, by itself, is not sufficient to promote learning—it's what you do next that counts.

Specifically, after you've finished reading and annotating the material, create study notes. The study notes should provide a summary of the key points, in outline form or in the form of concept maps. Either form of summary should supplement the annotations you've made on the printed page. (To practice making a concept map from a text, see **Try It! 4**.)

Furthermore, any notes you take should stand on their own. For instance, they should include enough information to be useful, whether or not you have the book or article on hand.

▶ **Use flash cards.** If you feel confident that the annotations you've written in the book are sufficiently comprehensive, you might consider taking notes on flash cards. **Flash cards** are simply index cards that contain key pieces of information that you need to remember.

Flash cards are particularly useful in subjects that present many small bits of information to remember, such as technical vocabulary words or math formulas. When you need to learn a new term, for instance, you can write the term on one side of a card and its definition on the other side.

One of the greatest virtues of flash cards is their portability. Because they are small, they can fit into your pocket or backpack, and you can look at them when you have a spare moment.

flash cards
Index cards that contain key pieces of information to be remembered.

Taking Notes on Material You Are Unable to Write On

Taking notes on materials that can't be written on or annotated digitally is a different story. Some digital textbooks and other online materials don't offer the opportunity of making online annotations. And traditional physical, hard-copy library books, magazines, journal articles, and materials on library reserve that are shared with others require a different approach.

Mapping Your Notes

Treat the lecture in Try It! 2 in Section 3.1 as if it were a passage in a textbook. Take notes using the strategies you've learned here and create a concept map. Then answer the following questions:

1. How did taking notes help you structure your concept map? Why would making a map be more difficult without notes?

2. How will your concept map make studying for a test easier? Do you think it's a more useful tool than notes alone? Why?

▶ **Approach the written material as you would a class lecture.** The techniques we discussed earlier for taking notes in class can all be adapted for taking notes from written material. In fact, the task is often easier, because—as is not the case with the spoken word—you'll be able to refer back to what was said earlier. It's all in black and white in front of you.

▶ **Laptops can be especially helpful in creating study notes.** If you're a good keyboarder, it's often easier and quicker to take notes using a word-processing program. However, don't be lured into typing too much. You need to be just as selective in what you input into your computer as you would be in taking notes during a class lecture.

▶ **Use the tricks of the trade we discussed earlier for taking notes from a class lecture.** Look for key ideas, definitions, quotations, and formulas, and include them in your notes. Use the headings that are included in the text, such as chapter and section titles. Bold or italic type is also a clue that an important point is being made. Graphs and charts often provide critical information.

▶ **Use the same form of notetaking that you use in class lectures.** If you write your notes in outline form, create an outline based on the written material. If you often create graphics such as concept maps, create them now. The point is to produce notes that are consistent with those you take during class lectures.

Taking Notes on the Job: Meetings of the Minds

The principles of good notetaking discussed in this chapter are useful not only in the classroom. They can also help you as you make your way in your career. For instance, you may need to take notes on lengthy memos or reports that detail company procedures you will need to master to do your job.

Furthermore, one of the most important settings in which you'll want to take effective notes is in meetings. For many people, meetings take up a good part of their professional workdays and being able to take effective notes can provide a significant career advantage.

Meetings are similar to class discussions. During a meeting, you will want to look for key topics and make notes of the ideas that receive the most emphasis or enthusiastic response. Note these areas and keep them in mind as likely priorities.

During meetings, tasks are often assigned. Not only do you want to clearly note what you are to do and when you are supposed to do it, but keeping track of what others are doing will also be helpful, because you may need to get information from them or otherwise coordinate efforts. For instance, if you are assigned the task of managing the development of your company's website, you'll want to clarify in your notes who has agreed to do what portion of the task.

Taking notes when others are speaking also shows that you are paying attention to what the speaker is saying. It's a kind of compliment that suggests you find what the speaker is saying to be so important that you will want to refer to it later.

Finally, notetaking plays another role: It can make seemingly interminable meetings appear to proceed faster by providing something for you to do that's more active than simply listening. In short, not only can notetaking provide you with a clear record of what occurred in a meeting, but it can also keep you engaged in what is going on.

Speaking *of* Success

Source: Courtesy of Yajaira Gijon

NAME: **Yajaira Gijon**

SCHOOL: **Columbia College Chicago, Chicago, Illinois**

HOME: **Chicago, Illinois**

Yajaira Gijon was the first in her family to attend college and receive a degree, but it took 10 years to achieve her goal.

"I didn't pay much attention in high school and my grades suffered," Gijon said, "but I pulled myself together and decided to go to community college. My parents were surprised but very supportive."

Gijon took an opportunity to work full time at a bilingual graphics design company during her first semester and as a result was going to school at night, taking a few courses each semester.

After four years she decided to pursue a fine arts degree at Columbia College Chicago, but it wasn't easy.

"The first semester was pretty tough," she said. "It was very competitive and the instructors pushed you a lot. I wasn't used to that. The next semester I had to rethink if I wanted to stay since I found it to be a frightening experience.

"But I told myself I just couldn't give up and returned the following semester, working full-time and going to school at night," Gijon added.

Realizing she needed to put an extra effort into her studies, Gijon made a commitment to being more involved.

"What I had to do was educate myself more and learn more about the design field," she explained, "and so I joined a design group. I would pick up magazines and read through them looking for ideas. I also developed a sketch book and journal, jotting down my ideas and noting what the latest trends were.

"Monday through Friday I would make an effort to be at school, at either the library or the lab," she said. "Every opportunity I had I was at the library or doing research on design trends in the lab. Being at school and seeing other students working hard motivated me."

For now Gijon wants to take a break before looking for work, but education is not far from her mind.

"I might work for a year and then go on to graduate school," she said. "I have an interest to go into teaching, and I want to come back and teach in my community and be a role model for others.

"The sacrifices of my parents coming to this country as immigrants inspired me to keep going," she added. "If they can do that, then I can do the same."

[RETHINK]

- Why do you think joining a design group was helpful to Gijon as she continued her studies?

- What advantages might Gijon receive by taking a year off before going to graduate school? Can you think of any disadvantages?

Looking **Back**

LO 3-1 Describe techniques for taking notes in class.

▶ The central feature of good notetaking is listening and distilling important information—not writing down everything that is said.

▶ Prepare for taking notes by identifying the instructor's and your own goals for the course, completing all assignments before arriving in class, and "warming up" for class by reviewing the notes and assignments from the previous class.

▶ Before writing notes, listen and think, processing the information that the instructor is attempting to deliver.

▶ Notes should be brief phrases rather than full sentences and, if possible, in outline form to reveal the structure of the lecture. Material written on the board should usually be copied word for word.

LO 3-2 Apply techniques for taking notes from written materials.

▶ Before leaving class, evaluate your notes, verifying that they are complete and understandable while there is still time to correct them.

▶ As soon as possible after class, actively rethink your notes.

LO 3-3 Explain methods for effective notetaking.

▶ Taking good study notes from written materials involves many of the principles that apply to taking good notes from oral presentations, though the source material can be consulted repeatedly, making it easier to get the information down accurately.

▶ Concept maps, outlines, and flash cards can be helpful tools for notetaking from textbooks.

[KEY TERMS AND CONCEPTS]

Active listening (p. 63)

Concept mapping (p. 72)

Flash cards (p. 74)

Hearing (p. 62)

Meta-message (p. 63)

Study notes (p. 72)

[RESOURCES]

ON CAMPUS

If you are having difficulty taking class notes effectively, talk with your course instructor. Bring your notes with you soon after a class has ended, and let the instructor assess what you are doing correctly and what could stand improvement.

If your problems persist, and you have great difficulty translating the spoken word into notes, then there's a small possibility that you suffer from an auditory learning disability. Be tested by a specialist to rule this out.

IN PRINT

Fiona McPherson's *Effective Notetaking* (Wayz Press, 2012) and Judy Kesselman-Turkel and Franklynn Peterson's *Note-Taking Made Easy* (University of Wisconsin Press, 2003) provide broad overviews of how to take good notes in class.

In addition, Deana Hippie's *Note Taking Made Easy!* (Scholastic, 2010) and Bobbi DePorter and Mike Hernacki's *Quantum Notes* (Learning Forum, 2000) provide strategies for increasing your listening and notetaking expertise.

ON THE WEB

The following sites on the Internet provide the opportunity to extend your learning about the material in this chapter. (Although the web addresses were accurate at the time this material was published, check the *P.O.W.E.R. Learning* Connect Library or contact your instructor for any changes that may have occurred.)

▶ Brigham Young University's Career and Counseling Center offers this page (**https://casc.byu.edu/note-taking**) on the Cornell Notetaking System. This notetaking system can help you improve the organization of your notes, while allowing you to make use of your existing strengths as a notetaker.

▶ A learning style model formulated by Richard M. Felder and Linda K. Silverman from North Carolina State University, The Index of Learning Styles is an online instrument used to assess preferences on four dimensions (active/reflective, sensing/intuitive, visual/verbal, and sequential/global) (**www.ncsu.edu/felder-public/ILSpage.html**).

The Case of . . .

One Big Mess

Andy Ward stared at the dozens of papers spread across the table. *Mess* was the only word to describe the pile of notes he'd taken for his Farm and Food Systems class that term.

As he studied for his final exam, he had to keep turning papers over to see what he'd written on the back. Pretty soon the lectures all got jumbled. He couldn't figure out which ideas were important. He hadn't tried to write down everything the instructor said, but now a lot of the one- and two-word phrases he'd jotted down made no sense to him. He skimmed through the textbook, hoping it would give him clues, but it was just too much material to absorb in one evening. His heart sank. He was probably going to fail the exam.

1. What are some of the mistakes you think Andy made in taking notes for this class?

2. What are some of the techniques for good notetaking in class that Andy might have used to make studying for his final exam easier?

3. How might Andy have used notetaking skills to make the textbook material more useful to him?

4. How could making concept maps have helped Andy study for his final?

5. Do you think Andy evaluates his notes during or after class? Do you think he ever rethinks them? What questions would you ask to help him perform these steps?

Learning Outcomes

By the time you finish this chapter you will be able to

» LO 4-1 Identify the kinds of tests you will encounter in college.

» LO 4-2 Explain the best ways to prepare for and take various kinds of tests.

» LO 4-3 Analyze the best strategies for answering specific kinds of test questions.

Taking Tests

Why on earth does a lab technician have to know algebra? wondered Chandra Farris. Yet here she was, nearing completion of her associate's degree, promised a position at the hospital of her dreams when she graduated—and the only obstacle in her path was a final algebra test. Her last test before graduation.

She had paid attention in class, made notes carefully, worked with a study group, and asked questions of her professor, and still she felt that every algebra concept she had ever struggled to understand was waiting to ambush her on this test. No two ways about it, this test—tomorrow's test—struck her with terror.

She kept reading and rereading her notes and her textbook, and time kept passing. Sleep seemed a remote possibility. She knew it was useless to keep force-feeding her brain for the sake of this one test, but she couldn't escape the feeling that her entire career, her whole future, was on the line.

Looking Ahead

Although many tests are not as critical as Chandra Farris's algebra final, tests do play a significant role in everyone's academic life. Students typically experience more anxiety over tests than over anything else in their college careers. If you're returning to college after a long break, or perhaps struggled with tests earlier in your academic career, you may find the prospect of taking a test especially intimidating.

But tests don't have to be so anxiety producing. There are strategies and techniques you can learn to reduce your fear of test taking. In fact, learning how to take tests is in some ways as important as learning the content that they cover. Taking tests effectively does not just involve mastering information; it also requires mastering specific test-taking skills.

One of the most important goals of this chapter is to take the mystery out of the whole process of taking tests. To do that, you'll learn about the different types of tests and strategies you can start using even before you take a test. You'll gain insight into how different kinds of tests work and how best to approach them, and you'll also learn about the various types of test questions and strategies for responding most effectively to each type.

This chapter also explores two aspects of test taking that may affect your performance: test anxiety and cramming. You will learn ways to deal with your anxiety and keep cramming to a minimum—but you will also learn how to make the most of cramming, if you do have to resort to it.

The chapter ends with suggestions for evaluating your performance toward the end of a test and for using what you learn to improve your performance the next time around.

» LO 4-1 Getting Ready

Tests may be the most unpopular part of college life. Students hate them because they produce fear, anxiety, apprehension about being evaluated, and a focus on grades instead of learning for learning's sake. Instructors often don't like them very much either, because they produce fear, anxiety, apprehension about being evaluated, and a focus on grades instead of learning for learning's sake. That's right: Students and instructors dislike tests for the very same reasons.

But tests are also valuable. A well-constructed test identifies what you know and what you still need to learn. Tests help you see how your performance compares with that of others. And knowing that you'll be tested on a body of material is certainly likely to motivate you to learn that material more thoroughly.

Journal Reflections

How I Feel about Tests

1. How do you feel about tests in general?

2. What are your first memories of being in a testing situation? What were your feelings, and why?

3. What makes a test "good" and "bad" from your perspective?

4. What factors contribute to your success or failure on a particular exam? Which of these factors are under your control?

5. What strategies do you use when taking tests to maximize your performance? Which have been particularly effective, and why?

However, there's another reason you might dislike tests: You may assume that tests have the power to define your worth as a person. If you do badly on a test, you may be tempted to believe that you've received some fundamental information about yourself from the instructor and the college, information that says you're a failure in some significant way.

This is a dangerous—and completely wrong—assumption. If you do badly on a test, it doesn't mean you're a bad person. Or stupid. Or that you don't belong in college. If you don't do well on a test, you're the same person you were before you took the test—no better, no worse. You just did badly on a test. Period.

In short, tests are not a measure of your value as an individual. They are only a measure of how well (and how much) you studied, and your test-taking skills. Tests are tools; they are indirect and imperfect measures of what we know. Someone with a great deal of knowledge can do poorly on a test; tension or going at too slow a pace can lead to unwelcome results in some cases. Another person may know considerably less and still do better on the test simply because he or she may have learned some test-taking skills along the way.

How we do on a test depends on a number of considerations: the kind of test it is, the subject matter involved, our understanding of test-taking strategies, and, above all, how well we prepare for it. Let's turn, then, to the first step in test taking: preparation. (The five steps are summarized in the P.O.W.E.R. Plan on the right.)

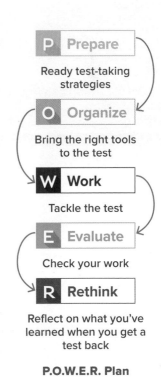

P Prepare

Ready test-taking strategies

O Organize

Bring the right tools to the test

W Work

Tackle the test

E Evaluate

Check your work

R Rethink

Reflect on what you've learned when you get a test back

P.O.W.E.R. Plan

Readying Your Test-Taking Strategies

Preparation for tests requires a number of strategies. Among the most important are the following.

Remember: Everything You Do in a Course Is Preparation for a Test

All the things you do during a course help to prepare you for a test. There is no surer way to get good grades on tests than to attend class faithfully and to complete all class assignments seriously and on time.

Preparing for tests is a long-term proposition. It's not a matter of "giving your all" the night before the test. Instead, it's a matter of giving your all to every aspect of the course.

Know What You Are Preparing For

Determine as much as you can about the test before you begin to study for it. The more you know about a test beforehand, the more efficient your studying will be.

To find out about an upcoming test, ask these questions:

▶ Is the test called a "test," "exam," "quiz," or something else? As you can see in **Table 4.1**, the names imply different things. For simplicity's sake, we'll use the term "test" throughout this chapter, but know that these distinctions exist, and they should affect the way you prepare.

▶ What material will the test cover?

▶ How many questions will be on it?

▶ How much time is it expected to take? A full class period? Only part of a period?

▶ What kinds of questions will be on the test?

▶ How will it be graded?

▶ Will sample questions be provided?

▶ Are tests from previous terms available?

▶ Will the instructor hand out a study guide?

▶ How much does the test contribute to my final course grade?

Match Test Preparation to Question Types

Test questions come in different types (see **Table 4.2**), and each requires a somewhat different style of preparation.

▶ **Essay questions.** Essay tests focus on the big picture—ways in which the various pieces of information being tested fit together. You'll need to know not just a series of facts, but also the connections between them, and you will have to be able to discuss these ideas in an organized and logical way. A good study tactic is to play instructor: After carefully reviewing your notes and other course materials, think of likely exam questions. Then, without looking at your notes

table 4.1   Quizzes, Tests, Exams . . . What's in a Name?

Although they may vary from one instructor to another, the following definitions are most commonly used:

Quizzes. A *quiz* is a brief assessment, usually covering a relatively small amount of material. Some quizzes cover as little as one class's worth of reading. Although a single quiz usually doesn't count very much, instructors often add quiz scores together, and collectively they can become a significant part of your final course grade.

Tests. A *test* is a more extensive, more heavily weighted assessment than a quiz, covering more material. A test may come every few weeks of the term, often after each third or quarter of the term has passed, but this varies with the instructor and the course.

Exams. An *exam* is the most substantial kind of assessment. In many classes, just one exam is given—a final exam at the end of the term. Sometimes there are two exams, one at the midpoint of the term (called, of course, a midterm) and the second at the end. Exams are usually weighted quite heavily because they are meant to assess your knowledge of all the course material covered up to that point.

table 4.2   Types of Test Questions

Essay	Requires a fairly extended, on-the-spot composition about some topic. Examples include questions that call on you to describe a person, process, or event, or those that ask you to compare or contrast two separate sets of material.
Multiple-choice	Usually contains a question or statement, followed by a number of possible answers (usually 4 or 5 of them). You are supposed to choose the best response from the choices offered.
True–false	Presents statements about a topic that are either accurate or inaccurate. You are to indicate whether each statement is accurate (true) or inaccurate (false).
Matching	Presents two lists of related information, arranged in column form. Typically, you are asked to pair up the items that go together (e.g., a scientific term and its definition).
Short-answer	Requires brief responses (usually a few sentences at most) in a kind of mini-essay.
Fill-in	Requires you to add one or more missing words to a sentence or series of sentences.

or your readings, answer each potential essay question, either aloud or by writing out the major points an answer should include. After you've answered the questions, check yourself by looking at the notes and readings once again.

▶ **Short-answer and fill-in questions.** Short-answer and fill-in questions are similar to essays in that they require you to recall key pieces of information

Source: © Kennedy Photography / Alamy

rather than finding them on the page in front of you. However, short-answer and fill-in questions—unlike essay questions—typically don't demand that you integrate or compare different types of information. Consequently, the focus of your study should be on the recall of specific, detailed information.

▶ **Multiple-choice, true–false, and matching questions.** While the focus of review for essay questions should be on major issues and controversies, studying for multiple-choice, true–false, and matching questions requires more attention to the details.

Almost anything is fair game for multiple-choice, true–false, and matching questions, so you can't afford to overlook anything when studying. True, these kinds of questions put the material right there on the page for you to react to—Did Columbus land in 1492, or not?—rather than asking you to provide the names and dates yourself (as in the case of the essay question). Nevertheless, to do well on these tests you must put your memory into high gear and master a great many facts.

It's a particularly good idea to record important facts on index cards. Either write them out by hand, or use one of several smartphone apps that help you create them. In addition, if you are using an e-textbook, the software may make it easy for you to create index cards automatically. They can be reviewed on your smartphone or computer or you can print them out.

Political reforms of progressive age:
– direct primaries: people vote for whom they want
   to run; not appointed
– initiative: people propose laws on their own
– referendum: gov. proposes; people say yes or no
– recall: people can remove politicians from office
   before they finish term

Endoplasmic reticulum (ER):
Smooth ER-makes fats (lipids)
Rough ER-has ribosomes which make proteins

Together, they make membranes for whole cell (for
plasma membrane, mitochondrion, etc.) Also make
more of themselves.

Source: © Kennedy Photography / Alamy

It also can be helpful to write the name of a particular concept or theory on one side of a note card, and then generate and write an example of it on the other side. Studying the cards will help ensure that you fully understand the concepts and theories and can generalize them to different situations.

Measure Your Test-Taking Style

Do you feel anxious at the very thought of a test, or are you cool and calm in the face of testing situations? Get a sense of your test-taking style by checking off every statement below that applies to you.

☐ **1.** The closer a test date approaches, the more nervous I get.

☐ **2.** I am sometimes unable to sleep on the night before a test.

☐ **3.** I have "frozen up" during a test, finding myself unable to think or respond.

☐ **4.** I can feel my hands shaking as I pick up my pencil to begin a test.

☐ **5.** The minute I read a tough test question, all the facts I ever knew about the subject abandon me and I can't get them back no matter how hard I try.

☐ **6.** I have become physically ill before or during a test.

☐ **7.** Nervousness prevents me from studying immediately before a test.

☐ **8.** I often dream about an upcoming test.

☐ **9.** Even if I successfully answer a number of questions, my anxiety stays with me throughout the test.

☐ **10.** I'm reluctant to turn in my test paper for fear I can do better if I continue to work on it.

If you checked off more than four statements, you have experienced fairly serious test anxiety. If you checked off more than six statements, your anxiety is probably interfering with your test performance. In particular, statements 3, 5, 6, 7, and 10 may indicate serious test anxiety.

If, based on your responses to this questionnaire and your previous experience, your level of test anxiety is high, what are some of the steps described in this chapter that might be helpful to you?

Deal with Test Anxiety

What does the anticipation of a test do to you? Do you feel shaky? Frantic, like there's not enough time to get it all done? Do you feel as if there's a knot in your stomach? Do you grit your teeth?

Test anxiety is a temporary condition characterized by fears and concerns about test taking. It is manifested in a very real physical reaction: your body is producing stress hormones as a reaction to your mental state of concern.

Almost everyone experiences test anxiety to some degree, though for some people it's more of a problem than for others. The real danger with test anxiety is that it can become so overwhelming that it can hurt test performance. (To assess your own test-taking style and the degree of anxiety around tests that you experience, see **Try It! 1**.)

You'll never eliminate test anxiety completely, nor do you want to. A little bit of nervousness can energize us, making us more attentive and vigilant. Like any competitive event, testing can motivate us to do our best. You might think of moderate test anxiety as a desire to perform at your peak—a useful quality at test time.

On the other hand, for some, anxiety can spiral into the kind of paralyzing fear that makes their minds go blank. There are several ways to keep this from happening to you:

1. *Prepare thoroughly.* The more you prepare, the less test anxiety you'll feel. Good preparation can give you a sense of control and mastery, and it will prevent test anxiety from overwhelming you.

test anxiety
A temporary condition characterized by fears and concerns about test taking.

2. *Take a realistic view of the test.* Remember that your future success does not hinge on your performance on any single exam. Think of the big picture: Put the task ahead in context, and remind yourself of all the hurdles you've passed so far.

3. *Eat right and get enough sleep.* Good mental preparation occurs when your body is well prepared.

4. *Learn relaxation techniques.* You can learn to reduce or even eliminate the jittery physical symptoms of test anxiety by using relaxation techniques. The basic process is straightforward: Breathe evenly, gently inhaling and exhaling. Focus your mind on a pleasant, relaxing scene such as a beautiful forest or a peaceful farm, or on a restful sound such as that of ocean waves breaking on the beach.

5. *Visualize success.* Think of an image of your instructor handing back your test marked with a big, fat "A." Or imagine your instructor congratulating you on your fine performance the day after the test. Positive visualizations that highlight your potential success can help replace images of failure that may fuel test anxiety.

6. Just before you take a test, *spend 10 minutes writing about your feelings regarding the upcoming exam.* It's a way to help free yourself of negative emotions, allowing you to concentrate better on the exam.

What if these strategies don't work? If your test anxiety is so great that it's getting in the way of your success, consider consulting a professional counselor or therapist. Many colleges provide a learning resource center or a counseling center that can provide you with personalized help. (To focus on dealing with math test anxiety, see the **Course Connections** feature.)

» LO 4-2 Studying for the Test

A key part of preparing for a test is a trial run-through. Like running practice trials before you participate in an actual race, it makes sense to ready yourself for the real event by taking a practice test.

Test Yourself

Once you feel you've mastered the material, test yourself on it. There are several ways to do this. Often textbooks are accompanied by websites that offer automatically scored practice tests and quizzes.

You can also create a test for yourself, Make it as close as possible to what you expect the actual test to be. For instance, if your instructor has told you the classroom test will be made up primarily of short-answer questions, your test should reflect that.

You might also construct a test and administer it to a classmate or a member of your study group. In turn, you could take a test that someone else has constructed. Constructing and taking practice tests are excellent ways of studying the material and cementing it into memory. (To be sure you're fully prepared for your next test, complete **Try It! 2.**)

Special Techniques for Dealing with Math Anxiety

For many students, the greatest test anxiety comes when they're taking a test involving math. Math seems to bring out the worst fears in some people, perhaps because it's seen as a discipline in which answers are either totally right or totally wrong, or because they've felt they've "hit the wall" and they'll never be able to understand a new concept, no matter how hard they try.

Such feelings about math can be devastating, because they can prevent you from doing well even if you know the material. If you suffer from math anxiety, keep these things in mind:

- Math is like any other subject: The greatest component of success is the effort you put in, not whether you have a "math gene" that makes you naturally good at math. It's not true that you are either born "good at math" or not. It's a cultural myth that "math is hard" and that somehow it's fine if you're not good at it.

- It's also not true that there's only one way to solve a math problem. Sometimes there are a variety of routes to coming up with a solution. And keep in mind that the solution to math problems often calls for creativity, not just sheer logic.

- It's a false stereotype that women are not as good at math as men, but it's a stereotype that many women buy. Research has shown that when men do badly on a math test, they're most likely to think that they haven't put in enough effort. But when women don't do well on a math test, they're three times more likely than men to feel that they don't have enough ability to be successful. That's an erroneous view of the world. Don't become a prisoner of stereotypes.

Use these special strategies to deal with math problems on exams:

BEFORE TESTS:

1. Math is cumulative, building on prior concepts and knowledge. Make sure you review math fundamentals before moving on to more advanced topics.
2. Ask questions in class. Don't be afraid that you'll ask the wrong question in the wrong way. Instructors want you to understand their subject.
3. Make use of review sessions and other study resources.
4. Practice, practice, practice. The more experience you have completing math problems under pressure, the better you'll do. Practice math problems using a timer in order to simulate an actual test.

DURING TESTS:

1. Analyze math problems carefully. What are the known quantities or constants, and what pieces of information are missing? What formula(s) or theorem(s) apply?
2. Consider drawing a diagram, graph, or probability tree.
3. Break down calculations into their component parts.
4. Check your math carefully.
5. Be neat and logical in your presentation, and show every step as you solve problems. Your instructor may give you partial credit if you lay out every step you're going through. In addition, some instructors may require you to show your work.

Complete a Test Preparation Checklist

It takes more than simply learning the material to prepare for a test. You also need a strategy that will help you understand what it is you are studying for. To do that, learn as much as you can about what the test will be like. The more you understand about the kind of test it will be and what it will cover, the better you'll be able to target your studying.

To focus your studying, complete the following test preparation checklist before your next test.

TEST PREPARATION CHECKLIST

- ☐ I know whether it's a quiz, test, or exam.
- ☐ I know what kinds of questions will be on the test.
- ☐ I understand what material will be covered.
- ☐ I know how many questions will be on the test.
- ☐ I know how long I will have to complete the test.
- ☐ I know how the test will be graded, and how the grade contributes to my final course grade.
- ☐ I obtained sample questions and/or previous tests, if available.
- ☐ I formed or participated in a study group.
- ☐ I used different and appropriate preparation strategies for different types of questions.
- ☐ I read and studied my class notes.
- ☐ I composed some questions of the kind that will be on the exam.
- ☐ I answered essay questions aloud.
- ☐ I actively memorized facts and details.
- ☐ I made and used flash cards.
- ☐ I created and used a test like the real test.

After completing the checklist, ask yourself these questions: How can I use this checklist to study more effectively for tests? How might completing the checklist change the way I study for tests? What new strategies might I follow to prepare for tests more effectively in the future?

From the perspective of . . .

A STUDENT You will take many types of courses during your academic career. Can you think of how test-taking strategies will work in an English course versus a science course?

Form a Study Group

study groups

Small, informal groups of students whose purpose is to help members work together and study for a test.

Study groups are small, informal groups of students who work together to learn course material and study for a test. Forming such a group can be an excellent way to prepare for any kind of test. Some study groups are formed for particular tests, whereas others meet consistently throughout the term.

Taking an online class? You can still form a study group by using Skype, Facetime, or other applications that allow you to communicate face to face virtually. It may seem a bit awkward, but the benefits of even a virtual study group are very real.

Study groups can be extremely powerful tools because they help accomplish several things:

▶ They help members organize and structure the material to approach their studying in a systematic and logical way.

▶ They allow students to share different perspectives on the material.

▶ They make it more likely that students will not overlook any potentially important information.

▶ They force members to rethink the course material, explaining it in words that other group members will understand.

There are some potential drawbacks to keep in mind. Study groups don't always work well for students with learning styles that favor working independently. In addition, "problem" members—those who don't pull their weight—may cause difficulties for the group. In general, though, the advantages of study groups far outweigh their disadvantages. (To set up your own study group, see **Try It! 3**.)

Study groups, made up of a few students who study together for a test, can help organize material, provide new perspectives, and motivate members to do their best. Do you think you would function well in a study group? Why or why not?
Source: © Peter M. Fisher/Fuse/ Getty Images

Use Your Campus Learning or Tutorial Center Resources

Many colleges have a learning center, tutorial center, or other office that can help you study for a test. Don't wait until after you do badly on a test to visit your campus learning or tutorial center. A visit prior to your first test is a good use of your time, even if you feel it's not essential. Just knowing what resources are available can boost your confidence.

Cramming: You Shouldn't, But . . .

You know, of course, that **cramming**—hurried, last-minute studying—is not the way to go. You know that you're likely to forget the material the moment the test is over because long-term retention is nearly impossible without thoughtful study. But . . .

   . . . it's been one of those weeks where everything went wrong.

   . . . the instructor sprang the test on you at the last minute.

   . . . you forgot about the test until the night before it was scheduled.

Whatever the reason, there may be times when you can't study properly. What do you do if you have to cram for an exam?

Don't spend a lot of time on what you're *unable* to do. Beating yourself up about your occasional failings as a student will only hinder your efforts. Instead, admit you're human and imperfect like everyone else. Then spend a few minutes developing a plan about what you can accomplish in the limited time you've got.

cramming
Hurried, last-minute studying.

Form a Study Group

The next time you have to prepare for a test, form a study group with three to five classmates. They may have a variety of study habits and skills, but all must be willing to take the group seriously.

The first time you meet, compare notes about what is likely to be on the test and brainstorm to come up with possible test questions. If the instructor hasn't given you detailed information about the test (i.e., number and types of questions, weighting, etc.), one of you should be delegated to ask for it. Plan to meet once more closer to the test date to discuss answers to the questions you've come up with, share any new insights, and quiz one another on the material.

After you've taken the test and gotten your results, meet again and evaluate the experience by answering the following questions:

1. Did you and the other members of the group find the experience useful?

2. Did participating in the study group make the members feel more confident prior to the test?

3. What aspects of the study group were most effective?

4. What aspects of the study group didn't work effectively?

5. What would you do differently the next time you use a study group?

The first thing to do is choose what you really need to study. You won't be able to learn everything, so you have to make choices. Figure out the main focus of the course, and concentrate on it.

Once you have a strategy, prepare a one-page summary sheet with hard-to-remember information. Just writing the material down will help you remember it, and you can refer to the summary sheet frequently over the limited time you do have to study.

Next, read through your class notes, concentrating on the material you've underlined and the key concepts and ideas that you've already noted. Forget about reading all the material in the books and articles you're being tested on. Instead, read only the passages that you've underlined and the notes you've taken on the readings. Finally, maximize your study time. Using your notes, index cards, and concept maps, go over the information. Read it. Say it aloud. Think about it and the way it relates to other information. In short, use all the techniques we've talked about for learning and recalling information.

Just remember: When the exam is over, material that you have crammed into your head is destined to leave your mind as quickly as it entered. If you've crammed for a midterm, don't assume that the information will still be there when you study for the final.

Cramming can be exhausting, but it is on occasion necessary. With the many family and personal responsibilities many students face, sometimes it can't be avoided. There are, however, strategies you can use to help you make the best use of limited time.
Source: © Pixtal/AGE Fotostock

In the end, cramming often ends up taking more time for worse results than does studying with appropriate techniques.

O Organize | Facing the Day of the Test

You've studied a lot, and you're happy with your level of mastery. Or perhaps you have the nagging feeling that there's something you haven't quite gotten to. Or maybe you know you haven't had enough time to study as much as you'd like, and you're expecting a disaster.

Whatever your frame of mind, it will help organize your plan of attack on the day of the test. What's included on the test is out of your hands, but you can control what you bring to it.

For starters, bring the right tools to the test. Have at least two pens and two pencils with you. It's usually best to write in pen because, in general, writing tends to be easier to read in pen than in pencil. But you also might want to have pencils on hand. Sometimes instructors will use machine-scored tests, which require the use of pencil. Or there may be test questions that involve computations, and solving them may entail frequent reworking of calculations.

You should also bring a watch to the test, even if there will be a clock on the wall of the classroom. You will want to be able to pace yourself properly during the test. Also, if you usually use a cell phone to determine the time, remember that some instructors may not allow you to look at them during the test.

Sometimes instructors permit you to use notes and books during the test. If you haven't brought them with you, they're not going to be much help. So make sure you bring them if they're permitted. (Even for closed-book tests, having such material available when you arrive in the classroom allows you a few minutes of review before the test actually starts.) And don't be lulled into thinking an open-book test is going to be easy. Instructors who allow you to use your notes and books during a test may not give you much time to look things up, so you still need to study.

On the day of a test, avoid the temptation to compare notes with your friends about how much they've studied. Yes, you might end up feeling good because many of your fellow classmates studied less than you did. But chances are you'll find others who seem to have spent significantly more time studying than you, and this will do little to encourage you.

In addition, you might want to plan on panicking. Although it sounds like the worst possible approach, permitting yourself the option of spending a minute feeling panicky will help you to recover from your initial fears.

Finally, listen carefully to what an instructor says before the test is handed out. The instructor may tell you about a question that is optional or worth more points or inform you of a typographical error on the test. Whatever the instructor says just before the test, you can be sure it's information that you don't want to ignore.

Taking a Test Online

If you will be taking the test online, either because you are enrolled in a distance learning class or because your face-to-face course instructor has assigned an online quiz, there are two key additional factors to consider as you get ready to take the test:

▶ Have your computer at the ready and have reliable access to the Internet.

▶ Be sure to know exactly when the test will be available online. You may be able to take the test only for a certain period. Miss that time, and you'll be out of luck.

≫ LO 4-3 Taking the Test

The instructor hands you the test, and it's time to start. Here are some proven strategies that will help you maximize your success.

 **Tackling the Test**

Take a deep breath—literally.

There's no better way to start work on a test than by taking a deep breath, followed by several others. The deep breaths will help you overcome any initial panic and anxiety you may be experiencing. It's OK to give yourself over for a moment to panic and anxiety, but to work at your best, use the relaxation techniques that we spoke about earlier to displace those initial feelings. Tell yourself, "It's OK. I am going to do my best."

Read test instructions carefully. Even if instructors talk about what a test will be like beforehand, at the last minute they may make changes. Consequently, it's critical to read the instructions for the test carefully. In fact, you should skim through the entire exam before you begin. Look at the kinds of questions and pay attention to the way they will be scored. If the point weighting of the various parts of the exam is not clear, ask your instructor to clarify it.

Knowing the point weighting is critical, because it will help you to allocate your time. You don't want to spend 90 percent of your time on an essay that's worth only 10 percent of the points, and you want to be sure to leave time at the end of the test to check your answers.

An initial read-through will also help you verify that you have every page of the exam and that each one is readable. It may also provide you with "intratest knowledge," in which terms defined or mentioned in one part of a test trigger memories that can help answer questions in another part of the test.

If there are any lists, formulas, or other key facts that you're concerned you may forget, jot them down now on the back of a test page or on a piece of scrap paper. You may want to refer to this material later during the test.

Once this background work is out of the way, you'll be ready to proceed to actually answering the questions. These principles will help you do your best on the test:

▶ **Answer the easiest questions first.** By initially getting the questions that are easiest for you out of the way, you accomplish several important things. First, you'll be leaving yourself more time to think about the tougher questions. In addition, moving through a series of questions without a struggle will build your confidence. Finally, working through a number of questions will build up a base of points that may be enough to earn you at least a minimally acceptable grade.

▶ **Write legibly and only on one side of the paper.** If an instructor can't read what you've written, you're not going to get credit for it, no matter how brilliant your answer. So be sure to keep your handwriting legible.

It's also a good idea to write your answers to essay questions on only one side of a page. This will allow you to go back later and add or revise information.

▶ **Master machine-scored tests.** Tests will sometimes be scored, in part, by computer. In such cases, you'll usually have to indicate your answers by filling in—with a pencil—circles or squares on a computer answer sheet.

Be careful! A stray mark or smudge can cause the computer scanner to misread your answer sheet, producing errors in grading. Be sure to bring a good eraser in addition to a pencil; the biggest source of mistakes in machine grading is incomplete erasing.

It's best to write your answers not only on the answer sheet, but also on the test itself (if the test is not intended for future reuse). That way you can go back and check your answers easily—a step you should take frequently. It's also a good idea to match up your answers on the test with the spaces on the answer sheet every five or so items. This will help you make sure you haven't skipped a space or gotten off track in some other way. If you catch such problems early, they're easy to fix.

A variant of machine-scored testing is online testing. In such cases, you'll be taking an exam on a computer outside of class. Keep in mind that you shouldn't wait until the final deadline to start your test. Technical difficulties may prevent you from logging in or not allow you enough time to finish. In addition, be sure to have paper and pencil available. Even though you use the computer to record your answers, you'll want to be able to jot down ideas and notes, and do calculations the traditional way: by hand.

> "Computerized test-scoring isn't perfect. Smudges can kill you. If your grade seems incorrect, ask to see the answer sheet."
>
> **Graduate, Physiology, Michigan State University, in S. Tyler,** *Been There, Should've Done That* **(Haslett, MI: Front Porch Press, 1997), p. 128.**

Use Strategies Targeted to Answering Specific Types of Test Questions

Every type of question requires a particular approach. Use the strategies below:

▶ **Essay questions.** Essay questions, with their emphasis on description and analysis, often present challenges because they are relatively unstructured. Unless you're careful, it's easy to wander off and begin to answer questions that were never asked. To prevent that problem, the first thing to do is read the question carefully, noting what specifically is being asked. If your essay will be lengthy, you might even want to write a short outline.

Pay attention to keywords that indicate what, specifically, the instructor is looking for in an answer. Certain action words are commonly used in essays, and you should understand them fully. For instance, knowing the distinction between "compare" and "contrast" can spell the difference between success and failure. **Table 4.3** defines common action words.

Use the right language in essays. Be brief and to the point in your essay. Avoid flowery introductory language. Compare the two sentences that follow:

> *"Management techniques have evolved to a point never before seen in the history of our country, or perhaps even our world."*
>
> *"Many new management techniques have been developed in recent years."*

The second sentence says the same thing much more effectively and economically.

Essays are improved when they include examples and point out differences. Your response should follow a logical sequence, moving from major points to minor ones, or following a time sequence. Above all, your answer should address every aspect of the question posed on the test. Because essays often contain several different, embedded questions, you have to be certain that you have answered every part to receive full credit. (After reviewing Table 4.3, complete **Try It! 4**.)

▶ **Short-answer and fill-in questions.** Short-answer and fill-in questions basically require you to generate and supply specific information. Unlike essays,

table 4.3 Action Words for Essays

These words are commonly used in essay questions. Learning the distinctions among them will help you answer essay questions effectively.

Analyze: Examine and break into component parts.

Clarify: Explain with significant detail.

Compare: Describe and explain similarities.

Compare and contrast: Describe and explain similarities and differences.

Contrast: Describe and explain differences.

Critique: Judge and analyze, explaining what is wrong—and right—about a concept.

Define: Provide the meaning.

Discuss: Explain, review, and consider.

Enumerate: Provide a listing of ideas, concepts, reasons, items, etc.

Evaluate: Provide pros and cons of something; provide an opinion and justify it.

Explain: Give reasons why or how; clarify, justify, and illustrate.

Illustrate: Provide examples; show instances.

Interpret: Explain the meaning of something.

Justify: Explain why a concept can be supported, typically by using examples and other types of support.

Outline: Provide an overarching framework or explanation—usually in narrative form—of a concept, idea, event, or phenomenon.

Prove: Using evidence and arguments, convince the reader of a particular point.

Relate: Show how things fit together; provide analogies.

Review: Describe or summarize, often with an evaluation.

State: Assert or explain.

Summarize: Provide a condensed, precise list or narrative.

Trace: Track or sketch out how events or circumstances have evolved; provide a history or timeline.

which are more free-form and may have several possible answers, short-answer and fill-in questions are usually quite specific, requiring only one answer.

Use both the instructions for the questions and the questions themselves to determine the level of specificity that is needed in an answer. Try not to provide too much or too little information. Usually, brevity is best.

▶ **Multiple-choice questions.** If you've ever looked at a multiple-choice question and said to yourself, "But every choice seems right," you understand what can be tricky about this type of question. However, there are some simple strategies that can help you deal with multiple-choice questions.

Understand Action Verbs in Essay Questions

Answer the following questions about the Second Amendment to the United States Constitution by outlining your responses to them, paying attention to the different action verbs that introduce questions.

The Second Amendment states:

A well-regulated militia, being necessary to the security of a free State, the right of the people to keep and bear arms, shall not be infringed.

1. Summarize the Second Amendment to the Constitution.

2. Analyze the Second Amendment to the Constitution.

3. Discuss the Second Amendment to the Constitution.

How do your answers differ for each of the questions? Which of the questions provoked the lengthiest response? Which of the questions could you answer best?

First, read the question carefully. Note any specific instructions. In most cases, only one answer will be correct, but some questions will ask you to select multiple items.

Then, *before you look at the possible answers, try to answer the question in your head.* This can help you avoid confusion over inappropriate choices.

Next, *carefully read through every possible answer.* Even if you come to one that you think is right, read them all—there may be a subsequent answer that is better.

Look for absolutes like "every," "always," "only," "none," and "never." Choices that contain such absolute words are rarely correct. For example, an answer choice that says, "A U.S. president has never been elected without having received the majority of the popular vote" is incorrect due to the presence of the word "never." On the other hand, less-absolute words, such as "generally," "usually," "often," "rarely," "seldom," and "typically" may indicate a correct response.

Be especially on guard for the word "not," which negates the sentence ("The one key concept that is not embodied in the U.S. Constitution is . . ."). It's easy to gloss over "not," and if you have the misfortune of doing so, it will be nearly impossible to answer the item correctly.

If you're having trouble understanding a question, underline key words or phrases, or try to break the question into different short sections. Sometimes it is helpful to work backwards, *Jeopardy!* style, and look at the possible answers first to see if you can find one that is clearly accurate or clearly inaccurate.

educated guessing

The practice of eliminating obviously false multiple-choice answers and selecting the most likely answer from the remaining choices.

Use an **educated guessing** *strategy*—which is very different from wild or random guessing. Unless you are penalized for wrong answers (a scoring rule by which wrong answers are deducted from the points you have earned on other questions, rather than merely not counting at all toward your score), it always pays to guess.

The first step in educated guessing is to eliminate any obviously false answers. The next step is to examine the remaining choices closely. Does one response choice include an absolute or qualifying adjective that makes it unlikely ("the probability of war *always* increases when a U.S. president is facing political difficulties")? Does one choice include a subtle factual error? For example, the answer to a multiple-choice question asking why Columbus took his journey to the new world that says "the French monarchy was interested in expanding its colonial holdings" is wrong because it was not the French, but the Spanish, monarchy that funded his journey.

▶ **True–false questions.** Although most of the principles we've already discussed apply equally well to the true–false questions, a few additional tricks of the trade may help you with this type of question. Begin a set of true–false questions by answering the ones you're sure you know. But don't rush; it's important to read every part of a true–false question, because key words such as "never," "always," and "sometimes" often determine the appropriate response. If you don't have a clue about whether a statement is true or false, here's a last-resort principle: Choose "true." In general, more statements on a true–false test are likely to be true than false. (The reason for this? It's because it's easier for an instructor to think of true statements than to make up believable false statements.)

▶ **Matching questions.** Matching questions typically present you with two columns of related information, which you must link, item by item. For example, a list of terms or concepts may be presented in one column, along with a list of corresponding definitions or explanations in the second column. The best strategy is to reduce the size of both columns by matching the items you're most confident about first; this will leave a short list in each column, and the final matching may become apparent.

About Academic Honesty

It's tempting: A glance at a classmate's test may provide the one piece of information that you just can't remember. But you owe it to yourself not to do it. Copying from a classmate's paper is no different from reaching over and stealing that classmate's calculator or cell phone. It is a violation of **academic honesty**, one of the foundations of civility in the classroom, as well as in society. Unless the work you turn in under your own name is your work, you are guilty of academic dishonesty.

Violations of academic honesty can take many forms. One form is **plagiarism**, taking credit for another's words, thoughts, or ideas. Academic dishonesty may also include using a calculator when it's not allowed, discussing the answer to a question, copying a computer file when it's unauthorized, taking an exam for another person, or stealing an exam. It can take the form of ripping a page out of a book in the library, or lying to an instructor about the reason for a late paper. It includes using your textbook or conferring with a friend when taking a closed-book exam in an online, distance learning course.

You may feel that "everyone does it," so cheating is not so bad. Wrong. Everyone doesn't do it, just as most people don't embezzle from their companies or steal from others. Although you may know of a few cases of exceptionally dishonest classmates, most of your classmates try to be honest—you just don't notice their honesty.

Whatever form it takes, academic dishonesty is just plain wrong. It lowers the level of civility in the classroom, it makes the grading system unfair, and it ultimately reduces the meaning of your grade. It certainly hinders academic and personal growth. It can't help but reduce one's self-esteem, and it robs the cheater of self-respect.

Finally, academic dishonesty violates the regulations of every college (rules that you should familiarize yourself with), and instructors feel it is their obligation to uphold standards of academic honesty. Violations of honesty policies will lead to any number of potentially devastating scenarios: failing the exam on which the cheating has taken place, failing the entire course, being brought before a disciplinary board, having a description of the incident permanently placed on your grade transcript, being placed on academic probation, or even being thrown out of school. A single instance of cheating can permanently prevent you from embarking on the career of your choice. Cheating is simply not worth it.

academic honesty
Completing and turning in only one's own work under one's own name.

plagiarism
Taking credit for someone else's words, thoughts, or ideas.

E Evaluate. # Taking Your Own Final Examination

The last few minutes of a test may feel like the final moments of a marathon. You need to focus your energy and push yourself even harder. It can be make-it-or-break-it time.

Tests for a Lifetime

If you think the last tests you'll ever have to take are the final exams just before you graduate from college, you're probably wrong.

Increasing numbers of professions require initial licensing exams, and some even require periodic exams to remain in good standing within the profession. For example, in some states, people who wish to become teachers must pass an exam. And even experienced teachers are required to take periodic tests throughout their careers to remain in the teaching field.

In short, good test-taking skills won't just bring you success in college. They're something that may benefit you for a lifetime as you pursue your career.

Save some time at the end of a test so you can check your work. You should have been keeping track of your time all along, so plan on stopping a few minutes before the end of the test period to review what you've done. It's a critical step, and it can make the difference between a terrific grade and a mediocre one. It's a rare person who can work for an uninterrupted period of time on a test and commit absolutely no errors—even if he or she knows the material backwards and forwards. Consequently, checking what you've done is crucial.

Start evaluating your test by looking for obvious mistakes. Make sure you've answered every question and haven't skipped any parts of questions. If there is a separate answer sheet, check to see that all your answers have been recorded on the answer sheet and in the right spot.

If the test has included essay and short-answer questions, proofread your responses. Check for obvious errors—misspellings, missing words, and repetitions. Make sure you've responded to every part of each question and that each essay, as a whole, makes sense.

Check over your responses to multiple-choice, true–false, and matching questions. If there are some items that you haven't yet answered because you couldn't remember the necessary information, now is the time to take a stab at them. As we discussed earlier, it usually pays to guess, even randomly if you must. On most tests, no answer and a wrong answer are worth the same amount—nothing!

What about items that you initially guessed at? Unless you have a good reason to change your original answer—such as a new insight or a sudden recollection of some key information—your first guess is likely your best guess.

Know When to Stop

After evaluating and checking your answers, you may reach a point at which there is still some time left. What to do? If you're satisfied with your responses, it's simply time to tell yourself, "Let it go."

Permit yourself the luxury of knowing that you've done your best, and hand the test in to your instructor. You don't have to review your work over and over just because there is time remaining and some of your classmates are still working on their tests. In fact, such behavior is often counterproductive, because you might start overinterpreting and reading things into questions that really aren't there.

Disaster! I've run out of time! It's a nightmarish feeling: The clock is ticking relentlessly, and it's clear that you don't have enough time to finish the test. What should you do?

Stop working! Although this advice may sound foolish, in fact the most important thing you can do is take a minute to calm yourself. Take some deep breaths to replace the feelings of panic that are likely welling up inside you. Collect your thoughts, and plan a strategy for the last moments of the test.

From the perspective of . . .

A LEGAL ASSISTANT Even though tests are uncommon in professional careers, deadlines are frequent occurrences. How might test-taking strategies help you when you are faced with a tight schedule?

If there are essays that remain undone, consider how you'd answer them if you had more time. Then write an outline of each answer. If you don't have time even for that, write a few keywords. Writing anything is better than handing in a blank page, and you may get at least some credit for your response. The key principle here: Something is better than nothing, and even one point is worth more than zero points.

Source: 68/Ocean/Corbis

The same principle holds for other types of questions. Even wild guesses are almost always better than not responding at all to an item. So rather than telling yourself you've certainly failed and giving up, do as much as you can in the remaining moments of the exam.

R Rethink | The Real Test of Learning

Your instructor is about to hand the graded exams back. All sorts of thoughts run through your head: How did I do? Did I do as well as my classmates? Will I be happy with my results? Will the results show how much I studied? Will I be embarrassed by my grade?

Most of us focus on the evaluative aspects of tests. We look at the grade we've received on a test as an end in itself. It's a natural reaction.

But there's another way to look at test results: They can help guide us toward future success. By looking at what we've learned (and haven't learned) about a given subject, we'll be in a better position to know what to focus on when we take future exams. Furthermore, by examining the kinds of mistakes we make, we can learn to do better in the future.

When you get your test back, you have the opportunity to reflect on what you've learned and to consider your performance. Begin by actively listening to what your instructor says as he or she hands back the test. You may learn about things that were generally misunderstood by the class, and you'll get a sense of how your performance compares with that of your classmates. You also may pick up some important clues about what questions will be on future exams.

Then examine your own mistakes. Chances are they'll jump out at you since they will be marked incorrect. Did you misunderstand or misapply some principle? Was there a certain aspect of the material covered on the test that you missed? Were there particular kinds of information that you didn't realize you needed to know? Or did you lose some points because of your test-taking skills? Did you make careless errors, such as forgetting to fill in a question or misreading the directions? Was your handwriting so sloppy that your instructor had trouble reading it?

Once you have a good idea of what material you didn't fully understand or remember, get the correct answers to the items you missed—from your instructor, fellow classmates, or your book. If it's a math exam, rework problems you've missed. Finally, summarize—in writing—the material you had trouble with. This will help you study for future exams that cover the same material.

Finally, if you're dissatisfied with your performance, talk to your instructor—not to complain, but to seek help. Instructors don't like to give bad grades, and they may be able to point out problems in your test that you can address readily so you can do better in the future. Demonstrate to your instructor that you want to do better and are willing to put in the work to get there. The worst thing to do is crumple up the test and quickly leave the class in embarrassment. Remember, you're not the first person to get a bad grade, and the power to improve your test-taking performance lies within you. (Now, take a deep breath and complete **Try It! 5.**)

Take a Test-Taking Test

Take the following test on test-taking skills, which illustrates every question type discussed in this chapter. Answers to all questions except short-answer and essay questions are provided at the end of this chapter.

Before taking the test, think of the test-taking strategies we've discussed in the chapter and try to employ as many of them as possible.

MULTIPLE-CHOICE SECTION

Choose one of the possible responses following each question.

1. Tests are useful tools for which of the following purposes?
- a. Identifying positive and negative learning traits.
- b. Predicting future academic and career success.
- c. Pinpointing strengths and gaps in academic knowledge.
- d. Determining intellectual or educational potential.

2. One of the main advantages of study groups is that
- a. The different members bring varied perspectives to the material.
- b. Every individual must contribute equally to the group.
- c. Group members can help one another during the test.
- d. Each member has to memorize only a fraction of the material.

3. Which of the following is the most effective way to deal with test anxiety during a test?
- a. Close your eyes for five minutes and visualize success on the test.
- b. Take a few breaths and tell yourself to remain calm.
- c. Return to earlier questions and reconsider your answers carefully.
- d. Remind yourself of the importance of the test.

MATCHING SECTION

_____**1.** Cramming	**A.** A question in which the student supplies brief missing information to complete a statement
_____**2.** Educated guessing	**B.** Hurried, last-minute studying
_____**3.** Essay question	**C.** A question in which the student must link information in two columns
_____**4.** Fill-in question	**D.** A question requiring a lengthy response in the student's own words
_____**5.** Matching question	**E.** Eliminating clearly false multiple-choice answers and selecting the best answer from the remaining choices
_____**6.** Multiple-choice question	**F.** Taking credit for someone else's words, thoughts, or ideas
_____**7.** Plagiarism	**G.** A question that requires selection from several response options

FILL-IN SECTION

1. Fear of testing that can interfere with test performance is called _____.

2. The assignment of different numbers of points to different sections of a test is called _____.

(continued)

TRUE–FALSE SECTION

1. True–false questions require students to determine whether given statements are accurate or inaccurate.
   T _____ F _____

2. You should never permit yourself to feel panicky during a test. T _____ F _____

3. The best way to prepare for an essay test is to review detailed factual information about the topic.
   T _____ F _____

4. In a multiple-choice question, the words "always" and "never" usually signal the correct response.
   T _____ F _____

5. A good evaluation strategy toward the end of a test is to redo as many questions as time permits.
   T _____ F _____

6. If you run out of time at the end of a test, it is best to write down brief notes and ideas in response to essay questions rather than to leave them completely blank. T _____ F _____

SHORT-ANSWER SECTION

1. What are five things you should find out about a test before you take it?

2. What is academic honesty?

ESSAY SECTION

1. Discuss the advantages of using a study group to prepare for an examination.

2. Why is academic honesty important?

(Answers can be found at the end of the chapter.)

After you have completed the test, consider these questions: Did you learn anything from taking the test that you might not have learned if you hadn't been tested? How effective were the test-taking strategies you employed? Were any types of strategies easier for you to employ than others? Were any types of questions easier for you to answer than others?

 WORKING IN A GROUP

Exchange your essay responses with a classmate, and critique the essay. How do the responses of your partner compare with your own?

Speaking *of* Success

Source: © Courtesy of Edmund Fixico

NAME: **Edmund Fixico**

SCHOOL: **Fort Berthold Community College, New Town, North Dakota**

Although he always had thoughts about going to college, until recently circumstances and opportunities were not right for Edmund Fixico.

"I had always planned to go to college, but I dropped out of high school in the eleventh grade," said Fixico. Two years later, he completed high school, but higher education remained a distant dream.

Fixico started work as a bricklayer at age 19 and continued for more than two decades before finally enrolling in college. His job and starting a family took much of his time and energy.

"I had to work, but also I knew I had to go back to school someday," he said. "My wife encouraged me, and finally—at the age of 42—I enrolled at Fort Berthold Community College."

Fixico, who is pursuing a degree in Human Services, had apprehensions about his return to school.

"I was concerned that everyone would be younger than me. But the average age at Fort Berthold is about 31, which made me feel more comfortable. I also wasn't sure I could still do many basic things, like math and writing. I felt I would have to learn everything over again in a short span of time," he added.

Fixico puts in long hours of studying, staying up late after the rest of his family has gone to bed. He also learned to ask for assistance from faculty and advisors.

"I'm pretty much a shy person, so it was hard for me to ask for help," he noted. "But the classes are small, and you have more time with the instructor. You can get to know them well, and they offered a lot of support."

One of the courses that proved to be a tremendous help was a class in study strategies. "One of my first classes had a writing assignment that asked us to describe what is going on in our lives, and so I wrote about starting college," said Fixico. "I also learned how to schedule my time because I work full time."

Fixico is determined to succeed, and he is making good progress toward his degree. A member of the Cheyenne-Arapo tribe of Oklahoma, he is motivated by a desire to show future generations of American Indians the value of a college education.

[RETHINK]

- Why do you think writing about his life helped Fixico develop study strategies?
- How did his reaching out for assistance to faculty and advisors help Fixico as an older student?

Looking Back

LO 4-1 Identify the kinds of tests you will encounter in college.

▶ Although tests are an unpopular fact of college life, they can provide useful information about one's level of knowledge and understanding about a subject.

▶ There are several types of tests, including brief, informal quizzes; more substantial tests; and even more weighty exams, which tend to be administered at the midpoint and end of a course.

LO 4-2 Explain the best ways to prepare for and take various kinds of tests.

▶ Good test preparation begins with doing the course assignments, attending class regularly, and paying attention in class. It also helps to find out as much as possible about a test beforehand and to form a study group to review material.

▶ If cramming becomes necessary, focus on summarizing factual information broadly, identifying key concepts and ideas, and rehearsing information orally.

▶ When you first receive the test, skim it to see what kinds of questions are asked, figure out how the different questions and sections will be weighted, and jot down complex factual information that is likely to be needed for the test.

▶ Answer the easiest questions first, write legibly, use only one side of each sheet of paper, mark answer sheets carefully, and record answers in the test book as well as the answer sheet.

LO 4-3 Analyze the best strategies for answering specific kinds of test questions.

▶ For essay questions, be sure to understand each question and each of its parts, interpret action words correctly, write concisely, organize the essay logically, and include examples.

▶ The best strategy for short-answer and fill-in questions is to be very sure what is being asked. Keep answers complete but brief.

▶ For multiple-choice questions, read the question very carefully and then read all response choices. Educated guessing based on eliminating incorrect response choices is usually a reasonable strategy.

▶ For true–false and matching questions, answer all the items that you are sure of quickly and then go back to the remaining items.

[KEY TERMS AND CONCEPTS]

Academic honesty (p. 99)

Cramming (p. 91)

Educated guessing (p. 98)

Plagiarism (p. 99)

Study groups (p. 90)

Test anxiety (p. 87)

[RESOURCES]

ON CAMPUS

Colleges provide a variety of resources for students having difficulties with test taking. Some offer general workshops for students, reviewing test-taking strategies. Furthermore, if you are planning to take a specific standardized test, you may be able to sign up for a course offered through your college (or through such commercial organizations as Princeton Review or Kaplan).

If you are experiencing difficulties in a specific course, you may be able to find a tutor to help you out. Some colleges have tutoring centers or campus learning centers that can provide one-to-one assistance. It's also important to speak to your instructor, who more than likely has encountered many students with similar problems and may have some useful test-taking strategies.

If you find that you are experiencing significant test anxiety when taking a test or in the days leading up to it, talk to someone at your campus counseling center or health center. They can help you learn relaxation techniques and can provide counseling to help make your anxiety manageable.

IN PRINT

Ace Any Test (Cengage Learning PTR, 2011, 6th ed.) by educator Ron Fry offers easy-to-follow strategies that can be used for all types of tests, from quizzes to the SAT.

Doc Orman's *The Test Anxiety Cure* (Stress Management Group, 2014) offers what the author describes as 10 root causes of test anxiety and how to deal with them.

You can find test strategies for all types of questions in *Test Secrets,* by The Complete Test Preparation Team (CreateSpace Independent Publishing Platform, 2013).

ON THE WEB

The following sites on the web provide opportunities to extend your learning about the material in this chapter. (Although the web addresses were accurate at the time the book was printed, check the *P.O.W.E.R. Learning* website Connect Library.)

▶ "Taking Multiple Choice Exams" is an online presentation from the University of Wisconsin—Eau Claire outlining a series of strategies and approaches for taking multiple-choice exams. **http://people.uwec.edu/ivogeler/multiple.htm**

▶ The University of Reading, England "Answering Exam Questions" site is a comprehensive collection of information on how to prepare for a variety of tests, including open-book and oral exams. **https://www.reading.ac.uk/internal/ studyadvice/StudyResources/Exams/sta-answering.aspx**

▶ "Dealing with Text Anxiety," prepared by the University of Alabama's Center for Academic Success, presents a three-step strategy for confronting text anxiety. **http:// www.ctl.ua.edu/CTLStudyAids/StudySkillsFlyers/TestPreparation/testanxiety.htm**

[ANSWERS TO THE ITEMS IN TRY IT! 5]

Multiple-choice: 1c, 2a, 3b

Matching: 1B, 2E, 3D, 4A, 5C, 6G, 7F

Fill-in: test anxiety, weighting

True—False: 1T, 2F, 3F, 4F, 5F, 6T

Short-answer:

1. Possible answers include what the test is called, what it will cover, how many questions will be on it, how much time it will take, what kinds of questions will be on it, how it will be graded, whether sample questions will be provided, and whether tests from prior terms are available.

2. Academic honesty is completing and turning in only one's own work under one's own name.

Essay:

1. Strong essays would include a brief definition of a study group, followed by a discussion of the advantages of using study groups (including such things as helping to organize and structure material, providing different perspectives, and rethinking material). A mention of the disadvantages of study groups would also be reasonable.

2. After starting with a brief definition of academic honesty, the bulk of the answer should concentrate on the reasons academic honesty is important and the consequences of academic dishonesty.

Images in this chapter: *Pencil on stack of notebooks:* © C Squared Studios/Photodisc/Getty Images; *Four students:* © Purestock/Getty images; *Apples:* © Isabelle Rozenbaum/PhotoAlto/Getty Images; *Man in blue shirt with laptop:* © sidneybernstein/iStock/Getty Images; *Group of happy business people:* ©Yuri/iStock/Getty Images.

The Case of . . .

The Big Freeze

Eddie Jackson had always done well on tests in high school, and he had no worries about a college midterm in business English. His entire preparation consisted of reading through a handout from his instructor on the use of punctuation, which he knew was a weak point for him.

The test surprised him. It contained 35 multiple-choice questions and a written composition. He'd never thought about the makeup of the test. He shrugged mentally and turned to page 1.

He got stuck on question 4, and his final answer made him doubt his answer to question 2. He went back and changed question 2, then hit another snag on question 6. But he kept working doggedly, often turning back to change an answer.

Then disaster struck. As he filled in the answer bubble for the last question, he noticed that there was one more row of bubbles than there should be. *He had skipped a question, and his answers were now all wrong.*

By the time he corrected his answer booklet, only 10 minutes remained. In a panic, he turned to the written composition, a business letter to an imaginary customer, and noticed for the first time that this section was worth 65 points. *He had spent the bulk of the testing period on multiple-choice questions worth only 35 points!*

Eddie took his pencil and quickly scribbled "Dear Mr. Jones:" at the top of the answer sheet. That's all he wrote. All sense of what a business letter should be left him. He couldn't think of a single thing to add.

1. What mistakes did Eddie make in his test preparation that probably harmed his performance?

2. What mistakes did Eddie make during the test that hurt him?

3. What should Eddie have done differently in calculating the amount of time to devote to each portion of the test? Why?

4. What specific strategies would have helped Eddie with the multiple-choice questions? What strategies could he have used on the essay?

5. If you were in Eddie's shoes, what would you do with only 10 minutes left in the test?

CHAPTER 5

Reading and Remembering

Learning Outcomes

By the time you finish this chapter you will be able to

» LO **5-1** Explain how reading style and attention span affect reading.

» LO **5-2** Identify how to improve concentration and read and remember more effectively.

» LO **5-3** Discuss how best to retain what you have read.

Maria Alcedo added up her reading assignments for the day. Two textbook chapters, three articles, and a 40-page study on nutrition. Maria knew she could get through it all. She prided herself on being a fast reader. But she'd never remember any of it.

Maria loved her classes, but she found the assigned readings boring. If only they were fiction. Maria loved novels. She could follow the most intricate plot line, and she never forgot any of the characters. However, textbooks and articles seemed to lack the glue that held her favorite stories together.

She dutifully plowed through all her assignments that night, but when she got to class the next morning, what she had read had turned into a jumble of facts and figures. How would she ever pass her exams?

Looking Ahead

For people like Maria, reading assignments are the biggest challenge in college. The amount of required reading is often enormous. Even skilled readers may find themselves wishing they could read more effectively and retain more of what they've read. On the job too, many people struggle with all the memos, e-mails, manuals, and so forth that they need to read.

Fortunately, there are ways to improve your reading and memory skills. In this chapter, we'll first go over a number of strategies for reading more effectively. You'll assess your reading style and your attention span, consider what you should do before you even start reading an assignment, and discover some ways of getting the most out of your reading.

Then we'll focus on memory and retaining what you've read. You'll learn how you can improve the memory skills you already have. We'll examine what memory is and why it sometimes fails us. Finally, you will become acquainted with specific ways to learn information so that you can recall it when you need to.

»LO 5-1 Sharpen Your Reading and Memory Skills

One of the reasons many people struggle with reading, especially in college, is that they feel they *shouldn't* have to struggle with it. Reading, after all, is something almost all of us master as children . . . right?

In fact, it is not so simple. Reading, as we will see in this chapter, involves more than just recognizing words. The task of reading large amounts of information and remembering the essential points takes time to master.

To begin, consider the way you read now. In other words, what kind of reader are you? Ask yourself first of all about your reading *preferences:* What do you *like* to read, and why? What makes you pick up a book and start reading—and what makes you put one down?

Before going any further, think about your own reading preferences by completing the **Journal Reflections**.

Journal Reflections

My Reading Preferences

Think about what you like and don't like to read by answering these questions.

1. Do you read for pleasure? If so, what do you read (e.g., magazines, newspapers, novels, humor, short stories, nonfiction, illustrated books)?

2. What makes a book enjoyable? Have you ever read a book that you "couldn't put down"? If so, what made it so good?

3. What is the most difficult book you are reading this semester? Why is it difficult? Are you enjoying it?

4. Think about when you read for pleasure compared with when you read material for a class. How does the way you read differ between the two types of material?

5. How well do you remember the last book or magazine you read for pleasure? Do you remember it better than your last college reading assignment? Why do you think this might be?

Read for Retention, Not Speed ✳

You may have come across advertisements on the web promoting reading "systems" that promise to teach you to read so quickly that you'll be reading entire books in an hour and whizzing through assigned readings in a few minutes.

Unfortunately, it's not going to happen. Research has shown that claims of speed-reading are simply groundless. But even if it were physically possible to read a book in an hour, ultimately it probably doesn't matter very much. If we read too fast, comprehension and retention plunge. Reading is not a race, and the fastest readers are not necessarily the best readers.

The act of reading is designed to increase our knowledge and open up new ways of thinking. It can help us achieve new levels of understanding and get us to think more broadly about the world and its inhabitants. Speed matters far less than what we take away from what we've read. That's not to say we shouldn't try to become more efficient readers who comprehend and recall more effectively. Ultimately, though, the key to good reading is understanding—not speed.

In describing how you can use the principles of *P.O.W.E.R. Learning* to become a better reader with a more complete memory of what you read, we'll focus on the type of reading that is typically called for in academic pursuits—textbook chapters, articles, handouts, and the like. However, the same principles will help you get more benefit and enjoyment out of your recreational reading as well. Crucially, the reading skills you learn and employ in the classroom will also help you read more efficiently and effectively on the job.

P Prepare Approaching the Written Word

[handwritten: Break down, Use plan for to plan for lecture]

P Prepare
Approach the written word

O Organize
Gather the tools of the trade

W Work
Get the most our of your reading

E Evaluate
Consider what it means and what you know

R Rethink
Get it the second time

P.O.W.E.R. Plan

Preparation to begin reading isn't hard, and it won't take very long, but it's a crucial first step in applying P.O.W.E.R. Learning (summarized in the P.O.W.E.R. Plan here). Your aim in preparation is to become familiar with **advance organizers**—overviews, section objectives, or other clues to the meaning and organization of new material—provided in the material you are reading. Most textbooks have them built in; for an example, look at the beginning of every chapter in this book, which includes a "Learning Outcomes" list and a "**Looking Ahead**" section. You can also create your own advance organizers by skimming material to be read and sketching out the general outline of the material you'll be reading.

Advance organizers pave the way for subsequent learning. They help you tie information that you already know to new material you're about to encounter. This connection between old and new material is crucial in helping build memories of what you read. If you approach each new reading task as something entirely new and unrelated to your previous knowledge, you'll have enormous difficulty recalling it. On the other hand, if you connect it to what you already know, you'll be able to recall it far better.

In short, the more we're able to make use of advance organizers and our own prior knowledge and experiences, the better we can understand and retain new material. (To prove the value of advance organizers, complete **Try It! 1**, "Discover How Advance Organizers Help.")

What's the Point of the Reading Assignment?

advance organizers
Outlines, overviews, objectives, and other clues to the meaning and organization of new material in what you are reading, which pave the way for subsequent learning.

Before you begin an assignment, think about what your goal is. Will you be reading a textbook on which you'll be thoroughly tested? Is your reading supposed to provide background information that will serve as a context for future learning but that won't itself be tested? Is the material going to be useful to you personally? Realistically, how much time can you devote to the reading assignment?

Your goal for reading will help you determine which reading strategy to adopt. You aren't expected to read everything with the same degree of intensity. Some material you may feel comfortable skimming; for other material you'll want to put in the maximum effort.

Understand the Point of View of the Material Itself

What are you reading—a textbook, an essay, an article? If it is an essay or article, why was it written? To prove a point? To give information? To express the author's personal feelings? Knowing the author's purpose (even if his or her specific point and message aren't yet clear) can help you a great deal as you read.

Discover How Advance Organizers Help

Read this passage. What do you think it means?

The procedure is actually quite simple. First you arrange items into different groups. Of course, one pile may be sufficient, depending on how much there is to do. If you have to go somewhere else due to lack of facilities, that is the next step; otherwise, you are pretty well set. It is important not to overdo things. That is, it is better to do too few things at once than too many. In the short run this may not seem important but complications can easily arise. A mistake can be expensive as well. At first, the whole procedure will seem complicated. Soon, however, it will become just another facet of life. It is difficult to foresee any end to the necessity for this task in the immediate future, but then one can never tell. After the procedure is completed, one arranges the materials into different groups again. Then they can be put into their appropriate places. Eventually, they will be used once more and the whole cycle will then have to be repeated. However, this is a part of life.[1]

If you're like most people, you don't have a clue about what this all means and won't be able to remember anything about it in five minutes. But suppose you had been given some context in advance, and you knew before reading it that the description had to do with washing laundry. Now does it all fall into place? Do you think it will be easier to remember? Read the passage once more, and see how having an advance organizer (in this case, *washing laundry*) helps out.

Start with the Frontmatter *（related to entire text (preface) of book — Global*

If you'll be using a text or other book extensively throughout the term, start by reading the preface and/or introduction and scanning the table of contents—what publishers call the **frontmatter.** Instructors often don't formally assign the frontmatter, but reading it can be a big help because it is there that the author has a chance to step forward and explain, often more personally than elsewhere in an academic book, what he or she considers important. Knowing this will give you a sense of what to expect as you read.

frontmatter
The preface, introduction, and table of contents of a book.

Create Advance Organizers

To provide a context for your reading, create your own advance organizers by skimming through the table of contents, which provides the main headings of what you will be reading. Textbooks often have chapter outlines, listing the key topics to be covered, which also provide a way of previewing the chapter content. As you read over the outline, you can begin to consider how the new material in the book may relate both to what you know and to what you expect to learn—from the reading assignment itself and from the course.

Textbooks also often have end-of-chapter summaries, and many articles include a final section in which the author states his or her conclusions. Take a look at these ending sections as well. Even though you haven't read the material yet and the summary probably won't make complete sense to you, by reading the summary, you'll get an idea of what the author covers and what is important.

Your instructor may also provide an advance organizer for readings. Sometimes instructors will mention things to pay particular attention to or to look for, like this: "When you read Thomas Paine's *Common Sense,* notice how he lays out his argument and what his key points are." Sometimes they will say why they assigned a reading. Such information provides clues that can help you develop a mental list of the reading's key ideas.

Create an Advance Organizer

Use any information you have available to create an advance organizer for a chapter in a text that you are using this term. Skim the section headings in the chapter, read the chapter summary, consult the book's frontmatter, and recall anything your instructor may have said about the chapter.

Complete the following statements to prepare your organizer:

1. The general topics that are covered in the chapter are . . .

2. The most critical topics and concepts in the chapter are . . .

3. The most difficult material in the chapter includes . . .

4. Words, phrases, and ideas that are unfamiliar to me include . . .

5. Ways that the material in this chapter relates to other material that I've previously read in the text include . . .

Use this Try It! as a starting point for advance organizers for future chapters in the book.

However you construct advance organizers, be sure they provide a framework and context for what you'll be reading; this framework and context can spell the difference between fully comprehending what you read and misunderstanding it.

Now it's time to put all this practice to good use. Create an advance organizer for a textbook chapter in **Try It! 2.**

Identify What You Need to Remember

Memorize what you need to memorize. Forget about the rest.

The average textbook chapter has something like 20,000 words. If you had to recall every word of the chapter, it would be nearly impossible. Furthermore, it would be a waste of time. Being able to spew out paragraphs of material is quite different from the more important ability to recall and deeply understand material in meaningful ways.

Within those 20,000 words, there may be only 20 different concepts that you need to learn. And perhaps there are only 10 keywords. *Those* are the pieces of information that should be the focus of your efforts to memorize.

How do you know what's so important that you need to recall it? One way is to use the guides built into most textbooks. Key concepts and terms are often highlighted or in boldface type. Chapters often have summaries that recap the most important information. Use such guideposts to understand what's most critical in a chapter.

Write down what you determine is important. Not only does putting critical information in writing help you manage what you need to remember, but the very act of writing it down makes it easier to memorize the information later.

In short, the first step in building a better memory of your reading is to determine just what it is that you wish to recall. By extracting what is important from what is less crucial, you'll be able to limit the amount and extent of the material that you need to recall. You'll be able to focus, laserlike, on what you need to remember.

Ⓞ Organize   Gathering the Tools of the Trade

It's obvious that the primary item you'll need to complete a reading assignment is the material that you're reading. But there are other essential tools you should gather, potentially including the following:

▶ A copy of the assignment, so you'll be sure to read the right material.

▶ A pad of paper and/or index cards for notetaking if the material is particularly complex. If you use a computer to take notes, get it ready.

▶ Pencils or pens to write notes in the margin, if it's a traditional paper book, and highlighters to indicate key passages in the text.

▶ Access to a dictionary, either online or as a hard copy. You never know what new words you'll encounter while you're reading. If a dictionary isn't easily accessible, you'll be tempted to skip over unfamiliar words—a decision that may come back to haunt you. All word processing software includes a dictionary, and there are also many good dictionaries available online (e.g., Merriam-Webster's at **www.m-w.com**, where you will also find an online thesaurus).

Give Yourself Time ✳

There's one more thing you need to prepare successfully for a reading assignment: enough time to complete it. The length of reading assignments is almost never ambiguous. You will typically be given a specific page range, so you will know just how much material you will need to cover.

Now get a watch and time yourself as you read the first three pages of your assignment, being sure to pay attention to the material, not the time! Timing how long it takes to read a representative chunk of material provides you with a rough measure of your reading speed for the material—though it will vary even within a single reading assignment, depending on the complexity of the material.

You'll also need to consider an aspect of your personal learning style: your reading attention span. **Attention span** is the length of time that a person usually is able to sustain attention. People with long attention spans can read for relatively lengthy periods without getting jumpy, while those with shorter ones can maintain attention only for a short while. You can get a general sense of this by using **Try It! 3**, "Discover Your Attention Span."

Use the three pieces of information you now have—the length of the assignment, your per-page reading speed at full attention, and your typical attention span—to estimate roughly how long it will take you to complete the reading assignment. For example, if you are asked to read 12 pages, you have found that you need approximately 4 minutes to read a page, and your reading attention span is, on average, 25 minutes long, you can expect your reading to take at least 60 minutes, assuming you'll take a short break when your attention begins to fade after 25 minutes.

In addition, you may need to interrupt your reading to look up words in the dictionary, get a drink, stretch, or answer the phone. You may also decide to break

attention span ✳
The length of time that attention is typically sustained.

Discover Your Attention Span

You should be aware of your attention span, the length of time you usually are able to sustain attention to a task, as you prepare for reading assignments. To get an idea of the length of your current attention span for reading, perform this exercise over the next few days.

1. Choose one of the textbooks that you've been assigned to read this semester.
2. Start reading a chapter, without any preparation, noting in the chart below the time that you start reading.
3. As soon as your mind begins to wander and think about other subjects, stop reading and note the time on the chart below.
4. Using the same textbook, repeat this process four more times over the course of a few days, entering the data on the chart below.
5. To find your reading attention span, calculate the average number of minutes across the five trials.

Trial #	Starting Time	Ending Time	Total Time
Trial #1	_____	_____	_____
Trial #2	_____	_____	_____
Trial #3	_____	_____	_____
Trial #4	_____	_____	_____
Trial #5	_____	_____	_____

Ask yourself these questions about your reading attention span:

1. Are you surprised by the length of your reading attention span? In what way?
2. Does any number in the set of trials stand out from the other numbers? For instance, is any number much higher or lower than the average? If so, can you account for this? For example, what time of day was it?
3. Do the numbers in your trials show any trend? For instance, did your attention span tend to increase slightly over the course of the trials, did it decrease, or did it stay about the same? Can you explain any trend you may have noted?
4. Do you think your attention span times would be very different if you had chosen a different textbook? Why or why not?
5. What things might you do to improve your attention span?

your reading into several short sessions, in which case your total reading time may be greater, since you will have to get reacquainted with the reading assignment each time you sit down again.

Remember that you can use this strategy for estimating the amount of time reading will take you for reading tasks outside the classroom, too. If your employer asks you to read a set of customer feedback forms, for example, you can figure out how much time in your day you'll need to block off to complete the work by factoring in the total length of all the forms, your per-page reading speed, and your attention span. Remember, though, that reading on the job is different from reading in a college library or at your desk at home. You can expect many more distractions as you try to read—co-workers asking questions, e-mails coming in, the phone ringing. Take into account these inevitable workplace distractions when making your reading time estimate.

Getting the Most Out of Your Reading and Using Proven Strategies to Memorize New Material

Once you've familiarized yourself with the material as a whole and gathered the necessary tools, it's time to get down to work and start reading. Here are several things that will help you get the most out of the reading process.

Stay Focused

The TV show you watched last night . . . your husband forgetting to meet you at the bus stop . . . the new toothbrush you need to buy for your daughter . . . your grumbling stomach. There are a million and one possible distractions that can invade your thoughts as you read. Your job is to keep distracting thoughts at bay and focus on the material you are supposed to be reading. It's not easy, but the following are things you can do to help yourself stay focused:

▶ **Read in small bites.** If you think it is going to take you 4 hours to read an entire chapter, break up the 4 hours into more manageable time periods. Promise yourself that you'll read for 1 hour in the afternoon, another hour in the evening, and the next 2 hours spaced out during the following day. One hour of reading is far more manageable than a 4-hour block.

▶ **Take a break.** Actually, plan to take several short breaks to reward yourself while you're reading. During your break, do something enjoyable—eat a snack, watch a bit of a ball game on television, text message a friend, or the like. Just try not to get drawn into your break activity to the point that it takes over your reading time.

▶ **Deal with mental distractions.** Sometimes problems have a way of popping into our minds and repeatedly distracting us. If a particular problem keeps interrupting your concentration—such as a difficulty you're having on the job—try to think of an action-oriented strategy to deal with it. You might even write your proposed solution down on a piece of paper. Putting it down in words can get the problem off your mind, potentially making it less intrusive.

▶ **Manage interruptions.** You can't prevent your children from getting into a fight and needing immediate attention. But there are some things you can do to reduce interruptions and their consequences. For instance, you can schedule reading to coincide with periods when you know you'll be alone. You can also plan to read less critical parts of assignments (such as the summaries or book frontmatter) when distractions are more likely, saving the heavier reading for later. Or, if you are a parent with small children, you can get them involved in an activity that they can perform independently so you'll be free to concentrate.

If you are reading a long assignment, taking a break can be a reward and reinvigorate you.
Source: © Purestock/Superstock

Textbook Tips: Starting Off on the Right Page

You've just come back from the bookstore, weighed down with a bookbag filled with the textbooks and other materials for the upcoming term. Now is the time to take some preliminary steps to make the most of your investment.

- Make sure you've bought the correct textbooks. Look at each syllabus from your classes to ensure you've bought the appropriate text and the right edition. Sometimes there are multiple sections of a course, and each section uses a different text. Be sure the book you've bought matches the description in the syllabus.

- Make the book your own. Write your name, e-mail address, and/or telephone number in the front of the book. If you misplace your book during the term, you want the person who finds it to be able to return it to you.

- Orient yourself to each of your textbooks. Take a quick look at each of the books, examining the table of contents, introduction, and/or preface (as we discussed earlier). Get a sense of the content and the general reading level of the book.

- Get yourself online. Many textbooks contain a card or insert with a password that gives you access to online material, sometimes including access to the complete book in an online format. Follow the directions and enter the book's website, making sure the password allows you to register. If you have trouble making the site work, call the tech support number; it should be included with the password.

Write While You Read

Writing is one of the most important aspects of reading. If you haven't underlined, jotted notes to yourself, placed check marks on the page, drawn arrows, constructed diagrams, and otherwise defaced and disfigured your book while you're reading, you're not doing your job as a P.O.W.E.R. reader.

The idea of writing on a book page may go against everything you've been taught in the past. (And of course you should never write on a library book or one that you've borrowed.)

However, once you've bought your book, *you own it and you should make it your own.* Don't keep your textbooks spotless on the off chance they will fetch a higher price if you sell them later. Instead, think of textbooks as documents recording your active learning and engagement in a field of study. In addition, you should look at your textbooks as the foundation of your personal library, which will grow throughout your lifetime. In short, writing extensively in your book while you're reading is an important tactic for achieving success. (For more on using textbooks, see the **Course Connections** feature.)

The ability to add your own personal notes, underlining, and other annotations to a clean text while you're reading is one of the reasons it usually pays to buy new, rather than used, textbooks. Why would you want a stranger's comments on something you own? Can you really trust that person's judgment over your own regarding what's important to underline? New books allow you to mark them up in your own personal style, without the distraction of competing voices.

If you have purchased an *electronic textbook, or e-book,* you'll be able to read it on a laptop computer, an iPad, or even a smartphone. E-books have several advantages over traditional books. You can easily follow links to visuals and interactive exercises, search for key terms, listen to music, watch embedded videos, and manipulate 3-D images. And, like traditional textbooks, you can highlight and take notes as you are reading, and save (and organize) your notes for future study.

Writing the Right Way

What should you be writing while you are reading? There are several things you should write down (or—if you are using an e-book—keyboard in to your electronic text):

▶ **Rephrase key points.** Make notes to yourself, in your own words, about what the author is trying to get across. Don't just copy what's been said. Think about the material, and rewrite it in words that are your own.

Source: © Mark Dierker/McGraw-Hill Education

Writing notes to yourself in your own words has several consequences, all good. First, you make the material yours; it becomes something you now understand and part of your own knowledge base. This is an essential aid to memorization. When you try to recollect your reading, you won't be trying to summon the thoughts of someone else—you'll be trying to remember *your own* thinking.

Second, trying to summarize a key point in your own words will make it very clear whether you truly understand it. It's easy to be fooled into thinking we understand something as we're reading along. But the true test is whether we can explain it to ourselves (or someone else) on our own, without referring to the book or article.

From the perspective of . . .

A STUDENT To truly retain what you are reading, you must give your reading your undivided attention. Make a list of your biggest distractions and consider strategies for avoiding those distractions when you read.

Source: © CMCD/Photodisc/Getty Images

Third, the very act of writing engages an additional type of perception—involving the physical sense of moving a pen or pressing a keyboard. This act will help you learn the material in a more active way.

Finally, writing notes and phrases will help you study the material later. Not only will the key points be highlighted, but your notes will quickly bring you up to speed regarding your initial thoughts and impressions.

▶ **Highlight or underline key points.** Very often the first or last sentence in a paragraph, or the first or last paragraph in a section, will present a key point. Before you highlight anything, though, read the whole paragraph through. Then you'll be sure that what you highlight is, in fact, the key information. Topic sentences do not always fall at the beginning of a paragraph.

Be selective in your highlighting and underlining. A page covered in yellow highlighter may be artistically appealing, but it won't help you understand the material any better. Highlight only the key information. You might find yourself highlighting only one or two sentences or phrases per page. That's fine. *In highlighting and underlining, less is more.* One guideline: No more than 10 percent of the material should be highlighted or underlined.

Keep in mind, too, as you highlight and underline that the key material you are marking is the material you will likely need to remember for exams or class discussions. To aid in your recall of such material, read it over a time or two after you've marked it, and consider also reading it aloud. This act will reinforce the memories you are building of the essential points in the assignment.

▶ **Use arrows, diagrams, outlines, tables, timelines, charts, and other visuals to help you understand and later recall what you are reading.** If there are three examples given for a particular point, number them. If a paragraph discusses a situation in which an earlier point does not hold, link the original point to the exception by an arrow. If a sequence of steps is presented, number each step.

For example, after you have annotated *this* page of *P.O.W.E.R. Learning,* it might look something like what is shown in **Figure 5.1.**

Particularly if your learning style is a visual one, representing the material graphically will get you thinking about it—and the connections and points in it—in new and different ways. Rather than considering the material solely in verbal terms, you now add visual images. The act of creating visual annotations will not only help you understand the material better but also ease its later recall. Practice this technique on the sample textbook page in **Try It! 4.**

▶ **Look up unfamiliar words in a dictionary.** Even though you may be able to figure out the meaning of an unfamiliar word from its context, use a dictionary anyway. This way you can be sure that what you think it means is correct. A dictionary will also tell you what the word sounds like, which may be important if your instructor uses the word in class.

 ▶ **Use your own reading system.** If you've already learned a reading system in the past and it works for you, use it. Many students have been taught the *SQ4R* method, which consists of six steps, designated by the initials *S-Q-R-R-R-R:*

• *Survey.* Give yourself an overview of the major points of the material.

• *Question.* Formulate questions about the material—either aloud or in writing—prior to actually reading a section of text.

Third, the very act of writing engages an additional type of perception—involving the physical sense of moving a pen or pressing a keyboard. This act will help you learn the material in a more active way.

Finally, writing notes and phrases will help you study the material later. Not only will the key points be highlighted, but your notes will quickly bring you up to speed regarding your initial thoughts and impressions.

Topic sentence ① **Highlight or underline key points.** Very often the first or last sentence in a paragraph, or the first or last paragraph in a section, will present a key point. Before you highlight anything, though, read the whole paragraph through. Then you'll be sure that what you highlight is, in fact, the key information. Topic sentences do not always fall at the beginning of a paragraph.

Read whole paragraph before highlighting

"What is reading but silent conversation?"

Walter Savage Landor, author, "Aristoteles and Callisthenes," *Imaginary Conversations* **(1824–53).**

Be selective in your highlighting and underlining. A page covered in yellow highlighter may be artistically appealing, but it won't help you understand the material any better. Highlight only the key information. You might find yourself highlighting only one or two sentences or phrases per page. That's fine. *In highlighting and underlining, less is more.* One guideline: No more than 10 percent of the material should be highlighted or underlined.

Reread key points to help memory

Keep in mind, too, as you highlight and underline that the key material you are marking is the material you will likely need to remember for exams or class discussions. To aid in your recall of such material, read it over a time or two after you've marked it, and consider also reading it aloud. This act will reinforce the memories you are building of the essential points in the assignment.

② ▶ **Use arrows, diagrams, outlines, tables, timelines, charts, and other visuals to help you understand and later recall what you are reading.** If there are three examples given for a particular point, number them. If a paragraph discusses a situation in which an earlier point does not hold, link the original point to the exception by an arrow. If a sequence of steps is presented, number each step.

Use visuals ⟶

For example, after you have annotated *this* page of *P.O.W.E.R. Learning,* it might look something like what is shown in **Figure 5.1.**

Particularly if your learning style is a visual one, representing the material graphically will get you thinking about it—and the connections and points in it—in new and different ways. Rather than considering the material solely in verbal terms, you now add visual images. The act of creating visual annotations will not only help you understand the material better but also ease its later recall. Practice this technique on the sample textbook page in **Try It 4.**

▶ **Look up unfamiliar words in a dictionary.** Even though you may be able to figure out the meaning of an unfamiliar word from its context, use a dictionary anyway. This way you can be sure that what you think it means is correct. A dictionary will also tell you what the word sounds like, which may be important if your instructor uses the word in class.

▶ **Use your own reading system.** If you've already learned a reading system in the past and it works for you, use it. Many students have been taught the *SQ4R* method, which consists of six steps, designated by the initials *S-Q-R-R-R-R:*

- *Survey.* Give yourself an overview of the major points of the material.
- *Question.* Formulate questions about the material—either aloud or in writing—prior to actually reading a section of text.

figure 5.1
Sample of Annotated Page

- *Read.* Read the material carefully and, even more important, actively and critically. While you are reading, answer the questions you have asked yourself.
- *Recite.* Describe and explain to yourself the material you have just read and answer the questions you have posed earlier.
- *Record.* Write in your textbook, make notes, or create flash cards.
- *Review.* Review the material, looking it over, reading end-of-chapter summaries, and answering the in-text review questions.

Memorize Key Material

Many of the reading strategies discussed above will help fix key material in your mind. Rephrasing key points, highlighting or underlining essential material and

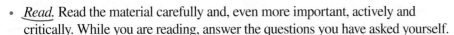

Mark Up a Book Page

First, working alone, read the excerpt in **Figure 5.2**. Then use the techniques we've discussed for marking up a page to highlight its key points.

Next, working in a group, compare and contrast your annotations with those of some classmates, and answer the following questions:

1. How do others' annotations differ from yours?

2. Why did they use the annotations they did?

3. Which annotation techniques worked best for you? Which did others prefer? Why?

4. How might these annotations help you remember what is important?

5. If there were different sorts of material presented on the page, such as mathematical formulas, would you use different kinds of annotations?

The more parents speak to their children, the better their children's language skills.

Understanding Language Acquisition: Identifying the Roots of Language

Anyone who spends even a little time with children will notice the enormous strides that they make in language development throughout childhood. However, the reasons for this rapid growth are far from obvious. Two major explanations have been offered: one based on learning theory and the other on innate processes.

The **learning-theory approach** suggests that language acquisition follows the principles of reinforcement and conditioning discussed in Chapter 6. For example, a child who utters the word "mama" is hugged and praised by her mother, which reinforces the behavior and makes its repetition more likely. This view suggests that children first learn to speak by being rewarded for making sounds that approximate speech. Ultimately, through a process of shaping, language becomes more and more like adult speech (Skinner, 1957).

The learning theory approach is supported by research that shows that the more parents speak to their young children, the more proficient the children become in language usage (see Figure 8-11). In addition, higher levels of linguistic sophistication in parents' speech to their young children are related to a greater rate of vocabulary growth, vocabulary usage, and even general intellectual achievement by the time the children are 3 years of age (Hart & Risley, 1997).

On the other hand, the learning theory approach is less successful when it comes to explaining the acquisition of language rules. Children are reinforced not only when they use proper language, but also when they respond incorrectly. For example, parents answer the child's "Why the dog won't eat?" as readily as they do the correctly phrased question "Why won't the dog eat?" Both sentences are understood equally well. Learning theory, then, has difficulty in providing the full explanation for language acquisition.

Pointing to such problems with learning theory approaches to language acquisition, Noam Chomsky (1968, 1978, 1991), a linguist, provided a ground-breaking alternative. Chomsky argued that humans are born with an innate linguistic capability that emerges primarily as a function of maturation. According to his analysis, all the world's languages share a similar underlying structure called a **universal grammar.** Chomsky suggests that the human brain has a neural system, the **language-acquisition device,** that both permits the understanding of the structure of language and provides strategies and techniques for learning the unique characteristics of a given native language.

learning-theory approach: The theory suggesting that language acquisition follows the principles of reinforcement and conditioning

universal grammar: Noam Chomsky's theory that all the world's languages share a similar underlying structure

language-acquisition device: A neural system of the brain hypothesized to permit understanding of language

figure 5.2
Sample Page to Annotate
Photo Source: © Sonda Dawes/Image Works

then rereading it, and creating visuals will all help you recall the information you've read.

Sometimes, though, these strategies are not enough. You may need to memorize a great deal of information, more than you'll be able to recall just through the process of reading, underlining, and so forth. Many people find extensive memorization daunting. But one of the good things about the work of memorization is that you have your choice of literally dozens of techniques. Depending on the kind of material you need to recall and how much you already know about the subject, you can turn to any number of methods.

As we sort through the various options, keep in mind that no one strategy works by itself. (And some strategies don't seem to work: For example, forget about supplements like gingko biloba—there's no clear scientific evidence that they are effective.[2]) Instead, try the following proven strategies and find those that work best for you. Feel free to devise your own strategies or add those that have worked for you in the past.

Rehearsal

Rehearsal. Think it again: rehearsal. Say it aloud: rehearsal. Think of it in terms of the three syllables that make up the word: re—hear—sal. OK, one more time—say the word "rehearsal."

rehearsal
The process of practicing and learning material.

If you're scratching your head over the last paragraph, it's to illustrate the point of **rehearsal**: to transfer material that you encounter into memory. If you don't rehearse information in some way, it will end up like most of the information to which we're exposed: on the garbage heap of lost memory.

To test if you've succeeded in transferring the word "rehearsal" into your memory, put down this book and go off for a few minutes. Do something entirely unrelated to reading this book. Have a snack, catch up on the latest sports scores on ESPN, or read the front page of the newspaper.

Are you back? If the word "rehearsal" popped into your head when you picked up this book again, you've passed your first memory test. You can be assured that the word "rehearsal" has been transferred into your memory.

Rehearsal is the key strategy in remembering information. If you don't rehearse material, it will never make it into memory. Repeating the information, summarizing it, associating it with other memories, and above all, thinking about it when you first come across it will ensure that rehearsal will be effective in pushing the material into memory.

Mnemonics

mnemonics
Formal techniques used to make material more readily remembered.

acronym
A word or phrase formed by the first letters of a series of terms.

Mnemonics. This odd word (pronounced in an equally odd fashion, with the "m" silent—"neh MON ix") describes formal techniques used to make material more readily remembered. **Mnemonics** are the tricks of the trade that professional memory experts use, and you too can use them to nail down the sort of information you will often need to recall for tests.

Among the most common mnemonics are acronyms. You're already well acquainted with **acronyms**, words or phrases formed by the first letters of a series of terms. For instance, though you may not have known it, the word "laser" is actually an acronym for "light amplification by stimulated emissions of radiation," and "radar" is an acronym for "radio detection and ranging." If you took music lessons, you may know that FACE spells out the names of the notes that appear in the spaces on the treble clef music staff ("F," "A," "C," and "E," starting at the bottom of the staff).

Do-It-Yourself Acronyms and Acrostics

In the first part of this Try It!, work individually to create an acronym and an acrostic.

1. Figure out an acronym to remind you of the names of the five Great Lakes, using the first letters of their names (which are Erie, Huron, Michigan, Ontario, Superior).

2. Devise an acrostic for the nine planets in order of their average distance from the sun. Their names, in order, are Mercury, Venus, Earth, Mars, Jupiter, Saturn, Uranus, Neptune, Pluto. (Bonus question: Because many astronomers no longer believe Pluto is a planet, devise an acrostic that omits Pluto and just contains the first eight planets.)

 WORKING IN A GROUP

After you've tried to create the acronym and acrostic, meet in a group and discuss these questions: How successful were you in devising effective acronyms and acrostics? Do some of the group members' creations seem more effective than others? Why? Is the act of creating them an important component of helping to remember what they represent, or would having them created by someone else be as helpful in recalling them? For your information, a common acronym for the Great Lakes is HOMES (**H**uron, **O**ntario, **M**ichigan, **E**rie, **S**uperior), and a traditional acrostic for the order of the planets is **M**y **V**ery **E**ducated **M**other **J**ust **S**erved **U**s **N**ine **P**izzas. (As for the bonus question that omits Pluto, future generations may use the acrostic My Very Educated Mother Just Served Us Noodles.)

The benefit of acronyms is that they help us to recall a complete list of steps or items. P.O.W.E.R. stands for—well, by this point in the book, you probably remember.

After learning to use the acronym "FACE" to remember the notes on the spaces of the music staff, many beginning musicians learn that the names of the lines on the staff form the acrostic, "Every Good Boy Deserves Fudge." An **acrostic** is a sentence in which the first letters spell out something that needs to be recalled. The benefits—as well as the drawbacks—of acrostics are similar to those of acronyms.

Although mnemonics are helpful, keep in mind that they have a number of significant shortcomings. First, they don't focus on the meaning of the items being remembered. Because information that is learned in terms of its surface characteristics—such as first letters that form a word—is less likely to be retained than information that is learned in terms of its meaning, mnemonic devices are an imperfect route to memorization.

There's another problem with mnemonics: Sometimes it takes as much effort to create a mnemonic device as it would to memorize the material in the first place. And because the mnemonic itself has no meaning, it can be forgotten.

Despite their drawbacks, mnemonics can be useful. They are particularly helpful when the material being memorized includes a list of items or a series of steps as you can see above in **Try It! 5.**

acrostic

A sentence in which the first letters of the words correspond to material that is to be remembered.

planets

Chunking Material

When we learn new material, we face a physical limitation of our brains: We can hold only a limited amount of information in our heads at any one time. Although the specific amount varies, it's generally around five to nine individual bits of information.

But there's a way around that limitation, known as chunking. A *chunk* is a grouping of information that can be stored in working memory, the memory store where information is processed before it moves into long-term memory. For example, a chunk can be a group of seven individual letters or numbers, permitting us to hold a seven-digit phone number (such as 226-4610) in working memory.

But a chunk also may consist of larger categories, such as words or other meaningful units. For example, consider the following list of 21 letters:

P B S F O X C N N A B C C B S M T V N B C

Because the list of individual letters exceeds seven items, it is difficult to recall the letters after one exposure. But suppose they were presented as follows:

PBS FOX CNN ABC CBS MTV NBC

In this case, even though there are still 21 letters, you'd be able to store them in working memory since they represent only seven chunks.

The principle of chunking can help us to store information more efficiently. Rather than considering individual bits of information, try to link them into meaningful groups. The larger the meaningful groupings, the more information you'll be able to recall.

Involve Multiple Senses

The more senses you can involve when you're trying to learn new material, the better you'll be able to remember. Here's why: Every time we encounter new information, all of our senses are potentially at work. For instance, if we witness a car crash, we receive sensory input from the sight of the two cars hitting each other, the sound of the impact, and perhaps the smell of burning rubber. Each piece of sensory information is stored in a separate location in the brain, and yet all the pieces are linked together in extraordinarily intricate ways.

What this means is that when we seek to remember the details of the crash, recalling a memory of one of the sensory experiences—such as what we heard—can trigger recall of the other types of memories. For example, thinking about the *sound* the two cars made when they hit can bring back memories of the way the scene looked.

When you learn something, use your body. Don't sit passively at your desk. Instead, move around. Stand up; sit down. Touch the page. Trace figures with your fingers. Talk to yourself. Think out loud. It may seem strange, but doing so increases the number of ways in which the information is stored.

Visualize

Visualization is a technique by which images are formed to ensure that material is recalled. For instance, memory requires three basic steps: the initial recording of information, the storage of that information, and, ultimately, the retrieval of the stored information. As you read the three steps, you probably see them as logical and straightforward processes. But how do you remember them?

You might visualize a computer, with its keyboard, disks, and monitor (see **Figure 5.3**). The keyboard represents the initial recording of information. The disk represents the storage of information,

visualization
A memory technique by which images are formed to help recall material.

Recording of information

Storage of information in memory

Display of information retrieved from memory

figure 5.3
Visualizing Memory

Try It!

The Memory Game

Return to the excerpt in Figure 5.2 (the same passage you used in **Try It! 4**). To help you memorize and retain what is meant by the *learning-theory approach,* review the material using each of the following strategies. Then answer the questions below.

1. Rehearse what is meant by the *learning-theory approach.* Put it in your own words. Think about it. Say your thoughts out loud. Associate it with other ideas that are familiar to you. Summarize it.

2. Read through the three paragraphs about the *learning-theory approach.* Try breaking the information into smaller chunks. Does each chunk still retain meaning? Can you sum up the information in each chunk in a phrase? Now, try stringing the chunks together to form a complete concept for *learning-theory approach.*

3. Create an acronym or acrostic to help you remember the basic principles of the *learning-theory approach.*

4. Visualize. Form clear, detailed images that represent the concepts of the *learning-theory approach* .

5. As you read through the material, involve multiple senses. Touch the photo in the excerpt. Move around the room. Trace the definition in the sidebar with your finger. Think out loud about what the author is saying.

Were any memory techniques more useful to you than others? If so, do you know why? Why might it be useful to use multiple techniques in memorizing material?

---

and the monitor represents the display of information that has been retrieved from memory. If you can put these images in your mind, it will help you to remember the three basic memory steps later. (You can test these memorization techniques in **Try It! 6.**)

Overlearning

Overlearning. Think back to when you were learning your basic multiplication facts ($1 \times 1 = 1$; $2 \times 2 = 4$; and so forth). Let's suppose you had put each multiplication problem on a flash card, and you decided to go through your entire set of cards, trying to get every problem right.

The first time you went through the set of cards and answered all the problems correctly, would you feel as if you'd memorized them perfectly and that you'd never again make an error? You shouldn't. You would need several instances of perfect performance to be sure you had learned the multiplication facts completely.

Lasting learning doesn't come until you have overlearned the material. **Overlearning** consists of studying and rehearsing material past the point of initial mastery. Through overlearning, recall becomes automatic. Rather than searching for a fact and going through mental contortions until perhaps the information surfaces, overlearning permits us to recall the information automatically, without even thinking about it. The more facts and mental operations that you have memorized through overlearning, the more quickly you can move through a test.

To put the principle of overlearning to work, don't stop studying at the point when you can say to yourself, "Well, I'll probably pass this test." You may be right, but that's all you'll do—pass. Instead, spend extra time learning the material until it becomes as familiar as an old pair of jeans.

overlearning
Studying and rehearsing material past the point of initial mastery to the point at which recall becomes automatic.

Muscle & Memory

What Does It Mean?
What Do I Know?

Evaluation is a crucial step in reading. You need to be able to answer the seemingly simple question: "What does all this mean?"

But there's another aspect to evaluation. You need to evaluate, truthfully and honestly, your own level of understanding. What do you know as a result of your reading? Evaluation, then, consists of the following steps:

▶ **Identify the main ideas and themes and their value** *to you personally.* Try to determine the take-home message of the material you've read. For example, the take-home message of a chapter on accounting ethics might be, "In the long run, honest accounting practices benefit the long-term health of any business."

Sometimes the main ideas and themes are spelled out, and at other times you will have to deduce them for yourself. Evaluating the main ideas and themes in terms of how they relate to you personally will help you understand and remember them more easily.

From the perspective of . . .

AN EDITORIAL ASSISTANT The ability to discern what is important within what you read is a key job function for editors. How might you apply your reading evaluation skills to an author's first draft?

Source: © Comstock/SuperStock

▶ **Prioritize the ideas.** Of all the information that is presented, which is the most crucial to the main message and which is the least crucial? Make a list of the main topics covered and try to rank them in order of importance.

▶ **Think critically about the arguments presented in the reading.** Do they seem to make sense? Are the author's assertions reasonable? Are there any flaws in the arguments? Would authors with a different point of view dispute what is being said? How would they build their own arguments?

▶ **Pretend you are explaining the material (talking—out loud!—about the material) to a fellow classmate who missed the assignment.** This is one time when talking out loud when no one is around is not only normal, but beneficial. Summarize the material aloud, as if you were talking to another person.

Talking out loud does two things. First, it helps you identify weak spots in your understanding and recall. Talking to yourself will help you nail down concepts that are still not clear in your own mind. Second, and equally important, because you are transforming the written word into the spoken word, you are thinking about the information in another way, which will help you remember it better.

▶ **Use in-text review questions and tests.** Many textbook chapters end with a quiz or a set of review questions about the material. Some have questions scattered throughout the chapter. Don't ignore them! Not only do such questions indicate what the writer of the book thought was important for you to learn, but they can also provide an excellent opportunity for evaluating your memory.

▶ **Team up with a friend or use a study group.** When it comes to evaluating your understanding of a reading, two heads (or more!) are often better than one. Working with a classmate or study group—especially with others who may have a different preferred learning style from your own—can help you test the limits of your understanding and memory of material, and assess areas in which you need work.

▶ **Be honest with yourself.** Most of us are able to read with our minds on cruise control. But the net result is not much different from not reading the passage at all. If you have drifted off while you've been reading, go back and reread the passage.

Dealing with Learning Disabilities

If you, like millions of people in the United States, have a learning disability of one sort or another, reading and remembering may prove to be particularly challenging. **Learning disabilities** are defined as difficulties in processing information when listening, speaking, reading, or writing; in most cases, learning disabilities are diagnosed when there is a discrepancy between learning potential and actual academic achievement.

One of the most common kinds of learning disabilities is *dyslexia,* a reading disability that produces the misperception of letters during reading and writing, unusual difficulty in sounding out letters, spelling difficulties, and confusion between right and left. Although its causes are not yet completely understood, one likely explanation is a problem in the part of the brain responsible for breaking words into the sound elements that make up language.

Another common disability is *attention deficit hyperactivity disorder* (or *ADHD*), which is marked by an inability to concentrate, inattention, and a low tolerance for frustration. For the 1 to 3 percent of adults who have ADHD, planning, staying on task, and maintaining interest present unusual challenges. Not only are these challenges present in college, but they also affect job performance.

People with learning disabilities are sometimes viewed as unintelligent. Nothing could be farther from the truth: There is no relationship between learning disabilities and IQ. For instance, dozens of well-known and highly accomplished individuals suffered from dyslexia, including physicist Albert Einstein, U.S. General George Patton, poet William Butler Yeats, and writer John Irving.

By the time they reach college, most people with learning disabilities have already been diagnosed. If you do have a diagnosed learning disability and you need special services, it is important to disclose your situation to your instructors and other college officials.

In some cases, students with learning disabilities have not been appropriately evaluated prior to college. If you have difficulties such as mixing up and reversing letters frequently and suspect that you have a learning disability, there usually is an office on campus that can provide you with guidance. One place to start is your college counseling or health center.

Many sorts of treatments, ranging from learning specific study strategies to the use of medication, can be effective in dealing with learning disabilities. In addition, colleges that accept support from

learning disabilities
Difficulties in processing information when listening, speaking, reading, or writing, characterized by a discrepancy between learning potential and actual academic achievement.

Many highly accomplished individuals suffer from learning disabilities, including Albert Einstein, who was dyslexic.
Source: © Library of Congress, Prints and Photographs Division

The Job of Reading

Memos. Annual reports. Instructions. Continuing education assignments. Professional journals.

Each of these items illustrates the importance of developing critical reading skills for on-the-job success. Virtually every job requires good reading expertise, and for some professions, reading is a central component. Polishing your reading skills now will pay big dividends when you enter the world of work. The better you are at absorbing and remembering written information, the better you'll be at carrying out your job.

For instance, in many corporations, vital information is transmitted through the written word, via e-mails, hard-copy memos, technical reports, or web-based material. The job of repairing broken appliances or automobiles requires reading numerous service manuals to master the complex computer diagnostic systems that are now standard equipment. Nurses and others in the healthcare field must read journals and reports to keep up with the newest medical technologies.

Furthermore, because not all supervisors are effective writers, you'll sometimes need to read between the lines and draw inferences and conclusions about what you need to do. You should also keep in mind that there are significant cultural differences in the ways people write and the type of language they use. Being sensitive to the cultural background of colleagues will permit you to more accurately interpret and understand what you are reading.

In short, reading is a skill that's required in virtually every profession. Developing the habit of reading critically while you are in college will pave the road for future career success.

---

the federal government have a legal obligation to provide people with diagnosed learning disabilities with appropriate support. This obligation is spelled out in the Americans with Disabilities Act, and it provides important legal protections.

However, just the fact that you are having trouble with reading assignments doesn't automatically mean that you have a learning disability. Not only is the kind of reading you do in college more difficult than reading in other contexts, but there's also more of it. It's only when reading represents a persistent, long-term problem—one that won't go away no matter how much work you do—that a learning disability becomes a possible explanation.

R Rethink | Getting It the Second Time

You're human, so—like the rest of us—when you finish a reading assignment you'd probably like nothing more than to heave a sigh of relief and put the book away.

By now you know that there's a crucial step you should take that will assist you in cementing what you've learned into memory: rethinking what you've read. If you do it within 24 hours of first reading the assignment, it can save you hours of work later.

The best way to rethink an assignment is to reread it, along with any notes you've taken. "Yeah, right," you're probably thinking. "Like I have time for that." The goal, though, is not a literal rereading. In fact, it isn't necessary to reread word for word. You already know what's important and what's not important, so you can skim some of the less important material. But it is wise to reread the more difficult and important material carefully, making sure that you fully understand what is being discussed and that you'll remember the key details.

> "Reading furnishes the mind only with materials of knowledge; it is thinking that makes what we read ours."
>
> **John Locke, author, *Of the Conduct of the Understanding*, 1706.**

What's most critical, though, is that you think deeply about the material, considering the take-home message of what you've read. You need to be sure that your understanding is complete and that you're able to answer any questions that you had earlier about the material. Rethinking should be the central activity as you reread the passage and your notes.

The benefits of rethinking the material can't be overstated. Rethinking transfers material from your short-term memory to your long-term memory. It solidifies information so that it will be remembered far better over the long haul.

Speaking *of* Success

Source: Courtesy of C'Ardiss Gardner

NAME: **C'Ardiss Gardner**

SCHOOL: **South Seattle Community College**

HOME: **Seattle, Washington**

When C'Ardiss Gardner began college, she was already familiar with challenge. She became a mother at age 16 and chose to finish high school while working two jobs to support her infant.

Despite the challenges, Gardner not only finished her high school requirements early but also had enough credits to start at the local community college. When she started at South Seattle Community College, not only was she taking classes, but she was working two part-time jobs. But eventually, she was forced to delay her college plans to take a third job to support herself. For three years she juggled work and child rearing.

But Gardner also had plans. She got married and reenrolled at South Seattle. After graduating with her associate's degree, she was accepted to four-year colleges around the country. She decided to move her family to the East Coast to attend Yale University. Gardner graduated from Yale with a B.A. in African-American Studies. She and her family returned to Seattle, where she now is raising three children, working as the registrar of a prep school, and studying for a master's degree in education at Seattle University.

"Attending school as an African-American student with a small child was very challenging. I did not come from a community that supported or encouraged kids like me to go to college," said Gardner.

"Even something as simple as writing was enough to set me apart from the other students, who had spent years learning how to write at a college level. I had to learn those things, and it was very difficult," she noted. "One of the most important things I learned was to access as many resources as I could to help learn skills I was lacking. Professors offered help by reading my drafts before I turned essays or papers in. By accepting help, I was able to improve my writing skills and improve my grades."

The skills Gardner developed while at South Seattle Community College laid the groundwork for her future academic success and became the foundation upon which she has been able to build the rest of her life. Not only has she been able to continue her education, but she plans to use her skills to help pave the way for other students to access education.

[RETHINK]

• How do you think Gardner's reading skills helped her achieve her academic successes?

• What types of resources do you think Gardner accessed to help her develop learning skills?

Looking
Back

Conceptualized

LO 5-1 Explain how reading style and attention span affect reading.

▶ The most important aspect of reading is understanding, not speed. Finishing a reading assignment quickly is far less important than understanding it fully.

▶ One problem people have with reading is a limited attention span. However, attention span can be increased with self-awareness and practice.

LO 5-2 Identify how to improve concentration and read and remember more effectively.

▶ Reading should be approached with a clear sense of purpose and goals, which will vary from assignment to assignment. Examining the frontmatter of a book and creating advance organizers is also useful.

▶ As you read, identify and focus on the key material you will need to remember later. Don't try to memorize everything you read.

▶ Maintain focus by breaking down the reading into small chunks, taking breaks as needed, dealing with distractions, and writing while reading.

▶ Many memory techniques are available to improve memorization. Rehearsal is a primary one, as is the use of mnemonics, such as acronyms and acrostics.

▶ Overlearning is a basic principle of memorization.

LO 5-3 Discuss how best to retain what you have read.

▶ Understanding of reading assignments can be cemented in memory by identifying the main ideas, prioritizing them, thinking critically about the arguments, using in-text questions and tests, and explaining the writer's ideas to someone else.

▶ Quickly rereading assignments and notes taken on them can greatly help in solidifying memories of what has been read.

[KEY TERMS AND CONCEPTS]

Acronym (p. 124)

Acrostic (p. 125)

Advance organizers (p. 112)

Attention span (p. 115)

Frontmatter (p. 113)

Learning disabilities (p. 129)

Mnemonics (p. 124)

Overlearning (p. 127)

Rehearsal (p. 124)

Visualization (p. 126)

[RESOURCES]

ON CAMPUS

If you are experiencing unusual difficulties in reading or remembering material, you may have a learning disability. If you suspect this is the case, take action. Many colleges have an office that deals specifically with learning disabilities. You can also talk to someone at your college's counseling center; he or she will arrange for you to be tested, which can determine whether you have a problem.

IN PRINT

The seventh edition of Joe Cortina and Janet Elder's book, *Opening Doors: Understanding College Reading* (McGraw-Hill, 2015), provides complete guidelines for reading textbooks and other kinds of writing that you will encounter during college. Another useful volume is *Breaking Through: College Reading* (Longman, 2015, 11th ed.) by Brenda Smith. In *Improving Your Memory* (Johns Hopkins, 2014, 4th ed.), Janet Fogler and Lynn Stern provide an overview of practical tips on maximizing your memory. Finally, Forrest King provides numerous memory improvement techniques in *How to Improve Memory* (CreateSpace Independent Publishing Platform, 2014).

ON THE WEB

The following sites on the Internet provide opportunities to extend your learning about the material in this chapter. (Although the web addresses were accurate at the time this material was published, check the *P.O.W.E.R. Learning* Connect Library or contact your instructor for any changes that may have occurred.)

▶ "Editor Eric's Greatest Literature of All Time: The Works" (**http://editoreric.com/greatlit/indexB.html**): Check out this lengthy list of books. While it is one person's interpretation of what constitutes great books, it nevertheless contains a variety of great literature, with links to outlines of each work.

▶ Increasing Textbook Reading Comprehension by Using SQ3R is the title of this site offered by Virginia Tech University (**http://www.ucc.vt.edu/academic_support_students/online_study_skills_workshops/SQ3R_improving_reading_comprehension/index.html**). It offers a clear and detailed outline on how to use the SQ3R method, as well as links to other reading comprehension aids such as critical reading, proofreading, and selective reading.

▶ Need a mnemonic? Have one you'd like to share? Then just go to **www.mnemonic-device.com/**, a site devoted entirely to mnemonics. This fun and educational site covers a variety of subjects from astronomy to weather.

▶ Mind Tools, a bookstore specializing in works on memory, offers a number of free online articles (**www.mindtools.com/memory.html**) detailing methods for improving memory. It includes examples of how each technique can be applied to such topics as remembering lists and foreign languages.

The Case of . . .
The Way He Studies

Roger Chen is working on his degree in criminal justice. He always begins a reading assignment by looking over the learning objectives for that day's chapter, something his professor stresses. Then he begins reading, using a highlighter to underline the important stuff, usually about every third sentence. He studies with headphones on because he read somewhere that music improves your concentration. And he usually has a basketball game on his laptop—no sound—which he checks every time he finishes reading a page or two. He likes to draw arrows from tables and charts to the material they represent. In fact, he likes to doodle. His margins are filled with the definitions of key terms and lots of pictures of dragons. Roger is not big on note cards or writing notes outside the book. "Keep it simple" is his motto. Right before a test, he skims through the highlighted material and looks over the charts and tables. He sometimes gives himself a short quiz aloud on the key words of the chapter. Roger does okay. He never fails a test, but he never gets more than a low B either.

1. What study techniques is Roger using that can help him understand and retain the material? How would you advise him to make the most of the techniques he's using?

2. What should Roger change to make his study habits more effective and efficient?

3. What new study techniques would you suggest to Roger to improve his performance in his courses?

4. What techniques might Roger use to memorize long lists or other key material from his reading?

5. How might Roger effectively use writing as a way to stay focused on his reading?

Choosing
Your Courses
and Academic
Program

Learning Outcomes

By the time you finish this chapter you will be able to

>> LO 6-1   Create a plan to prepare for the academic choices that college demands.

>> LO 6-2   Outline a strategy for choosing courses that ensures you are getting the most out of your studies.

>> LO 6-3   Explain the criteria for choosing your academic program.

Our Sustainable Planet. As she scrolled through the Shutesbury Community College website, this course title caught Sinda Dobbs's eye. Concerned about the Earth, and desperate to get her science requirement out of the way as painlessly as possible, Sinda registered for the course in her very first term. She had hated science in high school, but this course seemed safe. She'd do enough work to pass, check off the science requirement, and move on.

Her decision turned out to be more significant than she thought. To her surprise, she loved the course and found herself working hard and looking for more. Not only did she sign up for another environmental science course, she worked with her academic advisor to design an associate's degree program in environmental studies to prepare for continuing her education at a four-year college in the area.

In picking a course, she might well have chosen her life's work.

Looking Ahead

Our academic and professional careers are propelled by many forces, not the least of which is chance. Sinda Dobbs, like many other students, found a new direction while scrolling through her course list. Although she never would have predicted at the beginning of college that she would end up taking environmental science courses and pursuing a degree in environmental studies, her willingness to take a chance in selecting a course led to a new passion and to a career opportunity.

In this chapter we focus on choosing an academic program of study and major, one of the central challenges of college life. Not only do the choices we make color our entire college experience, but they also may determine the path we follow once we graduate.

This chapter begins by considering the many choices that you'll have to make as a routine part of attending college, including the choice of courses, instructors, and programs of study—and often the choice of whether to pursue a certificate or a degree leading to further education. Each of these choices has long-term implications. You'll learn ways to select courses each term that meet your personal needs and maximize your chances of getting the courses that will meet your personal goals.

Ultimately, the extent to which your college education benefits you is in your hands. By learning various strategies, you can act decisively to get the most out of your college experience.

>> LO 6-1

Making Academic Choices

It's a moment filled with promise.

A list of courses for the upcoming term appears on a computer screen before you. Many of them sound interesting. Each offers the possibility of new knowledge and therefore has the potential to change your life in significant ways.

As you work through the course list and begin to make your decisions, you will likely be feeling a wide range of emotions: anticipation over what you'll learn;

hope that the course can bring you closer to your dreams; fear that you won't be able to do well, and excitement that you're proceeding with your college career, taking another of the many small steps that will eventually add up to a complete journey though college.

Choosing what courses to take can be intimidating. But if you approach the problem thoughtfully, your final choices will make the best of the possibilities offered. Let's consider how to proceed, using the P.O.W.E.R. Plan.

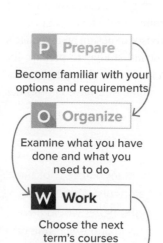

P Prepare

Become familiar with your options and requirements

O Organize

Examine what you have done and what you need to do

W Work

Choose the next term's courses

E Evaluate

Decide whether you are in the classes you need

R Rethink

Learn what you love and like what you learn

P.O.W.E.R. Plan

grade point average (GPA)

Also known as *quality point average*. A numeric average in which letter grades are transformed into numbers.

academic program (or major)

A specialization in a particular subject area, requiring a set course of study.

P Prepare | # Becoming Familiar with Your Options and Requirements

Choosing which courses to take requires that you take several significant preparatory steps before you jump in. These include the following.

Familiarize Yourself with Your College Catalog

Every college has a *catalog of courses and requirements*—which may be in a document located entirely online, published as a hard-copy booklet, or both. The catalog provides you with information about your education: what's offered, its cost, and the steps you need to take in obtaining a college degree.

College catalogs are actually legal documents that offer you a contract. If you are admitted to the college and you fulfill certain requirements (such as taking a particular set of courses, maintaining a certain level of grades, and—let us not forget—paying your tuition bills on time), you'll get something in return. That something is a college degree.

Because they outline contractual obligations, college catalogs are important documents. They provide a summary of what your institution expects and offers in a number of areas:

1. **Academic regulations.** Every college has strict rules, requirements, and policies; these are all spelled out in the college catalog. For example, to graduate you need a certain number of courses or course credits. Similarly, if you wish to add or drop a course, you must do so by a certain date.

   In addition, colleges often require that you maintain a certain grade point average. A **grade point average** (or **GPA**; also known as a *quality point average*) is a numeric average in which letter grades are transformed into numbers. Most colleges use a four-point scale in which A = 4, B = 3, C = 2, D = 1, and F = 0. In such a system, a 3.0 GPA is equivalent to a B average, while a 3.5 would be halfway between an A and a B.

   For example, if your five grades for a term were A, A, B, B, and C, and all the courses had the same number of credits, you would translate your grades into 4, 4, 3, 3, and 2. Next, you would sum the numbers and divide by the number of courses to find the average. That works out to [(4 + 4 + 3 + 3 + 2) ÷ 5], or a 3.2 GPA. In addition, if you have access to your transcript online, you may be able to find it there; your college may calculate your GPA for you each semester.

2. **Academic programs.** Most of the college catalog is a description of the school's academic departments and its programs of study or **majors**—areas of academic specializations in a particular subject area, requiring a set course of study.

Requirements for an academic program generally fall into two or three categories:

- *College-wide or university-wide requirements* that every student enrolled in the college must fulfill.

- *Major requirements.* These are specific requirements for each particular major. To major in an area, you must take a specified number of courses or credits in that area.

- *Academic unit requirements.* Finally, if the major falls within a broader academic unit (such as a school of education or school of business), that broader entity may have its own requirements for a degree. For example, an accounting major might have to complete not only the requirements for an accounting major, but also the requirements for the school of management, and the requirements for the university or college.

For instance, a student pursuing a liberal arts degree with a human services major might be required to fulfill requirements that apply to all students enrolled in the college, such as a specified number of English composition, humanities, social science, physical science, and math courses. In addition, the human services program will have its own separate requirements for its students to complete, such as taking no fewer than four or five human services courses.

The college requirements also provide information for students who have transferred from another college. For instance, transfer students may receive credit for only a certain number of courses or credits earned at their first institution. Or they may be required to take particular courses even if they already took them at their previous school.

If you attend a two-year community college, your college may also provide information on transferring to a four-year school. Many two-year colleges often have articulation agreements. *Articulation agreements* are formal agreements with local four-year colleges stating that these four-year colleges will automatically accept certain courses or credits taken at your current institution.

Articulation agreements may even spell out what groups or blocks of courses will be accepted, as a set, by a four-year college. Knowing what courses will automatically be counted at other colleges is crucial if you are thinking about transferring later.

3. **Course listings.** The list of requirements usually includes all the courses the school offers, even though not all of them may be offered every term. Courses are listed by department, and the descriptions typically include the course name, the number of credits the course provides, and a short description.

Sometimes course descriptions also name the instructors who teach the course and the time and place the class meets. However, this information may also be published separately.

4. Some courses have **prerequisites**—requirements that must be fulfilled before one can enroll. If the course has a prerequisite, this will be stated. Take these prerequisites seriously, because you will not be permitted to enroll in a course if you haven't completed the prerequisite for it. In addition, the prerequisite course may not be offered every term, so you may have to wait a year (or more!) before getting into the course you want.

prerequisites

Requirements that must be fulfilled before a student may enroll in a course or discipline.

Make an Appointment with Your College Advisor

college advisor (or college counselor)

Also called college counselor. An individual who provides students with advice about their academic careers.

The job of a **college advisor** (sometimes called **college counselor**) is to give you good, clear-headed advice. Your advisor will be someone who knows the ins and outs of the college's regulations, and whose experience in working with other students provides a good deal of knowledge in other areas as well. Advisors can help you figure out what classes to take, how to overcome academic bureaucracies, whom to go to about a problem, and generally how to prepare yourself for graduation and beyond. They can even provide information on extracurricular activities, volunteer opportunities, and part-time jobs.

Advisors are particularly busy at the beginning of each term (as well as when the course schedule comes out). Consequently, find out their office hours, schedule an appointment early, and be sure to keep your scheduled appointment. Don't go unprepared when you do go. **Figure 6.1** provides a checklist you should go through before your appointment.

Advisors can be tremendously valuable resources. Take some time to get to know your advisor as a person—and to let him or her get to know you. To get a better sense of who your own advisor is, complete **Try It! 1**, "Get to Know Your College Advisor."

> "It can be no dishonor to learn from others when they speak good sense."
> **Sophocles, author, *Antigone***

If you find that you and your advisor aren't a good match and you know of another advisor who is willing and qualified to advise you, you might consider making a switch. Just be sure you have given your original advisor a chance. It is not your advisor's fault, for example, that you missed your only chance

figure 6.1
Advisor Visit Checklist

——— Check the college catalog for information about the advisor, noting any potential links or conversational topics that might be used to open the meeting.

——— Be on time, be aware of how much time is scheduled for your appointment, and check the time frequently during the appointment.

——— Summarize who you are (e.g., hometown, high school, grades in high school, interests, high school or community activities, etc.) to begin the more formal part of the meeting.

——— List some or all of the courses you plan to take in the next term.

——— Prepare some questions about your course choices (e.g., difficulty of the courses, whether they match your interests, whether they will fulfill your requirements, what future courses or career choices they might lead to, personality of the instructors, etc.).

——— List the extracurricular activities you're considering.

——— Prepare some questions about these activities (e.g., how time-consuming, how interesting, what sorts of students participate in them, etc.).

——— Be prepared to ask about the advisor's impressions of the college.

——— Be prepared to ask the advisor to recommend activities, events, and the like on campus or off, and which to avoid.

——— List any other issues you would like to raise (e.g., impressions of the college so far, roommate issues, personal issues, etc.).

——— Be prepared to ask about the availability of the advisor in the future (e.g., office hours, calling outside office hours, etc.).

——— Remember to thank the advisor before leaving.

Get to Know Your College Advisor

It is helpful to get a feel for who your advisor is, so schedule a 15- to 30-minute appointment with him or her. Before you meet with your advisor, do some background research by looking at your college requirements. You can also usually find information on the background of faculty and staff, listing their titles, where they went to college and graduate school, what departments they teach in, and what their areas of academic interest are. In addition, many instructors have their own home pages that describe their background.

To learn more about your advisor, cover some of these topics when you meet:

- Philosophy of college advising
- Words of advice
- Things to try at the college
- Things to avoid at the college

After you have met with your advisor, answer the following questions:

1. How would you describe your advisor as a person?

2. What things did you learn that can help you?

3. How can you use your advisor's responses to take better advantage of what your college has to offer?

this year to take astronomy. Similarly, even though you may not like your advisor's message ("You still need to take a science course"), this doesn't mean that he or she doesn't have your best interests at heart. If you feel you can trust your advisor and speak with him or her frankly, you and your college career will have gained a valuable ally.

No matter how helpful your advisor is (or how unsupportive, for that matter), remember that ultimately *you* are responsible for your academic career. Advisors are human like the rest of us, they can't know everything, and they can make mistakes. You should double-check what your advisor tells you. Remember that in the end you need to take charge of your own college experience.

College advisors can play an important role in your academic career, providing valuable advice, helping you overcome problems, and making sure that you meet all the requirements needed to graduate.
Source: © Corbis

Organize

Examining What You Have Done and What You Need to Do

Where Are You?

If you've prepared well, you have a basic understanding of how the courses you are taking now or have already taken fulfill your college requirements. To figure out what you still need to do, you should organize a complete list of the requirements you need to fulfill to graduate.

Try It! 2, "Create a List of Required Courses," provides a form that you can complete. (Sometimes colleges will offer such a list—known as a *degree audit*—online. If yours does, you should check it frequently to make sure you are moving ahead in the right direction.)

Even if you have yet to decide on an academic program, you might now be taking courses to satisfy requirements for a program you are considering. Noting this on your list will help you make decisions and plan for the future.

If this is just the start of your college career, you'll probably have completed only a few of the requirements. Don't let the blank spaces on the form overwhelm you; the credits have a way of adding up quickly.

If you are farther along in your college career and have trouble remembering what courses you've taken, get a copy of your transcript from the registrar, or—if you have online access—print out a copy. The **registrar** is the official designated to oversee the scheduling of courses, the maintenance of transcripts, and the creation and retention of other official documents. (A **transcript** is the official record of the courses you've taken and the grades you received in them.)

It's also a good idea to check your transcript periodically to make sure it's accurate and to keep a record of course descriptions from your college catalog. (You can simply save a copy of each year's catalog, or if it is online, print out copies.) You might need the course descriptions if you plan to apply for a transfer to a four-year college or for certification to practice a particular occupation.

As you're recording the courses you've taken, remember that meeting graduation requirements may not be the same as meeting the requirements of your academic program. For instance, some schools not only require that you take and pass certain courses, but also require that you achieve a certain minimum grade in your courses as a whole. Or you may have to get a grade of C or better in a course for it to be counted toward your program of study or major. In this case, if you received a C– in the course, you'd still get credit toward graduation, but the course wouldn't count toward the number of credits you need in your academic program.

Confusing? You bet. That's why it's important to keep track of where you stand from the very start of your college career. (It's a good idea to keep all relevant information together on your computer or in a file folder.) There's no worse surprise than finding out a month before you thought you'd be graduating that you lack some critical requirement. Don't count on others to keep track of this information for you. No one knows more about what you've done than you do.

registrar

The college official designated to oversee the scheduling of courses, the maintenance of grades and transcripts, and the creation and retention of other official documents.

> "Choosing courses can make or break you in college. The better you are at it, the better your grades and the less your aggravation."
>
> **Student, University of Colorado,** in S. Tyler, *Been There, Should've Done That* **(Haslett, MI: Front Porch Press, 1997).**

transcript

A college's official record of courses taken and grades received by students.

Where Are You Going?

You should also use the information you have recorded to help determine which courses to take in the upcoming term. Once you have chosen an academic program, you can add those requirements to your record.

Try It! P O W E R

Create a List of Required Courses

Use the form below to list all of your required courses. The form covers both prerequisite courses (i.e., courses you must take before you can take other courses) and requirements imposed by your college, the college division of which your department is a part, and your department. In addition, the form allows you to indicate both credit requirements and grade requirements.

List of Required Courses							
Type of Course	Credits Required	Credits Completed	Grade Required	Grade Achieved	Whose Requirement?		
					College	Division	Department
I. Prerequisite Courses							
Total Prerequisite Courses							
II. Required Courses							
Total Required Courses							

What does the information in the chart tell you? How can you use it to plan your future course selections? What courses do you wish to take that are not requirements? How much leeway do you have to take nonrequired courses?

Now that you know where you are and where you are going, you are ready to start selecting courses to take you there.

>> LO 6-2 W Work

Choosing the Next Term's Courses

The course listings for the next term are published online or in print in a *course schedule*. The list is typically organized by department, with each course in the department having a number, such as "Business 111: The Contemporary Business World" or "Mathematics 214: Introduction to Statistics." Generally, the higher the number, the more advanced the course. The course schedule will tell you when and where the class meets and whether there are any prerequisites for the course.

Go with What You Know

Chances are, you already know of at least one or two courses you need to take in a given term. Perhaps this is the term you plan to fulfill your natural science or humanities requirement. There may be some courses you have been waiting to take, since some courses are taught only once a year. A good place to begin is to find out when these courses are given and where.

Draft a Personal Schedule for the Term

First, write down when the courses you absolutely have to take are scheduled. If, as is the case for many introductory courses in larger schools, you have a choice of times, choose one you prefer. In choosing times, take into consideration whether you are a "morning person," at your best first thing in the morning, or whether you usually drag yourself out of bed in the morning and don't fully function until noon. This will be the beginning of your time management for the upcoming term.

electives
Courses that are not required.

Next, choose **electives**—courses that are not required. Keep in mind broad considerations about the kinds of courses you need to take for your academic program and for graduation. But also consider courses that simply sound interesting to you. College offers the opportunity to discover who you are and what you like and do best, but the only way that can happen is if you take intellectual risks.

Try to balance easier and more difficult courses for a particular term. You don't want to load up on all highly challenging courses. In addition, signing up for too many courses in a single term—beyond the norm for you—can be self-defeating. (For more on choosing courses, see the **Course Connections** feature.)

To get started in deciding which courses to take for the upcoming term, complete **Try It! 3**, "Choose Your Courses."

Register for Courses

register
To enroll formally in courses.

The rest of the work of choosing courses consists of **registering**, or completing the college's paperwork to become formally enrolled in your chosen classes.

Meeting with your advisor is an essential step. Sometimes, in fact, it's mandatory, and you won't be allowed to register without your advisor's signature. But even if it's not required, it's a good idea to go over your proposed course of studies.

What Are Courses *Really* Like? The Covert College Catalog

Although the official college catalog is the place to start to identify courses that you need to take, there's a wealth of other sorts of unofficial information about courses that you can make use of. Tapping into this often-hidden body of knowledge can help you make informed judgments about which courses are best for you.

Among the sources of information about courses you're considering are these:

- **Current instructors.** Your current instructors know their colleagues and their reputations and may be willing to provide you with off-the-record suggestions.

- **Your classmates.** Ask your classmates for advice and experiences in particular classes, knowing this may be influenced by their own performance in the class. In addition, students have their own biases, and they are not always objective in their evaluations of instructors. For some, "easy course" equals "good course." That's why you should be extremely wary of material on such online evaluation sites as "Rate My Professor." Sometimes the students who provide comments have a dispute with the instructor, and the students who bother to provide comments often do not represent a fair sampling of views.

- **Instructor evaluations.** Sometimes schools permit access to instructor evaluations from previous terms. If these are available, they can be used to get an idea of how other students have reacted to a class you're considering taking. (Although you might be tempted to consider social media and public online ratings of instructors, be extremely suspicious of the information you find. Online ratings suffer from a variety of problems. You will have no idea how representative the online ratings are, because there's no way of knowing what percentage of a class is represented in the ratings. Furthermore, online rating systems often attract students with an ax to grind or students who care only about how easy a class is.)

- **Previous course syllabus.** An instructor may post a class syllabus online or may keep it on file in a departmental office. By examining the syllabus, you'll see exactly what a course covers (and how it compares with the official course description in the catalog).

- **Course instructors themselves.** Sit in on a class that you're thinking about taking, or talk with instructors during their office hours. There's nothing more direct than what you'll learn from the person who will be teaching the course in the upcoming term.

You may have overlooked something, or your advisor may be able to suggest some alternative courses that will work better for you.

Remember, though, that the ultimate responsibility for taking the right courses rests with you. Advisors sometimes make mistakes and overlook a requirement; ultimately, you know best what's right for you.

After meeting with your advisor, your next step will be to register. Course registration varies significantly from one school to another. In some cases, it's a matter of listing course numbers on a form, along with some alternatives.

Before registering online, make sure to review all of your course selections.

Source: © GM Visuals/Getty Images

1. Call the system at (555) 444-3214 (From On-Campus, call 4-3214)

2. Enter your student ID number ☐1☐2☐6☐-☐0☐4☐-☐9☐8☐1☐1

3. Enter your branch code ☐1 (Undergraduate = 1, Graduate = 2)

4. Enter your personal ID number (PIN) ☐6☐7☐7☐5

5. If the Schedule Confirmation you receive in the mail instructs you to get from your advisor a Registration Approval Code before add/drop, enter that code ☐☐☐☐

6. For each add, drop, or change you want to make, enter the appropriate action code from the list below and the schedule number for the course you want affected by that action.

Action Code*	Schedule Number of Course Requested	Dept	Course #	Section #	Crd	Day/Time
1 0	7 8 2 8 4 0	Psych	102	1	3	T-T 11:15-12:30
1 0	6 7 2 9 4 7	Engl	231	1	3	M-W-F 9:05-9:55
1 0	2 6 0 4 6 3	Phed	102	2	1	M 4:00-4:50
1 0	1 2 0 3 0 9	Latn	124	1	3	T-T 9:00-10:15
1 0	8 8 0 1 8 1	Hist	102	1	3	M-W-F 10:10-11:05
1 0	7 2 4 9 6 2	Phys	101	3	3	T-T 2:30-3:45
☐☐	☐☐☐☐☐☐					
☐☐	☐☐☐☐☐☐					
☐☐	☐☐☐☐☐☐					
☐☐	☐☐☐☐☐☐					

7. After completing the form, enter the online registration system at www.umass.edu/virtual-registrar and enter your username and password.

*Action Code	Action
10	**ADD** a course or Swap between sections of a course (To **SWAP**, simply add the new section; the old section will automatically be dropped from your schedule.)
30	**ADD** a course with **Pass/Fail** option or **CHANGE** existing course to **Pass/Fail**
90	**DROP** a course
80	**REMOVE Pass/Fail** or **Audit** option from existing course
50	**CHANGE** variable credit for an existing variable credit course
40	**ADD** a course with **AUDIT** grading option or **CHANGE** existing course to **AUDIT** grading
60	**LIST** your course schedule

Note: Action Codes 30 and 80 are not available to graduate students.
40 is not available to undergraduates.

figure 6.2
A Sample Telephone/Web Course Registration Worksheet

In most schools, you register for your courses using an automated system, online, or by using your cell phone. If your college uses web-based registration, you will be prompted to enter course information on a web form, and your registration will be accomplished completely online (see **Figure 6.2**).

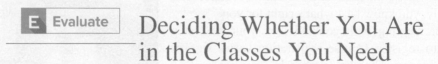

E Evaluate Deciding Whether You Are in the Classes You Need

Picture this horror story:

You go online to look at your grade report from the previous term. You're excited because you know you've done well. You're especially looking forward to seeing your Spanish grade because you know you were on the borderline between an A— and a B+. Instead you're

Choose Your Courses

Use the form below to make your course selections for the coming term. The form will allow you to verify that you are meeting course requirements, avoiding schedule conflicts, and signing up for instructors you want.

Course Selections

Term: _____

Course Name and Number	Credits	Required Course or Just for Fun?	Pre-requisites Met?	Have I Met the Grade Required?	Days Class Meets	Times Class Meets	Instructor Name	Instructor Permission Required?

After completing the chart, answer these questions: How does the next semester seem to be shaping up? Will you be able to take courses you *want* to take, as opposed to those you *need* to take? Have you encountered any conflicts and considered ways to deal with them? Have you made any choices that open you to new intellectual possibilities?

astounded to see that there is no grade listed for the Spanish class, but you've received an F in a French class that you didn't even take. That F pulls down your grade point average, and at the bottom of your grade report is an announcement that you are on academic probation.

Here's the explanation: Because of an error during registration, you were never formally enrolled in the Spanish course, even though you actually spent the entire term attending classes in the course. To compound the mistake, your instructor never noticed that you weren't on her class roster. At the end of the term, when she was filling out her grade report, she didn't notice that your name wasn't listed. So no grade was reported for Spanish.

At the same time, the instructor of the French class in which you were erroneously enrolled had to give you a grade at the end of the semester. Because you never completed any assignments or took any tests, your average for the semester was 0—warranting an F for the term. That F is what appeared on your grade report.

The situation—which is far more likely to occur at a large university than at a small college—might be seen as a comedy of errors if it weren't so painful. Fortunately, if this were actually your story, it would most likely have a happy ending—eventually. You would go to your college registrar, who would be able to tell you what to do to get the F erased and the appropriate grade added. Still, undoing the cascade of errors would take time and a considerable amount of effort.

From the perspective of . . .

AN OFFICE MANAGER Organizing schedules can be an integral part of organizing an office. What aspects of managing your course schedule might apply to managing an office?

Difficulties such as these are encountered by a surprising number of students every term. Many problems, however, can be avoided with a bit of "due diligence" on the part of the student. One key is to evaluate your success in registering.

First, be sure you are registered for the courses you think you are. In many schools, you can determine on the web whether you have successfully enrolled in the courses you want. If your college doesn't use an online registration system, you will be given a list of courses in which you are enrolled for the upcoming term.

Source: © Ingram Publishing/ Superstock

Second, whether you have online access or a hard copy, carefully look over the courses in which you are enrolled. Use the following checklist to determine how successful your efforts to register have been:

▶ Are the courses in which you are enrolled the ones you wanted?

▶ Are the times accurate? Are there any conflicts?

▶ Have any substitutions been made?

▶ Are you registered for the number of credits that you wanted to be registered for?

Third, if there are any problems, try to correct the situation immediately. If there has been a clerical or computer error, you should pay a visit to the registrar's office. Sometimes, though, you'll find that there was no mistake. Class sizes are almost always limited, and not every student who wants to enroll can do so, either because of physical limitations (the room can hold only a certain number of students) or because of educational considerations (learning may be maximized when only a small number of students are in the class).

When a course is overbooked, you have several alternatives. One is to sign up for another section of the course that is not overbooked. Another is to attempt to register for an entirely different course.

Finally, you may appeal directly to the course instructor. Instructors sometimes will permit particularly interested or motivated students to enroll in the class, even if the official capacity has been reached. You may find that approaching an instructor with a polite request may yield you a slot in the course after all.

If none of these alternatives works, you will have to add a course to the ones you have already registered for. How do you add courses after the registration period has ended? Often, you'll need to complete a special form. Depending on the timing of your request, the form may require the signature of the instructor whose course you are adding. In other cases, you may be able to add and drop courses online, depending on the course registration system your college uses.

Also keep in mind that if you drop a class during a term, you must do it officially, through the registrar and course registration system. Simply ceasing to attend doesn't mean you'll be dropped from the class list. Instead, you'll probably end up with a failing grade in the course unless you complete the necessary paperwork to officially drop the course.

"Help—I Can't Get into the Courses That I Need to Graduate!"

For some students, their efforts to register result in utter disaster. Sometimes most or all of their first choices are unavailable, and they end up enrolled in only a few of the courses they had requested. Or perhaps they cannot get into the one crucial course required for graduation.

Whatever the problem, there are several steps you can take to improve the situation:

▶ **Don't despair—act!** There is virtually no academic problem that can't be solved in some way. Focus your energies on finding a creative solution to the problem.

▶ **Identify classes that are still available and enroll in them.** There are probably many classes offered at your college that are still available. Registrars or departments often maintain lists of classes that have many openings.

▶ **Talk with your advisor.** Perhaps what you think of as an absolute requirement can be waived or appealed. Or maybe some other course can substitute for a particular required course.

▶ **Speak with individual course instructors.** It may be that the instructor of the course you need will make an exception and permit you to enroll; it can't hurt to ask.

▶ **Take necessary courses through another division at your college.** Some schools have Continuing Education divisions that offer courses in the evenings, on weekends, during the summer, or online. It may be the same course you would take as part of your normal curriculum, but in this case it is offered through a separate division of your college. The big drawback: you'll have to pay extra for the course, above and beyond normal tuition and fees.

▶ **Consider taking a must-have, required course at another college.** If you live in an area where there are other schools in the vicinity, it may be possible to enroll in a course that you simply must take at another school. It also may be possible to take the course using distance learning. **Distance learning** courses are taught at many institutions, and students participate via the web.

distance learning
The teaching of courses at another institution, with student participation via video technology or the web.

Before you take a course offered by a college other than your own, make sure that you'll receive credit for the course at your school. Also keep in mind that you'll probably have to pay for courses offered by other schools over and above what you've already spent for your own school's tuition.

Learning What You Love and Loving What You Learn

Take one step back. No, make that two steps back.

Stepping back and taking stock of where you are in your course of studies and where you're headed are absolutely essential tasks. In fact, they are among the most important things you can do during your college career. They can mean the difference between plodding through your courses, focused only on day-to-day deadlines and problems, and, alternatively, gaining a sense of satisfaction as you progress toward your own goals and see yourself growing as a person.

From the perspective of . . .

A STUDENT. Choosing a major that will lead to a career you love is a monumental decision. What factors in your life should you consider when making this choice?

Source: © Mark Andersen/Getty Images

When you do take stock, answer the questions in **Try It! 4**. If you're satisfied with your answers, feel affirmed in the choices you've made. You're on the right track, and you should feel secure in the knowledge that you're getting from college what you want to.

On the other hand, if you're less than satisfied with the answers you come up with, take action. Choose courses in the future that better match your goals. Consider changing your program of study or major to one that more closely reflects what you want to get out of college. And, if you're truly unhappy with the way your college career is proceeding, consider changing colleges.

Whichever option you choose, don't simply accept dissatisfaction with your college career. There are few times in our lives when we have the opportunity to partake of an experience that has the potential to raise us to new intellectual and emotional heights. College should be intellectually enlightening and exciting. We should be able to see how our education is preparing us for the rest of our lives. The worst thing we can do is let the time slip away without being confident that our college experience is the best experience possible.

Service Learning: Helping Yourself by Helping Others

service learning
Courses that allow a student to engage in community service activities while getting course credit for the experience.

As you make decisions about what courses to take, you should be sure to consider those that involve service learning. In courses with **service learning**, you engage in community service activities—while getting course credit for the experience.

Service learning is a win–win activity. It links classroom education to real-world community needs. As a student, you are able to gain valuable experience and knowledge that can give you greater insight into a subject area. You can build on the material that you are learning in class and apply that information outside the classroom to real-world situations. Students in a class can share their

Reflect on Your College Experience

As you proceed in college, take a few moments at regular intervals (e.g., once a semester, once a year) to rethink your entire college experience. With a small group of classmates, discuss your reactions to the following topics and questions:

COURSEWORK

- Are my courses moving me toward my educational, career, and personal goals?
- Are the classes I'm taking helping me meet my short- and long-term goals?
- Are the classes I'm taking meeting my expectations?

PERSONAL COMMITMENT

- Am I working hard to get the most out of the classes I'm taking?
- Am I doing my best in every class?
- Am I keeping the goal of learning—apart from doing well in classes—in mind as I progress through my classes?

PERSONAL GROWTH

- What personal growth am I experiencing?
- Am I becoming closer to the person I want to be?
- Are my critical thinking abilities growing?

COLLEGE

- Is my school providing me with the best educational experience possible?
- Am I learning not only in the classroom but also outside the classroom?
- Am I learning from my fellow students as well as my instructors?

CHANGES

- Is there anything (my course selections, my program, or my college) that I should consider changing?
- Have I made the best choices in the past? How can I remedy mistakes that I have made?

service-learning experiences, thereby expanding their understanding of the subject matter.

In addition, you can learn useful skills that can be helpful in your future career. Working outside the classroom can give you experience that will make you a more desirable job candidate. Finally, service learning can help you learn more about yourself and what your strengths and weaknesses are.

Your community is a winner, too. It receives critical support that immediately can improve the quality of life for its citizens. In fact, your efforts can have an impact that echoes for years.

Community service activities span a vast range. For instance, you might tutor an elementary school child in an after-school program as part of a course in elementary education. You'll learn firsthand about the reading process, while the skills (and perhaps motivation) of the child being tutored improve.

table 6.1 Service-Learning Possibilities

Here are just a few possibilities for service-learning activities:

- Develop a website for a social service agency.

- Participate in a "Big Brother" or "Big Sister" program.

- Raise funds for a local food bank.

- Register voters for the next election.

- Volunteer at a local government office.

- Help organize a Special Olympics for people with disabilities.

- Participate in an educational program to protect the environment.

- Help staff a shelter for battered women.

- Volunteer to feed the homeless.

- Organize a blood drive.

To learn of more service-learning opportunities, go to the website of the National Clearinghouse for Service-Learning Organizations, Networks, and Resources at **www.servicelearning.org**.

Or you might enroll in an abnormal psychology class and volunteer at a halfway house for patients with severe psychological disorders. You'll gain a firsthand understanding of disorders that would be impossible to gain simply from reading a textbook, while the patient may benefit from the social interaction you provide. Other examples of service-learning activities are shown in **Table 6.1**.

Whatever service-learning activity you do, there are several basic principles to keep in mind:

▶ **Ask questions.** Don't feel shy about asking for clarification of your responsibilities. It's the best way to maximize your learning. Remember, though, that the staff may be overworked and may not have time to immediately respond.

▶ **Maintain a positive outlook.** You may face challenges unlike those you've encountered before. You may see things that are upsetting and depressing. Keep your own good fortune in mind, and be grateful for the opportunity for growth that the experience is providing you.

▶ **Go with the flow.** You may not agree with everything that is being done at your placement site, but don't think that your ideas are necessarily better than those of the professionals who work there. Voice your concerns, but remember that you're at the site to help, not to make the rules.

▶ **Keep your commitments.** The staff depends on you. If you don't complete a task or show up, you are leaving someone in a lurch and shirking your responsibilities.

- **If you have concerns, discuss them with your supervisor and faculty sponsor.** Don't let your concerns fester. If you're asked to do things that you believe are inappropriate, discuss them with the appropriate person.

- **Keep a journal.** You'll probably be required to keep a journal of your experiences for the academic class attached to your service-learning experience. Even if you're not, keep a journal anyway. Writing in a journal offers a way of reflecting on the meaning of your experiences, as well as providing an enduring record of what you've accomplished.

Many students point to service learning as the high point of their college careers. And for most, it's not because of what they have gained personally—even though that's a significant part of it—but because of the difference they've made in improving the lives of others. To consider service learning further, complete **Try It! 5**.

»LO6-3 Choosing Your Academic Program

You attend a family gathering and encounter relatives you haven't seen for a while. What's the first question they ask when you say you're attending college? You can bet on it: "What's your major?"

Although one could argue that there are lots of other important questions that you could be asked—"What interesting things have you learned?" comes to mind—having a focus of study is an important part of college. An academic program, or major, is important because it focuses what we study, leading us to gain a good deal of expertise in a specific area.

Some students know what academic program they want to enroll in when they begin college; some don't have a clue. That's fine. No one says you should know right away.

In fact, some educators feel that it's better to delay choosing a program. Waiting gives you the opportunity to explore a range of possibilities and gain a more rounded education. Exposure to subjects such as history, art, and literature provides people with a shared background and sharpens critical thinking skills that are useful no matter what program or career is ultimately chosen.

If you're having trouble choosing an academic program, one strategy is to consider the kinds of activities you most like doing outside the academic arena. For example, if you've enjoyed coaching a youth soccer team, you might want to consider an education major.
Source: © Alistair Berg/Getty Images

Explore Service-Learning Opportunities

To find out about the service-learning opportunities available to you, complete the following activities:

A. Examine the courses offered at your college and identify three that contain service-learning components.

1. Course number and name _____
   What is the service-learning activity?

2. Course number and name _____
   What is the service-learning activity?

3. Course number and name _____
   What is the service-learning activity?

B. Identify three potential service-learning activities in your community by contacting social service agencies, food banks, the Red Cross, or religious organizations. You can also do research on the web.

1. Organization name _____
   What is the service-learning activity you might conduct?

2. Organization name _____
   What is the service-learning activity you might conduct?

3. Organization name _____
   What is the service-learning activity you might conduct?

 WORKING IN A GROUP

Compare your findings with those of other students in your class. What opportunities did you find? What service-learning opportunities might you seek out in the future? Discuss what you see as the advantages and disadvantages of service learning.

Journal Reflections

Focusing on Your Interests

The following questions are intended to lead you to explore areas of personal preference and interest that should inform your choice of a field of study. These questions are informal and designed to be answered briefly; more extended and formal "interest inventories" are available in your college's counseling office.

1. Do you think you would enjoy being told precisely what to do and how to do it, or would you rather work things out by yourself, without extensive instructions or supervision? What implications might your answer have for a choice of academic programs?

2. Are you ambitious and success oriented and not ashamed to admit that you'd like to earn a lot of money, or are success and money of secondary importance to you? What implications might your answer have for a choice of academic programs?

3. Are you the artistic type and do you enjoy performing, creating, and viewing/listening to artistic works, or is art of relatively little interest to you? What implications might your answer have for a choice of academic programs?

4. Do you enjoy working with others, or do you prefer to work on your own? What implications might your answer have for a choice of academic programs?

Furthermore, taking a variety of classes in a broad range of courses can lead to quite practical outcomes. Look at **Table 6.2**, which shows areas that employers want emphasized in colleges. The skill areas in which employers are interested can be attained only by taking a broad array of courses.

In addition, taking a variety of classes in a broad range of subjects can help you identify a field of study that you're really interested in. You might find after taking a civics course that you have a passion for legal studies. Or a physical science class may lead you to consider entering an engineering program. College is meant to be a time of exploration, and leaving yourself open to the future—and the unknown—is a completely reasonable thing to do. (To begin your own exploration of academic programs, complete **Try It! 6**, "Identify Major Attractions," on page 158.)

But what if you don't have any idea which field of study you wish to pursue? If you are still in your first year of college, you have time to make up your mind. But here are some approaches that should help as the time to declare your program choice (usually your second year) draws nearer.

table 6.2 What Skills Do Employers Want?

Knowledge of Human Cultures and the Physical and Natural World

• Science and technology	82%
• Global issues	72%
• The role of the United States in the world	60%
• Cultural values and traditions (U.S./global)	53%

Intellectual and Practical Skills

• Teamwork skills in diverse groups	76%
• Critical thinking and analytic reasoning	73%
• Written and oral communication	73%
• Information literacy	70%
• Creativity and innovation	70%
• Complex problem solving	64%
• Quantitative reasoning	60%

Personal and Social Responsibility

• Intercultural competence (teamwork in diverse groups)	76%
• Intercultural knowledge (global issues)	72%
• Ethics and values	56%
• Cultural values/traditions—U.S./global	53%

Integrative Learning

• Applied knowledge in real-world settings	73%

The percentages in the table refer to the percentage of employers that want colleges to "place more emphasis" on these essential learning outcomes.

Source: These findings are taken from a survey of employers commissioned by the Association of American Colleges and Universities 2006.

"I sat back thinking that the right major would just pop into my head. It didn't."

Senior, University of Connecticut, in S. Tyler, *Been There, Should've Done That* **(Haslett, MI: Front Porch Press, 1997).**

1. **Celebrate your indecision.** If you don't have to make a decision for some time, take advantage of the situation. Enjoy the fact that you're uncommitted and that you have an uncommon degree of freedom. In addition, remember that there are a lot of others in the position of not knowing what to study. Many students struggle to identify an academic program, and some change programs a number of times, just as most people change careers several times.

2. **Focus on your interests.** Take a long look inward, paying attention to what your interests are. What do you most like to do in life? What are your strengths and weaknesses? What do you want to get out of life? The more you know about yourself, the easier it will become to narrow down the choices for an academic program. Completing the **Journal Reflections**, "Focusing on Your Interests," on page 155 is a good place to start.

> "He who hesitates is sometimes saved."
>
> **James Thurber, author**

3. **Seek the help of others.** College campuses provide many resources to help their students choose a program (and also to help narrow the choices for potential careers). Talk to other students in areas that interest you. Find out what they like and don't like about the field and its requirements. You will probably find your interest in the program grows or diminishes depending on how you feel about the issues they mention.

   Speak with your advisor. If you've gotten to know your advisor, he or she can often provide reasonable, helpful information. For instance, you may be able to find out about the strengths and weaknesses of various departments.

   You can also turn to your college counseling or career center. Most colleges have offices that can provide information about the different academic programs, including information about career opportunities typically available to graduates of those programs. Sometimes it's possible to take tests that will help focus your choices, pinpointing how your interests, values, and personality type fit with particular careers.

4. **Be career oriented, but not too career oriented.** If you have a good idea about what career you wish to embark upon once you graduate, you can easily find out which skills are required to be successful in that field. Knowing what you'll need to gain entry into a field can help you determine a good academic program that will set you on the road toward your desired profession.

   Don't narrow your options too much, however. Students sometimes fear signing up for classes that don't seem to lead directly toward a career. Or they may avoid courses that seem to point them in the direction of a career that would be "unacceptable" to their parents or friends. One of the greatest sources of indecision in choosing a program of study stems from the mistaken notion that when you choose your program, you're also choosing a career.

   Don't fall into that trap. Follow your heart—not always your head—and pursue courses without regard to how they may broaden or narrow your future job opportunities. You may discover a passion, and an aptitude, that you never knew you had. Even if you are oriented toward a specific profession, remember that employers often prefer well-rounded employees over ones who are narrowly focused on a particular subject area.

5. **Always keep in mind that education is a lifelong enterprise.** Educational opportunities will continue to present themselves not just through the undergraduate years, but for the rest of your life.

College counseling and career centers are excellent sources of information on potential majors and occupations.
Source: © Digital Vision/Getty Images

Identify Major Attractions

To complete this assessment, check off each characteristic that applies to you. Then use the pattern of results to determine how closely your interests and personality style match with the characteristics of others who are already in a particular field of study.

Characteristic	Is This Me?	Possible Field of Study
• High interest in creative expression. • Appreciation of nonverbal communication. • Understanding of aesthetics. • Commitment to perfection. • Ability to manipulate form and shape.	_____ _____ _____ _____ _____	Arts (e.g., dance, drama, music, art, creative writing)
• Interest in organization and order. • Ability to lead and manage people. • Interest in practical problem solving. • Ambition and interest in financial incentives. • Can-do attitude. • Ability to simplify complexity.	_____ _____ _____ _____ _____ _____	Business
• Intense interest in solving real problems. • "Tinkerer" mentality a plus. • Extreme ability to focus on minute details. • Commitment to exactness and perfection. • Strong logical ability. • Ability to work alone for long stretches.	_____ _____ _____ _____ _____ _____	Engineering sciences (e.g., engineering, computer science)
• Interest in people. • Desire to solve real human problems. • Commitment to people more than money. • Tolerance of "messy" situations with multiple, partial solutions. • Insight and creativity. • Ability to work with people.	_____ _____ _____ _____ _____ _____	Helping professions (e.g., nursing, counseling, teaching, many areas of medicine)
• Interest in human emotions and motivations. • Interest in cultural phenomena. • Ability to integrate broad areas of study and inquiry. • Good skills of human observation. • Interest in the panorama of human life.	_____ _____ _____ _____ _____	Humanities (e.g., English literature, history, theater, film)
• Interest in words, word origins, and speech. • View of language as a science. • View of literature as human expression. • Appreciation of cultural differences as scientific phenomena.	_____ _____ _____ _____	Languages and linguistics

Characteristic	Is This Me?	Possible Field of Study
• Interest in physical performance. • Enjoyment of sports and athletics. • Commitment to helping others appreciate physicality. • Patience and perseverance. • Commitment to perfection through practice.	_____ _____ _____ _____ _____	Physical education
• Enjoyment of research questions; high level of curiosity about natural phenomena • Quantitative thinking a requirement; high comfort level with mathematics and statistics. • Minute problem-solving skills; great attention to detail. • Strong logical ability. • Ability to work with others.	_____ _____ _____ _____ _____	Physical, biological, and natural sciences (e.g., physics, astronomy, chemistry, biology, some areas of medicine)
• Interest in people as individuals or groups. • Ability to think quantitatively and qualitatively. • High comfort level with mathematics and statistics. • High level of creativity and curiosity. • Ability to work with others. • Interest in theory as much as problem solving.	_____ _____ _____ _____ _____	Social sciences (e.g., psychology, communication, sociology, education, political science, economics)
• Interest in the inner life. • Interest in highly theoretical questions. • Ability to think rigorously about abstract matters. • Appreciation of the human search for meaning.	_____ _____ _____ _____	Spiritual and philosophical studies

Use the results to focus on the kinds of courses and educational experiences that are involved in potential fields of study. Examining your responses may lead you toward some unexplored territory.

After you complete the chart, consider how you can use the information. Did you learn anything new about yourself or about various courses of study? Do your responses direct you toward a particular academic program? Do they direct you away from any particular program?

Consequently, regardless of your choice of academic program, you're not precluding the possibility of taking courses in other areas in the future. You may eventually end up in graduate school pursuing a master's degree, a doctorate, or an MD. You also may take courses periodically at local colleges even after you graduate, enrolling in them because they will help you advance in your career or simply because they interest you.

In addition, choosing an academic program is not an irreversible choice. Many students change programs at some point during college—just as most people change their careers several times over the course of their lifetimes.

In short, choosing an academic program is not a decision that places your life on a set, unchangeable course. Instead, it's one step in what can be a lifetime of learning.

Choosing a Job That's Right for You

It's a question no family member can resist asking, and one that you've probably asked yourself: What kind of work are you going to do when you graduate?

Happily, it's a question you don't have to answer, at least not yet. Although some students know from their first day in college what they want to do (and actually choose their college on that basis), many—perhaps most—don't decide on a career path until late in their academic career.

And that's fine. After all, one of the reasons you are in college is to expose yourself to the universe of knowledge. In one sense, keeping your options open is a wise course. You don't want to prematurely narrow your options and discard possibilities too early. And even if you're quite sure in your choice of careers, it doesn't hurt to explore new possibilities.

In the Career Connections features in previous chapters, we've discussed various strategies for exploring future professions. Here, in summary, are some steps to take to identify a career:

1. **Clarify the goal of your search.** There's no single perfect career choice. Some people search for the ideal career, assuming that they need to identify the one and only career for which they have been destined. The reality is that there are many careers they could choose that would make them equally happy and satisfied.

   Start with what you already know about yourself. You've already done a lot of mental work toward narrowing down a profession. Do you hate the sight of blood? Then you're probably well aware you're not cut out to be a nurse or veterinary assistant. Does the sight of a column of numbers bring an immediate yawn? Count out accounting and statistics.

   Awareness of your likes and dislikes already puts you on the road to identifying a future career. Knowing what you don't want to do helps identify what you do want to do and narrows down the kinds of occupations for which you're more suited.

2. **Gather information.** The more you know about potential careers, the better. Examine career-planning materials, read industry profiles, and visit relevant websites (such as the excellent Department of Labor site at **www.bls.gov/oco/**). Talk with career counselors. Discuss your options with people who work in professions in which you're interested. Find out how they chose their career, how they got their current job, and what advice they have for you.

   In addition, consider participating in an internship in a profession that you think might be attractive. *Internships* are off-campus, temporary work situations that permit you to obtain experience in a particular field. They are not always paid, but in many cases they can substitute for a course. For example, you might be able to receive three college credits for spending 10 hours a week at a work site during the course of a term.

   Internships are an excellent way to learn about a profession, up close and personal. Working as an intern will let you know the kinds of things employees do on a day-to-day basis and the responsibilities and duties of the profession you're interested in. You can gain experiences that you would not be able to get on campus.

3. **Narrow down your choices.** Once you've gathered enough information to give yourself a reasonable comfort level, narrow down the choices. If it's early in your college career, you don't need to make up your mind. If it's late and you feel the pressure to choose, then make the decision. Just do it. Remember, there's no single, absolutely correct decision; there are many right decisions.

   Whatever it is you ultimately choose as a career, think of it only as a first step. As the average life span continues to lengthen due to advances in medical technology, most people will pass through several careers during the course of their lives. By periodically taking stock of where you are and considering your goals, you'll be in a position to make career changes that bring you closer to your ideal.

Accepting Responsibility for Your Academic Performance

You received the highest grade in your class . . . you received an A on a paper . . . your instructor tells you your class participation was the best in the course.

Take pride in your success, and reflect on what you did to achieve it. If you're doing well academically, it's not an accident. It's because you've worked hard and put your intellectual capacities to full use.

On the other hand, each of us has moments of academic disappointment. When you get a poor grade in a course, it hurts. But even if you feel tempted to shrug it off publicly, don't make that mistake privately. It's just as important to take responsibility for and reflect on your academic disappointments as it is to accept your successes.

There is, of course, a great difference between reflecting on what has happened and blaming ourselves. When things go wrong, it's reasonable to reflect as a way to understand what went wrong. It is not useful, however, to spend time and energy blaming ourselves.

Learn from your mistakes. Consider why something went wrong, analyze what you could have done—or avoided doing—to prevent it, and seek ways of preventing a similar outcome in the future.

Remember, success occurs because we want it to and because we've worked hard to make it happen. It can happen every day if we allow it to. And success is not just reaching an endpoint, such as when we're handed our diploma. Success is a process. Any achievement that brings us closer to fulfilling our goals and dreams is a success.

> "Far and away the best prize that life offers is the chance to work hard at work worth doing."
>
> **President Theodore Roosevelt**

"Actually, I'm hoping what I'm going to be when I grow up hasn't been invented yet."

Source: © Barbara Smaller/The New Yorker Collection/The Cartoon Bank

Speaking *of* Success

Source: Courtesy of Dr. Alexa Irene Canady

NAME: **Dr. Alexa Irene Canady**

SCHOOL: **Michigan State University; University of Michigan Medical School**

As a young girl growing up just outside of Lansing, Michigan, Alexa Canady showed signs of a strong intellect and curiosity, but never realized it until her grandmother, taking a course in psychological testing, gave her an exam.

"I became a guinea pig for testing conducted by her class. After I scored exceptionally well on an exam, my grandmother's professor asked for further testing," Canady said. "A week later, the professor called our house during dinner. My mom came back to the table looking puzzled. 'He wants to know if Alexa is in any special programs—he says her intelligence testing is off the charts.' She looked at my father. 'That's odd,' my father said. 'Her scores at school are just average.'"

Alexa and her brother were the only black kids in their elementary school during the 1950s; it came as little surprise to her when she later found out that her teacher had lied to the school about her test results, attributing them to a white girl in her class.

Through perseverance, determination, and hard work, she became a National Achievement Scholar in 1967 and enrolled in Michigan State University, planning to pursue a career in mathematics. But things changed.

"I had trouble because I didn't know what I wanted to do," Canady said, noting she no longer felt a passion for math. "I had a crisis of confidence, and had lost mathematics as a dream."

Uncertain at this point, she took a suggestion from her brother to apply for a minority medical scholarship at Michigan. The move ignited her true passion, medicine, that propelled her on to become the first African American female neurosurgeon in the United States.

But there were still challenges as Canady pursued medical school, confronting a world dominated by men.

"It quickly became apparent that we were in a man's world. Professors frequently overlooked the women's raised hands, and most of the prestigious clubs and societies were all-male," she noted. "The white women in my class were shocked and outraged that they weren't being taken seriously. It was the first time they had felt pushed aside. But I just put my head down and worked harder. I was used to being disregarded," she said.

Never one to let adversity block her path, Dr. Canady strongly believes that hard work can overcome the biggest obstacles.

"Challenge yourself with the hardest courses and material you can find," said said. "At a certain point in your schooling, everyone is smart and the one who does the best works the hardest."

Source: National Women's Law Center, *Faces of Title IX (2012).* Accessed online, 4-22-15, **http://www.nwlc.org/title-ix/alexa-canady**

[RETHINK]

- Dr. Canady faced a number of challenges in pursuing her medical career, but says that through hard work she was able to overcome them. Describe a challenge in your own life that was overcome through hard work.

- How do you think Dr. Canady's experience regarding being lied to about her test scores helped form her determination to succeed?

Looking **Back**

LO 6-1 Create a plan to prepare for the academic choices that college demands.

▶ Making course choices involves finding out as much as possible about what your college has to offer. Your college's listing and description of courses, usually found online, is the best initial source of this information.

▶ An important source of information and personal guidance in college is your college advisor, who has training and experience in advising students on courses, instructors, requirements, and regulations.

LO 6-2 Outline a strategy for choosing courses that ensures you are getting the most out of your studies.

▶ In choosing courses, check out your selections with your academic advisor and then register for the courses. You should be prepared to choose different courses or course sections if your initial selections are unavailable.

▶ Verify that you have received your chosen courses, that the schedule of courses makes sense, and that your course schedule will help provide the number of credits needed to graduate.

▶ Be prepared to deal with errors during registration or cope with the unavailability of courses that you need to take.

▶ Reflect on your college experience regularly, verifying that course choices, academic performance, personal growth, choice of major, and your overall educational experience are satisfactory.

▶ In service-learning courses, students engage in community service activities while receiving course credit.

LO 6-3 Explain the criteria for choosing your academic program.

▶ Choosing a major involves first accepting a period of indecision, finding out more about yourself, seeking the help and advice of others, considering going beyond the traditional structure of your college major, trying out unusual courses, and taking career plans into account.

[KEY TERMS AND CONCEPTS]

Academic program (or major) (p. 138)

College advisor (or college counselor) (p. 140)

Distance learning (p. 149)

Electives (p. 144)

Grade point average (GPA) (p. 138)

Prerequisites (p. 139)

Register (p. 144)

Registrar (p. 142)

Service learning (p. 150)

Transcript (p. 142)

[RESOURCES]

ON CAMPUS

The obvious choice for information about courses is your advisor. Sometimes your advisor will be associated with a general program, such as liberal arts; sometimes with a particular department, such as English or Sociology; or sometimes with a collegewide academic advising center. Your course instructors also can often give good advice about what future courses to sign up for. Finally, don't forget about your fellow students; they can be an excellent source of information about the most interesting and exciting courses. If you'd like advice about future careers, visit your college career center. Not only will it have pamphlets and books on different jobs, but the staff also can often provide tests that can help you see how your personal strengths fit with potential programs and careers.

IN PRINT

The *Guide to College Majors* published by the Princeton Review (2010) provides a good overview of college majors, as does *Book of Majors 2015* (College Board, 2014).

Probably the most popular guide to careers is *What Color Is Your Parachute? 2016* (Ten Speed Press, 2016). In it you'll find ways to make decisions about choosing (and changing) professions, as well as ways to obtain a job.

ON THE WEB

The following sites on the Internet provide the opportunity to extend your learning about the material in this chapter. (Although the web addresses were accurate at the time this material was published, check the *P.O.W.E.R. Learning* Connect or contact your instructor for any changes that may have occurred.)

▶ "Selecting College Courses" **(www.advising.wayne.edu/hndbk/courses.php),** a guide offered by the Advising Center at Wayne State University, provides a solid list of questions to ask yourself when choosing your courses.

▶ Rutgers University provides a four-step plan that can help you with choosing a major, as well a four-year action plan on using your major to pursue a career. **http://cc.camden.rutgers.edu/choosing_a_major**

▶ Major Resource Kits are listed at the University of Delaware's Career Services Center **(www.udel.edu/CSC/students/major_resource_kits.html).** Dozens of majors are listed, ranging from Apparel Design to Women's Studies. Each major has a sample of job titles, types of employers, and resources for finding employment. This is a great site for getting ideas for future careers.

The Case of . . .
Program Interference

Tim Xiao knew he was a disappointment to his family. He had taken a year off after high school, saying he "needed time to figure things out." This was not the path that his sister—or his cousins, for that matter—had taken.

Now—at last—he was easing his way into higher education, starting with a two-year college. He was trying to show that he respected his parents' wishes, but in fact he was no closer to "figuring things out" than he had been a year earlier.

One key entry on his college registration form remained blank: "Intended Academic Program." Tim could think of nothing to write down. The assistant registrar said, "Just write 'Undecided,'" which he figured was the official college word for "Clueless." In fact, he had no idea what courses to take or what program to sign up for. He had no idea what he wanted to do with his life. His parents and his sister offered suggestions, but that didn't help at all.

1. What do you think is Tim's main reason for going to college? Is it a good reason?

2. What would you suggest Tim should do to clarify his thinking about college?

3. What seems to be Tim's main problem in choosing courses and an academic program? How would you advise him to think about the choice of courses and a program?

4. How can Tim find out more about himself? Why is this important in choosing a course of study?

5. Do you think Tim is taking this decision too seriously or not seriously enough? What advice would you give him about the importance of the choice of an academic program at this point in his college career?

Technology and Information Competency

Kendra Tamblin's parents always said she spent half her life online, and that may have been an understatement. She had her own laptop long before her friends did, and she was quick to join Facebook, set up a Twitter account, and participate in every new social site that the web offered. She'd had her own blog for years; she even posted to it occasionally. And lately her smartphone was increasing her online time dramatically.

When she learned that most of her college courses would require extensive use of the web, Kendra was delighted. She already understood every technical concept each instructor laboriously explained, and she even helped the other students figure out how to use their computers to find and participate in discussion groups, receive and turn in assignments, and find the instructor's lecture notes and class outlines.

It came as a complete surprise, then, when Kendra found herself missing deadlines and falling behind on assignments. When she thought about it, she realized that she hadn't adapted her computer habits to her new life as a college student. She had continued chatting with friends, posting comments on Facebook, and visiting favorite websites. Unhappily, she accepted that she would now have to transform her technological gadgets from toys to tools, and herself from player to user of technology.

Looking Ahead

The technology that Kendra was using in college didn't even exist 15 years ago. Education is changing, just like every other aspect of society, as "virtual" resources—e-mail, the web, texting, and so forth—become more and more a part of how we live our lives. Today, businesspeople hold meetings and instructors teach courses without even being in the same room with their co-workers or students.

Technology is making a profound difference in how we are taught, the ways we study and carry out our work, and how we communicate with our loved ones. It is changing the way we can access the vast quantities of information published each year—tens of thousands of books, journals, and other print materials, and literally billions of web pages. But successfully wading through all that information requires significant new skills in information competency that weren't necessary in the past.

In this chapter we discuss how technological advances increase your opportunities to achieve success in college and on the job. We'll first consider the basic educational uses of technology. We'll also talk about distance learning, an approach to education that involves studying with an instructor who may be thousands of miles away. Finally, we'll consider how you can use technology to develop information competency—locating and using both the information traditionally held in print *and* information created for, and in, the virtual world of cyberspace. Information competency is an essential skill in our increasingly technology-driven classrooms and offices.

Journal Reflections

Could I Live without Technology?

1. What do you use technology for most? Texting? E-mail? Surfing the web? Tasks at work? Classwork?

2. How much time do you spend using technology? How does it affect your social relationships?

3. What technological device could you live without? What devices could you *not* live without?

4. How much and what kinds of technology would you like to have in your courses? Why?

» LO 7-1 You and Technology

It's a great tool that can help you achieve success in your classes. It can save you hours of time on your job, whether you work in a cubicle or a garage. At the same time, it can be extremely frustrating, annoying, and maddening. And sometimes instead of saving time, it can eat up hours of your time.

"It," of course, is technology. Today it's as much a necessity to use technology as it was for you to learn to write using pen and paper earlier in your schooling. No one facing the job market in the twenty-first century will want to leave college without a strong working knowledge of a variety of technologies and what they can do for you. (To explore your feelings about technology and computers, complete the **Journal Reflections**.)

And if using technology is as familiar to you as brushing your teeth in the morning, be patient with those who are less at ease with it. An increasing number of students can be called *digital natives*—those who have used technology virtually their entire lives—and their experiences lead them to be considerably more tech savvy.

In fact, a *digital divide* separates students who have considerable and easy access to computers and technology from students for whom access to computers is difficult. The digital divide is especially pronounced between older and less affluent students and younger, more affluent students.

Technology and Your Academic Life

Even if you don't feel particularly proficient with technology in general, it already plays a big role in your life. Computers run your car's engine, make your digital camera work, allow you to record tunes on your iPod, and make sure the bus you're waiting for is running on time.

Technology has revolutionized academic life as well. Here are some of the ways you may encounter technology in your classes:

▶ **Course websites.** Most college courses have a website associated with them. The website may reside in a nationally developed course management software system (such as Blackboard, Moodle, or eCollege) with which your college may have a licensing agreement. In other cases, colleges develop their own course management systems.

Whatever course management system is used, the website will probably contain basic information about the course, such as a copy of the syllabus. Or it may provide important emergency updates, such as class cancellations or changes in paper due dates.

In other classes, the website may be much more elaborate and play a central role in the class. For instance, class websites that require a username and password for access may contain exercises and quizzes to be completed (and scored) online. All your grades for the class may be stored on the website, accessible to you at any time of the day or night.

In some classes, you may electronically deposit papers and essays onto the class website. Later, your instructor can read them online, post comments on your submissions, and return them to you on the website. You may carry out group projects or hold virtual discussions on the website. You may even be required to take your major tests and final exams on the website.

▶ **Textbook companion websites.** Most textbooks have a website that is tied to the book. The website typically includes chapter summaries, interactive reviews, flash cards, and practice tests. These resources, which are usually described in the preface to most textbooks, can be extremely valuable study tools.

▶ **Podcasts.** In some classes, instructors produce an audio or a video recording, called a **podcast**, of lectures or other instructional material relevant to the class. You can either access podcasts on the web or download them to a mobile device (such as a tablet or smartphone) that permits you to listen to and view them outside of class whenever you want.

▶ **Blogs.** Some instructors maintain blogs of their own. A **blog** is a kind of web-based public diary in which a writer offers ideas, thoughts, short essays, and commentary. If your instructor has a blog and tells you to read it, get in the habit of checking it routinely. Not only will it contain information relevant to the course that you'll need to know, but also it may reveal personal insights that can help you know your instructor better.

▶ **Classroom presentation programs.** Many instructors use technology during class. For example, rather than using transparencies and overhead projectors, an increasing number of instructors present material electronically using PowerPoint slides or some other presentation program. Presentation programs help instructors create professional-looking slides that contain not only text, but also graphics such as photos, charts, maps, and animations.

podcast
An audio or video recording that can be accessed on the Internet and viewed on a computer or downloaded to a mobile device.

blog
A web-based public diary in which a writer provides commentary, ideas, thoughts, and short essays.

lecture capture technology

Technology in which instructors upload in-class lectures, slides, and videos to a website, which students can later access to review the material presented in class.

▶ **Lecture capture technology.** In classes with **lecture capture technology**, instructors upload an audio or video recording of everything they say and do in the classroom, along with a feed of the PowerPoint slides or other material that is being presented. If you're in a class with lecture capture, you'll receive a link to the material and can review any or all of it later.

Lecture capture offers several advantages. For one thing, if you miss a class, you'll be able to review exactly what you missed. When studying for a test, you can review material with which you may be having trouble. And because the lecture capture is indexed to words on the PowerPoint slides, you can review key concepts, skipping to the material that is most important or hardest for you to understand and learn.

One of the key advantages of lecture capture is that it frees you up in class to focus on the big picture when taking notes. It relieves you of the sense that you need to write down everything on the PowerPoint slides and every detail the instructor discusses. Instead, you can be more engaged in class.

It's important not to use the availability of lecture capture technology as an excuse not to attend class. The classroom experience can't be recreated later, and you'll miss the opportunity to ask questions and engage in class discussions and other in-class work.

If you are lucky, your instructor might later place the slides projected in class onto the class website, where they can be reviewed after class. Sometimes instructors even put the slides on websites before class. That gives you the chance to print them out and bring them to class, writing class notes on them. (For tips on making best use of instructors' presentation programs in class, see the **Course Connections** box.)

From the perspective of . . .

A STUDENT What technology do you find intimidating in the classroom? What steps can you take to overcome your anxiety?

Using the Web

The web has revolutionized communication. And we haven't seen anything yet: Visionaries say it won't be too long before our refrigerators will order milk when supplies are running low or our physicians will be able to constantly monitor our vital organs.

The **web** (or, as it was originally called, the *World Wide Web*) provides a graphical means of locating and accessing information on the Internet. Using the web has become the standard way to find and use such information. The web provides a way to transmit typewritten text, visual material, and auditory information—graphics, photos, music, sound bites, video clips, and much more.

Source: © Rubberball/Getty Images

web

A highly graphical interface between users and the Internet that permits users to transmit and receive not only text but also pictorial, video, and audio information.

Getting the Most Out of Instructors' PowerPoint Presentations

Traditional "chalk-and-talk" lectures are a thing of the past in many classes. Instead, increasing numbers of instructors are using presentation programs such as PowerPoint to project material in their classes.

This newer technology calls for fresh strategies for taking notes and absorbing the information. Here are some tips:

- **Listening is more important than seeing.** The information that your instructor projects on screen, while important, ultimately is less critical than what he or she is saying. Pay primary attention to the spoken word and secondary attention to the screen.

- **Don't copy everything that is on every slide.** Instructors can present far more information on their slides than on a blackboard. Often there is so much information that it's impossible to copy it all down. Don't even try. Instead, concentrate on taking down the key points.

- **Remember that key points on slides are . . . key points.** The key points (typically indicated by bullets) often relate to central concepts. Use these points to help organize your studying for tests, and don't be surprised if test questions directly assess the bulleted items on slides.

- **Check to see if the presentation slides are available online.** Some instructors make their class presentations available on the web to their students, either before or after class time. If they do this before class, print them out and bring them to class. Then you can make notes on your copy, clarifying important points. If they are not available until after a class is over, you can still make good use of them when it comes time to study the material for tests.

- **Remember that presentation slides are not the same as good notes for a class.** If you miss a class, don't assume that getting a copy of the slides is sufficient. Studying the notes of a classmate who is a good notetaker will be far more beneficial than studying only the slides.

The Internet provides the backbone of virtual communication. Among its most common uses are the following:

- **E-mail. E-mail**, short for "electronic mail," offers a way for people to send and receive messages with incredible speed. On most college campuses, e-mail is the most common form of communication between students and faculty.

- **Text messaging (or texting). Text messaging (texting)** permits you to send short messages from mobile phones to other phones or e-mail accounts. Messages are typically limited to 160 or fewer characters. Using text messaging, you can communicate with others in real time. You can also sign up to receive automatic text messages, such as information about breaking news events. Most student-to-student communication uses text messaging.

- **Video messaging. Video message services** such as Skype or FaceTime allow users to communicate using video, voice, and instant messaging over the web. Skype alone has almost 7 million users. Video messaging is generally free, and it can be used on desktop computers, laptops, and smartphones.

e-mail
Electronic mail, a system of communication that permits users to send and receive messages via the Internet.

text messaging (texting)
Short messages sent from mobile phones to other phones or e-mail accounts.

video message services
Web services that let users communicate using video, voice, and instant messaging.

Using E-Mail Effectively

Although e-mail (illustrated in **Figure 7.1**) has become a major means of written communication for many of us, you may be unaware of some of the basics of how it works. For example, every e-mail address contains three basic elements:

▶ **Mailbox name.** The mailbox name—the name assigned to your account on an e-mail system—is often some variant of your own name (e.g., conan_obrien), though it may also be totally fictitious (e.g., hepcat9).

▶ **@.** The "at" sign.

▶ **Domain name.** The domain name is the name of the organization that hosts the e-mail "post office" to which the user subscribes—often an institution (e.g., umass.edu or mcgraw-hill.com), an Internet service provider (e.g., aol.com or earthlink.net), or a multifaceted system such as yahoo.com or hotmail.com. *Host computers* are connected directly to the Internet. You can usually tell what kind of an organization hosts an e-mail account by the last part of the address (the *extension*): for example, *.edu* is an educational organization, *.com* is a commercial organization, *.org* is a nonprofit or charitable organization, *.mil* is the military, and *.gov* is a governmental organization (see **Table 7.1**).

Many e-mail providers (e.g., Gmail, Yahoo! Mail) have their own, unique e-mail systems on which e-mail can be retrieved anywhere you have access to the web. Others use particular software programs such as Microsoft's Outlook or Outlook Express to send and receive mail; you must have that software installed on your computer to retrieve your e-mail. Sometimes colleges have their own unique e-mail system that you can access through your college website.

figure 7.1 E-mail
E-mail sent via Google's Gmail.
Source: © IanDagnall Computing/Alamy

table 7.1 Domain Extensions

E-Mail Address	Extension	Type of Organization
jasper.johns@asu.edu	.EDU	Arizona State University—educational
dowd@nytimes.com	.COM	*The New York Times*—commercial
send.help@redcross.org	.ORG	American Red Cross—charitable or nonprofit
general@army.mil	.MIL	United States Army—military
head.counter@census.gov	.GOV	U.S. Census Bureau—government

Writing Effective E-Mail Messages

Although you may communicate frequently with your peers via texting, most instructors are reluctant to give out their phone numbers. This means that you will most likely communicate with instructors via e-mail. Even if you are an experienced e-mail user, you can do several things to improve the effectiveness of the messages you send. Among the most important to keep in mind when writing formal e-mail messages:

▶ **Use an informative subject line.** Don't say "IMPORTANT" or "meeting" or "question." None of those help recipients sort out your message from the dozens of others that may be clogging their inboxes. Instead, something like "Reminder: supervisor applications due 5:00 pm 10/11" is considerably more useful. In addition, *always* use a subject line: Some recipients routinely delete messages without a subject line, fearing they contain viruses.

▶ **Make sure the recipient knows who you are.** If you are writing someone you know only casually, jog their memory with a bit of information about yourself. If you don't know them at all, identify yourself early in the message ("I am a college student who is interested in an internship . . . ").

▶ **Keep messages short and focused.** E-mail messages are most effective when they are short and direct. If at all possible, keep your message short enough that it fits on one screen without scrolling down to see the rest. The reason is simple: Recipients sometimes don't read beyond the beginning of a message. If you do need to include a good deal of material, number each point or set them off by bullets so recipients will know to read down.

▶ **Always check spelling and grammar before sending an e-mail.**

▶ **Try to include only one major topic per e-mail.** It's often better to write separate e-mails rather than including a hodgepodge of unrelated points in an e-mail. This is especially true if you want a response to each of the different points.

▶ **Put requests near the beginning of the e-mail.** If you want the recipient to do something in response to your message, respectfully put the request at the very beginning of your message. Be explicit, while being polite.

▶ **Keep attachments to a minimum.** If possible, include all relevant information in the body of your e-mail, unless requested to do otherwise. Large attachments clog people's e-mail accounts and may be slow to download. In addition, recipients who don't know you personally may fear your attachment contains a virus and will not open it.

▶ **Avoid abbreviations and emoticons in formal e-mails.** When writing texts and e-mails to friends, abbreviations such as AFAIK ("as far as I know"), BTW ("by the way"), CYA ("see ya"), OIC ("oh, I see"), and WTG ("way to go") are fine. So are **emoticons** (or **smileys**), which signal the emotion that you are trying to convey. However, they should be avoided in a formal e-mail. Recipients may not be familiar with them, and they may make your e-mail seem overly casual.

▶ **Above all, always be respectful and courteous.** It always pays to be polite. In fact, as we discuss next, there are certain guiding principles that govern civility on the web that you should always keep in mind when writing e-mails.

Netiquette: Showing Civility on the Web

Although e-mail and text communication is usually less formal than a letter, it is essential to maintain civility and demonstrate good etiquette, which in the technology world is known as *netiquette*. Here are some rules:

▶ **Don't write anything in an e-mail or text message that you'll regret seeing on the front page of your local newspaper.** Yes, e-mail and texts are usually private; but the private message you write can easily be forwarded by the recipient to another person or even scores of other people. Worse yet, it's easy to hit "reply all" when you mean simply to "reply": In this case, you might think that you are responding to an individual, when in fact the e-mail will go to everyone who received the message, along with you.

▶ **Be careful of the tone you convey.** It is harder in e-mails and texts to express the same kind of personality, and often the same degree of subtlety, that our voice, our handwriting, or even our stationery can add to other forms of communication. This means that attempts at humor and especially sarcasm can backfire.

If you're using humor, consider adding an emoticon to clarify the intent of your message if you are writing to someone you know well. Avoid emoticons in e-mails to people you don't know well. Better to err on the side of formality.

▶ **Never write anything in an e-mail or text message that you wouldn't say in person.** If you wouldn't say something in a face-to-face conversation, don't say it electronically.

▶ **Don't use all capital letters.** Using all caps MAKES IT LOOK AS IF YOU'RE SHOUTING.

▶ **Never send an e-mail or text message when you are angry.** No matter how annoyed you are about something someone has written in a message, don't respond in kind—or at least wait until you've cooled down. Take a deep breath, and wait for your anger to pass.

▶ **Be especially polite and professional when writing to instructors and on-the-job supervisors.** Instructors often get dozens, and sometimes hundreds, of e-mails and texts from students each week, and they are especially sensitive to messages that are inappropriate. Follow these guidelines to be sure your e-mail messages will receive maximum attention:

- Always use the subject line in e-mail messages, identifying the class you are in and describing the general topic of the e-mail (e.g., "Psych 100, Lec 3, exam query").

- Address instructors politely (as in "Dear Professor xx," as opposed to, say, "Yo, Prof!" or "Hey!"). Unless your instructor has specifically told you otherwise, never use his or her first name.

- Avoid the high-priority flag.

- Be concise. Make your point quickly, and try not to write more than a few paragraphs. Make one point per e-mail.

- Avoid emoticons, nonstandard abbreviations, and slang; you're writing an instructor, not a friend.

- Don't tell your instructor that you need to hear from him or her immediately. It's fine to convey that your concerns are urgent, but don't make demands. If there is a deadline involved—for instance, if you are facing a registration deadline—respectfully ask for a response before that date.

- At the end of every message, thank the instructor and be sure to sign your complete name.

- Finally, proofread what you've written and make sure your spell-check tool is on.

To consider e-mail and text message netiquette more closely, complete **Try It! 1**.

In-Person Netiquette: Using Technology Appropriately

In many situations, there are standards for appropriate use of technology. An instructor does not want you to answer a cell phone call while he or she is speaking; neither does your boss.

Follow these guidelines to ensure you don't offend anyone with how you use technology:

▶ **Turn off your cell phone in formal settings.** If you're in a meeting or a class, keep your cell phone off (or set on "vibrate" mode). Cell phones ringing at random times are distracting and annoying.

▶ **Don't send text messages or make calls while someone else is speaking.** It's obvious that you should be paying attention to what co-workers, classmates, or instructors are saying, rather than to what's going on in the rest of the world.

▶ **If you use your laptop to take notes, stay on task.** No matter how tempting it is to check your e-mail messages, text with a friend, check Facebook, or surf the web, avoid the temptation. Use your laptop to take notes, and nothing else.

▶ **Never use your cell phone to text answers to problems in class.** Cheating is cheating, whether done using high-tech or low-tech methods. Don't do it.

Protecting Yourself: Spam, Cybersecurity, and Online Safety

The downside of e-mail is *spam*—the virtual equivalent of junk mail. Spam may range from get-rich-quick schemes to advertisements for body enhancements or

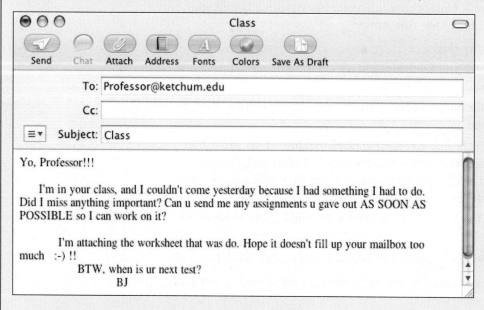
Using E-Mail Netiquette

Read the e-mail below, written by a student to his instructor, and respond to the questions that follow.

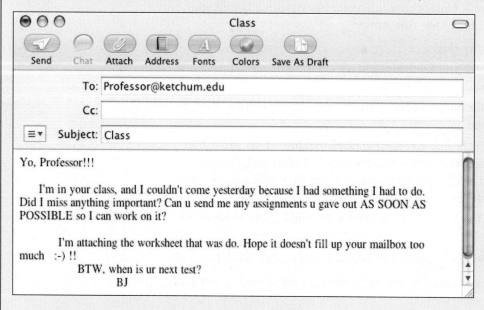

```
●●●                          Class
Send    Chat   Attach  Address  Fonts  Colors  Save As Draft

       To:  Professor@ketchum.edu
       Cc:
≡▾  Subject:  Class

Yo, Professor!!!

    I'm in your class, and I couldn't come yesterday because I had something I had to do.
Did I miss anything important? Can u send me any assignments u gave out AS SOON AS
POSSIBLE so I can work on it?

    I'm attaching the worksheet that was do. Hope it doesn't fill up your mailbox too
much  :-) !!
            BTW, when is ur next test?
            BJ
```

1. What rules of "netiquette" does the e-mail violate?

2. If you were the instructor to whom the e-mail message was sent, how do you think you would react to receiving it? What questions would you have about the message?

3. Based on the e-mail, what opinion might you have of the student who wrote it?

4. Rewrite the e-mail so that it is consistent with good netiquette.

pornography. Spam is more than a nuisance; it takes up valuable transmission resources ("bandwidth"), disk space, and computer time.

Some e-mail systems apply a filter that uses a few simple rules to separate e-mail you actually want to read from spam. Unfortunately, these systems are not perfect: They sometimes let junk through and can even at times dispose of messages you want. The only absolutely reliable way to deal with spam is to delete it yourself as quickly as possible.

Spam filters are one aspect of broader efforts to maintain security on computers. **Cybersecurity** refers to measures taken to protect computers and computer systems against unauthorized access or attack. Every computer connected to the web is subject to multiple attacks from *hackers,* criminals (and sometimes foreign governments) who illegally attempt to gain access to and tamper with information on your computer. In fact, the average computer connected to the web is attacked by hackers every 39 seconds, 24 hours a day.

cybersecurity

Measures taken to protect computers and computer systems against unauthorized access or attack.

Here are a few tips for dealing with spam:

▶ Consider using two e-mail addresses—one for personal messages and one for college and professional messages.

▶ When you choose a password, make it long (8 or more characters) and complex (include letters, numbers, punctuation, and symbols).

▶ Don't use the same password on every program.

▶ *Never* give anyone your password, and change your password frequently.

▶ Install anti-virus programs on your personal computer. It is essential to protect yourself from hackers by installing an anti-virus program such as McAfee or Norton Security.

▶ *Never* respond to e-mails that ask for personal or financial information, even if they appear to be legitimate. Such requests may originate in *crimeware*— programs that steal personal financial information. For instance, in a practice called *phishing,* spam or pop-up messages are used to trick you into disclosing bank account or credit card numbers, passwords, or other personal information.

  In a phishing scam, the e-mail appears to be from a legitimate source and asks you to update or validate information by providing account information. In reality, such messages are from con artists seeking to steal your identity. E-mails that contain promises of riches for little effort, offer deals that seem too good to be true, or threaten that accounts will be closed unless you provide information immediately are likely to be bogus.

▶ *Do not click* on any links in the e-mail message until you're sure it's real. Not only can such links lead to the disclosure of personal information about you, but they may lead to the secret installation of software that can spy on you.

▶ *Never* open an attachment from someone you don't know. Computer viruses, which can ruin everything on your hard drive, are often spread through e-mail attachments.

▶ Finally, if your e-mail program has a spam filter, periodically check your spam folder to make sure no legitimate e-mails may have been directed there by mistake.

Keeping Safe

There's an even darker side to the web than financial criminals looking to steal from you. Specifically, you need to be wary of sexual predators who use the web to identify potential victims. To help protect yourself, use these guidelines:

1. Don't give out personal information to strangers, such as your name, phone number, address, hometown, or future schedule—anything that can be used to identify you.

2. Never send photos of yourself or friends or family to someone you don't know.

3. Don't reply to e-mails that are offensive, weird, or distressing in any way.

4. If you plan to meet someone you've known only from the web, for example, from a dating site, be cautious. Meet them in a visible, public location. Even then, meet someone only in a visible, public location in which many people will be present. *Don't* have someone you don't know pick you up at your home. Tell a friend or family member whom you are meeting and where you are going, and stay sober.

5. If you do have problems with someone over e-mail, immediately contact your college or local police.

Social Networking Websites

Most college students use social networking websites such as Facebook.com or Twitter to stay in touch with their friends, acquaintances, and even total strangers. The number of users is huge: Facebook has more than 845 million active users and Twitter 140 million.

Facebook provides users with the ability to post information to friends who have access to their online profiles. Users can post updates and photos, exchange messages, list their personal interests, and share other information. Because it can be accessed on any computer or mobile device connected to the web, Facebook allows users to stay in constant touch with others.

Twitter allows users to send and receive short messages of up to 140 characters, called *tweets*. People can send short updates about what they are doing, offer opinions about events, or tell people where they are at a given moment. The tweets are sent to followers who have signed up to receive a person's tweets.

Although social networking websites offer many possibilities for interacting with friends, making new acquaintances, and sharing information, they need to be used appropriately. Remember that *what's posted on the web stays on the web*—potentially forever. Even if you delete information from a social networking site, it may still reside on someone else's computer.

Consequently, don't post information about yourself or photos that you wouldn't want your instructors, parents, or future employers seeing. For instance, faculty at colleges can—and sometimes do—read students' postings.

Furthermore, employers increasingly are using information posted on social networking sites in their hiring decisions. You might also want to consider maintaining two social media accounts: one for public consumption (that employers may read) and a personal account for close friends and family.

In short, be thoughtful of what you post about yourself. And be sure the privacy settings on your social network accounts are set in a way that protects your privacy.

At the same time, be an informed consumer of material you encounter on social networking websites. Some of the profiles contain bogus material or are entirely false. Individuals sometimes disguise their identities or make up false ones. It's important to verify whom you are communicating with before exchanging personal information.

» LO 7-2 Distance Learning: Classes without Walls

Do you find that your schedule changes so much from one day to the next that it's hard to fit in a course that meets at a regularly scheduled time? Interested in an unusual course topic that your own college doesn't offer? Want to take a class during the summer, but you live too far from your college's campus?

The solution to your problem may be to enroll in a **distance learning** course. Distance learning is a form of education in which students participate via the web or other kinds of technology. Although most distance learning courses are taught via the web, some use teleconferencing, fax, and/or express mail.

The key feature of distance learning courses is the nature of interaction between instructor and students. Rather than meeting in a traditional classroom, where the instructor, you, and the other students are physically present, distance learning classes are most often virtual.

Although some schools use "webcasts" of lectures with virtual discussion rooms or employ lectures on videotape or CDs, most students in distance learning courses will never sit through a lecture or even participate in a real-time conversation with students in the class. They may never even know what their instructor or classmates look like or hear their voices.

Most distance learning courses involve multiple students and an instructor assigned to the course. If you are taking a distance learning course, you may read lecture notes posted on the web, search and browse websites, write papers, and post replies, along with other students, to discussion topics posted by your instructor on a *message board.* You will see your instructor's and classmates' responses through comments they post on the web. You may be expected to read a textbook entirely on your own, and you may take online quizzes and exams.

You may already be familiar with the kinds of technologies used in distance learning courses, because many traditional, face-to-face courses already contain elements of distance learning. In **blended (or hybrid) courses**, instruction is a combination of the traditional face-to-face classroom interaction and a significant amount of online learning. Students in blended courses generally spend more time working alone or in collaboration with others online. They also may collaborate with fellow students outside of class on the web.

In contrast to blended courses, *all* instruction takes place online in distance learning classes that are fully online. If you take a distance learning class that is fully online, you will probably never meet your instructor and fellow students in person. However, you will get to know them through virtual interactions online.

On the other hand, in *self-paced distance learning courses,* students move ahead at their own pace. There is no "live" instructor or other students with whom to interact; all instruction occurs in pre-recorded formats. Grading is entirely computer-scored. Because your progress is entirely self-paced, you need to manage your time carefully. It's a lot easier to stay caught up on assignments than to try to catch up on them.

Distance learning is not for everyone. Whether you're a good candidate for it or not depends on your preferred style of course taking. Complete **Try It! 2** to see whether you are suited to learn at a distance.

Distance learning classes have both advantages and disadvantages. On the plus side, distance learning courses offer the following:

▶ **You can take a web-based distance learning course anywhere that you have access to the web.** You can be at home, at the office, or on vacation on the beach and still participate.

▶ **Distance learning classes are often more flexible than traditional classes.** You can participate in a course any time of the day or night, and you typically don't have to be in class at a specific time. This is particularly helpful for those with time-consuming family obligations such as child care.

▶ **Distance learning classes are often self-paced.** You may be able to spread out your work over the week, or you may fit the work into a single day.

distance learning
The teaching of courses at another institution, with student participation via video technology or the web.

blended (hybrid) courses
Courses in which instruction is a combination of traditional, face-to-face, and online methods.

Assess Your Course-Taking Style

Your preferred course-taking style—how you participate in classes, work with your classmates, interact with your teachers, and complete your assignments—may make you more or less suitable for distance learning. Read the following statements and indicate whether you agree or disagree with them to see if you have what it takes to be a distance learner:

	Agree	Disagree
1. I need the stimulation of other students, both inside and outside of class, to learn well.		
2. I need to see my teacher's face, expressions, and body language to interpret what is being said.		
3. I place a high value on class discussions.		
4. I prefer to hear information presented orally rather than reading it in a book or article.		
5. I'm not very comfortable asking for help when I don't understand something.		
6. I'm easily distracted, especially when reading.		
7. I'm not very well organized.		
8. I'm not very good at keeping track of time, pacing myself over long assignments, and holding to schedules.		
9. I'm not very good at writing.		
10. I'm not very patient.		

The more you disagree with these statements, the more your course-taking style is suited to distance learning. Interpret your style according to this informal scale:

Disagreed with 8–10 statements = Excellent candidate for distance learning.

Disagreed with 6–7 statements = Good candidate for distance learning.

Agreed with 5–7 statements = Probably better taking classes on campus.

Agreed with 8–10 statements = Avoid distance learning.

► **You may have more contact with your instructor than you do with a traditional class.** Even though you may not have face-to-face contact, you may have greater access to your instructor, via e-mail and the web, than in traditional classes. You can leave messages for your instructor at any time of the night or day; most instructors of distance learning classes respond in a timely manner.

- **Shy students may find it easier to "speak up" in a distance learning class.** You can think through your responses to make sure you are communicating just what you wish to say. You don't have to worry about speaking in front of other people. For many people, distance learning is liberating.

- **You can become a better writer.** Because distance learning usually involves more writing than traditional courses, you receive more practice writing—and more feedback for it—than in traditional classes.

On the other hand, distance learning has disadvantages that you should keep in mind:

- **You are a prisoner of technology.** If you lose access to a computer and the web, you won't be able to participate in the class until the problem is fixed.

- **You won't have direct, face-to-face contact with your instructor or other students.** Distance learning can be isolating, and students sometimes feel alone and lost in cyberspace.

- **You won't get immediate feedback.** In a distance learning class, it may be hours, or sometimes days, before you receive feedback on what you have posted to a message board, depending on how well the pace of other students matches your own.

- **Distance learning classes require significant discipline, personal responsibility, and time management skills.** You won't have a set time to attend class as you do in traditional courses. Instead, you must carve out the time yourself. Although instructors provide a schedule of when things are due, you have to work out the timing of getting them done.

Consequently many students believe that distance learning courses are more difficult than traditional classes. You must be focused and committed to keeping up with the course. You need to be prepared to work hard on your own for a substantial number of hours each week.

Despite these potential challenges to distance learning courses, they are becoming increasingly popular. More and more colleges are offering them. Many companies encourage employees with crowded schedules to take distance learning as a way of providing continuing education.

If you are considering taking a distance learning course, follow these steps, which are summarized in the P.O.W.E.R. Plan here.

 ## Identifying Distance Learning Course Possibilities

How do you find a distance learning course? In some cases, your own college may offer courses on the web and list them in your course catalog. In other cases, you'll have to find courses on your own.

The best place to look is on the web itself. By searching the web, you can find distance learning courses ranging from automotive engineering to zoology. Don't be deterred by the physical location of the institution that offers the course. It doesn't matter where the college is located because for most distance learning classes, you'll never have to go to the campus itself.

But before you sign up for a potential course that you would like to count toward your degree, *make sure that your own college will give you credit for it.* Check with your advisor and registrar's office to be certain.

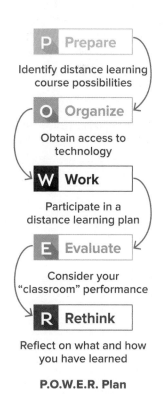

P Prepare

Identify distance learning course possibilities

O Organize

Obtain access to technology

W Work

Participate in a distance learning plan

E Evaluate

Consider your "classroom" performance

R Rethink

Reflect on what and how you have learned

P.O.W.E.R. Plan

Get Some Distance on the Problem

Working by yourself initially, see if you can find distance learning courses of interest to you. Start by checking your school's listing of courses to see what might be offered there. If you're already comfortable online, you might also try the following:

- *The Chronicle of Higher Education*'s Distance Education: Daily Updates (**chronicle.com**).
- Harvard Extension School's Distance Learning website offers a number of links and information on pursuing courses at Harvard (**www.extension.harvard.edu/distance-education**).

Try to find five courses you would be interested in and list them below. After you have completed your list, share your list with others in a group.

1. How diverse were the courses you were able to find?

2. Were particular subject areas better represented than others?

3. Why do you think this might be?

You should also find out what the requirements of a course are before you actually sign up for it. Check the syllabus carefully and see how it meshes with your schedule. If it is a summer course and you are going to be away from your computer for a week, you may not be able to make up the work you miss.

Finally, try to talk with someone who has taken the course before. Was the instructor responsive, providing feedback rapidly? If necessary, could you speak with the instructor by phone or via video technology such as Skype? Was the course load reasonable? (**Try It! 3** will help you work through the process.)

 ## Obtaining Access to Technology

Although you don't need to be a computer expert, you will need some minimal e-mail and web skills to take a distance learning course. If you don't have sufficient technological expertise, strengthen your computer skills by taking a computer course or workshop *before* you actually sign up for the distance learning course.

You'll also need access to a computer connected to the Internet. It doesn't have to be your own computer, but you will certainly need regular and convenient access to one. Make sure that the computer you plan to use has sufficient internal resources to quickly connect to the Internet; a very slow connection is frustrating.

Be sure to make all your arrangements for computer access before the start of a course. It can take several weeks to set up Internet service on a home computer if you don't have it already.

In addition, you should familiarize yourself with the course Learning Management System (LMS) before the course starts. The **Learning Management System (LMS)** is the software that delivers the distance learning course to your computer. It typically provides the course content such as online lectures or material to read, as well as a course syllabus, calendar, tests, and a way to track your grades.

The most common LMS's are Blackboard, Canvas, Moodle, Desire2Learn, and Angel. In some cases, a college will brand its LMS with its own name.

Although all LMS's are designed to work well with a variety of browsers, there are certain browsers that may work better with them than others. The common browsers are Mozilla Firefox, Google Chrome, and Safari. Be sure to use the browser that is recommended to be best for the LMS you will be using.

Participating in a Distance Learning Class

Successfully participating in a distance learning course involves several skills that are distinct from those needed for traditional classes. To get the most out of a distance learning course, you'll need to do the following:

- ▶ **Manage your time carefully.** You won't have the luxury of a regular schedule of class lectures, so you'll have to manage your time carefully. No one is going to remind you that you need to sit down at a computer and work. You will need every bit of self-discipline to succeed in a distance learning course.

- ▶ **Check in frequently.** Instructors may make crucial changes in the course requirements. Make sure to check for any changes in due dates or class expectations.

- ▶ **Find a cyberbuddy.** At the start of the semester, try to make personal contact with at least one other student in the class. You can do this by e-mailing, phoning, or actually meeting the student if he or she is geographically nearby. You can share study strategies, form a study group, and share notes. Connecting with another student can help you avoid feelings of isolation that may interfere with your success.

- ▶ **Make copies of everything.** Don't assume everything will go well in cyberspace. Make a printed copy of everything you submit, or alternatively have a backup stored on another computer.

- ▶ **Have a technology backup plan.** Computers may crash, your connection to the Internet may go down, or an e-mailed assignment may be mysteriously delayed or sent back to you. Don't wait until the last minute to work on and submit assignments, and have a plan in place if your primary computer is unavailable.

You might consider using a cloud storage system such as Dropbox or Google Drive. Even if your own computer crashes, you'll be able to access your computer files from any computer.

Considering Your "Classroom" Performance

As with any class, you'll be receiving feedback from your instructor. But unlike many courses, in which almost all the feedback comes from the instructor, much of the feedback in a distance learning course may come from your fellow students. Consider what you can learn from their comments, while keeping in mind that they are, like you, students themselves.

At the same time you'll be receiving feedback, you will likely be providing feedback to your classmates. Consider the nature of feedback you provide, and be sure that you use the basic principles of classroom civility. The following are some principles to keep in mind as you provide feedback to your classmates.

1. Think of the recipient of your feedback as a fellow student who will be as sensitive to a negative tone as you are.

2. Be constructive. Suggest specific ways in which the other student's work could be made better. Make it clear that you are trying to help improve the student's work.

3. Frame your criticism in a positive context, indicating that your comments are focused on one particular aspect of the student's work, not the entire work. For example, "I found your ideas on question 4 very perceptive. I think that the point you were making in the second sentence would be clearer if you gave a concrete example."

4. Don't get personal ("You really need to take a course in English grammar!"). Never criticize the student; simply provide feedback on the student's work.

5. Criticize a fact, statement, opinion, or act that you can point to, rather than communicating a vague feeling or a general sense of unease or displeasure.

6. State what you have observed; don't interpret it. ("In your discussion of Freud, I believe you meant 'superego' when you wrote 'ego.'" Not "Your misuse of Freud's terminology indicates a fundamental misunderstanding of Freudian psychology.")

7. Always make it clear that you are expressing your personal opinion. Use phrases like "The way I see it . . . ," "In my view . . . ," and "I believe that. . . ."

R Rethink | Reflecting on What and How You Have Learned

Distance learning is not for everyone. If your preferred learning style involves extensive, face-to-face interaction with others, you may find that your experience is less than satisfying. On the other hand, if you are at ease with computers and enjoy working on your own, you may find distance learning highly effective.

As you reflect on your distance learning experience, go beyond the technology and think about what, and how much, you have learned. Ask yourself whether you learned as much as you would have in a traditional class.

Most educational experts believe that distance learning will play an increasingly important role in higher education. Furthermore, because it offers an efficient way of educating people in far-flung locales, it is a natural means of promoting lifelong learning experiences. In short, the first distance learning class you take is likely not to be your last.

Also think about how your distance learning experience could have been more effective for you. And think about whether you were so absorbed by the technology that you lost sight of the real goal of the course: learning new material.

Fact Finding: Developing Information Competency

One of the greatest advances brought about by technology involves the area of research. More than ever, people require **information competency**, the ability to determine what information is necessary, and then to locate, evaluate, and effectively use that information. The sheer abundance of material available today makes information competency a critical skill.

We'll consider the ways in which you can use the two primary storehouses of information available today to boost your own level of information competency. One you can walk or drive to—the library. The other—the web—doesn't have a physical location. Both are indispensable in anyone's quest for information.

Libraries

No matter how imposing or humble their physical appearance, whether they contain only a few hundred volumes or hundreds of thousands of them, libraries are a good place to focus your efforts as you seek out and gather information. Although every library is different, all share two key elements: the material they hold—their basic collections—and tools to help you locate the material you need.

What Can Be Found in a Library's Basic Collection?

Libraries obviously contain books, but they typically have a lot more than that, including some or all of the following:

▶ **Periodicals.** *Periodicals* include specialized journals for professionals in a field, magazines, and newspapers. Many periodicals can now be found online.

▶ **Indexes and online databases.** An index provides a listing of periodical articles by title, author, and subject. Some indexes also provide a short summary, or *abstract*, of the contents of each article.

Most indexes come in electronic form known as an **online database**, an organized body of information on related topics. For example, the National Center for Biotechnology Information (NCBI) maintains *Medline,* an online public database that provides information on medical research. The advantage of online databases over traditional, print-based indexes is that the database sometimes provides the full text of material it identifies in a search.

▶ **Encyclopedias.** Some encyclopedias, such as the *Encyclopaedia Britannica* or *World Book Encyclopedia,* attempt to cover the entire range of knowledge, and they may take up many volumes. Others are more specialized, covering only a particular field, such as the *Encyclopedia of Human Behavior* or the *Encyclopedia of Religion.* Most are available online, although some are still printed as multivolume sets of books. Encyclopedias provide a good general view of a topic, but they lack depth. Use them at the earliest stage of your information hunt for an overview of key issues, and move from there to more specific and current sources.

> "Knowledge is of two kinds: we know a subject ourselves, or we know where we can find information upon it."
>
> **Samuel Johnson**

- ► **Government documents.** Census records, laws, and tax codes are some of the millions of government documents that are stored in libraries.

- ► **Musical scores.** The music to *Rent,* the Brahms *Alto Rhapsody,* and the Beatles' greatest hits are among the types of musical scores you can find in libraries.

- ► **Reserve collections.** Reserve collections hold items that instructors assign for a class. Although they are typically found, and accessed, online, sometimes they are in the form of material that may be physically removed from the library for a limited period of time. Reserve collections may contain not only books and articles, but also videos, CDs, laptops, and multimedia equipment.

Locating Information in a Library

The place to begin searching for information in a library is the library catalog. Catalogs list all materials that are held in the library and provide their location. Most library catalogs are computerized, though a few still use name cards filed in drawers or microform (microfiche or microfilm). You are usually able to access computerized catalogs from home or residence hall rooms as well as from computers housed in the library itself.

Library catalogs traditionally allow searches by title, author name, and subject; electronic catalogs also typically allow searching by keyword. Individual catalog entries generally include additional information about the material, such as the publisher, date of publication, number of pages, and similar information.

Say, for example, you're writing a paper about Ernest Hemingway. To find books he *wrote* in an electronic catalog, you would enter his name in the "author" field. You may be presented with the listing shown in **Figure 7.2**.

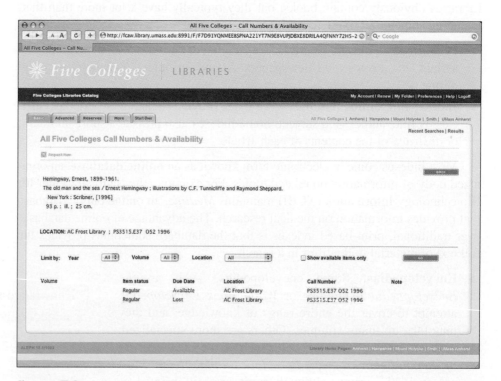

figure 7.2
Online Catalog Entry
Online catalog entry for a book called *The Old Man and the Sea.* Note especially the call number and due date: These will tell you where the book is to be found and whether it is on the shelves or is checked out.

Of course, you could also search for "Hemingway" as the subject, which would yield a list of books *about* him and his work; if you entered his name in a "keyword" search, the catalog would return a more comprehensive list of books both by *and* about him.

The key piece of information in a catalog entry is the book's **call number**, a code that tells you exactly where to find it. Most college libraries use the Library of Congress classification system, which assigns to each book a unique combination of letters and numbers.

Because the record illustrated in **Figure 7.2** is from an electronic search, it contains further helpful information. The word "Available" under "Due Date" tells you that one copy of the book has not been checked out by another patron and should be sitting on the shelf. You'll need to familiarize yourself with your library's particular system to know precisely how you can make most efficient use of the catalog. Chances are there's a handout or a posted set of instructions nearby.

Once you have identified the material you need and where it is located, you'll need to go find it. In all but the biggest libraries, you can simply go into the **stacks**, the place containing shelves where the books and other materials are kept, and—using the call number—hunt for it. In libraries with closed stacks, you must fill out a form with the call numbers of the books you want. A library aide will find the material and deliver it to a central location.

What if you go to the location in the stacks where the material is supposed to be and you can't find it? The material may be checked out, in use by someone else at that time, incorrectly shelved, or simply lost. Whatever the reason, *don't give up*. If the material is checked out to another user, ask a librarian if you can **recall** the material—a process by which the library contacts the person who has the book and asks him or her to return it.

If the librarian informs you that the material is not checked out, wait a few days and see if it appears on the shelf. Someone may have been using it while you were looking for it. If it was misshelved, the librarian may be able to find it. If the material is truly lost, you may be able to get it from another library through **interlibrary loan**, a system by which libraries share resources.

Finally, even if you do find exactly what you were looking for, take a moment to scan the shelves. Because books and other materials are generally grouped by topic, you may find other useful titles in the same place. One of the pleasures of libraries is the possibility of finding an unexpected treasure—material that your catalog search did not initially identify but that may provide you with exactly what you need.

Finding Information on the Web

The web is vast—sometimes frustratingly so. In fact, no one knows how much material exists on the web. Not only is more information added to the web every day, but the information also resides on thousands of individual computers.

Searching for materials in the library stacks can be frustrating if they are not on the shelves. However, you may unexpectedly find relevant and interesting material while browsing.
Source: © S. Olsson/PhotoAlto

Anyone with minimal web savvy and access to a *server* (a computer with a permanent Internet connection) can set up a personal website.

The fact that anyone can put information on the web is both the biggest asset and the greatest disadvantage of using the web as an information source. Because minimal computer skill is the only expertise a person needs to set up a web page, as much misinformation may be on the website as there is information. Consequently, keep the usual consumer rule in mind: Buyer beware. Unless a website has been established and is maintained by a reliable organization, the information it contains may not be accurate.

A number of key factors are involved in each web search. They include a browser, web pages, links, and search engines.

browser

A program that provides a way of navigating around the information on the web.

▶ **Browsers.** To use the web, your computer has to have a browser. A **browser**, as its name implies, is a program that provides a way of looking at the information on the web. Among the major browsers are Microsoft's Internet Explorer, Google Chrome, and Firefox's Mozilla.

Using a browser is a bit like taking a taxi: once you get in, you get where you want to go by providing an address. The address, also known as a URL (Uniform Resource Locator), identifies a unique location on the web, a *website* or a *web page* (one of the parts of a site).

From the perspective of . . .

A LAW ENFORCEMENT PROFESSIONAL Technology is changing the approach to many long-established career fields. What technology changes could potentially impact your chosen profession?

Web addresses are combinations of letters and symbols. They typically start off with "www.[domain_name].[xxx]"—the address of the hosting website (e.g., **www.iastate.edu** is the home page for Iowa State University). If you're looking for a subsite or a particular page on the site, the address becomes increasingly specific: **www.iastate.edu/visitors/**

Source: © RubberBall Productions

will take you to a "visitors" site—a collection of pages—hosted by **iastate.edu**. A *page* on that site—for example, **http://www.museums.iastate.edu/BAM.html**, which connects you with the Iowa State Museums—ends with a specific name, usually followed by ".htm," ".html," or ".shtml." Because most addresses begin with "http://," this part of the address is sometimes dropped in references to a site.

You can often get a decent idea of what kind of site you're going to by taking a careful look at the web address: you can tell that **www.mhhe.com/power**, for example, is a site that has something to do with "power" and is hosted by a commercial entity (which you might or might not recognize as McGraw-Hill Higher Education). (Hmm, might be worth checking out . . . .)

web page

A location (or site) on the web housing information from a single source and (typically) links to other pages.

▶ **Web pages.** Web pages are the heart of the web. A **web page** is a document that presents you with information. The information may appear as text on the screen, to be read like a book (or more accurately, like an ancient scroll). It might include a video clip, an audio clip, a photo, a portrait, a graph, or a figure. It might offer a news service photo of the president of the United States or a backyard snapshot of someone's family reunion.

▶ **Links.** Websites typically provide you with **links**— embedded addresses to other sites or documents that, at a click, cause your browser automatically to "jump" there. Just as an encyclopedia article on forests might say at the end, "See also Trees," web pages often refer to other sites on the web—only it's easier than with a book. You just have to click on the link with your mouse and—*poof!*—you're there.

▶ **Search engines.** A **search engine** is simply a computerized index to information on the web. When you know what information you want to find but don't have an address for it, a search engine can often steer you toward relevant sites.

"Go ask your search engine."

The various parts of the web are similar to the components of traditional libraries, as illustrated in **Figure 7.3**. A web browser is equivalent to a library card; it gives you access to vast quantities of material. Websites are like the books of a library; web pages are the book pages, where the content resides. Links are analogous to "see also" portions of books that suggest related information. And search engines are like a library's card catalog, directing you to specific locations.

link
A means of "jumping" automatically from one web page to another.

search engine
A computerized index to information on the web.

figure 7.3
Comparison of Library and Web
The various parts of the web are similar to the components of a traditional library.

Traditional Library | **Web**

Library card ⟷ Web browser

Book ⟷ Website

"See Also" pages ⟷ Web links

http://www.nbcnews.com
http://www.whitehouse.gov
http://www.umass.edu
http://www.ama-assn.org

Library catalog ⟷ Search engine

Locating Information on the Web

There is no central catalog of the contents of the web; instead, there are a number of different search engines. Furthermore, depending on the search engine you use and the type of search you do, you'll identify different information.

Search engines themselves are located on the web, so you have to know their addresses. After you reach the "home" address of a search engine, you enter your search terms. The search engine then provides a list of websites that may contain information relevant to your search.

Although most people are familiar with the most popular search engine, Google, there are actually many search engines. Others include (in order of popularity) Bing, Yahoo, Ask, AOL, Wow, and WebCrawler. Although they all are useful for searches on the Web, they do so using somewhat different strategies.

Some search engines, such as Yahoo!, specialize in organizing information by subject, making it easy to search for information on, say, different dog breeds, the Islamic religion, or car repair. Using Yahoo! for its subject directories is like searching for information using the subject entries in a library catalog.

Other search engines, such as Google, catalog many more pages than Yahoo! but don't group them by subject. Due to the breadth of their coverage, they might be more useful when you are looking for obscure pieces of information or for numerous sources for different perspectives on a topic. Using Google or AltaVista is like performing a keyword search in a library catalog.

Finally, a third type of search engine is exemplified by Ask.com. Known as metasearch tools, these sites send your search commands to other search engines, compiling the results into a single, unified list.

There's no single search engine that works best. Most people develop their own preferences based on their experience. The best advice: Try out several of them and see which works best for you. To get started, work through **Try It! 4**, "Work the Web: Information, Please!"

Becoming a Savvy Surfer

The process you use to search the web couldn't be easier—or more difficult. The vast amounts of material online and the relative ease of navigation afforded by the web make finding information quite simple; what is hard is finding appropriate information.

Consider a search in which you enter the question, "How do I use the web?" into the home page of Google. That search will identify over 3.5 *billion* websites related to the topic.

Using the list of sites generated by the search is simple. With your computer mouse, click on the site address of the relevant document, and the home page of the site will (eventually) appear on your computer screen. You can then take notes on the material in the same way you'd take notes on material in a book.

Many of the billions of sites Google returns, however, may be of little use. It's easy in such a search to end up in a virtual dead end, in which the information you have found is only minimally related to the topic you're researching. If you do find yourself at a site that's of no use to you, simply hit the "back" button on your browser until you return to where you started.

"First, they do an online search."

Source: © Arnie Levin/The New Yorker Collection/The Cartoon Bank

"Don't let that little glowing screen become an adversary. If you plan correctly, the computer can become your most useful tool at college—next to your brain."

Greg Gottesman, author

Work the Web: Information, Please!

Try to find the answer to the first question below on Google (**www.google.com**), Yahoo! (**www.yahoo.com**), *and* Bing (**www.bing.com**). Then use whichever search engine you prefer to find answers to the remaining questions.

1. What was the French Revolution and when did it occur?

2. Who is Keyser Soze?

3. What are the words of Dr. Martin Luther King Jr.'s "I have a dream" speech?

4. Are diesel engines more efficient than gasoline engines?

5. What is the ecu?

How easy was it for you to find the answers to the questions? Which search engine(s) did you prefer, and why?

How can you limit your search so that you find sites that are more directly relevant? The following tips can help you to get the most from a search:[1]

1. **Before you even begin to type anything into your computer, ask yourself the question you want answered.** Then identify the two or three important words in that question.

2. **Go to your favorite search engine.** Google is the most popular today, but preferences vary.

3. **Type three or four words into the search engine,** making sure they are spelled correctly. Then search. Note: You can do a few things here to limit the number of results returned, thus making your search more efficient. Most search engines allow you to use the following:

   - *Quotation marks,* to denote a phrase—words that should appear together, in a specific order (e.g., "animal rights").

   - *Plus signs,* used before terms that must appear in all results returned (+ "animal rights" + experimentation).

   - *Minus signs,* before terms you do not want to appear in results (+ "animal rights" + experimentation – fur).

   - *Boolean operators*—words like AND, OR, AND NOT, and NEAR (e.g., "animal rights" AND experimentation NOT fur).

Check the "Help" section of your preferred search engine for more precise information on limiting your searches.

4. **Open a new window,** type in a different set of search terms, and search again.

5. **Identify the common links between the two searches.** Read the very brief summaries provided.

6. **Open a word processing window.** Copy and paste the site's address into that window and follow it with an annotation of your own.

7. **See if you have found the answer you were looking for.** If not, reformulate your question to come up with new key words. If you have found the answer, you're done!

8. **Avoid the temptation to rely on Wikipedia pages.** Very often, a search will yield a Wikipedia entry. *Wikipedia* is a free online encyclopedia created through the joint efforts of dozens, hundreds, or even thousands of people. Anyone can create or edit an article, and it is assumed that the power of multiple contributors can ensure the accuracy of the article.

   The reality is that Wikipedia entries vary considerably in accuracy. Although some involve the collective knowledge of so many people that they are largely accurate, in some cases the material is suspect. Consequently, use information in Wikipedia entries as a starting place, not an endpoint. In some cases, in fact, instructors will not allow the use of material obtained solely from Wikipedia in their students' papers.

9. **Resist the temptation to simply cut and paste the material you've found into a new document.** It's too easy to succumb to plagiarism if you simply copy material. Instead, take notes on the material using the critical thinking and notetaking skills you've developed.

   Then save your notes. You can save your notes on a computer's hard drive, on a flash drive, or in the cloud (if you use Dropbox or Google Docs). You can also print out hard copies of what you create virtually.

   However you do it, *make sure you save material frequently and make backup copies.* Nothing is more frustrating than laboring over a document for hours and having it disappear into cyberspace.

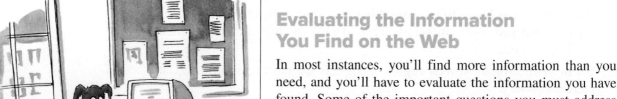

"On the Internet, nobody knows you're a dog."

Source: © Peter Steiner/The New Yorker Collection/www.cartoonbank.com

Evaluating the Information You Find on the Web

In most instances, you'll find more information than you need, and you'll have to evaluate the information you have found. Some of the important questions you must address before you can feel confident about what you've found include the following:

▶ **How authoritative is the information?** It is absolutely essential to consider the source of the material. Approach every piece of information with a critical eye, trying to determine what the author's biases might be. The best approach is to use multiple sources of information. If one source diverges radically from the others, you may reasonably question the reliability of that source.

Another approach is to consider the publisher of the material or sponsoring institution. For instance, sites established by well-known publishers and organizations

Using the Web at Work

The skills you learn at finding and sorting information on the web will have many uses in your working life. Nearly every modern office is equipped with Internet-ready computers. Your employer will probably expect you to be able to find specific pieces of information—addresses, dates, phone numbers, and so forth—using the web, regardless of your specific profession. Further, in many industries, web skills are crucial. Real estate agents, for example, need to be able to use the web to assess markets and post offerings; accountants need to be able to research costs; salespeople need to be able to get background on present and potential clients.

Even if you don't work in an office setting, you will find great use for the web. Whatever professional problem you are facing—from an engine you can't fix to a patient who won't cooperate—there are others who have faced it before, and probably more than one of these people have shared their experiences online. Your evaluation skills will be crucial in applying what you find on the web to your job, but it's likely that there is helpful, reliable information online to be found.

are more likely to contain accurate information than those created by unknown (and sometimes anonymous) authors. Remember, the web is completely unregulated: *Anyone* can put *anything* on the web.

▶ **How current is the information?** No matter what the subject, information is changing at a rapid rate. Consider whether what you've found is the most recent and up-to-date material. Compare older sources to newer ones to identify changes in the ways in which the topic is considered.

▶ **How well are claims documented?** Are there references and citations to support the information? Are specific studies identified?

A Final Word

The Information Age presents us with great promise and opportunity. Through the use of media such as e-mail and the Internet, we have at our fingertips the ability to communicate with others around the world. We can break the bounds of our physical location and reach across geography to learn about others. The computer keyboard truly can be said to contain keys to the entire earth and all of its people.

Speaking *of* Success

Source: Courtesy of Mara Lee Azlin

NAME: **Mara Lee Azlin**

SCHOOL: **Grossmont College, El Cajon, California**

For Mara Azlin, attending a community college was a chance not only to further her education, but also to pursue a profession that evolved from a personal family experience.

"Dealing with my son's leukemia got me interested in the medical field, and my observation of a young doctor's involvement with my father's heart valve transplant helped to guide me into the cardiovascular field," Azlin noted.

"My father was so sick when he finally went for medical help that all of the doctors except one said there was nothing that could be done. That young doctor was what my physiology teacher called a 'critical thinker.' He understood how the respiratory, cardiovascular, and urinary systems were integrated.

"I want to be that kind of doctor. And I was gratified during physiology class to learn the things that doctor knew from a teacher who emphasized critical thinking," she said.

Getting to school was not an easy road for Azlin. A long commute, having to work, raising two children, and attending classes five days a week were some of the challenges facing Azlin, but being an older student was probably the hardest.

"I was uncertain how I would fare when I first went back to college as an older student. But it has been very rewarding," she said. "If you don't try, you will never know what you are capable of. This is particularly important for older students thinking about returning to college.

"Entering college surrounded by younger people was daunting, but I found that my study habits and life experiences contributed in my favor, and I was near the top of the academic scale," Azlin added. "There are quite a few returning students my age, and the younger students are very accepting of us. There are even special programs to help those returning to college after a lengthy absence."

Her advice to someone thinking about going to college: "What are you waiting for? Get on board!"

[RETHINK]

- Do you think Azlin's experiences with the medical care system before being accepted helped her to be a better student?

- As an older student, how can technology make her academic pursuits easier?

Looking Back

LO 7-1 Explain how technology impacts you and your education.

▶ Course websites, textbook websites, podcasts, blogs, wikis, classroom presentation programs, individual response technology (IRT), and lecture capture technology are among the major educational uses of technology.

▶ The web includes e-mail, text messaging, video messaging, and search engines.

▶ E-mail and text messaging permit instant communication with others. Although college students tend to communicate more using text messaging, most student–instructor communication is conducted via e-mail.

LO 7-2 Describe strategies for effective distance learning.

▶ Distance learning is a form of education that does not require the physical presence of a student in a classroom. It is usually conducted over the web.

▶ Distance learning requires some adjustments for students, but it is increasingly popular.

LO 7-3 Discuss approaches for developing information competency.

▶ There are two main sources of information today: libraries and the web.

▶ Information in libraries is available in print form, electronic form, and microform.

▶ Library resources can be found through the use of the library catalog, which may be print-based but is increasingly likely to be computerized.

▶ The web is another major source of information. Web users access web pages (or sites) by using a browser, locate information by using search engines, and move from site to site by following links on each web page.

▶ Using the web effectively to find information can be tricky. It has many dead ends, false trails, and distractions, and the accuracy of the information presented as fact can be difficult to assess.

▶ Information on the web must be carefully evaluated by considering how reliable the source is, how current the information is, how well the source's claims are documented, and how complete the information is.

[KEY TERMS AND CONCEPTS]

Blended (hybrid) courses (p. 179)
Blog (p. 169)
Browser (p. 188)
Call number (p. 187)
Cybersecurity (p. 177)
Distance learning (p. 179)
E-mail (p. 171)
Emoticons (or smileys) (p. 174)

Information competency (p. 185)
Interlibrary loan (p. 187)
Learning Management System (p. 183)
Lecture capture technology (p. 170)
Link (p. 189)
Online database (p. 185)
Podcast (p. 169)
Recall (p. 187)

Search engine (p. 189)
Stacks (p. 187)
Text messaging (texting) (p. 171)
Video message services (p. 171)
Web (p. 170)
Web page (p. 188)

[R E S O U R C E S]

ON CAMPUS

If you are having difficulty connecting to or surfing the web, the first place to turn is your college's computer center. Most campuses have consultants who can help you with the technical aspects of computer usage.

If you need access to computers, most colleges have computer labs. Typically, these labs provide computers with web access, as well as printers. It's important to check their hours, as they usually are not open 24/7. In addition, you may have to wait in line for a computer, so it is a good idea to bring some other work to the lab so you have something to do while waiting. You may also need to provide printer paper if you want to print something out.

The librarians at your college library are the people to whom you should turn first if you need help in locating information. In recent years, librarians—most of whom hold advanced degrees—have undergone a significant change in what they do, and most are equally at home using traditional print material and searching electronic information storehouses.

IN PRINT

A good introductory guide to computers is Ron White's *How Computers Work* (Que, 2014, 10th ed.). A very comprehensive and in-depth look at online research can be found in *Librarian's Guide to Online Searching* (Libraries Unlimited, 2015, 4th ed.), by Suzanne S. Bell. Finally, Leslie Bowman's *Online Learning: A User-Friendly Approach for High School and College Students* (R&L Education, 2010) offers clear instruction on becoming an effective online learner.

ON THE WEB

Many sites on the web provide the opportunity to extend your learning about the material in this chapter. Although the web addresses were accurate at the time the book was printed, check the Connect Library or ask your instructor for any changes that may have occurred.

▶ Pretty much anything you want to know about high tech, from the definition of a smartphone to an explanation of Utopic Unicorn, can be found at Webopedia **http://www.webopedia.com/**. It also includes a list of the latest terms.

▶ The WWW Virtual Library (**www.vlib.org/**) is one of the oldest catalogs of the web, providing useful links to thousands of subjects.

▶ Yahoo! (**www.yahoo.com**) is a very popular Internet search engine and subject directory. Unlike Google, as a subject directory, Yahoo! allows browsing through prearranged categories (e.g., education, health, social science, and more). It also offers easy access to news, weather, maps, the Yellow Pages, and much more.

The Case of . . .
Caught in the Web

At 8 p.m., Tyson Dynes sat down at his computer to write his first college-level world history paper, due the next morning. He needed to summarize the basic facts of the Egyptian revolution of 2011 and express his thoughts about its causes and effects.

Searching Google under "Egypt," Tyson quickly found a long Wikipedia article, but it only briefly addressed the revolution. He started over, searching "Egyptian revolution." This led to another article, which he read for some time before realizing that the revolution he was reading about had taken place in 1952, not 2011. The clock was ticking.

Back to Google, this time adding "2011" to the search. Two hours later, he had read a wealth of facts about the revolution, but still had no basis for expressing his own thoughts—and had little time left in which to think. To gain some time, he pasted much of the factual text directly into his paper, changing some wording and content to sound more like him. For the interpretation section, he desperately searched Google under "meaning of the revolution in Egypt." He found an article that seemed good and copied much of it into his paper, changing it to sound less formal and intellectual.

1. How well did Tyson use his time in preparing his paper? What advice would you give him about the preparation stage of working on a paper?

2. It took Tyson three tries to get to information about the 2011 Egyptian revolution. What advice would you give him about using search engines more effectively?

3. Tyson ended up with a collection of facts and no time to digest them. Was his time-saving strategy of cutting and pasting text from a web article a smart solution?

4. What do you think of the ethics of Tyson's copy-and-paste strategy? Do you think it was just time saving, or was it plagiarism? Was changing the text the way he did enough to make the paper his own?

5. What criteria do you think Tyson used in judging that the article on the meaning of the revolution "seemed good"? What criteria should he have used? What use should he have made of the article?

8 Transfer Strategies: Making the Leap from Community College to a Four-Year School

Learning Outcomes

By the time you finish this chapter you will be able to

» LO **8-1** Discuss strategies for choosing a transfer college or university.

» LO **8-2** Explain how to transfer credits.

» LO **8-3** Identify strategies for adjusting to a new college.

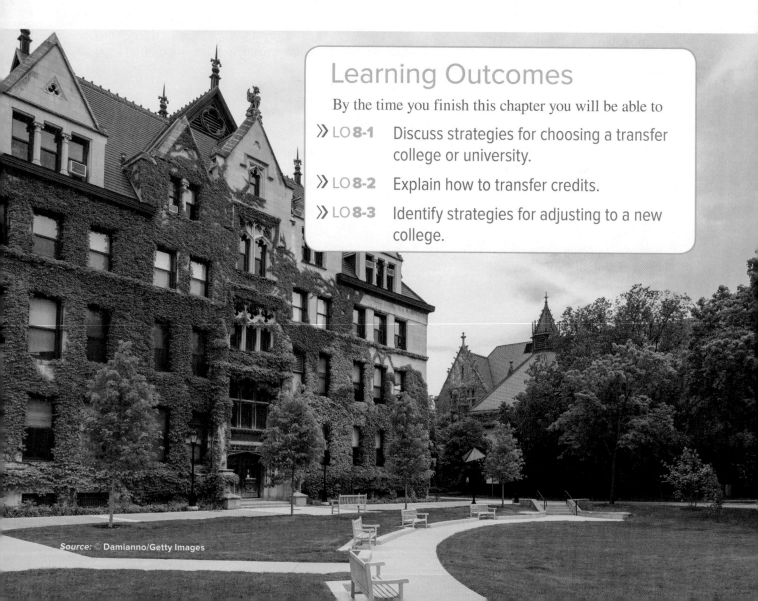

Source: © Damianno/Getty Images

Martine Franklin was thinking about transferring from Roxbury Community College in Boston to the University of Massachusetts in Amherst. She half loved the idea, and half dreaded it.

On the one hand, she would be leaving a small, comfortable student community in favor of a much larger campus. Would she simply get lost and sink without a trace?

On the other hand, she would be moving from a real city to a much smaller town. Would she be too much of a "city girl" to be happy in Amherst? Would her urban style clash with the cozy college town she envisioned Amherst to be? Would she stick out like a sore thumb?

She weighed her choices. On the plus side, UMass Amherst had more academic programs, sports, and extracurricular activities. It drew students from all over the world. Maybe it was time for Martine to stretch her wings a bit.

On the minus side, UMass Amherst was world famous and had high academic standards. Would Martine even be accepted for transfer? And if she was, would she succeed or be forced to drop out? Maybe it was better to stick with what she knew.

Plus–minus. How to decide?

Looking Ahead

The transition that Martine was contemplating—transferring from a two-year community college to a four-year college or university—is one that millions of students make each year. That doesn't make it any easier, though. Transferring from one school to another is no less challenging than the move from high school to college.

But it's a challenge that you can meet. With careful thought, preparation, and work, transferring can produce benefits that will help you for the rest of your life, both personally and professionally.

In this chapter we consider the transfer process. We address strategies for maximizing the credit you'll receive from your prior educational experiences. In addition, we consider the application process and how to choose among different educational institutions. Finally, we discuss ways of avoiding "transfer shock" when you move to a new college or university.

» LO 8-1 Mastering the Transfer Process

Transferring from one school to another is not just a matter of credits, units, and courses. It is a process that will have an impact on your life in significant ways.

Although it is a complicated process, transferring can be broken down into a series of steps that will help you navigate your way, following the P.O.W.E.R. Plan.

P Prepare Making the Decision to Transfer

Deciding whether to continue your education should not be done lightly. You'll need to consider a variety of factors, including academic, financial, and social considerations. However, in some ways the most important part of the process is considering the reasons why you may be thinking of transferring in the first place.

figure 8.1

Those Who Learn More Earn More: Earnings by Education Level and Unemployment Rate

Educational Degree Attained	Median Weekly Earnings in 2014	Unemployment Rate in 2014
Less than high school diploma	$ 488	9.0%
High school diploma	$ 668	6.0%
Some college, no degree	$ 741	6.0%
Associate's degree	$ 792	4.5%
Bachelor's degree	$1,101	3.5%
Master's degree	$1,326	2.8%
Doctoral degree	$1,591	2.1%
Professional degree	$1,639	1.9%

Source: U.S. Department of Labor, Bureau of Labor Statistics, April 2, 2015. http://www.bls.gov/emp/ep_chart_001.htm

P Prepare

Make the decision to transfer

O Organize

Get it together: Determine where you should transfer to

W Work

Apply to four-year schools

E Evaluate

Assess your options

R Rethink

Reconsider your choices

P.O.W.E.R. Plan

Why Transfer?

There are many good reasons to transfer—and some not-so-good ones. Let's start with the advantages of continuing your college education at a four-year institution:

▶ **You will have more career opportunities.** As we discuss in the **Career Connections** box, graduates of four-year schools have more opportunities in the job market and are more likely to get jobs that require sophisticated skills.

▶ **Your salary will be higher.** In 2014, graduates of four-year schools earned on average $15,912 more annually than graduates of two-year schools (see **Figure 8.1**). Over your lifetime, that adds up to a big difference. In addition, unemployment rates differ: The unemployment rate in 2014 for people with bachelor's degrees was lower by nearly two percentage points than for those with only associate's degrees.[1]

▶ **You will be better educated, understanding more about the world around you.** At its most basic level, college is about gaining an education, and the more college courses you take, the better educated you'll be. Don't underestimate the value of the knowledge you will gain if you continue your P.O.W.E.R. Plan education. You will be better informed about the world, have more basic knowledge, and have the opportunity to specialize in different areas.

▶ **You'll have more options.** By enrolling in a new school you may find a program of study that is not available at your present two-year school. This will open new options and directions for your education. You may have more opportunities to take advantage of an internship, study abroad, or even put together your own program of study. In short, the school to which you transfer may meet your own needs more effectively than your current college (also see the Career Connections feature).

▶ Ultimately, once you graduate from a four-year college, you'll have more options available to you. As a graduate of a four-year school, you'll have gained more knowledge, skills, and experiences to be better able to fit into and profit from a changing world—both professionally and socially. You'll be better able to adjust to the changes that will inevitably occur during your lifetime.

The Career Benefits of Transferring

A decision to transfer to a four-year college and continue your education is sure to produce benefits for your career that extend throughout your lifetime. More education translates into more career options, more income, and ultimately more career satisfaction.

For instance, many employers require that workers have, at a minimum, a bachelor's degree. They welcome the range of knowledge and skills that potential employees obtain during four years of education, compared to two. In some cases, you won't even be considered for a position without a four-year college degree, regardless of the skills you may have. Consequently, transferring opens up a variety of career choices that you would not have otherwise.

Similarly, transferring can lead to a higher salary. The average salaries of those with a bachelor's degree are nearly $15,000 a year higher than for graduates of two-year colleges. Furthermore, in some cases, salaries increase more rapidly for those with a bachelor's degree. Promotion opportunities may also be greater for those with more education.

Finally, your general satisfaction with your career may be higher with more education under your belt. By furthering your education, you are more likely to attain the benefits of college that we spoke of in the first chapter of the book, including having a better understanding of the world, a greater ability to deal with rapid societal changes, and more understanding of others from different cultures and backgrounds. Such capabilities not only will make your work life more rewarding and enriching—they also are likely to increase your general satisfaction with your life outside of work.

On the other hand, there are reasons for transferring that may not be so good. Wanting to transfer because you don't know what else to do, because your parents won't let you live at home anymore unless you enroll, or because your boyfriend or girlfriend is enrolling and you don't want to be away from him or her are all questionable reasons for transferring.

However, even these less-than-optimal reasons may have value if they at least get you thinking about the possibility of continuing your education. To delve into the reasons—pro and con—for transferring, complete **Try It! 1**.

Choosing Not to Transfer

In some cases, choosing *not* to continue your education is the right choice. For example, if you have had considerable academic difficulties, you may think twice about moving to a four-year school, where the academic challenges are often greater than those you're currently experiencing. Furthermore, if you have little academic motivation and continually have to force yourself to be engaged in your studies, transferring to a four-year institution may not be the right choice.

Also, depending on your area of study (such as a trade profession), a two-year program may be the wisest choice. You may also need a more flexible schedule, which may be more difficult to obtain at a four-year institution.

Keep in mind that choosing *not* to continue your education is not an irreversible decision. You could work for a few years and then go back to college. "It's never too late to learn" is an accurate statement, and you may later decide that the time is right.

Whatever choice you make, be sure that it is *your* choice—a thoughtful, reasoned, and logical decision that takes account of your needs and preferences. Don't do something just because everyone else is doing it. The more you think about your choices—which you can explore further in the **Journal Reflections**—the more committed you will be about your ultimate decision.

Why Consider a Transfer?

Examine your reasons for considering a transfer at this time by answering the questions below. Jot down notes in response to each question. Some reasons may seem more serious than others, but the purpose of this exercise is not to judge yourself, but to know yourself.

You may want to complete this exercise with the help of other people whose opinions you respect (such as fellow students, friends, parents, siblings, or other relatives). If you are comfortable with this approach, you may find that varied ideas, suggestions, and feedback can really help you sharpen your focus and identify your strongest reasons for considering a transfer.

I. ACADEMICS:

- Does your current institution offer enough courses that you are interested in?
- Are there specific courses that you would like to look for elsewhere?
- Is there an entire area of study (i.e., a major) that you would like to pursue in another institution?
- Do the courses you have taken seem too limiting or too easy?
- Have you not done well academically and do you think you might do better or find better teachers at another institution?
- Have the courses you've taken sparked an interest that you would like to pursue in a four-year college?
- Have you discovered that you are a more serious student and more interested in learning than you thought you were?

II. EXTRACURRICULAR ACTIVITIES:

- Does your current institution offer enough extracurricular activities?
- Are there particular sports, clubs, organizations, or other activities that you would like to try out, whether at a competitive level or at a less formal level, that are not offered at your current institution?
- Are you interested in experiencing, even just as a spectator, a higher level of student sports or performances?

 Organize

Getting It Together: Determining Where to Transfer To

Once you've made the decision to transfer to a four-year institution, you'll need to determine how to do it and decide what schools you're interested in applying to. Although it's never simple to transfer—you're dealing not just with the bureaucracy of your current institution but also with the one that you're seeking to transfer to—there are things you can do to simplify the process.

Begin with your own campus advisor. Almost all two-year colleges have a designated transfer advisor who can provide guidance. Even if there is no specific individual charged with providing transfer help, you can be sure that you'll find written material, on the web and in brochures and catalogs, that can help you out.

A transfer advisor can help you identify four-year institutions with which your present college has existing relationships. Those institutions are the schools that should be at the top of your list of most likely transfer possibilities. Why? Because agreements between colleges will make the most of what you've already accomplished, giving you

III. CAREER REASONS:

- Are you thinking of a career that is different from (e.g., more demanding or stimulating than) the ones that a two-year degree will enable you to pursue?
- Have you identified a specific career that you can't pursue any further at your current institution?
- Are you interested in a career that promises to pay better than the ones available with a two-year degree?
- Have you been looking for a job and found nothing that is right for you?
- Are you simply not ready to start a career, but don't yet know what you want to do?
- Are you trying to expand your career choices by educating yourself further?

IV. SOCIAL REASONS:

- Do you feel that you have "used up" or exhausted the social possibilities available at your current institution?
- Do you want a more active, campus-centered social experience than what's found at your current institution?
- Are you interested in meeting a greater number of students from different states, regions, countries, and/or cultural backgrounds?
- Do you simply feel that you need a "bigger pond" to swim in?

V. OTHER REASONS:

- Are you simply looking to make a fresh start in a different place?
- Are you considering a change for geographical reasons (e.g., different climate, different region)?
- Are you considering a change to a different setting (e.g., a switch from an urban environment to a more rural one, or vice versa)?
- Are you trying to get away from someone or something in your current school or neighborhood?
- Are you pursuing someone who is at the institution you are considering transferring to?
- Are you being pressured (e.g., by parents) to transfer to a four-year college?
- Can you identify any other reasons why you are considering a transfer?

academic credit for more, or even most, of the courses you've already taken. (We'll talk more about the specific types of agreements later in the chapter.)

Transferring to Four-Year Institutions That Don't Have Formal Arrangements

Don't limit your choices of transfer schools only to those with formal arrangements. Although it clearly will be easier to transfer to a four-year institution that has a formal agreement with your current school, almost every four-year school accepts community college transfers. It may be harder, and you may be forced to take some extra courses, but the trade-offs may be well worth it. Why should you consider transferring to a school that lacks an agreement with your current community college? There are several good reasons:

▶ **You may be seeking a specialized major that only certain colleges offer.** If you have well-established career goals that involve specific coursework or a specialized course of study, you may be limited in the four-year institutions that provide what you want.

▶ **You may wish to continue your education in another state or geographic locality.** Because formal agreements are usually arranged between state-supported institutions within the same state, you're unlikely to find four-year colleges with agreements in locations that are distant from your current school.

▶ **You are seeking new academic challenges.** Perhaps you have done well in your current school, but you feel you haven't been challenged. Transferring to an institution that is highly selective in its admissions requirements may give you the opportunity to take on more academic challenges.

▶ **You are seeking a college that is very different from your current institution.** You may currently be attending a small school, with a student body that is not very diverse and classes where you know everyone. Maybe, though, for the rest of your college career, you'd like to experience a much larger campus, with a more diverse student body and classes in which you hear a broader range of opinions.

Narrowing the Choices

Once you've done the background research on which four-year schools best fit your academic needs, you may have a fairly long list of possibilities. How do you narrow that list to a manageable few to which you will actually apply? Here are some things to take into consideration:

▶ **Does the college have the program you want?** Be sure that the school offers the program you want and that there's a strong likelihood that you'll be able to get into the program. Sometimes certain majors have their own admissions standards. You want to be confident that you'll be accepted into the program of your choice.

▶ **What are the philosophy and mission of the college?** Although every school has the basic goal of educating students, other aspects of school missions differ significantly from one college to the next. You'll find a statement of the philosophy and mission of most schools on the web or in a catalog. Use it to get a sense of what is important: Is the school oriented more to research than to teaching? Is there a religious affiliation? Is there an emphasis on student choice and freedom, or are there so many requirements that there is little room for experimentation?

Source: © Barry Winiker/Getty Images

Source: © Panoramic Images/Getty Images

The location and setting of a new school may be important factors to you. You may be looking for something entirely different from your current surroundings. Available housing or commuting time might also weigh heavily on your decision.

Journal Reflections

Should I Transfer?

Contemplate the reasons you might want to transfer by considering the pluses and minuses of your current college:

1. What are the things you like best about your current college experience?

2. What aspects of your current college experience do you like least?

3. What are the things you would miss most if you completed your schooling at your current school? How important are these things to you?

4. What might you gain if you transferred to a new college to continue your education? How important are these gains to you?

5. What would be the drawbacks of transferring to a new college?

▶ **How large is the college or university?** Schools vary significantly in size. The smallest four-year institutions have fewer than 1,000 students, and the largest over 50,000. Size matters: It sets the tone of the institution. Smaller schools offer more individual attention, and often classes are smaller than at larger schools.

At smaller schools, courses are typically taught only by faculty, but in larger universities with graduate programs, graduate students may do much of the teaching.

On the other hand, larger institutions may offer more courses in a greater variety of disciplines and often provide more services. Furthermore, even if their classes tend to be larger—and sometimes huge—the classes may break down into smaller sections with individual attention.

▶ **Where do you want to live?** There are four-year colleges and universities throughout the United States and Canada that can provide you with a fine education. You need to ask yourself whether location is an important consideration. How close to your family and friends do you want to be? Do you enjoy large cities, with their great cultural resources and sense of excitement, or do you prefer quieter, more rural areas where you can more easily enjoy natural resources? Do you intend to live at home and commute, or do you wish to live in a residence hall?

▶ **What is the student body like?** There are vast differences in the makeup of the student body of different colleges. You might want to consider the male–female ratio, the ethnic and racial composition of the students who attend, the number of foreign students, and the proportion of out-of-state to in-state students. You'll also want to check out the number of transfer students on campus and the number accepted each year. Finally, especially if you're an older student, you should check out the average age of the undergraduate student population on campus.

▶ **What extracurricular activities can you participate in?** Even if you haven't been a regular participant in activities outside the classroom at your current institution, you may wish to get more involved after you transfer. Consequently, determine what extracurricular activities are available at the schools you are considering. The possibilities can be staggering, including intramural sports, service organizations, student government, religious groups, theater and other arts groups, and campus publications.

▶ **Is student housing available?** One of the primary questions you need to ask yourself is where you intend to live. If you are thinking about living on campus, you'll need to know the options available to you. In addition to traditional residence halls, where you will probably have a double or triple room with the bathroom down the hall, many schools also have suites and apartments that you can share with only a few other students.

▶ **How much will it cost?** There are vast differences in the costs of different four-year schools. Public, state-supported schools are almost always less expensive than private colleges. However, even public four-year schools are usually more expensive than public two-year schools. Although financial aid packages at four-year schools may ease the sticker shock, you are still likely to end up paying more at a four-year college than you pay at a two-year school.

▶ **What is the school's reputation?** Although you won't find it in the school's promotional literature, try to find out something about the school's reputation. Among questions to ask are these: Are graduates highly regarded by employers? Are graduates readily admitted to graduate schools?

The only way to find answers to such questions is by asking as many knowledgeable people as possible. For example, your community college transfer counselor will have a good idea of the reputation of nearby four-year schools. Your instructors might also have some suggestions. Finally, you can consult college guidebooks (such as the *Fiske Guide to Colleges*) or the *U.S. News & World Report* annual rankings of colleges, which usually provide a fairly accurate picture of the strengths and weaknesses of four-year schools.

▶ **What is your own personal take on the school?** There is nothing like a campus visit to get a sense of what a college is like. If you can, take the time to visit the schools in which you are interested. Take a tour, talk to students, and get a general feel for the campus.

Don't be swayed by first impressions and irrelevant aspects of the visit—potential students tend to be less enthusiastic about a school if they visit on a cloudy, rainy day than if it's sunny and bright. But listen to your gut feelings. If you end up feeling that a school just isn't right for you, it probably isn't.

▶ **Will the four-year school accept me?** In making your decision about which schools to apply to, be sure to consider whether it is likely that you'll be accepted. Although some four-year colleges have formal agreements that they

Your Transfer Preferences

The questions below should help you define your preferences and narrow your options.

1. What are the two or three main reasons you are considering a transfer? (Use the list of reasons you generated as part of **Try It! 1**.)

2. Where do you want to live? What country, region, state, city, or area?

3. What type of setting do you prefer (i.e., urban, suburban, rural)?

4. How large a school do you want to attend (e.g., fewer than 5,000 students, between 5,000 and 10,000 students, or more than 10,000 students)?

5. What sort of student body do you prefer in terms of diversity, gender mix, geographical origins, and so on?

6. What potential major(s) are you considering?

7. What sort of academic standards and difficulty level do you want in a four-year college (high, moderate, relaxed)?

8. How much money are you prepared to pay each year? How large a loan are you willing to carry?

9. What other needs do you have (e.g., sports programs, religious affiliation, art or performance opportunities, student housing, handicapped accessibility, laboratory facilities, library, etc.)?

Use your answers to these questions to find four-year colleges that will meet your needs. You can do this by discussing your needs with a counselor at your current institution and/or by using a web-based college search tool, such as the *College Navigator* at **http://nces.ed.gov/collegenavigator/**, the college search tool at **www.petersons.com/college-search.aspx**, or the *Big Future* web page at **https://bigfuture.collegeboard.org/college-search**. If you find a school in your immediate area (i.e., commuting distance) or in your state, remember to find out if it has any kind of transfer arrangement with your current institution.

will accept every graduate of certain two-year schools who is in good academic standing and has a certain number of credits, most schools do not have such an arrangement.

Every college will evaluate your academic credentials before they accept you. You need to examine a college's degree of selectivity and realistically consider your chances of getting in. Some colleges have minimum standards for prior academic performance that they state up front; others apply some type of standards but don't explicitly say what they are. In any case, your prior academic performance (including your high school grades) will be taken into consideration.

Does this mean you should avoid taking a risk and rule out applying to a school that you'd really like to attend? Absolutely not. You lose nothing—except the application fee—by applying to a college even if you believe it's a toss-up as to whether you'll be accepted. The important thing is to apply to other schools as well, ranging from those where you're nearly certain you'll be accepted to those that are a stretch.

After you've examined the options, try to narrow your choices to no more than five. If you pick a range of schools—some relatively sure bets, some that are good possibilities, and perhaps a "stretch" school—you should be in good shape when admissions letters are sent out.

It's also important to create a backup plan in the event that none of your applications are successful. Be prepared to take action by rethinking your choices of schools. In addition, you might consider working for a year and reapplying or taking an additional class or two to improve your academic record. Preparing in advance for any eventuality is important.

To help you decide on the four-year school that you'd like to apply to, complete **Try It! 2**.

W **Work** | Applying to Four-Year Schools

If you've prepared and organized yourself adequately, you're now ready to apply. In some ways, applying is the easiest part of the process of transferring, since in essence, all you're doing is filling in the blanks on a variety of forms. Still, it's not simple, because there are quite a few steps you'll need to follow:

1. **Obtain an application from each college to which you are applying.** Sometimes you can download application forms from the web, whereas in other cases you will have to ask the school to mail you an application. It is even possible that your current college may have applications available.

2. **Make a list of the application deadlines.** Schools have deadlines for receiving all your materials. Sometimes there is a priority period during which your application will get preferential treatment. Miss the priority period, and you may lose your preference. In other cases, schools have a "rolling" admissions process, which means the earlier you get your application in, the earlier you will learn whether you have been accepted.

3. **Identify individuals who can provide you with a recommendation.** Because most schools require several recommendations, you will need to identify several people who can provide you with strong references. Look back over your academic career and think of the courses in which your performance was strongest or the classes in which an instructor took special notice of your talents. You can also ask counselors, employers, or members of the clergy who know you well to write a letter. Good recommendations can also be provided by high school teachers who knew you.

   Be sure to ask people if they are willing to write a recommendation well before any deadlines, and give them any forms provided by the college to which you are applying. Also include a stamped, addressed envelope to make it easy for them to return the recommendation.

4. **Arrange for transcripts and test scores to be sent.** You will need to send an official college transcript, listing the courses you have taken and your grades, to the colleges and universities to which you are applying (see also the accompanying **Course Connections** feature). In some cases they may also want a copy of your high school transcript.

   You also may need to send a copy of your standardized test scores, such as the SAT or ACT. You won't need to retake these examinations if you have already taken them; just arrange for the testing service to have them sent directly to the schools to which you are applying.

5. **Complete the applications.** Filling out forms is not fun. It takes effort and concentration. But it is important to complete each application carefully and legibly. You are providing a first impression that can make an impact, even in a small way, on the person deciding on your admission.

Documenting Your Courses

While you are gathering the information that you need to send to the colleges to which you are applying, there's one more step in the process: Gather documentation for every course that you have taken. What that means is to collect as full a description as possible of each course that you have completed (or in which you are currently enrolled).

There are several good reasons for documenting your courses. Sometime in the future, you may wish to take a course at your new institution that requires that you've already taken a prerequisite (a particular course that must be completed before one can enroll in the new course). For instance, you may want to take an abnormal psychology class that requires that you've already had an introductory psychology class. You may need to provide not just evidence that you've taken a course called "Introductory Psychology," but specifics about what the course consisted of.

In other cases, there may be a required course at the college to which you transfer that you've already taken. Having full documentation of the course content will make getting excused from the required course at your new institution considerably easier.

To document your prior courses, put together a separate folder for every course you've taken. At the very least, it should contain a syllabus for the course showing the course description and goals, textbook name, and topics covered. You can also include in the folder any papers or tests you've completed in the course.

Think of your course documentation in the same way you think of a medical insurance policy. You may never need to use it, but if you do, you'll be glad you have it.

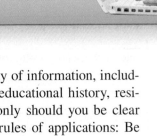

The application will undoubtedly ask for a variety of information, including your name, Social Security number, addresses, educational history, residency status, languages spoken, and so forth. Not only should you be clear in your answers, but you must follow the cardinal rules of applications: Be yourself and be honest.

If an application requires an essay, leave yourself plenty of time to write it. After you compose a first draft of the essay, it is perfectly acceptable to run it by others who are good writers to get their feedback. Use their comments to improve your essay. Remember that the essays are less a test of writing mechanics—although spelling, grammar, and organization matter—and more a way for the college to get a sense of who you are. Let your personality show through.

The last three steps in completing your applications are proofread, proofread, and proofread. You need to be sure that you have answered all the questions, that you've checked your spelling, and that everything is legible. Don't forget to sign the application, and then send it off—and wait!

Use the checklist in **Try It! 3** to keep track of your work.

E Evaluate Assessing Your Options

At some later point—it may be as short as a month or as long as six months—you will know how successful you have been. Whatever the outcome, you'll need to deal with your options.

If you've been accepted by most, or even all, of the schools to which you have applied, consider yourself lucky. But you still face some tough decisions because each school will have specific benefits and drawbacks.

Following the Application Trail

Use the running checklist below to keep track of the steps you will take in applying for admission to four-year colleges.

Application Step	Notes	Step Begun (Date)	In Progress	Step Completed (Date)
1. Obtain applications (enter college names)	Enter application deadlines below			
College 1:				
College 2:				
College 3:				
College 4:				
College 5:				
College 6:				
2. Identify and ask for references (enter name of each reference below)	Enter addresses, phone numbers, e-mail addresses below			
Reference 1:				
Reference 2:				
Reference 3:				
Reference 4:				
Reference 5:				
3. Follow up on references	Enter a check (✓) if a letter of recommendation has been sent			
Reference 1:				
Reference 2:				
Reference 3:				
Reference 4:				
Reference 5:				
4. Arrange transcript(s)	Enter contact information to obtain transcript (usually registrar's office)			
Transcript 1:				
Transcript 2:				
Transcript 3:				
5. Complete applications (fill out form, complete essay, proofread, mail)	Enter F for form, E for essay, P for proofread, and M for mail			
College 1:				
College 2:				
College 3:				
College 4:				
College 5:				
College 6:				
6. Keep track of results	Accepted? Financial aid?			
College 1:				
College 2:				
College 3:				
College 4:				
College 5:				
College 6:				

Although you probably considered the pros and cons of the colleges before applying, you are likely to have gained some new information from your letter of admission. Specifically, you may have learned how many of your prior credits will be accepted for transfer. Comparing what the different schools will permit you to transfer can help you make an informed decision.

Financial Aid Packages

Your acceptance letter may have brought another piece of information, this in the form of a number: the amount of financial support you are being offered. If financial aid makes a difference to you—and it most likely will—you must carefully evaluate the different financial packages.

Financial aid packages are not written in stone. You have nothing to lose by attempting to negotiate a better package, and there are two strong reasons for trying. First, financial aid is generally made up of several components, including direct scholarships, loans, and campus job earnings. The greater the direct scholarship offered, the better, since there is no payback or work required. Second, the overall size of the financial aid package can make the difference between whether you can afford to attend the school or not. Thus, it makes sense to try to ask for a larger overall package.

Although negotiating may seem daunting, it's important to make the effort. Here are the steps to follow:

▶ Call to make an appointment to speak with a financial aid officer.

▶ Prepare a case that shows why you need a better package. Remember that you can ask for a larger package overall and/or ask for a change in the specific components of the package. Justify what you are asking for by showing how the current financial aid offer is too small to allow you to afford attending the college.

▶ If your desired school's offer is smaller than that of another college, mention that. A college that knows you will definitely attend if it can provide a better offer has a greater incentive to provide more aid.

▶ Be polite as you present your case. Heavy-handed tactics will not work. You want the financial aid officer to do everything possible to permit you to attend the college.

To help you assess your options among several colleges that have accepted you for enrollment, complete **Try It! 4**.

| R Rethink |

Reconsidering Your Choices

If you've been accepted to a four-year school, the decision to attend takes on a life of its own. Before you enroll, though, take a moment to reassess your decision. Are you continuing your education for the right reasons? Are you doing it for yourself or to please someone else? Does the thought of taking more classes, spending late nights writing papers, and studying for tests fill you with dread and anxiety?

Unless you are fully committed to attending college, you should reconsider your decision to transfer. In most cases, you'll probably conclude that your decision to pursue a transfer to a four-year school was the right one. But if you are not sure, then systematically review your choices. For instance, you might want to work for a period before continuing your schooling. Many colleges will permit you to defer admission for a year, and that might be the right option for you to take at that point in time.

(To review the steps in transferring, see the P.O.W.E.R. Plan.)

Assessing Your Options

If you have several options to consider, complete this Try It! to organize your thoughts and weigh the options.

1. How closely does each college match the preferences you identified in **Try It! 2**? Use a scale of 1 to 4 to rate each college, where "1" = not a close match and "4" = a very close match. Then add the ratings in each column.

Your Preferences	Ratings (1 to 4, Higher Is Better)		
	College 1	College 2	College 3
1. Your main reasons for transferring:			
Reason 1			
Reason 2			
Reason 3			
2. Where you want to live			
3. Setting of school			
4. Size of school			
5. Student body			
6. Major(s)			
7. Academic standards			
8. Cost			
9. Other needs			
Total Preference Rating (highest possible rating is 44)			

2. Now look more closely at the cost of attending each college. Use the categories below to estimate what it would cost per year to attend each one. Then, in the last row, enter a "3" for the college with the lowest cost, a "2" for the next highest, and a "1" for the highest-cost college (assuming you are rating three colleges; note that the higher number indicates the most advantageous in terms of cost).

Your Preferences	College 1	College 2	College 3
Estimated Costs			
Tuition			
Room and board			
Textbooks and supplies			
Transportation			
Other expenses			
Total costs			

Your Preferences	College 1	College 2	College 3
Estimated Available Funds			
Savings or help from home			
Scholarships			
Loans			
College work programs			
Other work			
Other income			
Total funds available			
Costs minus funds			
Cost Rating (1 to 3, assuming three colleges; higher number corresponds to lower cost)			

3. Next consider how many credits from your current institution you will be permitted to transfer to each college. In the last row enter a "3" for the greatest number of transferable credits, a "2" for the next lowest, and a "1" for the lowest (assuming you are rating three colleges).

Your Preferences	College 1	College 2	College 3
Number of Credits Transferable			
Credit Transfer Rating (1 to 3, assuming three colleges; higher number corresponds to more credits transferable)			

4. Now consider your overall impression of each college, based on visits you have made or on other information. Rate each college on a scale from 1 to 4, where "1" = very unfavorable impression and "4" = very favorable impression.

Your Preferences	College 1	College 2	College 3
Overall Impression Rating (1 to 4, higher is better)			

5. Finally, add up your four separate ratings to produce a total rating for each college.

Your Preferences	College 1	College 2	College 3
Total Rating (= Total Preference Rating + Cost Rating + Credit Transfer Rating + Overall Impression Rating. Higher is better; highest possible rating is 54.)			

While you may use these ratings any way you want, or even ignore them, they may help you decide among your options.

» LO 8-2 Making the Most of Your Transfer Credits

Perhaps you are moving straight from a two-year college to a four-year school. Or perhaps your route has been a little more roundabout, and your earlier educational progress has come in fits and starts. Maybe you've had to suddenly leave college because of a business transfer or the need to take care of an ailing relative, and you have accumulated college credits from a number of schools.

Whether the route has been straight or winding, having your college credits evaluated to determine how many will be accepted for transfer to a four-year college is central to transferring. The outcome of this process is crucial, and it can determine how many and what courses you will need to take in the future. It can also save—or cost—you thousands of dollars.

Getting Credit Where Credit Is Due

The process of determining how much credit you will receive is complicated and the outcome can be affected by several factors, including these:

▶ **Where you earned the credits.** Unless a school is accredited (approved) by the appropriate state or regional authorities, courses will not be accepted for transfer. Although most two-year schools are accredited, if you have any doubts, you should check before beginning the process of transferring. Similarly, if you took a course through a continuing education program, the credits you earned may not count as college-level work (even if you received "continuing education credit" for them).

▶ **The grades you received in the course.** Many four-year colleges require a grade of C or better in order to accept a course.

▶ **When the credits were earned.** If the credits were earned many years earlier, some colleges will not accept them. This is especially true of programs in which there have been significant advances, such as computer technology and genetics.

▶ **The level of the courses.** In order to graduate from a four-year program, you will need to take a variety of lower- and higher-level courses. Some four-year programs will accept only a limited number of lower-level courses and will require you to take more upper-level courses when you transfer.

▶ **Residency requirements.** Virtually all schools require that you earn a certain number of credits on their campus. Consequently, the need to fit in the required number of courses at the new college may cause some previous credits to be disallowed.

All these factors, and many more depending on a particular college's regulations, enter into decisions about whether your prior credits can be transferred. Happily, though, matters can be much simpler if the college you wish to transfer

Source: © Denise Hager/Catchlight Visual Services/Alamy

to has a special arrangement with your current school. As we discuss next, such agreements can ease the transition significantly.

Transfer Agreements

In some cases, schools have done much of the work of transferring credits for you by entering into transfer agreements. Among the most common arrangements are the following:

▶ **Articulation agreements.** Most community colleges have **articulation agreements**, formal arrangements with selected four-year colleges that will automatically accept certain courses or credits taken at your current institution. Articulation agreements may even spell out what groups or blocks of courses will be accepted, as a set, by a four-year college to which you're considering applying.

For example, an articulation agreement might specify that English 1 at a community college is the equivalent of English 100 at a particular college covered by the agreement, and that History 2 is the equivalent of History 101. If you have taken one of the courses covered by the articulation agreement and achieved some specified minimum grade, credit for that course will automatically transfer to the four-year college.

Articulation agreements are often complicated and difficult to understand, but it's worth the time and effort to decipher what they say. They can save you literally hundreds of hours, permitting you to avoid repeating courses similar to ones you have already taken or scrambling to complete requirements at your new college.

In most cases, articulation agreements cover basic, general education courses. They typically do not cover more specialized, advanced courses counted toward a future major at the four-year institution to which you are transferring. There is an exception to this general rule, however: 2 + 2 plans.

▶ **2 + 2 plans.** Many state higher education systems have what are called 2 + 2 plans. A **2 + 2 plan** is a formal agreement between a community college and a four-year institution that permits students to transfer courses into a specific major or specialty program.

Courses a student takes at the community college level are applied not only to general education requirements at the new institution but also to a major or other specific program. In most cases, 2 + 2 plans are restricted to only a few selected majors, such as human services, nursing, computer technology, or engineering.

The main advantage of 2 + 2 plans is clear: They can provide you with a real head start after your transfer. The downside of a 2 + 2 plan is that it may tie you to a specific major earlier than you may want. Unless you are quite sure of what you want to specialize in, 2 + 2 plans may lead you to make a choice before you are ready to make it.

▶ **Priority enrollment plans.** Even if there is no formal agreement between a community college and a four-year state school to accept particular courses, some state four-year colleges have priority enrollment plans. In a **priority enrollment plan**, a four-year school gives preference to students from community colleges within the state when it considers which students to admit as junior-year transfers. Although priority enrollment does not guarantee admission, it provides potential transfer students from state community colleges with an advantage over other applicants.

articulation agreements
Formal arrangements with selected four-year colleges that will automatically accept certain courses or credits taken at your current institution.

2 + 2 plan
A formal agreement between a community college and a four-year institution that permits students to transfer courses into a specific major or specialty program.

priority enrollment plan
A plan in which a four-year school gives preference to students from community colleges within the state when it considers which students to admit as junior-year transfers.

The Appeal Process: When No May Not Mean No

You've completed Psychology 1, "Introduction to Psychology," at your community college, but the university to which you are transferring hasn't given you credit for it. What should you do?

Although you may think your hands are tied, you generally do have some options. Remember, transfer credit decisions are made not by a college but by a person who works for that college. Maybe that person was rushed, made a bad decision, or was simply in a bad mood when evaluating your previous courses.

If you feel that a mistake was made, you probably have the right to appeal the decision. Don't appeal it lightly or without considerable deliberation, but also don't be reluctant. You'll be seen not as a troublemaker but as a serious student who wants to right a possible academic wrong.

The first thing to do is try for an informal resolution. E-mail or call the office where the decision was made, contacting the person who made the initial decision. Ask if the decision can be reviewed, and be ready to show why you should be granted the credit.

If the informal route is ineffective, you may be able to file a formal appeal. An appeal may consist of a form, or it may be a letter stating your case. Find out what the specific process is, and be prepared for a lengthy procedure. Your appeal may be evaluated by a committee of faculty and administrators. Keep it brief and to the point and, as always, be sure you carefully proofread the document before you send it.

What arguments are most persuasive? The best is to clearly demonstrate that the course you have taken is, in fact, very similar to the one offered at your new institution. You can demonstrate the similarity by showing that the course syllabus and textbooks used in the two courses cover similar material. If the syllabus from the course you took does not show a significant course component that was actually included in the course, enclose additional handouts from the course, or ask the original course instructor to provide a "To Whom It May Concern" letter stating that the seemingly missing component was, in fact, covered in the course.

»LO 8-3 Making the Move: Mastering the Transition from Old to New College

You've done it! You've made the move from your previous school to your new one. However, your feelings of elation at being accepted may turn to anxiety and concern as you face the prospect of starting over. How you manage the transition can have repercussions for the rest of your college career.

Transfer Shock

Many students experience what has been called *transfer shock,* the feeling that their new college is so different from their old one that they will be unable to adjust. Students experiencing transfer shock may feel lonely and unhappy, and they may question their decision to transfer.

Why might you face transfer shock? A transfer to a new college presents a number of challenges, including these:

▶ **Time management issues.** Every college operates on a slightly different schedule and time frame. Your old college may have started the term in August and finished before the end-of-year holidays. Your new college may start later and finish the term after the first of the year.

The two schools may even have different term lengths. You might be changing from a semester system, in which the term consisted of 15 weeks, to a quarter system, in which terms last 10 weeks. What that means is that the rhythm of the terms will be completely different.

For example, in a quarter system, the term is nearly over at the same point in a semester system where you've just reached the midpoint of the course. Such changes in the timing of a course can be disorienting, and you need to prepare yourself for them by paying special attention to time management strategies.

▶ **More stringent academic requirements.** Your courses may be more rigorous, requiring greater effort. You may be reading and writing more than you were used to. Assignments may call for more higher-order thinking, and courses may present concepts that are more abstract. You also may have to take classes in technical subject areas in which you have little interest or natural ability.

If your classes are large, you may have to take multiple-choice exams, bubbling in your answers on machine-scored forms just as you did when you took the SAT or ACT standardized tests.

In addition, your classes may require the use of technology more extensively or in different ways than your community college did. Course assignments may be posted on a course website, and you may be expected to do homework online. You may need to develop new technology skills and have personal access to a computer.

▶ **Financial demands.** Four-year institutions are often more expensive than two-year colleges. Even if you have received a generous financial package from your new school, you still may face difficulties in making ends meet. In addition, if the courses are more challenging than those you've previously faced, you may have less time to work at a part-time job to help support yourself.

▶ **Roommate challenges.** If you previously lived at home and commuted to college, becoming a residential student will offer a stark contrast. You may live in a small room with two, three, or sometimes even four other students with whom you may have little in common. You'll share a bathroom with people you don't know and whose concerns about cleanliness and neatness may be very different from your own.

▶ **Commuting issues.** If you are a nonresidential commuter, you will have your own set of challenges that residential students don't need to worry about. For example, your new college may be farther from home than your old one, requiring a longer commute. In addition, once you arrive on campus, you may encounter parking problems. On some campuses, finding a parking space close to where your classes are will be a challenge.

If you are commuting to a school where most other students live on campus, you'll face other issues. For example, scheduling times to work on a group project will be more difficult. If you forget to pick up a book at the library, you may need to make a long trek back to campus.

- **College size differences.** If your new school is larger than your old one, you'll face other challenges. Bigger colleges mean more students, larger classes, and a bigger library. You will probably have to stand in longer lines. In large classes, there may be hundreds more students sitting with you in a huge lecture room than you've experienced before. The only thing smaller will be your view of the professor, who may be so far away from where you are sitting that you can barely see him or her.

    On the other hand, that doesn't mean that the skills you have developed in your earlier years of college are suddenly useless. If you have learned to use a computerized library catalog and find a book in the stacks at your old school, you'll undoubtedly quickly manage to do the same thing at your new school. Similarly, taking lecture notes in large classes requires the same set of skills as taking notes in small ones.

- **Diversity issues.** The student body of your community college might have been relatively homogeneous, consisting of students who grew up in the same geographic area and having little ethnic and racial diversity. Moving to a new four-year school may mean a more diverse student body, which can be challenging but can also be a great learning experience.

    For example, you may find yourself uncomfortable with the political attitudes advocated by classmates in your courses. You may hear speeches by people whose views you find puzzling or even objectionable. You may be assigned a residence hall roommate whose habits and customs you don't understand. Other classmates may practice religions that you've never even heard of.

    All this means is that you have to be open to people who are different from you. Realize that they have had experiences that are very different from the ones you've had, and that their perspective on the world may be quite dissimilar from yours. However, opening yourself to people who are different from you will enrich both your college experience and your education as a whole.

    In addition to facing these challenges, you will undoubtedly encounter challenges that are specific to your own situation. Use **Try It! 5** to consider the factors that might have the most impact on you.

Overcoming Transfer Shock

Although there are clearly many challenges in a transfer experience, you can use several strategies to diminish and even avoid the consequences of transfer shock. Consider these:

- **Knowledge is power.** Find out as much as you can about your new college before you get there. Read the information on the school website and in the catalog. Understand what is expected of you academically and the kinds of courses you need to take. Learn about the extracurricular activities and campus organizations that are available to you. Understand the technology resources that are available, such as where you can have access to a computer and how the library functions. The more you know about your school, the less anxiety you'll have.

- **Attend orientation.** Virtually all schools have an orientation program for new students. Don't ignore it even though you probably went through an orientation at your previous school. You'll receive valuable information, and you will meet transfer counselors who can give you advice on which courses to take. You will be introduced to the college's resources, and you'll find out how to sign up for courses. If you're living on campus, you'll also receive information about your residence hall.

Absorbing the Shock of a Transfer

Once you have decided to transfer to a four-year college, you can expect to feel some degree of transfer shock. A good way to lessen the effects of transfer shock is to prepare in advance for the shocks that you are most likely to experience and be ready to do something about them. Use this Try It! to consider likely shocks and prepare to absorb them.

In the first column, consider the most likely sources of discomfort under each category that applies to you. If you don't think you will experience any shock in that category, move on to the next. Then in the second column, try to come up with creative ways to deal with each possible shock.

This is an exercise that you may want to complete with a group of friends. It helps to put a lot of creativity and imagination from more than one mind to work in thinking up effective "shock absorbers" to call on in your first months at your new school.

Source of Potential Shock	What Can I Do about It?
Time management issues: • Different term schedule at new college? • Courses meet at different times of day? • Assignments due on shorter timeline? • Need to do part-time work to afford new college? • Less time structure and more responsibility to manage own time? • Other time issues?	
Academic issues: • Harder courses at new college? • Courses move at faster pace? • More reading and writing? • Need to spend more time in library? • Different types of tests? • Greater or different use of technology? • Other academic issues?	
Financial issues: • Hard to pay tuition and fees? • Worries about student loans? • Higher transportation costs? • More expensive books, and more of them? • Higher entertainment costs? • Higher cost for clothing and food? • Other financial issues?	

Source of Potential Shock	What Can I Do about It?
Roommate issues: • Not used to living with others? • Worried about not liking roommates? • Pressure to spend money and time to fit in with roommates' lifestyle? • Different standards of cleanliness, privacy, noise, and so forth? • Other roommate issues?	
Commuting issues: • Longer commuting time? • Parking problems? • Feeling left out of campus life? • Hard to make good friends? • Hard to schedule group study time with others? • Other commuting issues?	
College size issues: • Hard to find things? • Longer lines and waits? • Hard to pay attention or ask questions in large classes? • Large library hard to understand? • Confusing array of entertainment and social events? • Generally feeling lost and ignored? • Other size issues?	
Diversity issues: • Hard to understand other people's ideas, dress, habits? • Hard to relate to different backgrounds and experiences? • Hard to accept unusual ideas and practices? • Feeling that others are looking down on you? • Other diversity issues?	

▶ **Meet with your advisor.** At some point after you are accepted into your new college, you will be assigned an advisor. Meet this person as soon as possible, because he or she holds several keys to your academic future.

Your advisor will help you navigate through the maze of requirements that you will need to fulfill. He or she will help you choose courses, assist you in filling any gaps in your background, and generally advise you on the things you need to do to have a successful academic career. Good advisors can not only help you understand the things you need to do but also give guidance on the things you shouldn't do.

Getting involved in extracurricular activities can help alleviate transfer shock by providing opportunities to meet people with similar interests.

Source: © Blend Images - Hill Street Studios/Brand X Pictures/Getty Images

▶ **Seek out other transfer students.** Having friends who are going through the same thing you are can make the transfer experience much more manageable. Seek out other transfer students, because they will provide a sounding board for what you are going through and can also be a source of information you may have missed.

▶ **Find a mentor.** Get to know your instructors. Remember, they went into teaching because they enjoy interacting with and getting to know students. Even if you are in a large class with hundreds of other students, your instructor will enjoy meeting you. Choose an instructor who seems most approachable and likable, and stop by his or her office at the beginning of the term. Periodically drop in, just to say hello or to discuss an academic issue. You'll soon find yourself building a relationship with that individual. If you do that every term, you will develop a valuable network of instructors who will keep you feeling like you are a part of the academic community of the school.

▶ **Remember that you have done it before.** Keep in mind that this is not the first time you have started college. You did it several years ago, and you were successful enough to be accepted by your current school. You're also older than most typical beginning students, so you probably have a degree of maturity not seen in the average first-year college student. You know what college is like.

Your prior experiences and successes put you several steps ahead of most beginning students on the campus to which you have transferred. That doesn't mean the transition will be easy or stress-free. It does mean, though, that you can be more confident that you will master this new transition and be successful.

Speaking *of* Success

Source: Courtesy of Jordan M. Miller

NAME: **Jordan M. Miller**

SCHOOL: **Surry Community College, Dobson, North Carolina**

For Jordan Miller, there were three keys to academic success that permitted him to make a successful transition to college: developing good organizational skills, learning new reading strategies, and learning to speak up in class and ask the right questions. Until he mastered those skills, academic success was elusive.

"I was struggling in my junior year at high school," he recalled, "and noticed that my peers were preparing to go on to college and I wasn't even close to thinking about it."

One immediate solution was to find a personal place to study, which helped him organize his studying.

"Everyone has different study habits," he noted, "but for me, I had to find a place where I could always go to study. Before that, I was studying all over the house. But after I got more organized, I found a specific place to study and saw I could concentrate better, and things would go faster."

Miller's pursuit of new study habits and approaches were further expanded when he enrolled in Surry Community College and took a reading class.

"I noticed that when I would read something, by the time I reached the end of the page I forgot what I had read," he said. "Through a reading class at Surry, I began to slow my reading. I started to highlight sections and annotate important bits of information such as names and dates in the margins. This helped a lot.

"As a result I didn't have to go back and reread the book. Instead I could just review my notes and annotations," Miller added. "In addition, I noticed that I, as well as other students, would often skip over graphs and figures. But I came to the conclusion that they were very important.

Miller, who plans to continue his education at a four-year college, also overcame his fear of speaking up in class and asking questions, which proved to be a key skill.

"I always sat in the back of the class, but I found there were too many distractions. Just about anything would sidetrack me," he said. "As soon as I moved to the front, things changed.

"But I was scared to ask questions, fearing the other students would think I wasn't smart enough," Miller added. "It was only after I started asking questions that I realized that all my classmates had the same questions."

"I would urge all students to ask questions and seek out the teacher for explanations. And remember, if you have a question about the material, others probably have the same question, too," he said.

[RETHINK]

- How will overcoming his fear of speaking up be an advantage to Miller when he applies to a four-year college?

- Do you think Miller would have been as successful if he had gone directly from high school to a four-college? Why?

Looking Back

LO 8-1 Discuss strategies for choosing a transfer college or university.

▶ To prepare to transfer, consider the reasons why you should (or shouldn't) transfer.

▶ The organization step in the transfer process involves identifying schools to which you might consider transferring.

▶ The work of transferring involves the actual application process.

▶ To evaluate your options, consider the positive and negative aspects of schools to which you have been accepted, including the amounts of financial aid that have been offered.

▶ It's also important to rethink your choices to ensure you've made the right decisions.

LO 8-2 Explain how to transfer credits.

▶ Determining which credits will transfer is a central issue for transferring students.

▶ Many schools have articulation agreements—formal arrangements that determine which courses or credits will automatically transfer.

▶ Many states have 2 + 2 plans that permit students to transfer into specific majors or programs.

LO 8-3 Identify strategies for adjusting to a new college.

▶ Some students face transfer shock, which impedes the transition to their new college.

▶ Among the steps to combat transfer shock are getting as much information as possible, attending orientation, seeking out other transfer students, and finding a mentor.

[KEY TERMS AND CONCEPTS]

Articulation agreements (p. 215)   Priority enrollment plan (p. 215)   2 + 2 plan (p. 215)

[RESOURCES]

ON CAMPUS

To help plan a transfer from a two-year college to a four-year school, seek out your transfer advising office. Staff in that office will be well equipped to give you advice and information about the schools to which most students transfer. In addition, you can call or visit the transfer offices at the schools to which you are thinking about transferring.

IN PRINT

A variety of books provide useful information about the transfer process. Don Silver's *Community College Transfer Guide,* 2nd ed. (Adams-Hall Publishing, 2014) provides a good, concise treatment of the topic. Nadine Koch and K. William Wasson's *The Transfer Student's Guide to the College Experience* (Houghton Mifflin, 2002) is a good place for helpful information. In addition, Eric Freedman's *How to Transfer to the College of Your Choice* (Ten Speed Press, 2004) and Carey Harbin's *Your Transfer Planner* (Wadsworth, 1995) provide a variety of strategies to help you master the transfer process.

ON THE WEB

The following sites on the Internet provide opportunities to extend your learning about the material in this chapter. (Although the web addresses were accurate at the time the book was printed, check the P.O.W.E.R. Connect website for any changes that may have occurred.)

▶ Many colleges and universities offer in-depth information on transferring to their school. This link to the University of California system of universities **http://admission.universityofcalifornia.edu/transfer/index.html?PHPSESSID=dffad6a0c1ca0a9e8771b4ec9eade40f** provides a wide range of informational links, from how to transfer credits to a useful transfer planner.

▶ At **http://www.ccc.edu/colleges/washington/menu/Pages/Articulation-and-Transfer-Agreements.aspx**, you will find a comprehensive look at the articulation agreements of City Colleges of Chicago that encompass more than 200 programs at dozens of senior institutions. This example is followed by hundreds of other institutions of higher learning across the country.

The Case of . . .
The Undercover College Man

Lenny Manchaco's goal was simple: get a certificate and become a paramedic. He found a certification program at Greenfield Community College (GCC) and, using G.I. Bill money, he began taking courses. He figured he'd be out of school and on the job in less than two years.

But a funny thing happened. While he was taking a required pharmacology course, he became interested enough in the way drugs worked to sign up for a chemistry course at GCC. Then, during his management of cardiovascular emergencies course the next semester, he got sidetracked again and signed up for a biology course too.

Now he was one semester from his paramedic certificate, but his curiosity was aroused. Had he just kind of frittered away time and money on two nonrequired courses, or had he discovered something about himself? Maybe he was actually *made* for college.

The thought knocked him out. He was no brain—ask anyone at his high school or in the army. But still . . .

What if he took some more courses while working as a paramedic? Could he actually do something more serious with his interest in science?

1. What advice would you give Lenny about the possibility of continuing his education?

2. What would be the advantages of completing an associate's degree and then transferring to a four-year college?

3. What are the first steps Lenny should take to consider continuing his community college education and later transferring?

4. What should Lenny do to determine if his chemistry and biology credits might transfer?

5. How should Lenny identify schools to which he might transfer?

9 Diversity and Relationships

Learning Outcomes

By the time you finish this chapter you will be able to

» LO 9-1 Discuss why the increasing racial, ethnic, and cultural diversity of society is important to you.

» LO 9-2 Identify strategies to become more at ease with differences and diversity.

» LO 9-3 Build lasting relationships and learn to deal with conflict.

Source: © UpperCut Images/SuperStock

Paul Chudzik sank low in his seat, wishing he could disappear. The instructor had just asked his opinion, and all he'd been able to do was stammer and mumble. It was pretty much all he'd done since coming to this school in Chicago. Growing up in a Polish farming community hadn't prepared him for urban life, but he was dead set on earning a degree in computer information systems. He wanted to modernize the farm—make it a real business. But he hadn't imagined how college life would be in the city, surrounded by black, Latino, and Asian students. Even the white students felt foreign. Most of them were urban kids with street smarts he didn't have and couldn't imitate. He was afraid to open his mouth for revealing himself. A hick. An outsider. For the first time in his life, Paul found himself in the minority, and he didn't have a clue how to cope.

Looking Ahead

Whether you have skin that is black or white or brown, are Jewish or Muslim or Greek Orthodox or Hindu, were born in Cuba or Vietnam or Boise, are able-bodied or physically challenged, college presents a world of new opportunities. College permits you to encounter people with very different backgrounds from your own. If you take the opportunity to form relationships with a variety of individuals, you will increase your understanding of the human experience and enrich your life. This will also benefit you greatly in your career because whatever your field, you will inevitably find yourself in situations where success will depend on your ability to collaborate effectively with people different from yourself.

In this chapter, we consider how social diversity and relationships affect your life experience. We examine the increasing diversity of American society and consider the meanings and social effects of race, ethnicity, and culture. We look at practical strategies for acknowledging—and shedding—prejudice and stereotypes, and being receptive to others on their own merits.

We next discuss relationships from a broader perspective, exploring ways that you can build lasting friendships with others. Finally, the chapter discusses the conflicts that can arise between people and what you can do to resolve them.

» LO 9-1 Living in a World of Diversity

No matter where we live, our contacts with others who are racially, ethnically, and physically different from us are increasing. The web is bringing people from across the globe into our homes, as close to us as the computers sitting on our desks. Businesses now operate globally, so co-workers are likely to come from many different countries and cultures. Being comfortable with people whose backgrounds and beliefs may differ from our own is not only a social necessity, but virtually a requirement for career success.

By the mid-21st century, the percentage of people in the United States of African, Latin American, Asian, and Arabic ancestry will be greater than the percentage of those of Western European ancestry—a profound statistical, and social, shift.

Furthermore, it's not just racial and ethnic characteristics that constitute diversity. As you can see in the Diversity Wheel in **Figure 9.1**, diversity comprises characteristics such as gender, sexual orientation, age, and mental and physical characteristics. Layer on top of that factors such as education, religion, and income level, and the complexity of others—and ourselves—becomes apparent. In addition, people often have multiple diversities: One can be, for instance, a

figure 9.1

Diversity Wheel

Diversity is composed of many different characteristics, as exemplified by the Diversity Wheel.

anything and everything other people experience — Test

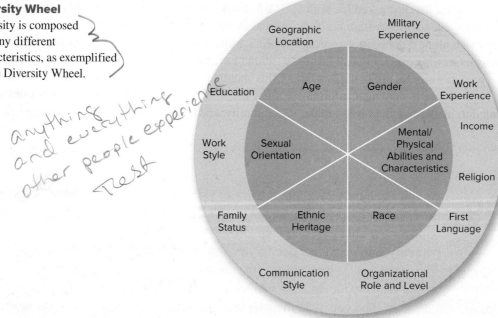

Test

race

Traditionally, biologically determined physical characteristics that set one group apart from others.

ethnicity — *eye of beholder*

Shared national origins or cultural patterns.

culture

The learned behaviors, beliefs, and attitudes that are characteristic of an individual society or population, and the products that people create.

hearing-impaired lesbian African American woman, evoking responses from others that reflect any, all, or none of these identities. (You can examine the diversity of your own campus by completing **Try It! 1**.)

Race, Ethnicity, and Culture

Are you African American or black? Caucasian or white or Euro-American? Hispanic or Latino? American Indian or Native American? Gay or lesbian? Physically challenged? A combination of various identities?

The language we use to describe our ethnic and racial group membership, and those of other people, is in constant flux. And what we call people matters. The subtleties of language affect how people think about members of particular groups, and how they think about themselves.

One of the difficulties in understanding diversity is that many of the terms we use are ill-defined and often overlapping. The term **race** is generally used to refer to obvious physical differences that set one group apart from others. According to such a definition, whites, blacks, and Asian Americans are typically thought of as belonging to different races, determined largely by biological factors.

Ethnicity refers to shared national origins or cultural patterns. In the United States, for example, Puerto Ricans, Irish Americans, and Italian Americans are categorized as ethnic groups. However, ethnicity—like race—is very much in the eye of the beholder. For instance, a Cuban American woman who is a third-generation citizen of the United States may feel few ties or associations to Cuba. Yet whites may view her as "Hispanic," and blacks may view her as "white."

Finally, **culture** comprises the learned behaviors, beliefs, and attitudes that are characteristic of an individual society or population. But it's more than that: Culture also encompasses the products that people create, such as architecture, music, art, and literature. Culture is created and shaped by people, but at the same time it creates and shapes people's behavior.

Determine the Diversity of Your Community

Try to assess the degree of diversity that exists in your community. *Community* can be a loosely defined term, but for this Try It! think of it as the group of people you encounter and interact with on a regular basis. When thinking of diversity, remember to include the many different ways in which people can be different from one another, including race, ethnicity, culture, sexual orientation, physical challenges, and so on.

1. List all of the groups in your community. Overall, how diverse would you say your community is?

2. Are there organizations in your community that promote diversity or work to raise the visibility and understanding of particular groups?

3. How diverse is your college's student body in terms of different racial, ethnic, or cultural groups? (You may be able to find statistics for this on your college's website.)

4. Is your college community more or less diverse than your community at large? Why do you think this might be?

5. How does the diversity in your community compare to the following statistics for the United States (as of the 2010 census)? White, 72 percent; Hispanic or Latino, 16 percent; black or African American, 13 percent; Asian, 5 percent; two or more races, 3 percent; American Indian and Alaska Native, .9 percent; Native Hawaiian and other Pacific Islander, .2 percent; other race, 6 percent. (Note: These percentages add up to more than 100 percent because Hispanics may be of any race and are therefore counted under more than one category.)

Race, ethnicity, and culture shape each of us to an enormous degree. They profoundly influence our view of others, as well as who we are. They affect how others treat us, and how we treat them in turn. They determine whether we look people in the eye when we meet them, how early we arrive when we're invited to dinner at a friend's house, and even, sometimes, how well we do in school or on the job.

Because many of us grew up in neighborhoods that are not ethnically diverse, we may have little or even no experience interacting with people who are different from us. Some college campuses don't have much diversity, either, and consequently, even in college, your exposure to people who have different backgrounds may be limited.

At some time, though, that will change. As the United States becomes increasingly diverse, it's not a matter of "if" but "when" you will be exposed to people who have

Workplace colleagues are increasingly diverse.
Source: © Monkey businessimages/iStock/Getty Images Plus/Getty Images

profoundly different backgrounds from your own. Whether in the workplace or the neighborhood in which you reside, living in a diverse environment will be part of your life.

Building Cultural Competence

Test

cultural competence
Knowledge and understanding about other races, ethnic groups, cultures, and minority groups.

We're not born knowing how to drive a car or cook. We have to learn how to do these things. The same is true of developing a basic understanding of other races, ethnic groups, and cultures. Called **cultural competence**, this knowledge of others' customs, perspectives, background, and history can teach us a great deal about others, as well as ourselves. Cultural competence also provides a basis for civic engagement, permitting us to act with civility toward others and to make the most of our contributions to society.

Building cultural competence proceeds in several steps, outlined in the P.O.W.E.R. Plan.

P Prepare

Accepting Diversity as a Valued Part of Your Life

P Prepare

Accept diversity as a valued part of your life

O Organize

Explore your own prejudices and stereotypes

W Work

Develop cultural competence

E Evaluate

Check your progress in attaining cultural competence

R Rethink

Understand how your own racial, ethnic, and cultural background affects others

P.O.W.E.R. Plan

In the title of her book on social diversity, psychologist Beverly Tatum asks, *"Why Are All the Black Kids Sitting Together in the Cafeteria?"*[1] She might just as well have asked a similar question about the white kids, the Asian American kids, and so forth. It often appears as if the world comes already divided into separate racial, ethnic, and cultural groups.

It's more than appearances: We form relationships more easily with others who are similar to us than with those who are different. It's easier to interact with others who look the same as we do, who come from similar backgrounds, and who share our race, ethnicity, and culture because we can take for granted certain shared cultural assumptions and views of the world.

But that doesn't mean that "easy" and "comfortable" translate into "good" or "right." We can learn a great deal more, and grow and be challenged, if we seek out people who are different from us. If you look beyond surface differences and find out what motivates other people, you can become aware of new ways of thinking about family, relationships, earning a living, and the value of education. It can be liberating to realize that others may hold very different perspectives from your own and that there are many ways to lead your life.

Letting diversity into your own life also has very practical implications: As we discuss in **Career Connections** (on page 232), learning to accept and work with people who are different from you is a crucial skill that will help you in whatever job you hold.

From the perspective of . . .

A STUDENT Having a varied classroom can help you see the world in a broader way. Have you ever had a classmate relate an experience that impacted your thought process?

Source: © PictureNet Corporation/Alamy

Journal Reflections

Thinking about Race, Ethnicity, and Culture

1. Were race and ethnicity discussed in your family as you were growing up? In what ways?

2. Do you demonstrate—through your behavior, attitudes, and/or beliefs—your own ethnic background? How?

3. Are there cultural differences between you and members of other races or ethnicities? What are they?

4. Are you proud of your ethnicity? Why?

5. Think what it would be like to be a member of a racial group or ethnicity other than your own. In what ways would your childhood and adolescence have been different? How would you view the world differently?

Organize

Exploring Your Own Prejudices and Stereotypes

Arab. Gay. African American. Hispanic. Female. Disabled. Overweight.

Quick: What comes into your mind when you think about each of these labels? If you're like most people, you don't draw a blank. Instead, a collection of images and feelings comes into your mind, based on what you know, have been told, or assume about the group.

The fact that we don't draw a blank when thinking about each of these terms means that we already have a set of attitudes and beliefs about them and the groups they represent. Acknowledging and then examining these preexisting assumptions is a first step toward developing cultural competence: We need to explore our own prejudices and stereotypes.

Diversity in the Workplace

Diversity, and issues relating to it, are a part of today's workplace. For example, in one California computer assembly company with several thousand employees, 40 different languages and dialects are spoken among people representing 30 nationalities.[2] Furthermore, employers must deal with issues ranging from whether time off for religious holidays should count as vacation time to whether the partner of a gay or lesbian worker should be covered by the worker's medical insurance.

The gulf in the workplace between people with different cultural backgrounds may be wide. For instance, an immigrant from Japan might consider it the height of immodesty to outline his or her accomplishments in a job interview. The explanation? In Japan, the general cultural expectation is that people should stress their incompetence; to do otherwise would be considered highly immodest.

The increasing diversity of the workplace means that increasing your cultural competence will serve you well. It will help you perform on work teams that are composed of people of different races and ethnic backgrounds. It will allow you to supervise people whose native language and customs may be different from yours. And it will help you to develop the skills to work for a boss from another country and cultural background.

Equally important, gaining cultural competence will help you respond to the legal issues that surround diversity. It is illegal for employers to discriminate on the basis of race, ethnic background, age, gender, and physical disability. Cultural competence will help you not only to deal with the letter of the law, but also to understand why embracing diversity is so important to getting along with others in the workplace.

prejudice *Test*

Evaluations or judgments of members of a group that are based primarily on membership in the group and not on the particular characteristics of individuals.

Test

stereotypes

Beliefs and expectations about members of a group that are held simply because of their membership in the group.

Prejudice refers to evaluations or judgments of members of a group that are based primarily on their membership in the group rather than on their individual characteristics. For example, the auto mechanic who doesn't expect a woman to understand auto repair or a job supervisor who finds it unthinkable that a father might want to take a leave for child care are engaging in gender prejudice. *Gender prejudice* is evaluating individuals on the basis of their being a male or female and not on their own specific characteristics or abilities. Similarly, prejudice can be directed toward individuals because of their race, ethnic origin, sexual orientation, age, physical disability, or even physical attractiveness. *Test*

Prejudice leads to discrimination. *Discrimination* is behavior directed toward individuals on the basis of their membership in a particular group. Discrimination can result in exclusion from jobs and educational opportunities. It also may result in members of particular groups receiving lower salaries and benefits.

Prejudice and discrimination are maintained by **stereotypes**—beliefs and expectations about members of a group. For example, do you think that women don't do as well as men in math? Do you agree that "white men can't jump"? Do you think that people on welfare are lazy?

If you answered yes to any of these questions, you hold stereotypes about the group being referred to. It is the degree of generalization involved that makes stereotypes inaccurate. Some women don't do well in math. But in fact many women do perfectly fine in math, and many men don't. Stereotypes ignore this diversity.

To develop cultural competence, it's important to identify our prejudices and stereotypes, and to fight them. Sometimes they are quite subtle and difficult to detect. For instance, a wealth of data taken from observation of elementary school classrooms shows that teachers are often more responsive to boys than to girls. The teachers don't know they're doing it; it's a subtle, but very real, bias.

Why does this happen? In part it's because we're exposed to stereotypes from a very young age. Parents and relatives teach them to us, sometimes unwittingly,

Career Connections

sometimes deliberately. The media illustrate them constantly and often in very subtle ways. For instance, African Americans and Latinos are often portrayed as unemployed or as criminals, women are less likely than men to be shown as employed, and gay men are frequently depicted as effeminate.

But it's not only stereotypes that lead us to view members of other groups differently from those of our own. For many people, their own membership in a cultural or racial or ethnic group is a source of pride and self-worth. There's nothing wrong with this. However, these feelings can lead to a less desirable outcome: the belief that their own group is superior to others. As a result, people inflate the positive aspects of their own group and belittle groups to which they do not belong. The result is continuing prejudice.

To overcome stereotypes and to develop cultural competence, we must first explore and identify our prejudices. To begin that process, complete **Try It! 2,** "Check Your Stereotype Quotient".

> "Prejudice is the child of ignorance."
> **William Hazlitt, essayist**

» LO 9-2

W | Work

Developing Cultural Competence

Although it's neither easy nor simple to increase your understanding of and sensitivity to other cultures, it can be done. Several strategies are effective:

▶ **Study other cultures and customs.** Take an anthropology course, study religion, or learn history. If you understand the purposes behind different cultural customs, attitudes, and beliefs, you will be able to understand the richness and meaning of other people's cultural heritage.

▶ **Travel.** There is no better way to learn about people from other cultures than to see those cultures firsthand. Vacations offer you the time to travel, and relatively inexpensive direct flights can take you to Europe, Asia, and other places around the globe. Sometimes, in fact, it's cheaper to take a transoceanic flight than to travel to closer locations in the United States.

If you can't afford airfare, take a car or bus ride to Mexico or Canada. In many parts of Canada, French is spoken and the culture is decidedly different from that in the United States (or the rest of Canada, for that matter).

Travel needn't be international, however. If you are from the northern states, head south. If you are from California, consider heading east. If you live in a large metropolitan area, travel to a less populated, rural spot. No matter where you go, simply finding yourself in a new context can aid your efforts to learn about other cultures.

▶ **Participate in community service.** By becoming involved in community service, such as tutoring middle school students, volunteering to work with the homeless, or working on an environmental cleanup, you get the opportunity to interact with people who may be very different from those you're accustomed to.

Travel provides us with an opportunity to become immersed in very different cultures and to see the world—and ourselves—through new eyes.
Source: © William Ryall 2010

Check Your Stereotype Quotient

Do you hold stereotypes about other people? How pervasive do you think they are? Respond to the following informal questionnaire to get a sense of your susceptibility to stereotyping:

1. When you see five African American students sitting together in a cafeteria, do you think that they are exhibiting racism? Do you think the same thing when you see five white students sitting together in a cafeteria?

2. When you are speaking with a person who has a speech-related disorder such as stuttering, are you likely to conclude that the person is less intelligent than a fluent speaker?

3. When an elderly woman can't remember something, do you assume her forgetfulness is because she is old or perhaps has Alzheimer's disease?

4. When an attractive blond female co-worker states an opinion, are you surprised if the opinion is intelligent and well expressed?

5. If a person with a mobility disorder were to turn down your offer for assistance, would you be offended and resentful?

6. If you found out that a star professional football player is gay, would you be surprised?

What do you think your answers tell you about yourself and your views of others?

 WORKING IN A GROUP

Compare your answers with those of your classmates. What do you think causes the similarities and differences in responses?

▶ **Don't ignore people's backgrounds.** None of us is color-blind—or blind to ethnicity or to culture. It's impossible to be completely unaffected by people's racial, ethnic, and cultural backgrounds. So why pretend to be? Cultural heritage is an important part of other people's identity, and to pretend that their background doesn't exist and has no impact on them is unrealistic at best and insulting at worst. It's important, though, to distinguish between accepting the fact that other people's backgrounds affect them and pigeonholing people, expecting them to behave in particular ways.

▶ **Don't make assumptions about who people are.** Don't assume that someone is heterosexual just because most people are heterosexual. Don't assume that someone with an Italian-sounding last name is Italian. Don't assume that a black person has two black parents.

▶ **Accept differences.** Different does not mean better. Different does not mean worse. Different just means not looking, acting, or believing exactly the same as you. We shouldn't attach any kind of value to being different; it's neither better nor worse than being similar.

In fact, even people who seem obviously different on the surface probably share many similarities with you. Like you, they have commitments to family or loved ones; they have fears and anxieties like yours; and they have aspirations and dreams, just as you do.

The important point about differences is that we need to accept and embrace them. Think about some differences you may have with people who are similar to you. Perhaps you really can't stand baseball, yet one of your childhood friends has followed the game since he was 5 and loves it. Chances are you both accept that you have different tastes and see this difference as part of who each of you is.

Checking Your Progress in Attaining Cultural Competence

Because cultural groups are constantly changing, developing cultural competence is an ongoing process. To evaluate where you stand, ask yourself the following questions. Be honest!

▶ Do I make judgments about others based on external features, such as skin color, ethnic background, cultural customs, gender, weight, or physical appearance?

▶ Who are my friends? Do they represent diversity or are they generally similar to me?

▶ Do I openly express positive values relating to diversity? Do I sit back passively when others express stereotypes and prejudices, or do I actively question their remarks?

▶ Am I educating myself about the history and varying experiences of different racial, ethnic, and cultural groups?

▶ Do I give special treatment to members of particular groups, or am I even-handed in my relationships?

▶ Do I recognize that despite surface differences, all people have the same basic needs?

▶ Do I feel so much pride in my own racial, ethnic, and cultural heritage that it leads me to look less favorably upon members of other groups?

▶ Do I seek to understand events and situations through the perspectives of others and not just my own?

Diversity in the Classroom

The increasing diversity of classrooms presents both opportunity and challenge. The opportunity comes from the possibility of learning on a firsthand basis about others and their experiences. The challenge comes when people who may be very different from us call into question some of our most fundamental beliefs and convictions.

Here are some ways that you can be better equipped to deal with the classroom challenges involved in diversity:

- **Present your opinions in a respectful manner.** Don't get annoyed or angry when others disagree with your point of view. Be tolerant of others' perspectives and their thinking.

- **Don't assume you can understand what it's like to be a member of another race, ethnicity, cultural group, or gender.** Talk about your own experiences, and don't assume you know what others have experienced.

- **Don't treat people as representatives of the groups to which they belong.** Don't ask someone how members of his or her racial, ethnic, or cultural group think, feel, or behave with respect to a particular issue. No single individual can speak for an entire group. Furthermore, group members are likely to display little uniformity on most issues and in most behaviors. Consequently, this type of question is ultimately impossible to answer.

- **Seek out students who are different from you.** If you are assigned a group project, volunteer to work with others who are different from you. You may learn more working with others who are dissimilar than working with those who are like you.

- **Don't be afraid to offer your opinion out of concerns for "political correctness."** If you offer an opinion in a respectful, thoughtful, and tolerant manner, you should feel free to voice your opinion. Even if your views are minority opinions, they deserve to be considered.

 Rethink

Understanding How Your Own Racial, Ethnic, and Cultural Background Affects Others

If you are a member of a group that traditionally has been the target of prejudice and discrimination, you probably don't need to be told that your race, ethnicity, and cultural background affect the way that others treat you. But even if you are a member of a traditionally dominant group in society, the way in which others respond to you is, in part, a result of others' assumptions about the group of which you are a part.

In short, both how we view others and how we ourselves are viewed are affected by the groups to which we—and others—belong. But keep this in mind: No matter how different other students, co-workers, or community members are from you in terms of their race, ethnicity, and cultural background, they undoubtedly share many of the same concerns you do. Like all of us, they question themselves, wonder whether they will be successful, and fret about making ends meet. Bridging the surface difference between you and others can result in the development of close, lasting social ties—a topic we consider next.

Building Lasting Relationships

Few of us lead our lives in isolation. There's a reason for this: Relationships with others are a critical aspect of our sense of well-being. The support of friends and relatives helps us feel good about ourselves. In fact, studies have found that our physical and psychological health may suffer without friendships. The social support of others acts as a guard against stress and illness. And if we do get sick, we recover more quickly if we have a supportive network of friends.

Our relationships with others also help us understand who we are. To understand our own abilities and achievements, we compare them with those of others who are similar to ourselves. Our attitudes, beliefs, and values are influenced—and shaped—by others. We are who we are largely because of the people with whom we come in contact.

"I have met the most amazing individuals and made the most incredible friends in such a short amount of time."

Student, Wittenberg University, Sponholz, M., & Sponholz, J. (1996). *The Princeton Review College Companion*, p. 24. New York: Random House.

Making Friends

Although some of us naturally make friends with ease, for others making friends is more difficult. But building relationships is not a mystery. Here are several ways to go about it:

▶ **Invest time in others.** There's no better way to demonstrate that you are interested in being friends than investing time. Relationships need to be nourished by the commitment of time. You can't expect friendships to flourish unless you spend time with people.

▶ **Reveal yourself.** Good friends understand each other. The best way to make that happen is to let others get to know you. Be open and honest about the things you like and dislike. Talk about where you come from, what your family is like. By honestly communicating your beliefs and attitudes, you give others the chance to learn those things you have in common.

▶ **Show concern and caring.** This is really the substance of friendship and the basis for the trust that develops between friends. Don't be afraid to show your interest in the fortunes of others and to share the sadness when they suffer some setback or loss.

▶ **Be open to friendships with people who are very different from you.** Don't assume the only "appropriate" friends are your peers who are similar to you, such as other college students. Open yourself to friends who are older, who are younger, who work at your school, and who are different from you in fundamental ways.

▶ **Recognize that not everyone makes a good friend.** People who put you down, consistently make you feel bad, or behave in ways that violate your own personal standards are not friends. Choose your friends based on the good feelings you have when you are with them and the concern and care they show for you. Friendship is a two-way street.

The R-Word: Relationships

Relationships move beyond friendship. They occur when two people feel emotionally attached, fulfill each other's needs, and generally feel interdependent. When a true relationship exists, several components are present:

▶ **Trust.** Relationships must be built on a foundation of trust. We need to be able to count on others and feel that they will be open with us.

▶ **Honesty.** No relationship can survive if the partners are not honest with one another. Each partner must share a commitment to the truth. Your life does not have to be a completely open book—it's the rare individual who has no secrets whatsoever—but it is important to be honest about your fundamental beliefs,

What you *don't* say matters. Close, lasting relationships are often built on good listening skills.
Source: © John Giustina/The Image Bank/Getty Images

values, and attitudes. Those in good relationships accept one another, blemishes and all. A relationship based on untruths or even half-truths lacks depth and meaning.

▶ **Mutual support.** Healthy relationships are characterized by mutual support. A partner's well-being should have an impact on you, and your well-being should affect your partner. In good relationships, the partners seek out what is best for both, and they act as advocates for and defend each other.

▶ **Loyalty.** The mark of a good relationship is loyalty. Loyalty implies that relationship partners are supportive of each other, even in times of adversity and difficulty.

▶ **Acceptance.** In good relationships small annoyances don't get in the way of the deeper connection between you and another person. We don't have to like everything others do to maintain relationships with them. We don't even have to appreciate or approve of every aspect of their personality. What is crucial is the willingness to accept others as they are without constantly yearning for changes.

▶ **Willingness** to embrace change. Change is part of everyone's life. As people grow and develop, they change. So do relationships.

We need to accept change as a fundamental part of relationships and build on that change. In fact, we need to welcome change. Although change brings challenges with it, it also helps us to understand ourselves and our own place in the world more accurately.

It is only natural that some relationships will fade over time. People sometimes outgrow each other. That's inevitable. What's important is not to live in fear that your relationship is so fragile that you have to avoid or ignore changes in each other. Instead, both partners should do their best to accept transformations in the relationship as a part of life.

Loneliness

loneliness

A subjective state in which people do not experience the level of connection with others that they desire.

Loneliness is a subjective state: We can be totally alone and not feel lonely, or we can be in the midst of a crowd and feel lonely. Loneliness occurs when we don't experience the level of connection with others that we desire. There are also different types of loneliness. Some of us feel lonely if we lack a deep emotional attachment to a single person, which can occur even if we have many friends. Others feel loneliness because they believe they don't have enough friends.

The reality is that there is no standard that indicates the "right" number of relationships. There's no standard against which to measure yourself and the number, and kind, of relationships that you have. It's something you need to decide.

Remember, also, that loneliness is not inevitable. There are several strategies you can use to deal with the feeling. You can become involved in a new activity, volunteering for a service organization or joining a recreational sports league. If you don't work, consider taking a job if it fits with your academic schedule. Not only will you have some more income, you'll have the chance to socialize with co-workers and perhaps form bonds of friendship with them, as well. You should also take advantage of the social opportunities you do have. Even if you don't think of yourself as a "people person," accept invitations from people you know to parties and other gatherings. You never know when you might meet someone you truly connect with.

What if your feelings of loneliness are extreme and you experience a sense of complete isolation and alienation from your classmates? If the feeling persists, it's wise to talk to a health service provider, college counseling center, or a trusted family member. Although everyone feels isolated at times, such feelings shouldn't be extreme. Counselors can help you deal with them.

» LO 9-3 Communicating in Relationships

Communicating well in personal relationships is a blend of talking and listening. Not only does it help to do both well, but it is also important to know when it's time to listen and when it's time to speak up. Listening is an often overlooked skill in personal relationships. We may be so busy trying to communicate our feelings and interests that we overlook the need of the other person to be heard. As friendships develop into personal relationships, simply talking isn't enough. How you express yourself, especially in moments of difficulty, can be very important to getting your message across.

Being a Good Listener: The Power of Supportive Silence

When it comes to building relationships, how you listen is sometimes more important than what you say. The silence involved in listening is a powerful force, one that can bind us more closely to others.

You may already have discussed the art and science of listening as it applies to academic success. The same principles that promote learning about lecture topics also promote learning about our friends. You can't call yourself a good friend without knowing what others are like and what they are thinking. Good listening is one of the ways to enhance your understanding of others.

When we are heard, we appreciate it because we get the message that our listeners care about us, not just about themselves. Similarly, when we listen, we show that we have respect for those who are speaking, are interested in their ideas and beliefs, and are willing to take the time to pay attention to them.

There are several ways you can improve your ability to listen:

1. **Stop talking!** Are you the kind of person who revels in telling stories about what happened to you? Do you wait eagerly for others to finish what they are saying so that you can jump in with a response? Do you accidentally cut other people off or finish their sentences while they are speaking?

   No one likes to be interrupted, even in casual conversation. In more personal relationships, it is a sign of not respecting what the other person has to say and is hurtful.

2. **Demonstrate that you are listening.** Linguists call them "conversational markers"—those nonverbal indications that we're listening. They consist of head nods, uh-huhs, OKs, and other signs that we're keeping up with the

conversation. Eye contact is important too. Listening this way shows that we're paying attention and are interested in what the other person is saying.

In addition, don't multitask. If you're having a serious conversation, turn off your cell phone. If it does ring, don't look at caller ID. Even glancing at your phone for a moment shows you're not paying full attention.

3. **Use reflective feedback.** Carl Rogers, a respected therapist, developed a very useful way to lend support to someone and draw him or her out. In **reflective feedback**, a listener rephrases what a speaker has said, trying to echo the speaker's meaning. For example, a listener might say, "as I understand what you're saying . . . ," or "you seem to feel that . . . ," or "in other words, you believe that. . . ."

In each case, the summary statement doesn't just "play back" the speaker's statements literally. Instead it is a rephrasing that captures the essence of the message in different words.

Reflective feedback has two big benefits. First, it provides speakers with a clear indication that you are listening and taking what they're saying seriously. Second, and equally important, it helps ensure that you have an accurate understanding of what the speaker is saying.

4. **Ask questions.** Asking questions shows that you are paying attention to a speaker's comments. Questions permit you to clarify what the speaker has said, and he or she can move the conversation forward. Further, people feel valued when others ask them about themselves.

5. **Admit when you're distracted.** We've all had those moments: Something is bothering you and you can't get it out of your mind, or you've simply got to finish something and don't really have time to chat. If at the same time someone wants to engage you in conversation, your distraction will undoubtedly show, making the other person feel you are not interested in her or him.

The way to deal with this situation is to admit that you're distracted. Simply saying, "I'd love to talk, but I've got to finish reading a chapter," is enough to explain the situation to a classmate who wants to talk about his date.

It's Not Just Talk: Avoiding and Handling Conflicts in Relationships

Listening communicates a great deal in personal relationships; but as discussed previously, it is also important to put yourself forward. Generally, close relationships are built on good communication, so day to day there may be no problem in this regard. But when misunderstandings or conflicts occur—as they definitely will from time to time—communication can fall apart. In these situations your ability to communicate in words is tested, and more sensitive listening and more careful ways of saying what you think and feel are needed.

The Subject Is "I" and Not "You"

Suppose a close friend says something with which you disagree: "All you guys are the same—you expect to get everything your way!" You might respond by directing anger at the other person, directly or indirectly accusing the person of some imperfection. "You're always looking for something to complain about!" Such responses (and, as you will notice, the initial statement) typically include

---

reflective feedback
A technique of verbal listening in which a listener rephrases what a speaker has said, trying to echo the speaker's meaning.

"The reason why we have two ears and only one mouth is that we may listen the more and talk the less."
Zeno of Citium, philosopher

the word *you*. For instance, consider these possible responses to indicate disagreement: "*You* really don't understand"; "*You're* being stubborn"; and "How can *you* say that?"

These types of statements cast blame, make accusations, express criticism, and make assumptions about what's inside the other person's head. And they lead to defensive replies that will probably do little to move the conversation forward: "I am *not*!"; "I do so understand"; "I'm not being stubborn"; and "I can say that because that's the way I feel."

A far more reasonable tactic is to use "I" statements. **"I" statements** cast responses in terms of yourself and your individual interpretation. Instead of saying, for example, "You really don't understand," a more appropriate response would be, "I think we're misunderstanding each other." "You're not listening to me" could be rephrased as "I feel like I may not be getting my point across." And "Why don't you call when you're going to be late?" becomes "I worry that something has happened to you when you don't call if you are going to be late." In each case, "I" statements permit you to state your reaction in terms of your perception or understanding, rather than as a critical judgment about the other person. (Practice using "I" statements in **Try It! 3**.)

"I" statements
Statements that cast responses in terms of oneself and one's individual interpretation.

From the perspective of . . .

A HUMAN RESOURCES SPECIALIST Relationships are a key part of a successful professional environment. What might you need to know about fostering positive relationships in your professional life?

Source: © Burke/Triolo Productions/Brand X Pictures/ Corbis

Resolving Conflict: A Win–Win Proposition

Even with careful attention to putting our own feelings forward instead of making accusations, whenever two people share their thoughts, concerns, fears, and honest reactions with each other, the chances are that sooner or later some sort of conflict will arise.

Conflict is not necessarily bad.

Often people are upset simply by the fact that they are having a conflict. It is as though they believe conflicts don't occur in "good" relationships. In fact, however, conflict is helpful in some important ways. It can force us to say what is really on our minds. It can allow us to clear up misconceptions and miscommunications before they begin to undermine the relationship. It can even give us practice at resolving conflicts with others with whom we might not share such good relations.

Outside the context of close relationships, conflict is not necessarily a bad thing, either. In the working world, conflict is often inevitable. Yet as in relationships, conflicts on the job can be beneficial. Misconceptions can be cleared up and new processes devised when co-workers engage in honest, productive discussion.

Like anything else, though, there are good ways to resolve conflict, and there are bad ways. Good ways move people forward, defining the problem and promoting creative problem solving. Bad ways make the situation worse, driving people apart rather than bringing them together.

Switch "You" to "I"

Working in a group or in pairs, turn the following "you" statements into less aggressive "I" statements. For example, a possible "I" statement alternative to "You just don't get it, do you?" would be "I don't think I'm making my feelings clear."

1. You just don't get it, do you?

2. You never listen to what I say.

3. You never try to see my point of view.

4. You don't really believe that, do you?

5. You always try to control everything and never let me make any decisions.

6. You never give me credit for anything.

7. Stop changing the subject!

8. You're not making sense.

9. You keep distorting what I say until I don't even know what point I'm trying to make.

10. You always use "you" statements when we disagree. Try using an "I" statement once in a while.

The following are some fundamental principles of conflict resolution that you can use when conflict occurs in personal and professional relationships:

▶ **Stop, look, and listen.** In the heat of an argument, all sorts of things that otherwise would go unsaid get said. If you find yourself making rash or hurtful statements, stop, look at yourself, and listen to what you and the other person are saying.

Stopping works like a circuit breaker that prevents a short circuit from causing a deadly fire. You've probably heard about counting to 10 to cool off when you're angry. Do it. Take a break and count to 10 . . . or 20 . . . or more. Whether you count to 10 or 100, stopping gives you time to think and not react rashly.

▶ **Defuse the argument.** Anger is not an emotion that encourages rational discourse. When you're angry and annoyed with someone, you're not in the best position to evaluate logically the merits of various arguments others may offer. It may feel exhilarating to get our fury off our chests in the heat of an argument, but you can bet it isn't taking anyone any closer to resolving the problem.

Don't assume that you are 100 percent right and the other person is 100 percent wrong. Make your goal *solving the problem* rather than winning an argument.

▶ **Get personal.** Perhaps you've heard others suggest that you shouldn't get personal in an argument. In one sense that's true: Accusing people you're arguing with of having character flaws does nothing to resolve real issues.

At the same time, you should be willing to admit personal *responsibility* for at least part of the conflict. The conflict would not exist without you, so you need to accept that the argument has two sides and that you are not automatically blameless. This creates some solid ground from which you and the other person can begin to work on the problem.

▶ **Listen to the real message.** When people argue, what they say is often not the real message. There's typically an underlying communication—a subtext—that is the source of the conflict.

It's important, then, to dig beneath what you're hearing. If someone accuses you of being selfish, the real meaning hidden in the accusation may be that you don't give anyone else a chance to make decisions. Remember, arguments are usually about behavior, not underlying character and personality. What people *do* is not necessarily synonymous with who they *are*.

If you rephrase the person's statement in your own mind, it moves from an insult ("You're a bad person") to a request for a change of behavior ("Let me participate in decision making"). You're much more likely to respond reasonably when you don't feel that the essence of your being is under attack.

▶ **Show that you're listening.** It's not enough only to listen to the underlying message that someone is conveying. You also need to acknowledge the *explicit* message. For example, saying something like "OK. I can tell you are concerned about sharing the burden on our group project, and I think we should talk about it" acknowledges that you see the issue and admit that it is worthy of discussion. This is a far more successful strategy than firing back a countercharge each time your co-worker makes a complaint.

▶ **If you are angry, acknowledge it.** Don't pretend that everything is fine if it isn't. Ultimately, relationships in which the partners bottle up their anger may suffer more than those in which the partners express their true feelings. If you're angry, say so, but do it in a way that is noncombative.

- **Ask for clarification.** As you're listening to another person's arguments, check out your understanding of what is being said. Don't assume that you know what's intended. Saying something like "Are you saying . . ." or "Do you mean that . . ." is a way of verifying that what you *think* someone means is really what is meant.

- **Make your requests explicit.** If you're upset that your spouse leaves clothes lying around your apartment, remarking that he or she is a "pig" shows more than that you are angry. It also shows that your intent is to hurt rather than to solve the problem.

  It's far better to be explicit in your concerns. Say something like "It would make me feel better if you would pick up your clothes from the floor." Couching your concern in this way changes the focus of the message from your spouse's personality to a specific behavior that can be changed.

- **Always remember that life is not a zero-sum game.** Many of us act as if life were a *zero-sum game,* a situation in which when one person wins, the other person automatically loses. It's what happens when you make a bet: If one person wins the bet, the other person loses.

  Life is not like that. If one person wins an argument, it doesn't mean that others automatically have to lose it. And if someone loses an argument, it doesn't mean that others have automatically won. In fact, all too often conflict escalates so much that the argument turns into a lose–lose situation, where everyone ends up a loser.

  However, life can be a win–win situation. The best resolution of conflict occurs when both parties walk away with something they want. Each may not have achieved *every* goal, but both will at least have enough to feel satisfied.

- **Finally, if a relationship involves emotional or physical abuse, you must seek help and end the relationship.** If a partner is emotionally or physically abusive to you, seek assistance from trained counselors. Don't wait. It is virtually impossible to deal with abuse on your own. Your college counseling center, mental health center, or medical center can offer you help. If you are physically threatened or injured, call 911.

When Relationships Are Over: Dealing with Endings

Not all relationships last a lifetime. Sometimes they just wind down, as the two people involved slowly lose interest in maintaining their partnership. At other times they break apart, as disagreements build and there is not a strong enough bond to hold the two parties together. Or there may be an abrupt rupture if some event occurs that destroys one partner's feeling of trust.

Caring for others is rewarding, but risky. When relationships don't work out, their endings can be painful, even devastating, for a time. Even when relationships evolve naturally and change is expected, the transformation in a relationship may not be easy. Parents die. Children grow up and move away from home. Siblings get new jobs on the other side of the country.

In the aftermath of a failed relationship, there are things you can do to ease the pain. The first is simple: Do *something.* Mow the lawn, clean out the closets, go for a run, see a movie. It won't completely get your mind off your loss, but it beats languishing at home, thinking about what you might have done differently or what could have been. Also, accept that you feel bad. If you're not experiencing unhappiness over the end of a relationship, it means that the relationship wasn't terribly meaningful in the first place. Understand that unhappiness normally accompanies the end of a relationship, and allow yourself your natural emotional response.

Finally, and perhaps most important, talk about your sadness. Seek out a friend or a relative. Discussing your feelings will help you deal with them better. If your sadness over a relationship feels totally overwhelming or continues for what you perceive to be too long a time, talk to a counselor or other professional. He or she can help you gain a better understanding of the situation and perhaps help you understand why you are taking it so hard.

Remember, there is one sure cure for the heartache of a lost relationship: time. The pain will eventually fade to a point where it is no longer difficult to manage. As the saying goes, time does heal virtually all wounds.

Speaking *of* Success

Source: Courtesy of Nichole Whitney Philipp

NAME: **Nichole Whitney Philipp**

SCHOOL: **Delaware County Community College, Media, Pennsylvania**

MAJOR: **Chemical engineering**

For Nichole Philipp, there was never any question that she would go to a two-year community college. Her father and sister both attended Delaware County Community College, and the location was ideal. But it also was best suited to her academic needs.

In her two years at Delaware County, Philipp maintained a 4.0 cumulative average, and she was one of 50 community college students in the nation to be named a New Century Scholar. But college wasn't without its challenges.

"Reading and math were very difficult for me in elementary and high school," said Philipp. "Having learned how to weld when I was 7, and having worked on cars most of my life, I knew I wanted to pursue engineering. I thought that a community college would not only offer me the opportunity, but also be better at providing a one-on-one connection with the faculty."

Pursuing a degree in engineering was challenging, particularly as the only female in her engineering class.

"Being the only woman was difficult at first, trying to earn the respect of your classmates and having to prove yourself. But I was determined to succeed, and once I started to do well, everyone came around."

In an effort to commit herself to school, Philipp said she treated going to school as if it were a job.

"I would come in at 8:00 in the morning and not leave until 4:00 in the afternoon," Philipp explained. "I found that people who go to college really need to work three hours for every single class that they're in."

Strong planning and time management skills were keys to Philipp's academic success.

"I would sit down at the beginning of the week and would plan my studies, laying them out, hour by hour," she explained. "You need to learn good time management and to set goals. I think it's important to really think about the fact that no one is forcing you to go college, and it's up to you how you perform," Philipp said.

[RETHINK]

- What kinds of stereotypes did Philipp likely face as she pursued her engineering degree?

- Do you think Philipp's being named a New Century Scholar helped her earn the respect of her classmates?

Looking Back

LO 9-1 Discuss why the increasing racial, ethnic, and cultural diversity of society is important to You.

▶ The diversity of the United States—and of U.S. college campuses—is increasing rapidly, and the world is becoming smaller as television, radio, the Internet, the web, and international commerce bring people and cultures closer together.

▶ Being aware of diversity can allow you to accept the challenge and opportunity of living and working with others who are very different from you.

LO 9-2 Utilize strategies to become more at ease with differences and diversity.

▶ Cultural competence begins with accepting diversity by seeking out others who are different from you, as well as exploring your own prejudices and stereotypes.

▶ You can learn about other cultures by traveling to other countries and geographic areas. It also helps to accept differences simply as differences.

LO 9-3 Build lasting relationships and learn to deal with conflict.

▶ Relationships not only provide social support and companionship, but also help people understand themselves.

▶ The central components of good relationships are trust, honesty, mutual support, loyalty, acceptance, and a willingness to embrace change.

▶ Listening is an important skill for relationship building, demonstrating that the listener really cares about the other person.

▶ Conflict is inevitable in relationships, and sometimes it is useful because it permits us to clear up misconceptions and miscommunications before they escalate.

▶ Although the end of a relationship can be very painful, the pain does subside over time.

[KEY TERMS AND CONCEPTS]

Cultural competence (p. 230)
Culture (p. 228)
Ethnicity (p. 228)

"I" statements (p. 241)
Loneliness (p. 238)
Prejudice (p. 232)

Race (p. 228)
Reflective feedback (p. 240)
Stereotypes (p. 232)

[RESOURCES]

AT SCHOOL

Anyone who feels he or she is facing discrimination based on race, gender, ethnic status, sexual orientation, or national origin should contact a college official *immediately*. Sometimes there is a specific office that handles such complaints. If you don't know which campus official to contact, speak to your academic advisor or someone in the dean's office and you'll be directed to the appropriate person. The important thing is to act and not to suffer in silence. Discrimination not only is immoral, but is against the law.

IN PRINT

Beverly Tatum's "*Why Are All the Black Kids Sitting Together in the Cafeteria?" And Other Conversations about Race* (HarperCollins, 2003 rev. ed.) explores race, racism, and the everyday impact of prejudice.

In *Readings for Diversity and Social Justice* (Routledge, 2013, 3rd ed.), editors Maurianne Adams and Warren Blumenfeld compile a comprehensive collection of essays covering a wide variety of social issues.

Finally, Joseph Folger, Marshall Poole, and Randall Stutman's *Working through Conflict: Strategies for Relationships, Groups, and Organizations* (Allyn & Bacon, 2013) suggests a variety of practical approaches to resolving conflict.

ON THE WEB

The following sites on the web provide the opportunity to extend your learning about the material in this chapter. (Although the web addresses were accurate at the time this material was published, check the *P.O.W.E.R. Learning* Connect website or contact your instructor for any changes that may have occurred.)

▶ "Communication Improvement" (**www.colorado.edu/conflict/peace/treatment/ commimp.htm**) is an outline posting by the Conflict Research Consortium at the University of Colorado. It includes a lengthy section on improving communication, with added links to improving listening skills and conflict resolution.

▶ This site provides a comprehensive look at language and culture covering all aspects of communication, from speech to body language, as used by cultures around the world. (**http://anthro.palomar.edu/language/default.htm**).

▶ "Race Relations" (**racerelations.about.com**), a comprehensive site on About.com, discusses topics ranging from affirmative action to white privilege. Hundreds of links are provided for more in-depth discussions and background on a variety of subjects, including race relations, hate crimes, gay/lesbian issues, and many other topics.

The Case of . . .
The Lose–Lose Team

Shannon Jones slammed down her book and stomped out of the room. Men! They always thought they ruled the world. They always had to control everyone and everything.

Watching Shannon's stormy exit, Jomo Okafor sighed. White people. They always had to have the last word. Always had to be the boss.

Shannon and Jomo had been assigned to work as a team on a project for their accounting class, but right from the start they'd bickered about everything. How the research should be done. Which sources they would use. How their findings should be presented. The only thing they agreed on was that the project should be a big success.

After the blow-up, Shannon told her sister, "Jomo's got great ideas. He's really creative. But he never listens to anything I say."

Jomo told a co-worker, "Shannon's quick. She's very smart. But she's a control freak. She acts like I'm her assistant."

The bottom line: Shannon and Jomo's project is due next week, and they've barely started the work.

1. How are stereotypes affecting Shannon's and Jomo's abilities to communicate with each other?

2. Can you identify with either Shannon's or Jomo's feelings? Have you ever been quick to dismiss someone's disagreement with you as being racist or sexist?

3. Do you think Shannon and/or Jomo view their disagreements as a zero-sum game? What advice would you give them to work more effectively as a team?

4. How could Shannon or Jomo defuse an argument before it gets to the blow-up point? What advice could you give them to improve their listening skills?

5. How could Shannon and Jomo use "I" statements to improve their communication?

10

Money Matters

Learning Outcomes

By the time you finish this chapter you will be able to

» LO **10-1** Explain how to develop a financial philosophy and its value.

» LO **10-2** Discuss strategies for managing your money.

» LO **10-3** Describe approaches to paying for your college education.

Source: © **PhotoDisc/Getty Images**

Jonathan Chen worked 60 hours a week all summer. By the time classes started, he'd banked enough money to take him comfortably through the school year. Or so he thought. But first his rent increased $100 a month. Then his car needed new front brakes and new shocks. Another $1,200. He spent a few weekends in Kansas City with friends, which, he was amazed to find, set him back $600. On top of all that, his roommate liked to eat well. The grocery bill was costing Jonathan $50 more a week than he'd figured. He didn't say anything about it because he didn't want to seem like a cheapskate, but . . .

In November, as he withdrew the money to pay his rent, he got up the courage to ask for his balance. The truth hurt. The money that was meant to see him through the year was three-quarters gone.

Looking Ahead

Jonathan Chen's story is hardly unique. Our finances present us with many challenges. Money plays a large role in our lives. It can determine where we go to college, where we live, and what jobs we take. It is the source of many of our problems and stress, forcing us to find a balance between what we need and what we want.

This chapter will show you how to manage your money. It begins by discussing the process of preparing a budget and identifying your financial goals—the basis for money management. The chapter goes on to examine ways you can keep track of your spending and estimate your financial needs and resources, and it discusses ways to control your spending habits and save money.

Education is one of the largest financial expenditures anyone encounters in life. Knowing the best ways to meet the costs of a college education—finding loans, grants, and scholarships—can give your finances a big boost and help you avoid graduating with thousands of dollars of debt. You will also learn what to do if your personal finances get out of control and discover how to stop the downward spiral of unpaid bills, defaulted loans, and unfavorable credit ratings. The chapter ends by suggesting ways to develop a financial philosophy.

» LO 10-1 Building a Financial Philosophy

Do you know where your money goes? Do you spend more than you think you should? Do you never have quite enough cash to buy the things you want?

Answering these questions and understanding the role money plays in your life is the first step of wise money management. To begin getting a grip on your finances, answer the questions in the **Journal Reflections** exercise.

Exploring your views of money is the first step in developing a meaningful financial philosophy, a way of viewing the role that money plays in one's life. For example, there's a famous line from *Jerry Maguire,* the Tom Cruise movie about a sports agent, in which an athlete claims his family motto is "Show me the money." That blunt statement might be used to illustrate one financial philosophy—that life revolves around money.

Others would disagree. For instance, some take the opposite viewpoint, arguing that money controls too many people and is a major source of stress. To combat an obsession with money, living a frugal existence in which money plays virtually no role is seen as the key to happiness.

Whether you choose to follow the path of Jerry Maguire or a more frugal existence, the important thing is to develop your own personal financial philosophy. Consider the role that money plays in your life. How much does money motivate what you do? Are you interested in becoming rich, or do you tend to think more in terms of simply having enough to have a comfortable life, without lots of

Journal Reflections

My Sense of Cents

Answer the following questions about your financial sense.

1. How much money do you now have in your pockets and wallet? (Guess first, then look.) How close did you come?

2. Do you know how much money you typically spend in a month, including money spent on food, lodging, and other items?

3. How good a sense of your finances do you think you have? How secure do you feel in your understanding of where your money goes?

4. How important is money to you? Why?

5. Research shows that although winning the lottery or other large sums of money brings an initial surge in happiness, a year later the winners' level of happiness returns to what it was before.[1] Why do you think this is true in general, and would it be true for you?

luxuries? What activities bring you the greatest satisfaction in life? Do those activities require a certain level of income? Explore these questions further in **Try It! 1**.

Developing a financial philosophy is the first step to gaining control over the role money plays in your life. The next step is to build a budget, a way of determining how you already use money and a plan for the future.

» LO 10-2 Managing Your Money

budget

A formal plan that accounts for expenditures and income.

If you have money problems—and there's virtually no one who doesn't have some concerns about finances—the solution is to develop a budget. A **budget** is a formal plan that accounts and plans for expenditures and income. Taking your goals into account, a budget helps determine how much money you should be spending each month, based on your income and your other financial resources. Budgets also help prepare for the unexpected, such as the loss of a job or an illness that would reduce your income, or for sudden, unanticipated expenses, such as a major car repair.

Discover Your Personal Financial Philosophy

Begin to create a personal financial philosophy by completing this Attitudes Toward Money questionnaire.

	Strongly Disagree	Disagree	Neutral	Agree	Strongly Agree
1. Money is essential for happiness.					
2. Having money guarantees happiness.					
3. Money makes no difference to one's happiness.					
4. More money equals more happiness.					
5. Having enough to live modestly on, money doesn't make much of a difference.					
6. I frequently worry about money.					
7. I frequently daydream about having a lot of money.					
8. If I suddenly had to live on very little money, I could adjust easily.					
9. If I suddenly won a lot of money, I would go on a spending spree.					
10. If I suddenly won a lot of money, I would share it with my relatives.					
11. If I suddenly won a lot of money, I would give a large percentage to charity.					
12. If I found a substantial amount of cash in a bag, I would try hard to find its rightful owner.					
13. If I could carry out of a burning building only a briefcase full of $100 bills or my pet dog, I would take the dog.					
14. I plan to make a lot of money in my career.					
15. I plan to make only enough money to live in reasonable comfort.					
16. It's great to have money.					
17. Money is a necessary evil.					
18. Money is the root of all evil.					

(continued)

After completing the questionnaire, answer these questions about your sources of satisfaction.

1. Which activities that you engaged in over the last 5 years have given you the greatest satisfaction?

2. How much money did those activities cost?

3. How would you spend your time if you could do anything you chose?

4. How much money would this cost each year?

PERSONAL FINANCIAL PHILOSOPHY

Based on the results of your Attitudes Toward Money questionnaire and the sources of your satisfaction, sum up your personal financial philosophy here in a short paragraph:

Budgeting on the Job

If you've ever held a job, the salary you received was determined, in part, by your employer's budget.

Although they may not always be accessible to every employee, budgets are part of the world of work. Regardless of who the employer is—be it a small dry cleaning business or the massive federal government—there is a budget outlining anticipated income and expenditures. Managers are expected to keep to the budget, and if their expenditures exceed what is budgeted, they are held accountable.

For this reason, the ability to create and live within a budget is an important skill to acquire. Not only will it help keep your own finances under control, but it will also prepare you to be financially responsible and savvy on the job—qualities that are highly valued by employers.

Although all budgets are based on an uncomplicated premise—expenditures should not exceed income—budgeting is not simple. There are several times during the year that require especially large expenditures, such as the start of a semester, when you must pay your tuition and purchase books. Furthermore, your income can be erratic: It can rise and fall depending on overtime, whether another member of your family starts or stops working, and so forth. But a budget will help you deal with the ups and downs in your finances. Learning budgeting skills can also help you at work, as discussed in this chapter's **Career Connections**.

Most of all, a budget provides security. It will let you take control of your money, permitting you to spend it as you need to without guilt because you have planned for the expenditures. It also makes it easier to put money aside because you know that your current financial sacrifice will be rewarded later, when you can make a purchase that you've been planning for.

Budgeting is very personal: What is appropriate for one person doesn't work for another. For a few people, keeping track of their spending comes naturally; they enjoy accounting for every dollar that passes through their hands. For most people, though, developing a budget—and sticking to it—does not come easily.

However, if you follow several basic steps—illustrated in the P.O.W.E.R. Plan—the process of budgeting is straightforward.

> "There was a time when a fool and his money were soon parted, but now it happens to everybody."
>
> **Adlai Stevenson, politician**

P | Prepare — Identifying Your Financial Goals

Your first reaction when asked to identify your financial goals may be that the question is a no-brainer: You want to have more money to spend. But it's not that simple. You need to ask yourself *why* you want more money. What would you spend it on? What would bring you the most satisfaction? Purchasing an iPad? Paying off your debt? Saving money for a vacation? Starting a business? Paying for college rather than taking out loans?

You won't be able to develop a budget that will work for you until you determine your short- and long-term financial goals. To determine them, use **Try It! 2**, "Identify Your Financial Goals."

P | Prepare
Identify financial goals

O | Organize
Determine expenditures and income

W | Work
Make a budget that adds up

E | Evaluate
Review the budget

R | Rethink
Rethink financial options

P.O.W.E.R. Plan

Identify Your Financial Goals

Determining your financial goals will help set you on the path to securing your financial future. Use this Try It! to get started.

Step 1. Use the planning tool below to identify and organize your financial goals:

SHORT-TERM GOALS

What would you like to have money for in the short term (over the next 3 months)? Consider these categories:

Personal necessities (such as food, lodging, clothes, household supplies, transportation, loan and credit card payments, medical and child care expenses):

Educational necessities (such as tuition, fees, books, school supplies, computer expenses):

Social needs (e.g., getting together with family, friends, and others; clubs and teams; charitable contributions):

Entertainment (e.g., movies and shows, trips, recreation, and sports):

Other:

MID-RANGE GOALS

What would you like to have money for soon (3 months from now to a year from now), but not immediately? Use the same categories:

Personal necessities:

Educational necessities:

Social needs:

Entertainment:

Other:

LONG-RANGE GOALS

What would you like to have money for 1 to 3 years from now? Use the same categories:

Personal necessities:

Educational necessities:

Social needs:

Entertainment:

Other:

Step 2. Now put each of your lists in **priority** order.

Short-term priorities:

Mid-range priorities:

Long-range priorities:

What does the list tell you about what is important to you? Did you find any surprises? Would you classify yourself as a financial risk taker or someone who values financial security?

 WORKING IN A GROUP

Compare your priorities with those of your classmates. What similarities and differences do you find, and what can you learn from others' priorities?

Determining Your Expenditures and Income

Organize

Do you open your wallet for the $10 that was there yesterday and find only a dollar? Spending money without realizing it is a common affliction.

Keeping to a budget is a constant balancing act. For example, even though you know you'll need to purchase books at the start of each semester, you can't predict exactly how much they will cost.
Source: © Keith Srakocic/AP Images

There's only one way to get a handle on where your money is going: Keep track of it. To get an overview of your expenditures, go through any records you've kept to identify where you've spent money for the last year—old checks, rent and utility receipts, and previous college bills can help you.

In addition, keep track of everything you spend for a week. *Everything.* When you spend $1.00 for a candy bar from a vending machine, write it down. When you buy lunch for $4.99 at a fast-food restaurant, write it down. When you buy a postage stamp, write it down.

Record your expenditures in a small notebook or on your smartphone. It may be tedious, but you're doing it for only a week. And it will be eye-opening: People are usually surprised at how much they spend on little items without thinking about it.

Make a list of everything you think you'll need to spend over the next year. Some items are easy to think of, such as rent and tuition payments, because they occur regularly and the amount you pay is fixed. Others are harder to budget for because they can vary substantially. For example, the price of gasoline changes frequently. If you have a long commute, the changing price of gasoline can cause substantial variation in what you pay each month. (Use **Table 10.1** to estimate your expenditures for the coming year.

When you are listing your upcoming expenditures, be sure to include an amount that you will routinely put aside into a savings account that pays you interest. It's important to get into the habit of saving money. Even if you start off small—putting aside just a few dollars a week—the practice of regularly putting aside some amount of your income is central to good financial management.

Determine Your Income Sources

You probably have a pretty good idea of how much money you have each month. But it's as important to list each source of income as it is to account for everything you spend.

Add up what you make at any jobs you hold. Also list any support you receive from family members, including occasional gifts you might get from relatives. Finally,

Source: © Michael Maslin/The New Yorker Collection/The Cartoon Bank

table 10.1   Estimated Expenditures, Next 12 Months

Category	Now to 3 Months from Now	3–6 Months from Now	6–9 Months from Now	9–12 Months from Now
Personal Necessities				
Food				
Shelter (rent, utilities, etc.)				
Clothing				
Household supplies				
Transportation (car payments, gas, car repairs, bus tickets, etc.)				
Loan and credit card payments				
Medical expenses				
Childcare expenses				
Other				
Educational Necessities				
Tuition and fees				
Books				
School supplies				
Computer expenses				
Other				
Social Needs				
Relationships				
Clubs and teams				
Charitable contributions				
Other				
Entertainment				
Movies and shows				
Trips				
Recreation and sports				
Other				
Total				

table 10.2 Estimated Income, Next 12 Months

Category	Now to 3 Months from Now	3–6 Months from Now	6–9 Months from Now	9–12 months from Now
Wages				
Family support				
Financial aid				
Tuition reductions				
Loan income				
Scholarship payments				
Other				
Interest and dividends				
Gifts				
Other				
TOTAL				

include any financial aid (such as tuition reductions, loan payments, or scholarships) you receive from your college. Use **Table 10.2** to record this information. When you do, be sure to list the amounts you receive in terms of after-tax income.

W Work | Making a Budget That Adds Up

If you've prepared and organized your budget, actually constructing your budget is as easy as adding 2 + 2. Well, not exactly; the numbers will be larger. But all you need to do is add up your list of expenses, and then add up your sources of income. In a perfect world, the two numbers will be equal.

But most of the time, the world is not perfect: Most of us find that our expenditures are larger than our income. After all, if we had plenty of excess cash, we probably wouldn't be bothering to make a budget in the first place.

If you find you spend more than you make, there are only two things to do: Decrease your spending or increase your income. It's often easiest to decrease expenditures because your expenses tend to be more under your control. For instance, there are many things you can do to save money, including the following:

▶ **Control impulse buying.** If you shop for your groceries, always take a list with you, and don't shop when you're hungry.

▶ **Make and take your own lunch.** Brown-bag lunches can save you a substantial amount of money over purchasing your lunches, even if you go to a fast-food restaurant or snack bar.

- **Read the daily newspaper and magazines at the library or online.** Not only do college libraries subscribe to many daily newspapers and magazines, but major newspapers and magazines are also online.

- **Check bills for errors.** Computers make mistakes, and so do the people who enter the data into them. So make sure that your charges on any bill are accurate.

- **Cut up your credit cards and pay cash.** Using a credit card is seductive: When you take out your plastic, it's easy to feel as if you're not really spending money. If you use cash for purchases instead, you'll see the money going out.

- **Make major purchases only during sales.** Plan major purchases so they coincide with sales.

- **Share and trade.** Pool your resources with friends. Carpool, share resources such as computers, and trade clothes.

- **Live more simply.** Is cable TV an absolute necessity? Is it really necessary to eat out once a week? Do you buy clothes because you need them or because you want them? If you don't have an unlimited service plan, do you really need to send so many text messages? Could you move to a less expensive cell phone plan?

Bag it! One way to cut down on expenditures is to reduce everyday expenses, such as by making your own lunch rather than grabbing a bite at a campus snack bar. Even small savings like this can add up fast.
Source: © Don Smetzer/Alamy

There are as many ways to save money as there are people looking to save it. But keep in mind that saving money should not necessarily be an end in itself. Don't spend hours thinking of ways to save a dime, and don't get upset about situations where you are forced to spend money. The goal is to bring your budget into balance, not to become a tightwad who keeps track of every penny and feels that spending money is a personal failure. To help you get started, get a sense of your current style of saving money in **Try It! 3**.

Finally, it's important to remember that budgets may be brought into balance not only by decreasing expenditures, but also by increasing income. The most direct way to increase income is to get a part-time job that will accommodate your academic schedule, or to work a few more hours at a job you already have.

The majority of all students enrolled in college work at some point. Although working adds to the time management challenges you will face, it does not necessarily mean that your grades will suffer. In fact, some students who work do better in school than those who don't work because those with jobs need to be more disciplined and focused. In addition, a part-time job in an area related to your future career may prove to be helpful in getting a job after you graduate.

On the other hand, working too much can be harmful. Jobs take a toll not only in hours away from your studies, but also in added stress. Consequently, it's sometimes better to take out a student loan to cover college costs than to work excessive amounts. Obviously you don't want to thoughtlessly get into debt because you don't want to burden your future with loan payments. But the well-thought-out use of loans, if they allow you to focus on your studies, may be a good investment in your future.

Try It! P O W E R

Determine Your Saving Style

Read each of the following statements and rate how well it describes you, using this scale:

1 = That's me

2 = Sometimes

3 = That's not me

	1	2	3
1. I count the change I'm given by cashiers in stores and restaurants.			
2. I prepare food at home and rarely eat in restaurants or order take-out meals.			
3. I don't buy something right away if I'm pretty sure it will go on sale soon.			
4. I shop tag sales and secondhand stores for used items whenever possible.			
5. I always remember how much I paid for something.			
6. I carpool or commute by bus or subway.			
7. I have money in at least one interest-bearing bank account.			
8. I look for discount coupons, two-for-one deals, and special promotions before shopping or dining out.			
9. If I lend money to someone repeatedly without getting it back, I stop lending it to that person.			
10. I share resources (e.g., CDs, books, magazines) with other people to save money.			
11. I'm good at putting money away for big items that I really want.			
12. I believe most generic or off-brand items are just as good as name brands.			

Add up your ratings. Interpret your total score according to this informal guide:

12–15: Very aggressive saving style

16–20: Careful saving style

21–27: Fairly loose saving style

28–32: Loose saving style

33–36: Nonexistent saving style

What are the advantages and disadvantages of your saving style? How do you think your saving style would affect your ability to keep to a budget? If you are dissatisfied with your saving style, how might you be able to change it?

Reviewing Your Budget

Budgets are not meant to be set in stone. You should review where you stand financially each month. Only by monitoring how closely actual expenditures and income match your budget projections will you be able to maintain control of your finances.

You don't need to continually keep track of every penny you spend to evaluate your success in budgeting. As you gain more experience with your budget, you'll begin to get a better sense of your finances. You'll know when it may be possible to consider splurging on a gift for a friend, and when you need to operate in penny-pinching mode.

The important thing is to keep your expenditures under control. Review, and if necessary revise, your budget to fit any changes in circumstances. Maybe you receive a raise at your job. Maybe the cost of gas goes down. Or maybe you face a reduction in income. Whatever the change in circumstances, evaluate how it affects your budget, and revise the budget accordingly.

R Rethink — Reconsidering Your Financial Options

If all goes well, the process of budgeting will put you in control of your financial life. Your expenditures will match your income, and you won't face major money worries.

In the real world, of course, events have a way of inflicting disaster on even the best-laid plans:

▶ You lose your job and can't afford to pay next month's rent.

▶ Your washing machine breaks down and needs a $300 repair. You don't have $300.

▶ Your parents run into financial difficulties, and you feel you need to help support them.

▶ Your car suffers collision damage, and repairing it will cost $1,500. If you pay for repairs, you can't afford a tuition payment.

All of us face financial difficulties at one time or another. Sometimes it happens suddenly and without warning. Other times people sink more gradually into financial problems, each month accumulating more debt until they reach a point at which they can't pay their bills.

However it happens, finding yourself with too little money to pay your bills requires action. You need to confront the situation and take steps to solve the problem. The worst thing to do is nothing. Hiding from those to whom you owe money makes the situation worse. Your creditors—the institutions and people to whom you owe money—will assume that you don't care, and they'll be spurred to take harsher actions.

These are the steps to take if you find yourself with financial difficulties (also see **Table 10.3** below).

▶ **Assess the problem.** Make a list of what you owe and to whom. Look at the bottom line and figure out a reasonable amount you can put toward each debt. Work out a specific plan that can lead you out of the situation.

table 10.3 Steps in Dealing with Financial Difficulties	
Assess the Problem	Make a list of what you owe and to whom. Figure out a reasonable amount you can put toward each debt. Work out a specific plan.
Contact Each of Your Creditors	Start with your bank, credit card companies, and landlord. Explain the situation. Show them your plan to pay off debt.
See a Credit Counselor	If you cannot work out a repayment plan on your own, visit a credit counseling service.
Stick to the Plan	Once you have a plan, make a commitment to stick to it. Your bank or creditor can help you identify a credit counselor.

If you have multiple loans, there are two main approaches to paying off what you owe. The *avalanche model of debt reduction* suggests paying off loans with the highest interest rate first. That helps reduce the accumulation of interest charges. In contrast, the *snowball model of debt reduction* emphasizes paying off loans with the lowest balance first. By paying off the smaller debts, you'll have more money to pay off other loans. In addition, it gives you a psychological boost to rid yourself of at least some debt.

Both methods work. What's important is making a choice and having a plan.

▶ **Contact each of your creditors.** Start with your bank, credit card companies, and landlord, and continue through each creditor. It's best to visit personally, but a phone call will do.

When you speak with them, explain the situation. If the problem is due to illness or unemployment, let them know. If it's due to overspending, let them know that. Tell them what you plan to do to pay off your debt, and show them your plan. The fact that you have a plan demonstrates not only what you intend to do, but also that you are serious about your situation and capable of financial planning.

If you've had a clean financial record in the past, your creditors may be willing to agree to your plan. Ultimately it is cheaper for them to accept smaller payments over a longer time than to hire a collection agency.

▶ **See a credit counselor.** If you can't work out a repayment plan on your own, visit a credit counseling service. These are nonprofit organizations that help people who find themselves in financial trouble. (Make sure the individuals you seek out are legitimate; there are scams in which individuals pose as credit counselors. Your bank or a creditor can help you identify a reputable one, or call the National Foundation for Credit Counseling at 1–800–388–2227 or visit its website at **www.nfcc.org**.)

▶ **Stick to the plan.** Once you have a plan to get yourself out of debt, follow it. Unless you diligently make the payments you commit to, you'll find your debt spiraling out of control once again. It's essential, then, to regard your plan as a firm commitment and stick to it.

Credit Cards

"Congratulations! You've been preapproved for a gold card! Just send us your signature on the enclosed authorization form, and we'll rush you your card."

Have you ever gotten such a letter in the mail? Millions of people in the United States are regularly enticed to receive credit cards in just such a manner, and college students are especially attractive targets. In many cases, it doesn't even matter if you have income; the mere fact that you're a college student is sufficient to win you approval to receive a card.

Credit cards are not necessarily bad. In fact, used appropriately, they can help get you through brief periods when you must make a purchase—such as replacing a tire for your car—but temporarily don't have enough money to do so. But it's easy to fall into debt. That's why the average credit card debt owed by college students is over $2,700. And about 10 percent of college students owe more than $7,000.

> "It is difficult to learn the meaning of fiscal responsibility, especially when you've got a new VISA and there's a great-looking sweater in the shop window. It's even harder when the sweater is on sale."
>
> **Lauren Pass, student, Grossmont Community College, Gottesman, G. (1994).** *College Survival.* **New York: Macmillan. P. 206.**

You don't want to be years past your college graduation and still paying for a slice of pizza you purchased in your first month on campus. That's why it's important to consider the use of credit cards very carefully.

There are several questions you should ask when deciding whether to get and use a credit card:

1. **Is there an annual fee?** Many cards charge an annual fee, ranging from $20 to $100 a year. You need to determine whether the advantages of the card are worth the cost of an annual fee.

2. **What is the interest rate?** Interest rates—the percentage of the unpaid balance you are charged on credit cards—vary substantially. Some interest rates are as low as 12 percent per year, while some are as high as 25 percent per year. If the rate is 25 percent, you will be charged an additional $250 each year if you owe an average of $1,000. Furthermore, although some interest rates are *fixed,* meaning that they don't vary from month to month, others are *variable,* which means they change

It's easy for most college students to get credit cards, and even easier to use them once they have them. The hard part comes later—paying the bills.
Source: © Incamerastock/ICP-Tech/Alamy

each month. How much they change is tied to various factors in the overall economy. To get a better sense of how interest rates add up, complete **Try It! 4,** "Maintain Your Interest."

3. **Do I need a credit card?** There are good and bad reasons for getting a credit card.

The Pluses of Credit Cards

▶ **Establishing a good credit history.** If you've ever owed money to a bank or your college, a computer file exists describing your payment history. If you have never missed a loan payment and always pay on time, you have a good credit history. If you haven't paid on time or have missed payments, your history will reflect this. Negative information can stay in a file for 7 years, and it can keep you from getting future loans, so it's important to establish and keep a clear credit history. (To get a copy of your credit report, complete **Try It! 5**, "Learn What Your Credit History Shows.")

Maintain Your Interest

Suppose you saw a $275 television set on sale "for a limited time" for $240. The $35 discount tempts you. The trouble is you don't have $240 to spare. But you *do* have a credit card—and you decide to buy the TV with the card and pay it off over time.

The advantages of this strategy are that you get the discount and have immediate use of the television set. The main disadvantage is that you will end up paying more than the $240 figure that you have in mind as the bargain price for the TV. In fact, depending on how high your credit card's interest rate is, how long you take to pay your bill in full, and how large each monthly payment is, you may wipe out most or all of the $35 savings that caused you to make the purchase in the first place. The more slowly you pay off the loan, the more money you pay for the television set.

For example, suppose you use a card with an annual interest rate of 12 percent, compounded monthly, meaning that the interest charge is applied each month rather than at the end of the year—making the true annual rate 12.68 percent. (Some cards even compound on a *daily* basis, resulting in a real interest rate that is even higher.) At the end of a year, assuming you pay $10 per month toward the $240 purchase, you will have paid $120 and still have $143.61 to pay. At the end of two years, you would end up paying $35 in interest on top of the $240 purchase price.

The 12-month calculation is illustrated in the first table below. To see how much of a factor the interest rate is, complete the second table, which shows the same purchase on a credit card with a 20 percent annual (approximately 1.67 percent monthly) interest rate, compounded monthly. (These calculations can also be figured automatically on several websites, including **www.bankrate.com** and **www.quicken.com.**)

Credit Card Payments: 12% Interest, Compounded Monthly (1% per month)

	Month 1	2	3	4	5	6	7	8	9	10	11	12
Unpaid balance	$240.00	$232.40	$224.72	$216.97	$209.14	$201.23	$193.24	$185.18	$177.03	$168.80	$160.49	$152.09
Plus interest of	2.40	2.32	2.25	2.17	2.09	2.01	1.93	1.85	1.77	1.69	1.60	1.52
Minus payment of	10.00	10.00	10.00	10.00	10.00	10.00	10.00	10.00	10.00	10.00	10.00	10.00
Balance due	$232.40	$224.72	$216.97	$209.14	$201.23	$193.24	$185.18	$177.03	$168.80	$160.49	$152.09	$143.61

Credit Card Payments: 20% Interest, Compounded Monthly (approx. 1.67% per month)

	Month 1	2	3	4	5	6	7	8	9	10	11	12
Unpaid Balance	$240.00	$234.01	$227.92	$221.72	$215.42							
Plus Interest of	4.01	3.91	3.81	3.70								
Minus payment of	10.00	10.00	10.00	10.00	10.00	10.00	10.00	10.00	10.00	10.00	10.00	10.00
Balance due	$234.01	$227.92	$221.72	$215.42								

How much would the $240 TV set cost if you bought it with this higher-rate card, paying $10 per month for 12 months and then paying the remaining balance by check? How does this compare with the nondiscounted purchase price of $275?

Learn What Your Credit History Shows

Big Brother is alive and well, at least in terms of your credit history. If you've ever had a credit card in your own name, taken out a student loan, or simply received an unsolicited offer for credit in the mail, there's probably a computer file describing who you are, where you live, and your financial history. It shows how high your credit lines are on every credit card you have, if you've ever been late on a payment, and a considerable amount of additional information.

Even worse: Many people's credit histories are riddled with errors. That's why it's important to check the record periodically. To get a complimentary copy of your credit report, go to the website maintained by the three major credit companies (Transunion, Experian, and Equifax): **www.annualcreditreport.com**.

Be prepared: You will be asked for a variety of information, including your name, address, Social Security number, birthdate, prior addresses for the past 5 years, and other names (like a maiden name) you may have been known by. In addition, you may be asked to sign up for future reports for a fee; if you don't want them, say "no." Eventually, you will receive an online copy of your credit report.

Once you get your credit report, check it carefully. If you find any mistakes, contact the credit bureau and explain the error. They are legally responsible for investigating the report and correcting the file. It's a good idea to check your file once a year.

▶ **Emergency use.** Few of us carry around enough cash to deal with emergencies. A credit card can be a lifesaver if we're on a trip and the car breaks down and needs emergency repairs.

▶ **Convenience.** Sometimes it's just easier to make purchases using a credit card. For instance, we can make purchases over the telephone or online if we have a credit card. Furthermore, credit cards not only provide a record of purchases, but also give us limited consumer protection should a product prove to be defective.

"Graduates, faculty, parents, creditors . . ."

Source: © Arnie Levin/The New Yorker Collection/The Cartoon Bank

The Minuses of Credit Cards

On the other hand, there can be significant drawbacks to the use of credit cards. Potential problems include the following:

▶ **Interest costs can be high.** As you saw in **Try It! 4**, the interest rate on credit card purchases can be significant. Unless you pay off your entire balance each month, your account will be charged interest, which can add up rapidly.

▶ **It's too easy to spend money.** Credit cards are so convenient to use that you may not realize how much you're spending in a given period. Furthermore, spending can become addictive. Unless you're careful, you can end up exceeding your budget by a significant amount.

▶ **If you're late in making your payments or exceed your credit limit, your credit rating will be damaged.** Credit card companies have long memories, and any mistakes you make will be reflected in your credit record for close to a decade. That may prevent you from buying a car or house in the future and jeopardize your ability to take out student loans.

▶ **You become susceptible to identity theft.** *Identity theft* occurs when your credit card number (or Social Security number) and name are used by someone fraudulently. Identity thieves may use your credit information to make purchases, open new credit card accounts in your name, open new phone accounts, or even rent a house in your name. They can change the address on existing accounts so you don't even know that they are running up bills in your name. Detecting identity theft is one of the reasons you should examine your credit card statements—in fact all your financial statements, such as bank accounts—very carefully every month.

» LO 10-3 Paying for College

College costs vary greatly from one school to another, but they are substantial everywhere. The average public community college costs $7,703 per year; the average four-year public college costs $15,014; and the average four-year private college costs $32,790.[2]

Nothing about college is cheap. It takes enormous expenditures of three often scarce commodities: energy, time, and money. Perhaps surprisingly, many students find money the easiest of them to find. Although it's not simple to get financial aid, and no one is going to walk up to you and offer you an all-expenses-paid scholarship, you can find many sources of funding for your education if you are persistent.

To find this money, however, you will need to spend ample amounts of the other two scarce commodities: time and energy. The entire process of securing financial aid takes a considerable amount of preparation because you need to identify potential sources of funds and then apply for them. You should assume the process will take somewhere between several weeks and several months, depending on the type of aid you're applying for.

Identifying the Different Types of Funding Available

Funding for college comes in three basic categories: loans, grants, and scholarships. Although each supplies you with funds for college, they do so in very different ways.

Loans

loan

Funds provided by a bank, credit union, or other agency that must be repaid after a specified period of time.

When you receive a **loan**, a bank, credit union, or other agency provides funds that must be repaid after a specified period of time. A loan carries a particular interest rate, which is stated as an annual percentage rate. Think of a loan as renting money: As long as you have the use of someone else's money, you have to pay them "rent" for the privilege. Banks and other lending agencies make money through the interest they charge on loans, just as they do with credit cards.

For example, suppose a bank gives you a $5,000 loan that has an interest rate of 8 percent per year. Not only must you pay back the $5,000 over a specified period, but you must pay the bank interest of 8 percent on the balance that you owe on the loan. Obviously the higher the interest rate, the more you are paying for the privilege of borrowing the bank's money.

Getting the Most Out of Your Classes:
How Cutting Classes Costs

Think about how much college costs you each term. Go ahead and add it up: tuition, books, transportation, housing, food, supplies, etc., etc. It's a pretty hefty sum.

Now count the number of hours you're in class during the term. If you divide the number of hours into the amount you spend on college, you'll come up with a dollar value that shows how much every hour of the courses in which you're enrolled is worth.

What you'll immediately see is that every class is worth a great deal. For most students, missing a day's worth of classes is the equivalent of giving up $50 at the very minimum. Students attending expensive private colleges may be losing hundreds of dollars.

If all the other reasons for not missing a class aren't convincing enough, then think in these economic terms. Giving away something you've paid for is irrational. It's really no different from buying thousands of dollars' worth of music downloads and then throwing them away, one by one, over the course of the semester. Only in the case of your college courses, what you're giving up is far more precious—your education.

Consequently, resolve to get your money's worth out of your courses by attending them faithfully. Not only will you benefit economically, but you'll maximize your chances for learning the material and ultimately being successful in your college career and beyond.

Three factors must be considered when you receive a loan: the stated amount of the loan (called the **principal**), the interest rate (stated as a percentage), and the length of the loan (referred to as the **term** of the loan). All three factors are important because they determine how much your payments will be when you pay the loan back.

Remember, too, that initial interest rates don't always last the life of a loan. *Variable interest rate loans* have interest rates that rise and fall according to some index. So a low initial interest may increase over time, forcing you to pay more.

Many loans for college have an enormous advantage over loans you'll take out for other purchases, such as a car or a house, because payments on college loans are *deferred* until you graduate and (presumably!) begin to earn an income—that is, it is often not necessary to start paying back the loan until you graduate. Depending on the type of loan you take out, interest on the loan is either paid for by the government while you are enrolled in college or deferred until you graduate.

Several national loan programs, sponsored by the federal government, lend money to students. The major ones include the following:

principal
The stated amount of a loan.

term
The length of time for which money is lent.

> "If you would be wealthy, think of saving as well as getting."
>
> Benjamin Franklin

▶ **Stafford loans.** Stafford loans are available to any student who is registered at least half-time and is a U.S. citizen or permanent resident. They provide from $5,500 to as much as $12,500 a year.

Stafford loans come in two types: subsidized and unsubsidized. *Subsidized Stafford loans* are awarded through colleges on the basis of student financial need. For subsidized loans, the government pays interest until repayment begins, typically after the student graduates. *Unsubsidized Stafford loans* do not require demonstration of financial need. Interest is not paid by the government; instead, it accumulates while the student is in college. However, the student doesn't have to make any payments until after graduation, when both principal and accumulated interest must be repaid over a specified period, which is up to 10 years.

- **PLUS loans (for parents).** If your parents support you and claim you as a deduction on their income tax return, they may take out a PLUS loan. PLUS loans can cover up to the full amount of a student's cost of college attendance and can be paid back over a 10-year period.

- **Perkins loans.** Perkins loans have a low interest rate. They are awarded on the basis of exceptional financial need, as determined by a student's college. The loans are made by a school's financial aid office.

College loans like these are relatively easy to get, though more difficult in the wake of the 2008 stock market crash and subsequent recession. It is also essential to remember that someday you'll need to pay them back. And many students are paying back a great deal. For instance, the average indebtedness is more than $9,000 for community college students and $25,250 for 4-year college students.[3] The total amount of student debt is staggering: Students and their parents in the United States owe one *trillion* dollars in debt, which is more than what is owed on credit cards.

Because college graduates often start off earning less than they thought they would, high levels of debt can lead to difficulties. More than half of graduates feel burdened by their debt, and a quarter report having significant problems paying back their loans. Consequently, think hard when taking out a loan, and consider how much you'll have to pay back each month after you graduate.

Grants

grant

An award of money that does not have to be repaid.

A **grant** is money that does not have to be repaid. Obviously it's more advantageous to receive a grant than a loan. And not surprisingly, it's harder to qualify for grants than loans—harder, but not impossible. Several grant programs exist that can help reduce the amount you'll need to pay for college. They include the following:

- **Pell grants.** Based on need, Pell grants are provided to undergraduate students who have earned no previous degrees. They are awarded by college financial aid offices, which follow a formula provided by the federal government. Every student who meets certain need criteria is eligible for a Pell grant, ensuring that the neediest students receive some support.

- **Federal Supplemental Educational Opportunity Grants (FSEOG).** The government supplies FSEOGs to every college, which then provide these grants to needy students. Unlike Pell grants, which are guaranteed to every eligible student, FSEOGs are in limited supply. Once a college awards its allotment for a given year, no other awards are possible.

- **Work-study grants.** Work-study grants provide jobs for undergraduates with financial needs. The jobs are typically related to a student's course of study or involve community service work, and part of the salary is paid by the government. Because a work-study position is often part of a student's total package of financial aid, it is generally considered a grant, even though work is required.

Scholarships

scholarship

An award of money to a student based on need or merit.

Scholarships are support awarded by colleges, organizations, and companies. Like a grant, a scholarship is money that does not have to be repaid. Most scholarships are based primarily on a student's financial need, although some are based on merit. For instance, students with exceptional academic or athletic abilities may receive a scholarship even though they wouldn't necessarily qualify under typical need-based measures.

The most frequent source of scholarships is one's own college, which may give money to reduce tuition and fees. But there are literally thousands of organizations that provide scholarships, ranging from companies such as Microsoft to nonprofit groups, such as the Boy Scouts and Girl Scouts.

The federal government also provides some scholarships to students whose family income does not rise above certain levels. These include the following:

▶ **Hope scholarship.** The Hope scholarship is a tax credit that helps free up funds for college. There is an annual maximum credit of $2,500.

▶ **Lifetime learning tax credit.** This tax credit is targeted to older students who are going back to school, changing careers, or taking courses to upgrade their skills, as well as to juniors and seniors in four-year colleges. Families can receive a 20 percent tax credit for the first $10,000 of tuition and fees, and the amount will increase in future years.

Whatever the source of financial aid, you almost always will have to maintain minimum standards of academic success and progress through your program of study to be eligible for continued aid. The federal government, in particular, requires that you have to be making what is officially called *satisfactory academic progress,* as defined by your particular college.

Researching Possible Sources of Financial Aid

As you can see, there are many sources of financial aid. The biggest problem often is finding them.

Your first stop on your search for sources of financial aid should be your college's financial aid office. Every college has one, and it tends to be one of the busiest places on campus.

Most student aid offices contain a great deal of information about possible sources of aid. But that's only a starting point. The library and the web also contain many types of information that can direct you to specific possibilities. One place to get started is the Federal Student Aid Information Center in Washington, which can be reached at 1-800-4-FED-AID (1-800-433-3243) or on the web at **studentaid .ed.gov/students/publications/student_guide/index.html**. The center will send you the "Student Guide," which describes programs that account for almost three-fourths of all financial aid awarded to students.

Keep in mind, however, that where money is involved, there are scams. Do not pay money to someone who offers to identify obscure scholarships that will yield you thousands of dollars. It's unlikely that anyone could find sources that you couldn't find yourself through careful research. Be especially wary of websites that ask for a credit card number to provide you with online information. The results are likely to be disappointing. (The websites we provide at the end of the chapter are completely reputable.)

Whatever the potential source of financial aid, you'll be asked to bare your financial soul. There will also be forms galore. Before actually completing the forms, it will be important to gather the information you will need. If you are being supported by your parents, they will have to complete some of the forms.

"Good day, Madam. I'm working my son's way through college."

Source: © J.B. Handelsman/The New Yorker Collection/ The Cartoon Bank

Keep track of deadlines! If you miss a deadline for applying for financial aid, you'll be out of luck; no exceptions are made. You'll just have to wait for another aid cycle.

Finally, make sure you know what your needs are. The typical costs of college include not only tuition but also fees, books, and supplies, as well as associated costs, such as transportation, housing, food, and child care.

Applying for Financial Aid

It may seem that for every dollar in aid you get, there is a different line to complete on a complicated form. Prepare yourself for a blizzard of paperwork.

Following are the steps in applying for financial aid:

► **Speak with a financial aid counselor at your school.** Because the best source of financial aid is your own college, make an appointment to discuss your needs with a campus financial aid counselor or officer. In addition to giving you the most up-to-date information about possible sources of aid, the college financial aid officer can provide you with the forms you need to fill out and a list of the deadlines you need to meet.

► **Decide how much aid you need.** It's important to ask for just the right amount of aid, neither too little nor too much. If you ask for too little aid, you may be strapped for funds during the school term. It's much more difficult to get aid in the middle of a term than during the normal application period.

At the same time, don't apply for more financial aid than you actually need. First, there is an issue of equity: What you get in aid may reduce the pool for others, and if you receive surplus aid you may be preventing other students from getting their fair share. Second, you don't want to load yourself up with unnecessary debt. Most graduates pay from $150 to $175 a month to pay off their student loans; you don't want to end up with so much debt that your loan payments are even higher than this.

► **Fill out your college's application for financial aid.** Colleges have their own forms to apply for financial aid. Carefully fill the form out, making sure you file it before the required deadline. In fact, the earlier you get the form in, the better: Most schools have a limited pool of funds, and the earlier you get your application in, the higher your chances of getting an appropriate share of the financial aid pie.

► **Write a personal letter to accompany your application.** If you think there are factors that affect your ability to pay for college which are not adequately reflected in the application—such as a recent job loss—write a letter to the financial aid officer describing them.

► **Complete a Free Application for Federal Student Aid (FAFSA) and Financial Aid PROFILE.** The FAFSA and PROFILE are standard forms used to assess a student's financial capabilities and determine how much the student and family can be expected to contribute toward college expenses. One or both of the forms are used by almost every college. They require a great deal of information, including past, present, and expected income from all sources. Copies of several tax returns from prior years are also required.

Be scrupulously honest when you complete the forms, which you can do on the web at **www.fafsa.ed.gov** (for the FAFSA) and **profileonline.**

collegeboard.com (for the PROFILE). If you fail to include a source of income that is later discovered by a financial aid provider, you may be required to immediately repay any aid that you have received. In addition, you may face disciplinary measures that put your education in jeopardy; in the worst case, you may even face legal charges.

▶ **Wait.** It takes time for loan applications to be processed and financial aid decisions to be made. Be prepared to wait, and consider contingency plans for various possibilities.

Your Financial Aid Package

Sometime later, when the college has had time to consider your application for aid, you will receive an official response. This is most likely to be in the form of a "package"—a combination of loans, grants, scholarships, and perhaps an offer of an on-campus job. This is the time for a thorough evaluation of the offer. Consider the various elements of the package carefully to determine whether, taken together, they will fully meet your financial needs.

Keep in mind that you may not have to accept every element of the package that is offered to you. For instance, you may decide to accept a scholarship but turn down a loan. That decision may mean that you'll have less debt after you graduate but that you'll have to work more hours at a part-time job—a trade-off that you may or may not wish to make.

What if the package doesn't seem sufficient? The most important thing is not to give up. A polite visit or call to the financial aid office is in order.

When you speak to someone from financial aid, lay out your difficulty with the package. If the aid is so low that you won't be able to attend that college, let the financial aid office know. If you had noted special circumstances in a letter, ask if they were taken into account. (Sometimes letters and other vital pieces of information get overlooked.) Ask if there is a formal appeal process and, if there is, ask how to begin it.

Your main goal is to get the financial aid office to take a second look at your application. By being polite and to-the-point in your dealings with the office staff, you stand a better chance of having them reevaluate your application.

Having good grades will help your chances of getting the financial aid office to take a second look, and poor grades will hurt: If you are not doing well in your classes, you have less bargaining power.

What if the school is unable to come up with a greater level of support? The first step is to ask the staff of the financial aid office for advice. They may be able to suggest an approach that you initially overlooked. The second step is to redouble your research efforts. You may be able to take out a loan to make up the deficit. Finally, consider alternatives to full-time college attendance. It may be preferable to attend school part-time while working than to give up college altogether or to get so much into debt that it will be hard to pay off your loans.

Above all, don't give up! If it's important enough to you, you will be able to find some way to afford an education.

Keeping in Mind the Value of a College Education

Our present focus on paying for college has led us, of necessity, to focus on the dollars and cents of education. Without a doubt, college is expensive. On the other side of the equation, there's no question that having a college education has vast financial value: People who are college graduates earn nearly twice as much money each year as those with only high school degrees.

But the money we spend on education buys us far more than a better salary. It gives us a better understanding of the world and its people, insight into who we are, better job opportunities, and a chance to befriend people who share the common goal of becoming well-educated citizens of a global society.

It would be terribly shortsighted to put a price tag on education, deciding, in effect, that if you must pay a lot you won't bother with an education. You may need to choose your school according to the tuition it charges and the financial aid package it offers you, but that's not the same as choosing to skip college altogether because it is going to be financially stressful. An experience that will permit us to reach our potential is worth *everything*.

Speaking *of* Success

Source: © Jeremy Sutton-Hibbert/Alamy

NAME: **Tom Hanks**

SCHOOL: **Chabot Community College, Hayward, California**

Tom Hanks is considered one of the biggest and most successful figures to ever come out of Hollywood. To what does he attribute his success? You might be surprised to learn that much of what makes Tom Hanks so successful was the education he received at Chabot College in Hayward, California.

Self-admittedly not the best student out of high school, Hanks noted that Chabot offered exactly what he needed.

"I graduated from high school as an underachieving student with lousy SAT scores, and knowing I couldn't afford tuition for college anyway, I sent my final set of stats to Chabot because it accepted everyone and was free," he said.

Much of Hanks's transformation as a student came from his approach to selecting the classes he was interested in.

"I made Chabot's dean's list taking classes I loved (oral interpretation), classes I loathed (health, a requirement), classes I aced (film as art—like Jean Renoir's

Golden Coach and Luis Buñuel's *Simon of the Desert*), and classes I dropped after the first hour (astronomy, because it was all math).

"Classes I took at Chabot have rippled through my professional pond. I produced the HBO mini-series *John Adams* with an outline format I learned from a pipe-smoking historian, James Coovelis, whose lectures were riveting. Mary Lou Fitzgerald's Studies in Shakespeare taught me how the five-act structures of *Richard III, The Tempest* and *Othello* focused their themes. And a public speaking class was able to force us to get over our self-consciousness."

As a result of his own personal experience, Hanks feels that his choice was an excellent path to not only getting an education, but pursuing a profession.

"That place made me what I am today," he said.

Source: Tom Hanks, "I Owe It All to Community College: Tom Hanks on His Two Years at Chabot College," *The New York Times,* January 14, 2015, A25.

[RETHINK]

- What do you think Hanks means when he says, "That place made me what I am today"?

- Based on the courses Hanks liked, what profession could he have pursued other than acting?

Looking Back

LO 10-1 Explain how to develop a financial philosophy and its value.

▶ Exploring your views of money is the first step in developing a meaningful financial philosophy.

▶ It is important to understand how you view the role of money in your life.

LO 10-2 Discuss strategies for managing your money.

▶ Concerns about money can be significantly reduced through the creation of a budget by which spending and income can be planned, accounted for, and aligned with your goals.

▶ Budgets provide security by helping you control your finances and avoid surprises.

▶ The process of budgeting involves identifying your financial goals, keeping track of current expenses and estimating future expenses, and making the necessary adjustments to keep income and spending in balance.

LO 10-3 Describe approaches to paying for your college education.

▶ Loans for education are available with reasonable interest rates and conditions, especially the ability to defer paying the loans back until after graduation. Several federal programs offer loan guarantees, interest subsidies, and lower interest rates.

▶ Grants offer money without requiring repayment. They are harder to receive than loans because they are typically reserved for people with exceptional financial need.

▶ Scholarships are usually awarded by colleges and other institutions based on either financial need or academic, athletic, or other abilities.

▶ Ultimately, it is important to consider the value of college beyond its costs. A college degree leads to a significantly higher salary (college graduates earn nearly twice as much as those with only a high school degree). In addition, a college education offers a better understanding of the world and insight into ourselves.

[KEY TERMS AND CONCEPTS]

Budget (p. 252)

Grant (p. 270)

Loan (p. 268)

Principal (p. 269)

Scholarship (p. 270)

Term (p. 269)

[RESOURCES]

ON CAMPUS

The bursar's or treasurer's office handles money affairs. Not only does it collect money owed for tuition, but it also may perform other services, such as cashing checks.

If you are receiving financial aid, there is usually a financial aid office devoted to the complexities of scholarships, loan processing, and other forms of aid. The personnel in the office can be very helpful in maximizing your financial aid package as well as in solving financial problems related to your schooling. If you have a problem with your finances, see them sooner rather than later.

IN PRINT

Paying for College without Going Broke 2014, by Kalman Chany (Princeton Review, 2013), includes many practical tips for finding ways to finance a college education. *The Ultimate Scholarship Book 2015,* by Gen and Kelly Tanabe (Supercollege, 2014), offers a variety of ways to identify scholarships to pay for college.

Emily Sawtelle's *How to Make a Simple Budget and a Winning Financial Plan* (Saverie Books, 2012) offers helpful guidance on financial management. In addition, Michelle Higgins's *College Poor No More* (New Year Publishing, 2015) offers dozens of easy tips on how to be frugal without the sacrifice.

ON THE WEB

The following websites provide additional information about money matters. (Although the web addresses were accurate at the time this material was published, check the *P.O.W.E.R. Learning* Connect Library or contact your instructor for any changes that may have occurred.)

▶ College Answer (**www.collegeanswer.com/index.jsp**) is a valuable, time-saving tool for students and their parents who are trying to identify sources of funds to pay for college. Through this service you can receive information about scholarships, fellowships, grants, work study, loan programs, tuition waivers, internships, competitions, and work cooperative programs.

▶ "Finaid: The SmartStudent Guide to College Financial Aid" (**www.finaid.org**) provides a free, comprehensive, independent, and objective guide to student financial aid. It was created by Mark Kantrowitz, author of *The Prentice Hall Guide to Scholarships and Fellowships for Math and Science Students.* The site's "calculators" page (**www .finaid.org/calculators/**) offers loads of online calculators, including College Cost Projector, Savings Plan Designer, Expected Family Contribution and Financial Aid Calculator, Loan Payment Calculator, and Student Loan Advisor (undergraduate).

▶ "Money Management" (**http://www.ndm.edu/admissions/financial-aid/ money-management**/), sponsored by Notre Dame of Maryland University, offers a variety of links covering everything from debt management to loan forgiveness programs.

▶ *Federal Student Aid* is a comprehensive resource on the types of student financial aid from the U.S. Department of Education. It provides information on how to apply for grants, loans, and work-study through the Federal Student Aid office. This publication is available in pdf form on the U.S. Department of Education's website at **https://studentaid.ed.gov/resources#funding.**

The Case of . . .

Creative Financing

Lynn Abrams grew up in a house where a little money had to go a long way. As a child, the answer to most of her requests was "We can't afford that." When she started college, she was deluged with credit card offers. Tired of scrimping, she accepted every offer. With five new cards and $10,000 worth of credit, Lynn felt like she'd won the lottery.

Lynn had applied for financial aid and received almost enough to cover her tuition for the semester. She put the rest of her tuition and all of her fees on one credit card. She rented an apartment, paying the security deposit and rent for the first month with a cash advance from another card. A cash advance on a third card got her the (used) wheels she needed to get to campus. No more buses for her! She assigned the fourth card to cover food and entertainment which, as the semester progressed, included some very pricey meals out and an even more expensive weekend away. Card number five bought her the kind of wardrobe she'd always dreamed of.

Four weeks into the semester, Lynn received her first credit card bills. Shock did not begin to describe her reaction as she stared at the five statements. In one month, she'd not only used her entire $10,000 credit—she'd overspent her limit by several hundred dollars on three of the cards. Their angry notices informed her she must pay the over-limit amounts *at once*. But Lynn had no money, and her rent was due.

1. What should Lynn do now to start addressing her problem? What steps should she take immediately?

2. Can you suggest some approaches Lynn can take to deal with the problem of the rent she needs to pay for next month?

3. How do you think Lynn exceeded her credit card limits by so much? What advice would you give her to avoid a similar mistake in the future?

4. From the evidence in this story, do you think Lynn understands the difference between want and need? How would you suggest she evaluate her spending priorities to avoid repeating this financial disaster?

5. What steps might Lynn take to decrease her expenses? What might she do to increase her income?

Learning Outcomes

By the time you finish this chapter you will be able to

» LO **11-1**   Explain what stress is and how to control it.

» LO **11-2**   Discuss what is involved in keeping well physically.

» LO **11-3**   Describe strategies for keeping well mentally.

Juggling: Stress, Family, and Work

After a long day of classes, a shift at his part-time job, and dinner with his dad, Dennis Hanson was finally able to settle down to his studies. Good thing, too. The midterm test in his media arts class was tomorrow.

He'd just begun reviewing his notes when his phone rang. He checked the caller. His dad. Anger and exhaustion flooded him. It wasn't fair. He'd visited his father every day since his stepmother's death. He cooked for him, made phone calls, ran errands. And still his dad called two or three times a day, interrupting him in class and at work, eating heavily into his study time.

In the wake of his irritation, he felt guilt. His dad was alone and grieving, with no one but Dennis to talk to. Sighing, Dennis answered the phone. Twenty minutes later, he returned to his notes. But it was midnight now and he was dead tired. He climbed into bed fully dressed and turned out the light. He couldn't cope with another thing.

Looking Ahead

Dennis Hanson's got a lot on his plate at the moment, but even in ordinary circumstances, the many hats we wear—student, parent, child, employee—can leave us stressed about how we're going to meet all the demands we face. College can often intensify this. Almost a third of first-year college students report feeling frequently overwhelmed with all they need to do.[1]

Coping with stress is one of the challenges that college students face. The many demands on your time can make you feel that you'll never finish what needs to get done. This pressure produces wear and tear on your body and mind, and it's easy to fall prey to ill health as a result.

However, stress and poor health are not inevitable outcomes. In fact, by following simple guidelines and deciding to make health a conscious priority, you can maintain good physical and mental health. It's not easy to balance the many responsibilities of study and work and family, but it is possible.

This chapter covers the ways you can keep fit and healthy during—and beyond—college. It offers suggestions on how you can cope with stress, improve your diet, get enough exercise, and sleep better. It will also discuss how particularly challenging stressors can result in posttraumatic stress disorder or even suicide.

»LO 11-1 Living with Stress

Stressed out? Tests, papers, job demands, family problems, volunteer activities . . . it's no surprise that these can produce stress. But it may be a surprise to know that so can graduating from college, starting your dream job, falling in love, getting married, and even winning the lottery.

Virtually *anything*—good or bad—is capable of producing stress if it presents us with a challenge. **Stress** is the physical and emotional response we have to events that threaten or challenge us. It is rooted in the primitive "fight or flight" response wired into all animals—human and nonhuman. You see it in cats, for instance, when they're confronted by a dog or other threat: Their backs go up, their fur stands on end, their eyes widen, and ultimately they either take off or attack. The challenge stimulating this revved-up response is called a *stressor*. For humans, stressors can range from a first date to losing a wallet to experiencing a tornado or hurricane.

stress
The physical and emotional response to events that threaten or challenge us.

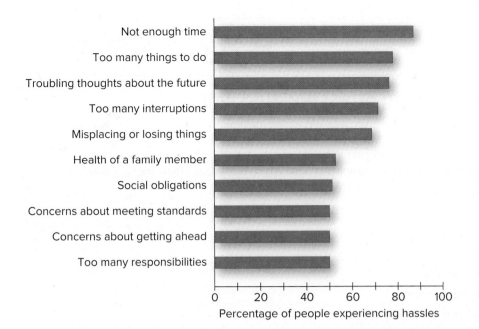

figure 11.1
Daily Hassles
Source: © K. Chamberlain and S. Zika, "The Minor Events Approach to Stress: Support for Use of Daily Hassles," *British Journal of Psychology* 81 (1990), pp. 469–481.

Bar chart labels (top to bottom): Not enough time; Too many things to do; Troubling thoughts about the future; Too many interruptions; Misplacing or losing things; Health of a family member; Social obligations; Concerns about meeting standards; Concerns about getting ahead; Too many responsibilities.

X-axis: 0 20 40 60 80 100 — Percentage of people experiencing hassles

Because our everyday lives are filled with events that can be interpreted as threatening or challenging, stress is commonplace in most people's lives. There are three main types of stressors:

1. **Cataclysmic events** are events that occur suddenly and affect many people simultaneously. Tornadoes, hurricanes, and plane crashes are examples of cataclysmic events.

2. **Personal stressors** are major life events that produce a negative physical and psychological reaction. Failing a course, losing a job, and ending a relationship are all examples of personal stressors. Sometimes positive events—such as getting married or starting a new job—can act as personal stressors. Although the short-term impact of a personal stressor can be difficult, the long-term consequences may decline as people learn to adapt to the situation.

3. **Daily hassles** are the minor irritants of life that, singly, produce relatively little stress. Waiting in a traffic jam, receiving a bill riddled with mistakes, and being interrupted by noisy machinery while trying to study are examples of such minor irritants. However, daily hassles add up, and cumulatively they can produce even more stress than a single larger-scale event. (**Figure 11.1** indicates the most common daily hassles in people's lives.)

cataclysmic events
Sudden, powerful events that occur quickly and affect many people simultaneously.

personal stressors
Major life events that produce stress.

daily hassles
The minor irritants of life that, by themselves, produce little stress, but which can add up and produce more stress than a single larger-scale event.

What Is Happening When We Are Stressed?

Stress does more than make us feel anxious, upset, and fearful. Beneath those responses, we are experiencing many different physical reactions, each placing a high demand on our body's resources. Our hearts beat faster, our breathing becomes more rapid and shallow, and we produce more sweat. Our internal organs churn out a variety of hormones.

In the long run, these physical responses wear down our immune system—our body's defense against disease. We become more susceptible to a variety of diseases, ranging from the common cold and headaches to strokes and heart disease. In fact, surveys have found that the greater the number of stressful events a person

Assess Your Susceptibility to Stress-Related Illness

Are you susceptible to a stress-related illness? The more stress in your life, the more likely it is that you will experience a major illness.

To determine the stress in your life, take the stressor value given beside each event you have experienced and multiply it by the number of occurrences over the past year (up to a maximum of four), and then add up these scores.

87	Experienced the death of a spouse
77	Got married
77	Experienced the death of a close family member
76	Got divorced
74	Experienced a marital separation
68	Experienced the death of a close friend
68	Experienced pregnancy or fathered a pregnancy
65	Had a major personal injury or illness
62	Were fired from work
60	Ended a marital engagement or a steady relationship
58	Had sexual difficulties
58	Experienced a marital reconciliation
57	Had a major change in self-concept or self-awareness
56	Experienced a major change in the health or behavior of a family member
54	Became engaged to be married
53	Had a major change in financial status
52	Took on a mortgage or loan of more than $10,000
52	Had a major change in use of drugs
50	Had a major conflict or change in values
50	Had a major change in the number of arguments with your spouse
50	Gained a new family member
50	Entered college
50	Changed to a new school
50	Changed to a different line of work
49	Had a major change in amount of independence and responsibility

experiences over the course of a year, the more likely it is that he or she will have a major illness (see **Try It! 1**, "Assess Your Susceptibility to Stress-Related Illness").

Handling Stress

Stress is an inevitable part of life. In fact, a life with no stress at all would be so boring and uneventful that you'd quickly miss the stress that had been removed.

47	Had a major change in responsibilities at work
46	Experienced a major change in use of alcohol
45	Revised personal habits
44	Had trouble with school administration
43	Held a job while attending school
43	Had a major change in social activities
42	Had trouble with in-laws
42	Had a major change in working hours or conditions
42	Changed residence or living conditions
41	Had your spouse begin or cease work outside the home
41	Changed your major
41	Changed dating habits
40	Had an outstanding personal achievement
38	Had trouble with your boss
38	Had a major change in amount of participation in school activities
37	Had a major change in type and/or amount of recreation
36	Had a major change in religious activities
34	Had a major change of sleeping habits
33	Took a trip or vacation
30	Had a major change in eating habits
26	Had a major change in the number of family get-togethers
22	Were found guilty of minor violations of the law

Scoring: If your total score is above 1,435, you are in a high-stress category and therefore more at risk for experiencing a stress-related illness.

But keep in mind the limitations of this questionnaire. There may be factors in your life that produce high stress but are not listed. In addition, a high score does not mean that you are sure to get sick. Many other factors determine ill health, and high stress is only one cause. Other positive factors in your life, such as getting enough sleep and exercise, may prevent illness.

Still, having an unusually high amount of stress in your life is a cause for concern. If you do score high, you may want to take steps to reduce it.

Source: M. B. Marx, T. F. Garrity, and F. R. Bowers, "The Influence of Recent Life Experience on the Health of College Freshmen," *Journal of Psychosomatic Research* 19 (1975), pp. 87–98.

That doesn't mean, though, that we have to sit back and accept stress when it does arise. **Coping** is the effort to control, reduce, or tolerate the threats that lead to stress. Using the P.O.W.E.R. principles (illustrated in the P.O.W.E.R. Plan) can help you to cope with the stress in your life, regardless of its cause or intensity.

coping
The effort to control, reduce, or learn to tolerate the threats that lead to stress.

P Prepare Readying Yourself Physically

Being in good physical condition is one excellent way to prepare for future stress. Stress takes its toll on your body, so it makes sense that the stronger and fitter you

P Prepare

Ready yourself
physically

O Organize

Identify what is causing
you stress

W Work

Develop effective
coping strategies

E Evaluate

Ask yourself if your
strategies for dealing with
stress are effective

R Rethink

Place stress in
perspective

P.O.W.E.R. Plan

are, the less negative impact stress will have on you. For example, a regular exercise program reduces heart rate, respiration rate, and blood pressure at times when the body is at rest—making us better able to withstand the negative consequences of stress.

If you drink a lot of coffee or soda, a change in your diet may be enough to reduce your stress. Coffee, soda, chocolate, and a surprising number of other foods contain caffeine, which can make you feel jittery and anxious even without stress; add a stressor, and the reaction can be very intense and unpleasant.

Eating right can alleviate another problem: obesity. Being overweight can bring on stress for several reasons. For one thing, the extra pounds drag down the functioning of the body. This can lead to fatigue and a reduced ability to bounce back when we encounter challenges to our well-being. In addition, feeling heavy in a society that acclaims the virtues of slimness can be stressful in and of itself.

O Organize

Identifying What Is Causing You Stress

Of course stress is not just a question of diet and exercise. To cope with stress, you need to understand what causes it. In some cases it's obvious—a series of bad test grades in a course, a family problem that keeps getting worse, a job supervisor who seems to delight in making things difficult. In other cases, however, the causes of stress may be more subtle. Perhaps your relationship with your wife or husband is rocky, and you have a nagging feeling that something is wrong.

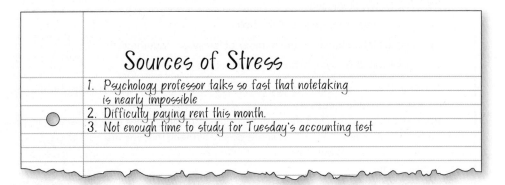

Sources of Stress

1. Psychology professor talks so fast that notetaking is nearly impossible
2. Difficulty paying rent this month.
3. Not enough time to study for Tuesday's accounting test

Whatever the source of stress, you need to pinpoint it. To organize your assault on stress, then, take a piece of paper and list the major circumstances that are causing you stress. Just listing them will help put you in control, and you'll be better able to figure out strategies for coping with them.

W Work

Developing Effective Coping Strategies

A wide variety of tactics can help you deal with stress once you've identified its sources. In addition to the lifestyle changes just outlined, among the most effective approaches to coping are these:

▶ **Take charge of the situation.** Stress is most apt to arise when we are faced with situations over which we have little or no control. If you take charge of the situation, you'll reduce the experience of stress. For example, if several work assignments are given to you all on the same day, you might try recruiting a co-worker to help lighten your load.

▶ **Don't waste energy trying to change the unchangeable.** There are some situations that you simply can't control. You can't change the fact that you have come down with a case of the flu, and you can't change your performance on a test you took last week. Don't hit your head against a brick wall and try to modify things that can't be changed. Use your energy to improve the situation, not to rewrite history.

> "There is more to life than increasing its speed."
>
> Mahatma Gandhi

▶ **Look for the silver lining.** Stress arises when we perceive a situation as threatening. If we can change how we perceive that situation, we can change our reactions to it. For instance, if your information technology instructor requires you to create a difficult computer program in a very short time, the saving grace is that you may be able to use this skill to your advantage in getting a high-paying job down the road. (You can practice finding the silver lining in **Try It! 2.**)

▶ **Talk to friends and family. Social support**, which is assistance and comfort supplied by others, can help us through stressful periods. Turning to our friends and family and simply talking about the stress we're under can help us tolerate it more effectively. Even anonymous telephone hotlines can provide us with social support. (The U.S. Department of Health and Human Services maintains a master toll-free number that can provide telephone numbers and addresses of many national helplines and support groups. You can reach it by calling 1-800-336-4797.)

social support
Assistance and comfort supplied by others in times of stress.

▶ **Relax.** Because stress produces constant wear and tear on the body, it seems logical that practices that lead to the relaxation of the body might lead to a reduction in stress. And that's just what happens. Using any one of several techniques for producing physical relaxation can prevent stress. Among the best relaxation techniques is *meditation*. Though often associated with its roots in the ancient Eastern religion of Zen Buddhism, meditation, a technique for refocusing attention and producing bodily relaxation, is practiced in some form by members of virtually every major religion.

Meditation reduces blood pressure, slows respiration, and in general reduces bodily tension. You can learn about practicing meditation online, at the library, or at a meditation center in your area.

Source: © Blend Images/Punchstock

From the perspective of . . .

A STUDENT The educational process can be stressful. When you consider your career path, what are the areas of stress you may need to address?

Look for the Silver Lining

Consider the following list of potentially stressful situations. Try to find something positive—a silver lining—in each of them. The first two are completed to get you started.

Situation	Silver Lining
1. Your car just broke down, and repairing it is more than you can afford right now.	1. This is the perfect time to begin exercising by walking and using your bicycle.
2. Your boss just yelled at you and threatened to fire you.	2. Either this is a good time to open an honest discussion with your boss about your job situation, OR this is a good time to get a more fulfilling job.
3. You have two papers due on Monday, and there's a great concert you want to go to on Saturday night.	3.
4. You just failed an important test.	4.
5. You're flat broke, you promised your friend you'd visit him, and you can't afford the plane ticket right now.	5.
6. Your last date went poorly, and you think your girlfriend/boyfriend was hinting that it was time to break up.	6.
7. You just found out you missed the due date for your mortgage payment.	7.
8. You just got cut from a sports team or club activity you loved.	8.
9. Your best friend is starting to behave coldly and seems not to enjoy being with you as much as before.	9.
10. You just realized you don't really want to pursue the career you're training for in college.	10.

 WORKING IN A GROUP

After you have considered each of these situations individually, discuss them in a group. What similarities and differences in others' responses did you find? Evaluate the different responses, and consider whether—and why—some ways of reframing the situations were better than others.

▶ **Keep your commitments.** Suppose you've promised a friend that you'll help him move, and you've promised yourself that you'll spend more time with your children. You've also been elected to the student body governing board, and you've made a commitment to bring more speakers to campus. Now you are facing all the demands connected to these commitments and feeling stressed.

You may be tempted to cope with the feeling by breaking some or all of your commitments, thinking, "I just need to sit at home and relax in front of the television!" This is not coping. It is escaping, and it doesn't reduce stress. Ducking out of commitments, whether to yourself or to others, will make you feel guilty and anxious and will be another source of stress—one without the satisfaction of having accomplished what you set out to do. Find ways to keep your promises.

Asking If Your Strategies for Dealing with Stress Are Effective

Just as the experience of stress depends on how we interpret circumstances, the strategies for dealing with stress also vary in effectiveness depending on who we are. So if your efforts at coping aren't working, it's time to reconsider your approach. If talking to friends hasn't helped ease your stress response, maybe you need a different approach. Maybe you need to see the silver lining or cut back on some of your commitments.

If one coping strategy doesn't work for you, try another. What's critical is that you not become paralyzed, unable to deal with a situation. Instead, try something different until you find the right combination of strategies to improve the situation.

R Rethink Placing Stress in Perspective

It's easy to think of stress as an enemy. In fact, the coping steps outlined in the P.O.W.E.R. Plan are geared to overcoming its negative consequences. But consider the following two principles, which in the end may help you more than any others in dealing with stress:

▶ **Don't sweat the small stuff . . . and it's all small stuff.** Stress expert Richard Carlson[2] emphasizes the importance of putting the circumstances we encounter into the proper perspective. He argues that we frequently let ourselves get upset about situations that are actually minor.

So what if someone cuts us off in traffic, or does less than his or her share on a group project, or unfairly criticizes us? It's hardly the end of the world. If an unpleasant event has no long-term consequences, it's often best to let it go. One of the best ways to reduce stress, consequently, is to maintain an appropriate perspective on the events of your life.

▶ **Make peace with stress.** Think of what it would be like to have no stress—none at all—in your life. Would you really be happier, better adjusted, and more successful? The answer is "probably not." A life that presented no challenges would probably be, in a word, boring. So think about stress as an exciting, although admittedly sometimes difficult, friend. Welcome it, at least in moderation, because its presence indicates that your life is stimulating, challenging, and exciting—and who would want it any other way?

Keeping Well: Physical Health

Eat right. Exercise. Get plenty of sleep.

Pretty simple, isn't it? We learn the fundamentals of fitness and health in the first years of elementary school.

Yet for millions of us, wellness is an elusive goal. We eat on the fly, stopping for a bite at the drive-in window of a fast-food restaurant. Most of us don't exercise enough, either because we feel we don't have time or because it's not much fun. And as for sleep, we're a nation in which getting by with as little sleep as possible is seen as a badge of honor.

For many college students, these bad habits are only made worse by the need to manage so many different sets of responsibilities. It is hard to concentrate on keeping well when you also need to keep your children cared for, your boss happy, your schoolwork complete, your household managed. Personal health can easily get lost in the shuffle of all these competing demands. At the end of the day, too many students feel as if they've run themselves ragged just trying to do the minimum to meet their many obligations.

> "The first wealth is health."
>
> **Ralph Waldo Emerson, author and poet**

Yet your health is too important to ignore. There are strategies you can use to balance your commitments, and you can begin to eat properly, exercise effectively, and sleep better. Approaches to accomplishing these goals include the following:

Eating Right

▶ **Eat a variety of "whole" foods, including fruits, vegetables, and grain products.** Strive to eat a range of different foods. If you make variety your goal, you will end up eating the right foods. You can learn more about maintaining variety in your diet by visiting the government website (**www.choosemyplate.gov**) that describes the food guide "plate" and allows you to construct a personalized eating plan.

▶ **Avoid processed foods.** Make an effort to choose whole foods, or foods in a state as close as possible to their natural state: brown rice is better than white rice, and both are better than a preservative-filled, packaged "rice casserole" mix.

▶ **Avoid foods that are high in sugar and salt content.** Read product labels carefully and beware of hidden sugars and salts. Many ingredients that end in *-ose* (such as dextrose, sucrose, maltose, and fructose) are actually sugars; salt can lurk within any number of compounds beginning with the word *sodium*.

▶ **Seek a diet low in fat and cholesterol.** The fat that is to be especially avoided is saturated fat—the most difficult for your body to rid itself of.

▶ **Remember: Less is more.** You don't need to walk away stuffed from every meal. Moderation is the key. To be sure you don't eat more than your body is telling you to eat, pay attention to internal hunger cues.

Source: © Corbis Premium Collection/Alamy

Evaluate Your Eating Habits

When you are busy or stressed, it's easy to eat mindlessly. But thinking about your eating habits puts you in a position to improve them.

Place a check before each statement that is true for you. Then check your score below.

____ 1. I eat fast food more than once a week.

____ 2. I often snack while watching TV or surfing the Internet.

____ 3. My social interactions with others almost always include eating and drinking.

____ 4. If I start a bag of potato chips or a pint of ice cream, I tend to finish it in one sitting.

____ 5. I drink more than 24 ounces of soda a week.

____ 6. When hungry, I tend to snack on whatever's at hand, mostly packaged foods.

____ 7. I rarely or never check the labels of the food and drink products I consume.

____ 8. If everyone's getting pizza, I'll go along, even if I just ate a full meal.

____ 9. I keep plenty of junk food at hand when I'm studying.

____ 10. In a typical week, there is more than one day when I don't eat fresh fruit and/or vegetables.

Count up your check marks. 0–2: You are mindful of what and when you eat. If you're also exercising, you're probably healthy and fit. 3–5: You need to think more about what you eat. Before you open that bag of chips or order a triple burger, ask yourself, Am I actually hungry? Could I make a better food choice here? 6 or more: You are currently sapping the energy you need in your busy life, and you are compromising your health for the future. Review the tips in this chapter for more healthful eating. Bon appétit!

▶ **Schedule three regular meals a day.** Eating should be a priority—a definite part of your daily schedule. Avoid skipping any meals. Breakfast is particularly important; get up early enough to eat a full meal.

▶ **Be sensitive to the hidden contents of various foods.** Soda and chocolate can contain substantial quantities of caffeine, which can disrupt your sleep and, along with coffee, become addictive. Many cereals—even those labeled "low fat"—contain a considerable amount of sugar or salt. Pay attention to labels. And watch out for fast foods: Research finds that eating fast foods just a few times a week leads to significant weight gain over the long run.[3]

▶ **If you want to lose weight, follow a sensible diet.** There's really only one proven way to lose weight: Control your food portions, eat a well-balanced diet, and increase the amount of exercise you get. Quick-fix, fad diets are ineffective. (And, of course, consult a physician before making any major changes in your diet.) See **Try It! 3** to evaluate your eating habits.

Making Exercise a Part of Your Life

Exercise produces a variety of benefits. Your body will run more efficiently, you'll have more energy, your heart and circulatory system will run more smoothly, and you'll be able to bounce back from stress and illness more quickly.

▶ **Choose a type of exercise that you like.** Exercising will be a chore you end up avoiding if you don't enjoy what you're doing.

Staying Alert in Class

If you're having trouble staying alert and—even worse—staying awake in class, the best solution is to get more sleep. Short of that, there are several strategies you can try to help you stay awake:

- Throw yourself into the class. Pay close attention, take notes, ask questions, and generally be fully engaged in the class. You should do this anyway, but making a special effort when you're exhausted can get you through a period of fatigue.

- Sit up straight. Pinch yourself. Stretch the muscles in different parts of your body. Fidget. Any activity will help you thwart fatigue and feel more alert.

- Eat or drink something cold in class (if your school and instructor permit it). The mere activity of eating a snack or drinking can help you stay awake.

- Avoid heavy meals before class. Your body's natural reaction to a full stomach is to call for a nap—the opposite of what you want to achieve.

- Stay cool. Take off your coat or jacket and sit by an open window. If it's warm, ask your instructor if there's a way to make the classroom cooler.

- Take off *one* shoe. This creates a temperature difference, which can be helpful in keeping you awake.

▶ **Incorporate exercise into your life.** Take the stairs instead of elevators. When you're on campus, take the longer way to reach your destination. Leave your car at home and walk to campus or work. If you drive, take the parking space farthest from the building to which you're heading.

▶ **Make exercise a group activity.** Exercising with others brings you social support and turns exercise into a social activity. You'll be more likely to stick to a program if you have a regular "exercise date" with a friend.

▶ **Vary your routine.** You don't need to do the same kind of exercise day after day. Choose different sorts of activities that will involve different parts of your body and keep you from getting bored. For example, for cardiovascular fitness, you might alternate between running, swimming, biking, or using a cardio training machine.

One note of caution: Before you begin an exercise program, it is a good idea to have a physical checkup, even if you feel you're in the peak of health. This is especially true if you're starting an exercise program after years of inactivity. You also might consult a personal trainer at the gym to set up a program that gradually builds you up to more vigorous exercise.

Getting a Good Night's Sleep

Do you feel as if you don't get enough sleep? You probably don't. Most college students are sleep deprived, a condition that causes them to feel fatigued, short-tempered, and tense. Sleep deprivation makes staying alert in class nearly impossible (see the **Course Connections** feature).

Ultimately, insufficient sleep leads to declines in academic, work, and physical performance. You can't do your best at anything if you're exhausted—or even tired.

Often the solution to the problem is simply to allow yourself more time to sleep. Most people need around eight hours of sleep each night, although there are wide individual differences. In addition to sleeping more, there are also some relatively simple changes you can make in your behavior that will help you to sleep better. They include the following:

▶ **Exercise more.** Regular exercise will help you sleep more soundly at night, as well as help you cope with stress that might otherwise keep you awake.

▶ **Have a regular bedtime.** By going to bed at pretty much the same time each night, you give your body a regular rhythm and make sleep a habit.

▶ **Use your bed for sleeping and not as an all-purpose area.** Don't use your bed as a place to study, read, eat, or watch TV. Let your bed be a trigger for sleep.

▶ **Avoid caffeine after lunch.** The stimulant effects of caffeine (found in coffee, tea, and some soft drinks) may last as long as 8 to 12 hours after it's consumed.

When we have more responsibilities than time, sleep is often the first thing to suffer. Getting an appropriate amount of sleep can actually help you get more done in the time you do have.
Source: © Rob Melnychuk/Getty Images

▶ **Drink a glass of milk at bedtime.** Your mom was right: Drinking a glass of milk before you go to bed will help you get to sleep. The reason: Milk contains a natural chemical that makes you drowsy.

▶ **Avoid sleeping pills.** Steer clear of sleeping pills. Although they may be temporarily effective, in the long run they impair your ability to sleep because they disrupt your natural sleep cycles.

▶ **Don't try to force sleep on yourself.** Although this advice sounds odd, it turns out that one of the reasons we have trouble sleeping is that we try too hard. Consequently, when you go to bed, just relax, and don't even attempt to go to sleep. If you're awake after 10 minutes or so, get up and do something else. Go back to bed only when you feel tired. Do this as often as necessary. If you follow this regimen for several weeks—and don't take naps or rest during the day—eventually getting into your bed will trigger sleep.

» LO 11-3 Keeping Well: Mental Health

Our physical well-being is one piece of the puzzle that leads to overall well-being. The other aspect of wellness is mental health. Let's next consider some of the threats to well-being related to mental health.

Juggling Your Responsibilities

▶ **Identify your priorities.** Taking your child to the dentist or studying for a final exam are examples of tasks that absolutely have to be accomplished. Updating your blog or cleaning out your garage are things that can be left to another day. This distinction seems obvious, yet too often we allow lower-priority tasks to

Anticipating Job Stress

Students are not the only ones who have to cope with stress. It's also one of the prime hazards of the world of work. Illnesses related to job stress result in costs of $150 billion each year.

Consequently, taking potential stress into account should be an important consideration when choosing a profession. Asking yourself the following questions can help you identify the factors that may induce stress on the job:

- How much control over working conditions will I have? (The more control an employee has in day-to-day decision making, the lower the level of stress.)

- What are the demands of the job? Will I face constant demands to do more work and to work more quickly? (Higher work demands create a more stressful work environment.)

- What is the tolerance for error? (Some occupations, such as air traffic controller, have no margin for error, while others, such as many white-collar professions, give workers a second chance if they make a mistake.)

- How closely do my abilities and strengths match the requirements of the job? (A good match between one's abilities and the demands of a job is the best insurance against an unduly stressful work environment.)

- How well do I cope with stress?

If your coping skills are good, you may be suited for entering a high-stress occupation. But if you have difficulty dealing with stress, choosing a career in a field that produces less stress makes more sense.

crowd out the high-priority ones. Identify what is most important for you to achieve, and use your time and energy to accomplish these high-priority goals.

▶ **Use proven time management techniques.** There are only 24 hours in a day. Often, though, it can seem there is 25 hours' worth of work to do—or more. To get a handle on your schedule, use the strategies outlined in Chapter 2. Creating daily to-do lists, calendars, and so forth will be a huge help in effectively meeting your many responsibilities.

▶ **Communicate with others about your obligations.** Remember that the people in your life—bosses, family members, instructors, fellow students—can't know you are managing a wide set of responsibilities unless you *tell them*. And while you can't expect special treatment just because you have a child at home or a second job to go to, you'll be surprised at how understanding others will be of your circumstances. Additionally, by communicating with those around you, you can work with them to find solutions when your life starts to feel overwhelming.

▶ **Multitask.** Don't draw strict limits regarding what you do and when. If you have a free 20 minutes at your job, use the time to catch up on reading for classes. When your children are napping, see if there is work for your job you can accomplish at home. You don't want to fill every spare minute with work, but you want to take advantage of the gaps in your hectic day.

Posttraumatic Stress Disorder (PTSD)

Some students who have been exposed to severe personal stressors experience **posttraumatic stress disorder**, or **PTSD**, in which a highly stressful event has

posttraumatic stress disorder (PTSD)

A psychological disorder in which a highly stressful event has long-lasting consequences that may include reexperiencing the event in vivid flashbacks or dreams.

long-lasting consequences that may include reexperiencing the event in vivid flashbacks or dreams. An episode of PTSD may be triggered by an otherwise innocent stimulus—the sound of a textbook dropping to the floor, for example—that leads a person to reexperience an extremely stressful past event.

An estimated 20 percent of veterans returning from Afghanistan and Iraq show symptoms of PTSD. Victims of child abuse or rape may also suffer from PTSD, as may rescue workers facing overwhelming situations, or victims of natural disasters or accidents that produce shock and feelings of helplessness.[4]

Symptoms of posttraumatic stress disorder may include emotional numbing, sleep difficulties, interpersonal problems, alcohol and drug abuse, and in some cases, suicide. For instance, the suicide rate for military veterans, many of whom participated in the Iraq and Afghanistan wars, is twice as high as for nonveterans.

Depression and Suicide

Almost no student passes through college without at least occasionally feeling depressed. The stress of college life can lead to feeling sad, unhappy, and even hopeless on occasion.

Most of the time, depression is a normal reaction to distressing circumstances. It may occur in response to the death of a loved one, the end of a relationship, failure at an important task, or any number of events. Usually the depression is temporary, and people return to their normal emotional state.

For some students, however, depression is more than fleeting. Around 3 percent of people suffer from *major depression*, a psychological disorder in which depression is severe and lasts more than two weeks. Major depression can occur without any obvious cause, and students who suffer from it feel extremely sad, hopeless, tired, and worthless.

Major depression ultimately can lead to suicide. But suicide can occur for other reasons. For instance, some—but not all—people who commit suicide are perfectionists, are socially inhibited, or suffer from extreme anxiety when they face any social or academic challenge. In other cases, though, none of those characteristics are present.

Several warning signs indicate when a student's problems may be severe enough to justify concern about the possibility of a suicide attempt. They include

▶ School problems, such as missing classes and a sudden change in grades.

▶ Frequent incidents of self-destructive behavior, such as careless accidents.

▶ Loss of appetite or excessive eating.

▶ Withdrawal from friends and peers.

▶ Sleeping problems.

▶ Signs of depression, tearfulness, or overt indications of psychological difficulties, such as hallucinations.

▶ A preoccupation with death, an afterlife, or what would happen "if I died."

▶ Putting affairs in order, such as giving away prized possessions or making arrangements for the care of a pet.

▶ An explicit announcement of suicidal thoughts.

If you know someone who shows signs that he or she is suicidal, urge that person to seek professional help. You may need to take assertive action, such as enlisting the assistance of family members, counselors, or instructors. This is especially true if people say they feel urges to harm not only themselves but others. Talk of hurting oneself or others is a serious signal for help, not a confidence to be kept.

For immediate help with a suicide-related problem, you can call the following national hotlines, which are staffed with trained counselors: 800-784-2433 or 800-448-3000.

Speaking *of* Success

Source: Courtesy of Siyu Lu

NAME: **Siyu Lu**

SCHOOL: **Edmonds Community College, Lynnwood, Washington**

MAJOR: **Associate of Arts in Business; Associate of Technical Arts Degree in Accounting**

Coming to the United States from China at age 17 with little knowledge of English, and facing homelessness, would seem like nearly insurmountable challenges for anyone. But armed with a strong desire for an education, Siyu Lu was more than determined to succeed, and the opportunities afforded by her local community college proved to be the solution.

Five years later, Lu is getting ready to move on to a four-year college, carrying with her a collection of various academic honors, numerous scholarship awards, and valuable academic skills.

Constantly working on improving her English, Lu developed a strict set of studying approaches to help her reach academic success.

"When reading textbooks, I took review notes and made flash cards to help me remember the material. If a publisher's website and study guides were available, I usually took as many practice exercises as I could," Lu said. "In addition, I stopped by instructors' offices frequently."

To help finance her education, Lu worked 20 hours per week part-time during school and full-time during breaks in the academic year, which forced her to learn time management techniques.

"I took 15 credits a term, which means I needed to study about 60 hours per week. In addition, I liked participating in campus and community activities," she said. "Being active meant balancing my activities and managing my time. I used a weekly planner that helps me plan and keep track of deadlines. Each week it took me about half an hour to plan my week and complete my 'time management log.'"

Lu's long-term goal is to pursue a B.A. degree in accounting and finance and then use her skills to help nonprofit ogranizations.

"My career goal is to become a financial analyst whose specialty is taxation," she explained. "While working as a financial analyst, I would like to establish a nonprofit organization that promotes family financial literacy and educates the public about personal finances management.

"There are so many options and possibilities out there. Figure out and be faithful to who you are and what you like," she added. "Taking charge of your life means knowing what you have done, being passionate about what you are doing, and feeling motivated about what you are going to do."

[RETHINK]

- How do you think Lu's use of a weekly planner helped her to deal with stress?
- What do you think Lu means when she says "Taking charge of your life means knowing what you have done"?

Looking Back

LO 11-1 Explain what stress is and how to control it.

▶ Stress is a common experience, appearing in three main forms: cataclysmic events, personal stressors, and daily hassles. Not only is excessive stress unpleasant and upsetting, but it also has negative effects on the body and mind.

▶ Coping with stress involves becoming prepared for future stress through proper diet and exercise, identifying the causes of stress in one's life, taking control of stress, seeking social support, practicing relaxation techniques, training oneself to redefine and reinterpret stressful situations, and keeping one's promises.

LO 11-2 Discuss what is involved in keeping well physically.

▶ For all people, keeping fit and healthy is both essential and challenging. Balance your responsibilities by identifying your priorities and using time management techniques.

▶ It is vital to learn to eat properly, especially by eating a variety of foods on a regular schedule and by restricting your intake of fat, cholesterol, sugar, and salt.

▶ Exercise is valuable because it improves health and well-being. Choosing exercises that we like, making everyday activities a part of exercise, and exercising with others can help form the habit of exercise.

▶ The third key element of good health is sleeping properly. Good exercise and eating habits can contribute to sound sleep, as can the development of regular sleeping habits and the use of sleep-assisting practices.

LO 11-3 Describe strategies for keeping well mentally.

▶ Strategies for juggling responsibilities include identifying your priorities, using time management techniques, communicating with others about your obligations, and multitasking effectively.

▶ In posttraumatic stress disorder, or PTSD, a highly stressful event has long-lasting consequences that may include reexperiencing the event in vivid flashbacks or dreams.

▶ In extreme cases, stress can lead to posttraumatic stress disorder and suicide.

[KEY TERMS AND CONCEPTS]

Cataclysmic events (p. 281)

Coping (p. 283)

Daily hassles (p. 281)

Personal stressors (p. 281)

Posttraumatic stress disorder (PTSD) (p. 292)

Social support (p. 285)

Stress (p. 280)

[RESOURCES]

ON CAMPUS

Many colleges have mental health counselors that can help you deal with emotional problems. If you are depressed, have trouble sleeping, or experience other problems in coping with the challenges of life, speaking with a counselor can be extremely helpful. Check with your school's counseling center or health center to identify someone appropriate with whom to speak.

IN PRINT

Kelci Lucier's *College Stress Solutions: Stress Management Techniques to *Beat Anxiety *Make the Grade *Enjoy the Full College Experience* (Adams Media, 2014) offers an array of information to ease the stress.

A Mindfulness-Based Stress Reduction Workbook for Anxiety by Bob Stahl and Florence Meleo-Meyer (New Harbinger Publications, 2014) offers insights and practical exercises.

Your Body: The Science of Keeping It Healthy (*Time,* 2013), from the editors of *Time* magazine, is a practical owner's manual for maintaining a healthy body and lifestyle.

ON THE WEB

The following sites on the web provide the opportunity to extend your learning about stress, health, and wellness. (Although the web addresses were accurate at the time this material was published, check the *P.O.W.E.R. Learning* Connect Library or contact your instructor for any changes that may have occurred.)

▶ The American Dietetic Association's website not only provides information for its professional members, but also includes updated consumer tips and articles (**www.eatright.org/Public/**). Features include strategies for smart grocery shopping, discussion of the latest fad diets, and guidelines for healthy eating.

▶ "What Coping Strategies are Effective?" (**http://stress.about.com/od/ frequentlyaskedquestions/f/coping_strategies.htm**), on **About.com**, offers in-depth and comprehensive information on coping with stress. Dozens of links cover teens through the elderly, self-assessment, psychotherapy, and relaxation techniques.

The Case of . . .

The Pile-Up

"Get your coats and shoes on!" Lena Olveras called out to her two daughters, who were dawdling over their cereal. Lena stuffed their lunches into paper bags, located her car keys and book bag, grabbed her jacket, helped 3-year-old Shelby with her shoes, and . . . they were out the door!

After leaving Shelby at day care, Lena drove across town to drop her older daughter at school. Traffic was a mess, but she finally cleared the logjam and headed out to campus. She mentally reviewed the day ahead. Classes until 3. Then her part-time job at the pharmacy. Pick up the girls from day care and after-school at 7. Dinner at 8—she'd have to stop by the store; the refrigerator was empty. Bedtime at 9. Study until midnight. Somewhere she'd squeeze in a load of laundry.

Lena took a deep breath and tried to smile. She was strong. She'd get through the day. The trouble was, *all* her days looked like this. And that was only if nothing went wrong.

1. What stressors are regularly present in Lena's life? What can she perhaps change, and what must she live with?

2. Do you see any silver linings in Lena's situation? What advice could you give her about changing her perceptions to ease her feelings of stress?

3. How might Lena use social support to make her life easier?

4. Why would it be important for Lena to practice good eating habits and exercise regularly? What advice could you give her?

5. What specific techniques might help Lena to juggle her responsibilities more easily?

Careers

Learning Outcomes

By the time you finish this chapter you will be able to

» **LO 12-1** Identify your career goals and ideal job.

» **LO 12-2** Describe how to a create career portfolio and its advantages.

» **LO 12-3** Discuss strategies for identifying references and interviewing well.

Carolene Drarnetz had worked hard to prepare for her interview for a job as a computer technician at a local hospital. She had read the hospital's mission statement online, learned what it considered its strengths, and found the types of care it specialized in. She had even read about its computer services department. As the final touch, she had visited a friend who worked at the hospital to pick her brain and check out the work environment.

She had also anticipated the types of questions she might be asked and practiced good answers to them, referring to her past job and school experiences. She was ready.

But when the interviewer, seemingly out of the blue, asked her, "How many golf courses are there in the United States?" she froze. How should she know? And more important, what did golf courses have to do with hospital computers?

Looking Ahead

Luckily for Carolene, what she later called the "golf course crisis" was a turning point. Once she got beyond her initial shock, she realized that the aim of the question was to test not her knowledge of golf courses but her problem-solving skills. After first considering the population of the United States, which she knew was around 310 million, and then guessing at how many of those people might play golf, and using this number to work out how many courses might be needed to accommodate them, she was able to come up with a rough estimate of how many courses there might be. The interviewer, clearly satisfied, moved on to other, more predictable questions.

Job interviews can be anxiety-producing events. But they are just one of a series of challenging activities that are part of the process of finding a job. In the last few chapters of *P.O.W.E.R. Learning*, we've been looking at skills that are usually applied in a classroom setting: notetaking, test taking, and so forth. In this chapter, we explore strategies that will help you in the world of work. We address ways to identify your career goals and the best methods to achieve them. To put it simply, we consider the things you need to know to get the job you want.

»LO 12-1 Career Planning

P Prepare

Identify your career goals

O Organize

Find career opportunities

W Work

Create a career portfolio

E Evaluate

Get feedback on your résumé and cover letter

R Rethink

Reconsider your career choices

P.O.W.E.R. Plan

At this point, you're in college to learn the skills to start down a specific career path. That means you've made up your mind about your career . . . right?

In fact, the answer is no. Even those on their way to acquiring training to work within a particular field need to think and plan carefully with regard to their professional ambitions.

For instance, imagine you are on your way to earning a degree in accounting. Clearly you've made an important decision about your career. But consider these questions: Do you want to work independently or as an employee of a business? If you want to work for a business, would you rather it be a small company or a large corporation? Do you want a job that will pay less initially but at which you can advance, or would you rather trade the possibility of moving up the ladder for a better starting salary?

Further, do you want to work locally, or would you be willing to relocate for the right job? What kind of hours are you willing to work? What kind of hours *can* you work, given the demands of family and other obligations?

These are just some of the questions people need to answer as they approach their careers. Keep in mind that you don't need to have all the answers right now. Few people know *exactly* how they'd like their professional lives to unfold. What's important to realize is that even if you've chosen a field, you still have lots of decisions to make and options to choose from as you pursue your career. Remember that career planning is not a decision you make once. Rather, it is an ongoing process. (To explore your thinking about work and careers, complete the **Journal Reflections**.)

Journal Reflections

Thinking about Work

At some point in your life, you've almost surely had a job. Maybe you have one right now. And whether you realize it or not, there's no doubt you have developed some strong ideas about what it's like to work. Take some time now to consider your thoughts about work more fully.

1. What was most rewarding about the best job you ever had: the ability to earn money, social aspects involving your fellow employees, enjoyment of the work itself, or something else?

2. What would you see as the positive and negative aspects of supervising other people? Would you like to supervise others at some point in your career?

3. How important is the amount of money that you're paid for the work you do?

4. Do you see work as something you must do in order to earn a living, or something that is a central and important aspect of life in and of itself?

5. How important is variety in what you do? How important is stability in what you do?

P Prepare ## Identifying Your Career Goals

Some people take a job for the money. Some people take a job for the health benefits. Some people show up at work because they love to crunch numbers or treat patients or cook filet mignon. Other people go to the office because they believe that hard work is the key to happiness.

These are all valid reasons for doing a job. As you think about the kind of job you want to find, it's essential to consider your own goals. Apart from what you might do during the day, do you want a job that helps others? A job that pays very well? One with flexible hours? Is having an impact on future generations important to you? Use **Try It! 1** to identify your long-term career goals.

Identifying Your Long-Term Career Goals

Consider each of these areas as you determine your long-term goals:

- Achievement
- Advancement opportunities
- Challenge
- Contribution to society
- Control, power
- Creativity

- Financial security
- Friendships with co-workers
- Helping others
- Independence
- Leadership
- Learning new things

- Loyalty
- Prestige
- Recognition from others
- Security
- Variety
- Working with others

Using this list, create a set of your three most important occupational goals. For example, three primary goals might be to (1) be challenged to reach my potential, (2) work with others in a cooperative environment, and (3) make a lasting contribution to society. However, don't be influenced by these examples—choose goals that are your own.

My Primary Career Goals Are to:

1.

2.

3.

Stating your career goals up front, even before you consider the range of jobs that you have to choose from, is important. Identifying your goals helps you know what it is that *you* want out of work. Future employers are interested in what you bring to your job, rather than how well a job fulfills your important goals. It's crucial that you consider what has significance to you before making career decisions. If a career opportunity doesn't fulfill your major goals, it will not be a good choice for you.

 Finding Career Opportunities

Research, research, research. That's the name of the game when it comes to charting your career. Even if you know the general direction you want your career to take, you'll want to get a feel for the specific opportunities within your chosen field, as well as how your field is developing and changing. Be sure to keep notes about what you find. Your notes don't have to be elaborately written or suitable for handing in to an instructor. Just keep them simple, legible, and organized, and make sure that they include the source of the information you're describing.

Books and Websites

A good first step in obtaining career information is the U.S. Department of Labor's *Occupational Outlook Handbook (OOH)*. The *OOH*, published every two years, categorizes occupations into 11 broad groupings. It provides information on kinds of work, working conditions, job outlook, earnings, education and training requirements, and expected job prospects.

You can also visit the website of the Bureau of Labor Statistics of the Department of Labor at **www.bls.gov/ooh/**, which provides a wealth of additional information. Among the most interesting features of this website is a compilation in its *Occupational Outlook Handbook* of the most up-to-date information on the hottest professions in terms of projected future growth. (This information, summarized in **Table 12.1**, must be used with care: The mere fact that a job is expanding rapidly doesn't necessarily mean that there are huge numbers of openings. A quickly growing profession may have only a few openings, and even with rapid growth, the absolute number of jobs may still be relatively small in coming years.)

Source: © Mark Andersen/Getty Images

From the perspective of . . .

A STUDENT Part of your growth as a student involves an honest assessment of career possibilities. What careers appeal to you most?

You are likely to find the *OOH,* and a wealth of other information, either in the career center of your college or in its library. In addition, almost every public library has a reference section on careers, and state employment centers often have extensive materials to help identify careers.

In addition to books, you may find CDs, pamphlets, and other helpful material at career centers, libraries, and employment centers. These resources also may offer on-site computers with software that can help you gather job-related information. For example, the *Discover Career Guidance and Information System* and *SIGI PLUS (System of Interactive Guidance and Information)* are widely used computer programs that have proven helpful to those engaged in career searches.

Home healthcare aides, forensic science technicians, and dental hygienists are all career areas on the rise. Have you considered any of the careers on this list?

Personal Interviews

To get an up-close-and-personal look at a profession, another strategy is to talk with people who are already in it. People love to talk about their jobs, whether they love them or hate them, so don't be afraid to ask for a meeting or information session regarding their profession. You don't need a lot of their time—just enough

table 12.1   Occupations with the Fastest Growth, Projected 2012–2022

OCCUPATION	GROWTH RATE, 2012–2022	2012 MEDIAN PAY
Industrial-organizational psychologists	53%	$83,580 per year
Personal care aides	49%	$19,910 per year
Home health aides	48%	$20,820 per year
Insulation workers, mechanical	47%	$39,170 per year
Interpreters and translators	46%	$45,430 per year
Diagnostic medical sonographers	46%	$65,860 per year
Helpers—brickmasons, blockmasons, stonemasons, and tile and marble setters	43%	$28,220 per year
Occupational therapy assistants	43%	$53,240 per year
Genetic counselors	41%	$56,800 per year
Physical therapist assistants	41%	$52,160 per year
Physical therapist aides	40%	$23,880 per year
Skincare specialists	40%	$28,640 per year
Physician assistants	38%	$90,930 per year
Segmental pavers	38%	$33,720 per year
Helpers—electricians	37%	$27,670 per year
Information security analysts	37%	$86,170 per year
Occupational therapy aides	36%	$26,850 per year
Health specialties teachers, postsecondary	36%	$81,140 per year
Medical secretaries	36%	$31,350 per year
Physical therapists	36%	$79,860 per year

Source: U.S. Bureau of Labor Statistics (2014). *Occupational Outlook Handbook, 2012–2022: Labor Statistics Bureau Bulletin 2800*. Washington, DC: U.S. Government Printing Office.

to get an inside view of what it's like to work in their profession. Here are some questions you might want to ask:

▶ What's your typical day like?
▶ How did you find your job?
▶ What are the best and worst aspects of being in your profession?
▶ What would you look for in someone who wants to enter your field?

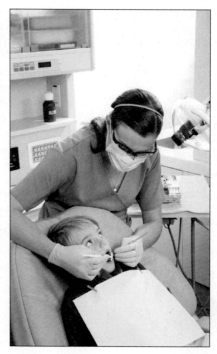

Source: © Jeff Cadge/Photographer's Choice/ Getty Images

Source: © Brand X Pictures/PunchStock

Source: © UpperCut Images/Getty Images

Keep in mind, of course, that the answers you get will be the opinions of one individual, reflecting his or her unique, personal experience. That's why it's a good idea to talk to several practitioners of a particular occupation, and to consider what they say in the context of other research that you have conducted.

Be sure to write a thank-you note following an interview. Not only is this a common courtesy, it serves the additional purpose of reinforcing who you are and your interest in the profession. You never know: One day they might have a job opening, and you might want to ask them for a job!

》LO 12-2 W Work Creating a Career Portfolio

The research you've done on career options forms the foundation for creating a career development portfolio. A **career portfolio** is a dynamic record that documents your skills, capabilities, achievements, and goals, as well as providing a place to keep notes, ideas, and research findings related to careers. Such a portfolio will provide an easy-to-access history of your job-related activities, and it will include material that will be helpful for you and, later, for potential employers. You'll want to keep and update your career portfolio as long as you are pursuing a career.

Your career portfolio will consist of two main parts. The first part, background information, will hold information to help you keep track of your accomplishments and notes on your research; the second part, which includes your resume and cover letter, will be material that you share with potential employers.

Your career portfolio can be either a traditional paper document or an online e-portfolio. Some colleges provide online templates or "wizards" that guide you through the process of creating a career portfolio. E-portfolios have the advantage of being easily modified, and—since they reside on the web—they are accessible anywhere you have access to the web.

career portfolio

A dynamic record that documents your skills, capabilities, achievements, and goals, as well as providing a place to keep notes, ideas, and research findings related to careers.

Instructors as Career Guides

Each of your instructors has a job—that of college instructor. But despite the similarity in job titles, each got that job in a different way, using different tactics and strategies. Each followed his or her own particular career path and has a distinct educational background. Furthermore, your instructors may have had a variety of positions, and possibly a number of previous careers, prior to becoming college instructors.

You can learn a great deal about career opportunities and the process of getting a job by talking to your course instructors about their own careers. Set up an appointment with each of your course instructors, and ask questions such as these:

- What is your educational and professional background?
- How did you get your current job?
- What students have you had that have been particularly successful careerwise? What qualities did they have that set them apart from other students of yours?
- What general advice do you have for someone looking for a job?
- Knowing me from your course, what skills would you encourage me to work on and develop in order to increase my chances of successfully getting a job?

You can gain valuable insights into navigating a career from your course instructors. Furthermore, talking with your course instructors can help you get to know them better, and it may eventually pave the way for you to ask them for letters of recommendation. Instructors also sometimes get leads on jobs, and if they know your career goals, they may pass the leads on to you. Finally, if you build a relationship with your instructor, it may help you do better academically in your course—no small benefit!

Career Portfolio Part I: Background Information

The information in this section of your career portfolio is meant to help you make career-related decisions and record your thinking about your career. This part is for your eyes only. Although you will draw on the material for the public part of your career portfolio that potential employers will see, think of it as your own private repository of information.

▶ **Basic personal data.** Keep a record of data and identification numbers that you think you'll never forget—but that even with the best intentions, you probably will be unable to remember at the least opportune moment. For example, include your Social Security number, addresses (home and college), college ID number, and telephone numbers. If you're a renter, keep a record of your landlord's name and address; you might need a credit reference one day.

▶ **Career research notes.** Whether you have notes collected from books, web-based research, or interviews with people in a particular occupation, they belong in your career portfolio. They will provide a record of your career-related activities.

▶ **Syllabus and outline from courses you have taken.** Include a copy of the syllabus and course outline of every course you take, along with the grade you received in the course. The information contained in a course syllabus and outline will serve to jog your memory about the material the course covered. Without these materials, you're at the mercy of your memory when you're trying to recall the content of a course you may have taken several years earlier that has direct relevance to your career.

For further documentation relating to your courses, you could include a copy of the course description from the college catalog and, if the class had a list of competencies that students were to attain, a copy of these as well.

▶ **Transcripts.** Include the most recent version of your transcript, listing the courses that you took, credits earned, and grades you received in your classes.

▶ **Your personal history.** If someone were to write your biography, what are the key events that you'd want him or her to know about?

The events that would be included in your biography can form the core of a list that you should make of every significant experience you've had. Although the list should include every employment-related experience you've had, even part-time jobs or summer jobs when you were in high school, don't limit yourself only to job experiences. Also include other accomplishments, such as the military service or community service you have performed. Personal events that have had a major impact on who you are, such as notable athletic achievements, should also earn a place in your personal history. Use **Try It! 2** to help make this list, which you'll use later to create a resume.

▶ **Long-term career goals.** Your career portfolio should include the statement of your long-term career goals that you developed in **Try It! 1**.

▶ **Writing samples.** Add examples of your best writing. These can be papers that you've handed in for classes or other writing you have done on your own or on the job. The idea is to have a sample of your writing easily available should a potential employer ask for one.

▶ **Credentials.** Include copies of any credentials you have earned. For example, place in the portfolio a copy of diplomas you have earned, certificates of workshop or training participation you have received, proof of noncredit continuing education courses you have taken, and the like. You never know when an employer might want to see documentation of your accomplishments.

Career Portfolio Part II: Resume and Cover Letter

This section of your career portfolio encompasses information that you will share with potential employers. Whereas the material in the first part of your portfolio provides the background for your career planning, this is the public face of your portfolio.

Think of the components of the first part as the equivalent of the backstage of a play, with a director and crew working behind the scenes to pull things together. In contrast, this second part of the portfolio is the play the audience sees—the part that should proceed flawlessly. You want the critics to offer nothing less than raves for your production.

The two primary elements that belong in the second part of your career portfolio are your resume and your cover letter.

Resume

A resume (pronounced res-oo-may) is a brief summary of your qualifications for a job. It is the first thing that potential employers see and should serve to arouse

Cataloging Your Personal History

	Activity or Event	When It Took Place	Where It Occurred (e.g., company, hospital, social agency)	Responsi-bilities or Activities	Skills or Talents Used	Achievements, Results, or Insights
Did you work during or before high school or college?						
Were you a member of any clubs or other organizations in high school or college?						
How many paid jobs have you held?						
Have you performed any community service?						
Have you had any personally significant life experiences?						
Have you ever been called upon to exercise skills or talents you didn't know you had?						
Have you ever solved a tough problem and felt great satisfaction?						
Have you ever worked in a group to solve a problem?						
Have you ever organized a complex task on your own?						
Have you ever led a group in the performance of a large task?						
What is the best thing you have ever done?						

WORKING IN A GROUP

Compare your responses to those of other students in the group. What are the unique capabilities that you have—the things that set you apart from others in the group? How could you take advantage of those unique capabilities when you are seeking a job?

their interest. Actually, a human may not even initially see it: An increasing number of employers use computers to screen resumes. The computers look for key skills, and if they are lacking, they send an automatic rejection.

Consequently, the resume must be crafted with great precision and care. If you've created a personal history statement earlier for Part I of your career portfolio, use it to get started.

The key elements of a resume include the following and are illustrated in a sample resume in **Figure 12.1**.

figure 12.1
Sample Resume

ALEJANDRO D. WEBB
1334 Russel Lane, Brooksville, FL 34603
352 - 555 - 1877 e: alejwebb@gmail.com

JOB OBJECTIVE—To obtain a position as a paralegal

WORK EXPERIENCE
Law offices of Brandon and Shields, Brooksville, FL
Office Manager
May 2011 - Present

- Oversaw logistics of law office of twelve people; was responsible for scheduling, filing, copying, and managing administrative staff.
- Devised new office-wide filing system for records of completed cases.
- Researched and implemented new office-wide benefits package.
- Responsible for balancing monthly facilities budget.
- Occassionally accompanied attorneys to court to provide organizational support.

Amelia D. Rafael, P.A., Jacksonville, FL
Administrative Assistant
October 2010–April 2012

- Managed schedule, correspondence, and files for high-profile Jacksonville attorney.
- Aided in creating documents and organizing evidence for $13 million class action case.

EDUCATION
Central Florida University
AD Paralegal Studies, June 2015

HONORS AND AWARDS
Academic Dean's List
Frederick Stein Prize for Outstanding Writing

CAMPUS AND COMMUNITY ACTIVITIES
Latino Students Organization
Volunteer, Holling Street Soup Kitchen

PROFESSIONAL MEMBERSHIP
Florida Paralegal Association

PARTICULAR SKILLS
Proficient in all Microsoft Office programs
Fluent in Spanish

REFERENCES
Available upon request

- **Contact information.** Include your name, address (current and permanent if they're different), phone number(s), and e-mail address. *Don't* include your sex, age, race, or marital status. Not only are they irrelevant, but employers who take them into consideration are breaking antidiscrimination laws.

- **Job objective.** If you are targeting a specific job, include a specific objective (such as "to obtain a position as a buyer for a major retail department store"). However, if you're willing to be flexible, provide a more general job objective (for example, "to obtain an entry-level position in retail sales").

- **Education.** Include the colleges you've attended or are currently attending, with the actual or anticipated year of graduation and degree or certificate earned.

- **Awards and honors.** If you've won any awards or honors (such as membership in an honors program or inclusion on the dean's list), mention them. If you have none that you want to include, leave this category off your resume.

- **Campus and community activities.** Include activities in which you've participated, and indicate any in which you've had a leadership role. You want to demonstrate that you are an involved, contributing member of your community.

- **Professional memberships.** Do you belong to any professional organizations that are relevant to the job you'll be seeking? If so, include them.

- **Work experience.** List your experience, starting with your most recent job and working backward. Include the job title, dates, and your major on-the-job responsibilities.

  Don't feel you need to include every job you've ever held (for example, leave out the occasional pet sitting). Instead, focus on the key positions that illustrate your ability to hold a job and carry out responsibilities. In fact, it is sometimes appropriate to use what is known as a *functional resume,* in which you organize your experience according to specific skills or functions, rather than chronologically.

  Functional resumes are particularly helpful if you are changing careers or are re-entering the job force after a long period in which you weren't working. Whether you use a traditional, chronologically organized resume, or a functional resume to present your work experience, always remember that the focus should be on how your past work can get you a job in the profession you want in the future.

- **Particular skills.** Do you know how to program in Linux? Can you speak Spanish fluently? Are you a certified lifeguard? Can you use an Excel spreadsheet or PowerPoint?

  Include a brief list of the special skills you have. Once again, make sure that the skills you list are related to the job you're seeking. For example, if you're seeking a job in information technology, Linux programming is relevant, but it may not be if you're looking for a job in medical services.

- **References.** A "reference" category is optional, but if you include it, simply say, "References available upon request." Don't list specific names, but have them available should you be asked for them. (We'll discuss whom to ask and how to obtain references later in the chapter.)

As you create a resume, keep in mind some general rules. First, keep it short. In a resume, less is more. Generally, resumes should be no longer than one page.

Second, make it look good. Your resume should appear professional. Use plenty of white space, with one-inch margins on every side. Use strong action words, such as those in **Table 12.2.** Avoid articles (such as "the," "a," and "an") and pronouns (such as "I" or "we"); don't write in full sentences.

Third, you should prepare several versions of your resume: edit-ready and PDF versions. *Edit-ready* versions are in word processing programs such as Word, Google Docs, or OpenOffice. An edit-ready version can be printed as a hard copy or sent online as an e-mail attachment. You should also save your edit-ready version as a *PDF file, using your word-processing software or Adobe Reader*. The advantage of a PDF file is that it maintains the formatting precisely, ensuring that your resume looks its best.

Finally, proofread, proofread, and proofread again. You want to be sure that no typographical errors or misspellings find their way into your resume.

▶ The same rules hold for the second element of Part II of your career portfolio, your cover letter, which we discuss next. Before moving on, though, get a start on creating a resume by completing **Try It! 3**.

table 12.2	Action Words	
Using strong action words and making sentences short will help you prepare a professional and eye-catching resume. Here is a list of action words to get you started. Use words that best describe what you do and who you are.		
Achieved	Directed	Investigated
Administered	Discovered	Launched
Advised	Drafted	Led
Aided	Edited	Managed
Approved	Educated	Moderated
Arranged	Enabled	Monitored
Archived	Established	Negotiated
Assigned	Evaluated	Operated
Assisted	Examined	Organized
Authored	Expanded	Oversaw
Budgeted	Expedited	Performed
Built	Extracted	Recommended
Calculated	Facilitated	Recruited
Cataloged	Fashioned	Regulated
Chaired	Forecasted	Remodeled
Classified	Formulated	Reported
Coached	Founded	Restored
Collected	Granted	Reversed
Compiled	Generated	Reviewed
Computed	Guided	Saved
Conducted	Identified	Scheduled
Contracted	Illustrated	Solved
Controlled	Improved	Strengthened
Coordinated	Increased	Summarized
Counseled	Influenced	Supervised
Created	Informed	Trained
Critiqued	Initiated	Translated
Delegated	Inspected	Trimmed
Demonstrated	Installed	Tutored
Designated	Instituted	Upgraded
Designed	Instructed	Validated
Developed	Integrated	Worked
Devised	Interviewed	Wrote
Diagnosed	Invented	

Creating a Resume

It's time to use some of the pieces you have been thinking about and working on to create a resume. You have explored your ideas about your occupational goals (**Try It! 1**), and you have gathered important elements of your personal history (**Try It! 2**). Now put the pieces together by filling in this worksheet. Then use the worksheet to create a clean, one-page resume that you can have reviewed and proofread.

CONTACT INFORMATION

Your name, address, phone number(s), and e-mail address.

JOB OBJECTIVE

Use your ideas about your occupational goals. Write one statement, beginning with the word "To," that sums up your goals. Be specific only if you are applying for a job you understand and want to focus on; otherwise state your goals broadly and generally.

EDUCATION

List any colleges attended, including your current college, starting with the most recent. If you have taken college courses without being formally enrolled, list those too.

AWARDS AND HONORS (OPTIONAL)

List any honors you have received. Academic honors are of primary importance, but honors and awards from social and community groups (e.g., 4-H, Red Cross, Rotary Club) may be worth including if they testify to personal characteristics that may help you gain employment, such as leadership, perseverance, or a sense of civic duty.

CAMPUS AND COMMUNITY ACTIVITIES (OPTIONAL)

List any clubs, teams, or activities in which you have participated since high school. (Include high school activities only if they were significant and are related to your career goals.) Also list community activities in which you have participated, especially those in which you had a leadership role.

PROFESSIONAL MEMBERSHIPS (OPTIONAL)

List any professional organizations related to your career goals of which you are or have been a member. Professional organizations are groups such as the Modern Language Association; any of a number of national honor societies; the National Student Speech, Language, and Hearing Association; National Art Education Association; Student Sports Medicine Association; American Criminal Justice Association; and the like.

WORK EXPERIENCE (IF YOU'VE HAD ANY)

List all jobs you have had, including paid jobs (on campus and off), apprenticeships, internships, and similar "real" jobs. List your most recent work experience first and work backward through time. Include the title of the job, organization for which you worked, dates of work, and major responsibilities. Understand that you may be asked about any of the jobs you list, including your reasons for moving to the next job.

PARTICULAR SKILLS (OPTIONAL)

List anything you are particularly good at that might transfer to a work setting—for example, the ability to speak a foreign language, to fix computer hardware problems, to write and debug software programs, to repair engines, to create websites, and so forth. You can draw this list from your academic, work, and even personal/recreational life.

REFERENCES

Available on request.

Cover Letter

Although your resume is the centerpiece of your presentation to potential employers, your cover letter is no less important. It shows that you can string words together into well-crafted sentences, and it gives you the opportunity to bring life to the list of qualifications on your resume. It also gives you the opportunity to say how enthusiastic you are about the job for which you're applying and to illustrate how well your qualifications match the job requirements.

In writing a cover letter, keep in mind the perspective of the person who is reading it. Potential employers have a problem that they need to solve: identifying someone to do work that they need done so much that they're willing to pay someone to do it. The better you can provide them with a solution to this problem, the more attractive you will be.

What this means is that your cover letter should be oriented toward helping employers solve *their* problem, not toward how the job will solve *your* problems. Consequently, don't talk about how you think the job will fulfill you as a person or how much you need it to pay your bills. Instead, orient your letter toward describing how well your own unique qualifications match the specific job requirements.

Although every cover letter should be tailor-written to a specific position (see the two sample letters in **Figure 12.2**), they typically contain the following elements:

▶ **Introduction: Catching the reader.** Describe why you are writing, how you learned about the job, and why you are interested in it. Emphasize the connection between the position requirements and your qualifications.

▶ **Letter body: Drawing in the reader.** Here's where you describe, in very brief terms, who you are and what makes you unique. Highlight major accomplishments and qualifications from your personal history.

   You can also include information that does not appear on your resume; for instance, if you paid for your education entirely on your own, mention that fact. In addition, you can write about what you hope to accomplish on the job.

   Finally, show that you know something about the organization to which you are applying. Do some homework to learn about the employer, and state specifically what you find attractive about working for this employer.

▶ **Conclusion: A call for action.** End the letter by restating your interest in the position and suggesting that you would like to discuss the position further. State that you are available to meet for an interview. Thank the employer for considering your application.

Like your resume, the cover letter should read well and look good. Before you send it, be sure to proofread it carefully.

The point of including a sample cover letter in your career portfolio is to be ready at a moment's notice to revise the sample and send it off. Job opportunities sometimes appear unexpectedly, and it will be much easier for you to respond quickly, and respond well, if you already have a sample letter on file.

Unless you are certain of the job you'll be seeking in the future, you might want to prepare several cover letters, targeted at the different job possibilities you are considering. In addition, the act of writing cover letters for a variety of professions may actually help you come to a decision regarding the path you ultimately choose to follow.

July 29, 2016

Mr. Reginald Pelly
Assistant Vice President
Jackson & Fentin Legal Offices
New York, NY 10011

Dear Mr. Pelly:

Jennifer Windsor, at WorldWide, advised me of an opening in your company for a paralegal. From my enclosed resume, you will find that both my experience and my education fully meet the requirements you have outlined for the position.

My current position as a paralegal at a small legal practice has given me experience in dealing with deadlines and working closely with others. Having served as a paralegal for six years, I can relate to the needs of lawyers as well. My colleagues consider me both outgoing and diplomatic, traits that have served me well in my work as a paralegal.

I will contact you Monday to learn if we can meet for an interview.

Sincerely,

Martina L. Veschova

Enclosure: Resume

figure 12.2
Two Sample Cover Letters

One final note about your career portfolio: Keep in mind that it is a work in progress, a living document that is meant to be revised as your interests and aspirations change. That's why it is a good idea to keep your career portfolio both in a virtual form and as a hard copy. By creating an e-portfolio, you will be able to make revisions easily. An e-portfolio also simplifies the process of producing an updated version of your resume and cover letter for an actual job opening.

Martin L. Chen

14A Orchard Street
Boise, Idaho 83702   email: marlchen@mrnr.com   Phone: 207 889-3763

July 29, 2016

Ms. Arlene Washington
Director, Human Services
Mercy General Hospital
18 Medical Plaza
Chicago, IL 60604

Dear Ms. Washington:

I am writing in response to the position advertised July 22, 2013, in the *Chicago Tribune* seeking a Lead Cost Analyst Accountant. My professional experience and education match well with the position requirements listed. Enclosed is my resume.

In addition to being self-motivated, I work well under pressure and welcome new challenges and opportunities. Among some of my accomplishments are the following:

- Analyzed, defined, and produced appropriate budgets for wages and salary costs, materials, expenses, and workload.
- Provided extensive, timely, and appropriate reporting for all aspects of the various budgets.
- Investigated variations from budget.
- Performed cost benefit analyses and assisted with capital expenditure proposals.

My experience in supervising a team of four co-workers has taught me patience and has strengthened my organizational skills. My greatest satisfaction in a job comes from selecting, training, and motivating personnel. I believe I have the qualities that can help a department become more efficient and productive.

I am familiar with Mercy General Hospital from news stories on breakthrough cancer research conducted there, and I have further researched your hospital and its contributions to medicine. I feel there is a good fit between my career goals and your needs. I welcome the opportunity to discuss the position further, and look forward to hearing from you soon. Thank you for your consideration.

Yours truly,

Martin L. Chen

Enclosure

figure 12.2
Two Sample Cover Letters (*continued*)

 **Evaluate** ## Getting Feedback on Your Resume and Cover Letter

After you have created the key elements of your career portfolio—your resume and cover letter—it's time to evaluate their effectiveness. Start by asking a trusted person, such as one of your course instructors or someone on the staff of your college's career center, to review what you've created. Ask him or her to provide honest and concrete suggestions because the more feedback you receive, the better the finished product will be.

Once you've received an initial review, one of the best strategies is to ask individuals working in the field in which you're interested to review your resume and cover letter. Requesting feedback from one or two people who are already working in your desired profession, particularly if they have hired people in the past, serves several purposes. First, your reviewers will be in the best position to know what employers are looking for, and they can tell you how to present yourself most effectively. Not only can they help you say the right things, but they can also help you avoid saying the wrong thing.

But there's an extra bonus from seeking advice from someone currently working in the field: You become a known quantity to them, and at some point in the future they may have a job opening and you may spring to mind. Or if you contact them in the future, they may be able to steer you to a job opening.

R Rethink

Reconsidering Your Career Choices

Going through the process of identifying your goals, researching careers, and building a career portfolio may lead you to solidify your ideas about which occupation you'd like to pursue. That's great—that's the point of career exploration.

But even if you are sure about what you intend to do professionally, it's important to take some time to reconsider your choices. The most important thing is to avoid what psychologists call "foreclosure." Foreclosure is making a premature decision and sticking with it so persistently that you ignore other possibilities, even ones that hold considerable promise. Keeping an open mind by reconsidering your choices will help you be sure that you've made the best decisions.

From the perspective of . . .

A SECOND-CAREER EMPLOYEE It is possible to work for years in one field before deciding on a new career path. What are some things to consider if you are contemplating a second career?

Source: © Jack Hollingsworth/ Getty Images

What if you haven't been able to narrow things down? What if you're still completely up in the air about what path you'd like to pursue? First, realize that it's natural to be undecided. It's almost inevitable that you'll have some uncertainty with regard to decisions as important as where you work.

Also, keep in mind that even if you are certain about the general shape you want your career to take, there will inevitably be moments of backtracking and reconsideration. Very few people take one job at one organization and work there until they retire. The point is that you will have many opportunities to rethink your decisions. Don't feel that any one decision will forever shape the rest of your career or your life.

If you're close to graduation and you still don't have a clue about what you want to do, then maybe you need to rethink your approach. Assuming you've considered various possibilities, you may want to reconsider the career-planning strategies you've been using. Ask yourself these questions:

> "Far and away the best prize that life has to offer is the chance to work hard at work worth doing."
> Theodore Roosevelt

▶ Have you been too restrictive or too selective in considering possibilities?

▶ Have you done sufficient research?

▶ Have you rejected job opportunities that seem somewhat interesting without carefully considering what they have to offer?

▶ Have you underestimated (or overestimated) your skills?

▶ Have you taken full advantage of all the resources your college offers in terms of career planning?

» LO 12-3 Acting On Your Career Plans
Your References: Who Says What about You

Getting the job you want sometimes can hinge less on what you say about yourself and more on what others say about you. A good reference can make the difference between getting a job and getting passed over. A bad reference can destroy your chances of being offered a position.

That's why finding just the right people to supply potential employers with a reference can be the key to obtaining the job you want. It is critical to identify people who are willing to speak on your behalf well before you face a deadline.

Identifying People to Provide References

Several categories of individuals can provide you references, including

▶ Former job supervisors.

▶ Colleagues in previous positions.

▶ Class instructors.

▶ Community service supervisors.

▶ Coaches, club advisors, or heads of professional groups to which you belong.

▶ People who can provide character references (e.g., clergy).

The most effective references come from people who know you well—very well—and can speak about your skills, abilities, accomplishments, motivation, and character. In addition, people who can address the specific requirements of the job you're seeking (especially those who have worked with you in environments similar to that of the potential job) are highly effective.

The least effective references are those from family members or friends or, even worse, friends of friends. For instance, a reference from someone famous who happens to play tennis occasionally with your uncle will rarely be helpful unless that person knows you well. Remember a key rule of references: The ability

Starting Over: Once You Have a Job You Want

What's the best time to start looking for a job? When you already have one and don't need to find a new position.

Even if you feel happy and secure in your job, it makes sense to be prepared for the unexpected. Perhaps you'll get a new boss whom you find it difficult to work with, or your current job's activities and requirements change for the worse. Or maybe the company will downsize or be merged with another corporation, causing widespread layoffs.

For a variety of reasons, then, you'll want to keep your resume and career portfolio updated, even if you've just started a new job. You will want to stay in contact with the people who have provided you with references in the past.

Above all, take every opportunity to learn new skills. As the economy and technology change, you'll want to have cutting-edge skills that will allow you to compete effectively.

In short: Be prepared!

of a reference provider to describe in detail *your* strengths and *your* accomplishments is considerably more important than the identity of the reference provider, whatever *his or her* strengths and accomplishments.

The necessity of having people to act as references points out the importance of networking. Even while you're in college, it's critical to build up a network of people who can vouch for you. To network effectively, be sure to keep in touch with people who know and like you. And try to expand your network of contacts. For example, whenever you're at a social event, talk to people you don't know and don't just hang out with people you're familiar with.

Asking for a Reference

When choosing someone to be a reference, **always ask permission**. Never give out the names of people who you think will provide references without asking them beforehand. Not only is seeking permission common courtesy, but asking first avoids violating another rule of references: *No reference is better than a bad reference.* You need to check that the reference someone provides will be an explicitly positive one.

Although you can't directly ask someone if they can provide a positive reference (it's very hard for someone to tell you straight out that they can't), you can approach the issue indirectly. When asking someone to serve as a reference, ask them if they have any reservations. If they do, no matter how minor, turn to someone else to provide the recommendation.

You should also offer some guidelines for those providing recommendations. Let them know why you're asking them in particular, and remind them of the context in which they've known you. If there is something you'd like them to specifically address in providing you with a reference—such as, for example, the unusual creativity you showed in a previous position or the fact that you wrote exceptionally good papers in a class—let them know. The more explicit information you can provide them, the better.

Using the Web in Your Job Hunt

The web has changed the rules for conducting a job search. It permits you to post your resume and have the potential for thousands of possible employers to screen it. It also permits employers to post their job needs and have the potential for thousands of possible employees to see them. You can even apply for jobs online. Internet services can help you to conduct automated searches, exposing you to job listings in your chosen field and letting you receive e-mails containing job postings that fit your skills.

The advantages of electronic job searches—such as the potentially wide exposure of your resume—come at some potential costs. First, your resume quite likely will be "read" by a computer. That means you must be extremely precise and follow some specific stylistic rules to avoid its being misread or ignored. Second, there are security issues, since you never know who may be reading your resume.

In using the web for a job search, you need to cast your net widely. Although general-interest job sites such as **monster.com** and **careerbuilder.com** post millions of jobs each year, there are more focused boards that can help you identify possible jobs in specific industries (see **Table 12.3**). In addition, most large companies post job openings on their own websites.

There are several general guidelines to follow when posting your resume on an online employment site:

▶ Be very precise in the words you employ. For example, use action verbs and other words that are standard within an industry.

▶ Use simple type styles, such as Arial, Calibri, or Times New Roman.

▶ Avoid elaborate formatting, such as tabs or italics.

▶ Use a standard 80 characters per line.

▶ As always, proofread, proofread, proofread. A typographical error is more than embarrassing: Computers screening your resume may reject your application before a human ever sees it because they do not recognize a misspelled word.

table 12.3 Finding the Right Site on the Web	
Specific Sites	
www.HigherEdJobs.com	Teaching
www.EngineerJobs.com	Engineering
www.ShowBizJobs.com	Acting
www.Medzilla.com	Doctors, nurses
www.RXCareerCenter.com	Pharmaceuticals
www.HR.com	Human resources
www.dice.com	Information technology
www.LegalStaff.com	Legal
www.AgCareers.com	Agriculture

Source: Farquharson, L. (2003, September 15). Find a job. *The Wall Street Journal,* p. R8.

Social Networking and Job Searches

A key strategy for finding a job is to make use of your online social networks. Membership in sites such as LinkedIn, Facebook, and Twitter allows you to alert others that you are seeking a job. For example, you can use LinkedIn's professional headline or status box to say that you are seeking a new position. You can also use a status update in Facebook to alert others that you're in the job market.

When looking for a job, it's important to expand your social network as much as you can. Think hard about everyone you know and invite them to join your network. Remember that it's not just the people you know who may lead to a job, but the friends and acquaintances of the people you know. So the wider your social network, the better your chances of coming in contact with someone who knows about a job opportunity.

Job Interviews: Putting Your Best Foot Forward

For a potential employer who has never met you, a job interview puts a face to what has previously been an impression based on mere words written on a page. The interview is your chance to show who you are, to demonstrate your enthusiasm for a potential position, and to exhibit what you can bring to a position.

The fact that interviews are so important may make them seem intimidating and overwhelming. However, remember that the mere fact that you've been invited to an interview means you've overcome some of the highest hurdles already. Furthermore, you can follow a variety of concrete strategies to ensure that you maximize the opportunity an interview presents. Among the most important are the following.

Before the Interview

▶ **Learn about the potential employer.** It's important to learn as much as you can about the position and the company that is offering it. Go to the potential employer's website and find out as much as you can about the organization's management style and company culture. Then try to find magazine and newspaper articles to gain a sense of the success and effectiveness of the organization. The bottom line: If an interviewer asks, "What do you know about our organization?" be prepared to answer, "Quite a bit because I've researched it thoroughly."

▶ **Prepare with questions.** Come to the interview prepared with questions. Think up a set of questions and write them down so you can remember them—it's perfectly fine to refer to them during the interview. Having targeted questions shows that you've spent time thinking about the position. (Don't ask about salary during the interview; salary issues are usually addressed if you get an actual job offer.)

▶ **Prepare answers.** Finally, come prepared with answers to likely questions. For instance, it shouldn't be a surprise if an interviewer asks you to "tell me about yourself." So have an answer ready, a two- or three-minute response that touches on your career goals, your skills, your experiences, and your personal traits. Obviously this is a lot to cover in just a few minutes, so practice it until you can do it comfortably within that short time frame. Going longer than three minutes runs the risk of boring your interviewer. Furthermore, don't just practice it by yourself. Have someone else listen to it and give you feedback.

Other favorite interview questions include "What are your major strengths and weaknesses?" "Why do you want to leave your current position?" "What are your major qualifications?" "What are your short-term and long-range goals?" and "Why should I hire you?" Although you can't prepare for every possible question in advance, thinking through some of the most likely possibilities will help you feel more confident and ready to deliver polished responses.

During the Interview

▶ **Be punctual.** Allow yourself enough time to arrive well ahead of the scheduled interview. That will help you find a parking space, locate the building and room, and generally get composed.

▶ **Dress appropriately.** Wear the right clothes for the interview. Stop by beforehand to see how people dress. If you're unsure of how formal to be, keep in mind that it's almost always better to be overdressed than to be underdressed. This is not the time to make a fashion statement. You want to look professional.

▶ **Use your social skills effectively.** Shake hands firmly, and look the interviewer in the eye. Show that you're interested in the interviewer as a fellow human being, not just as someone who might give you a job. Listen attentively to what he or she has to say, and be responsive. Above all, try to think confidently. Thinking positive, confident thoughts will help you appear positive and confident.

▶ **Ask questions.** If you have prepared for the interview, you've got some questions to ask about the organization with which you're looking for a job. Be sure to ask them. Interviewers almost always ask if you have any questions, but if they don't, try to work them in when you sense that the interview is almost over. It's also a good idea to ask about the hiring process the employer is using. Ask how

Interviews can be a nervous experience, but preparation and a coolheaded approach can make all the difference. Don't forget that you are interviewing a potential employer, as well as being interviewed as a potential employee!
Source: © Zia Soleil/The Image Bank/Getty Images

"Rule No. 1: Just be yourself. Unless, of course, you're sloppy, lazy, or otherwise undesirable, in which case, be someone else. Be ready to humbly sell yourself, and if someone asks about your weak points, say, 'Occasionally I just work too hard.'"

Rainbow Rowell, *The Daily Nebraskan* in Combs (1998). *Major Success*. Berkeley, CA: Ten Speed Press, p. 103.

long it will be before they will be making a decision and when you are likely to be hearing from them again.

▶ **Above all, be yourself and be honest.** You do yourself no favor by pretending to be someone other than who you are. Getting a job under false pretenses virtually guarantees that neither you nor your employer ultimately will be satisfied with your job performance. You may end up doing things you don't like to do and may not be very good at, and neither you nor your employer will find that acceptable for long. (To get experience interviewing, complete **Try It! 4**.)

After the Interview

▶ **Evaluate your interview performance.** Are you pleased with how you presented yourself in the interview? What did you do particularly well? What things could you have done better?

Jot down your impressions of the interview while they're still fresh in your mind and place them in your career portfolio. These notes will be valuable when you prepare for future interviews.

▶ **Consider if you still want the position.** Suppose, for a moment, you were actually offered the job. Do you really want it?

It's important to ask yourself whether, given what you learned about the position, you would accept it if it were actually offered to you. You probably found out things about the position that interested you, and others that may be worrisome. Evaluate the job, and if there are too many negatives, rethink whether you'd actually want it.

However, unless there are so many negatives that you're certain that under no circumstances would you take the job, don't withdraw your application. It may be that if you are offered the job, you could negotiate with your potential employer to eliminate the factors that you find undesirable.

▶ **Write a thank-you note.** It's common courtesy to thank someone for giving you his or her time during an interview.

It's also strategically important. It shows that you are polite and can be counted on to do the right thing. It demonstrates your interest in the job. And it gives you one more opportunity to show you have the "right stuff."

Although you shouldn't turn your thank-you note into a sales pitch, do indicate your continued interest in the position. Write about the aspects of the job that were of particular interest to you and explain how you can see yourself fitting in well with the company.

▶ **Follow up.** If you haven't heard from the employer in a few weeks, and it's past the point where you were told you'd be contacted, it's perfectly reasonable to e-mail or call. The purpose is not to badger the employer into hiring you—that's not going to work—but to simply check up on where the process stands. Of course, it also serves another purpose: to remind a potential employer of your continued interest in the position. You can also use the opportunity to provide additional information or to inform the employer of another job offer.

Interviewing

Nothing will prepare you better for an upcoming interview than a number of prior interviews. To get practice interviewing, ask an instructor, a person who has had experience in hiring, or even a fellow student to role-play an interview with you in which they will interview you, the potential job applicant. Tell them that you will prepare for your role carefully and that you will treat the practice interview seriously.

Follow these steps:

- Choose a company or organization that you would like to work for, and provide the person who will interview you with some details about it, such as information from the company website.
- You should also research your chosen company as a potential interviewee would, to gain enough knowledge to answer potential interview questions well.
- Write down a few questions you would expect to be asked, and prepare notes and/or responses to them. If you have difficulty thinking up likely questions, turn to the web. Many websites list the most popular interview questions; some even provide suggested responses. One such site operating at the time of publication is **http://jobsearch.about.com/od/interviewquestionsanswers/a/interviewquest.htm**. Be aware, however, that interviewers are aware of such websites, too, and have come to regard "canned" answers with disgust. The best use of such sites is to find the questions and come up with your own answers.
- Hold the interview. You should be serious and try to play your role well. If you like, you can "dress the part" to help you set the right tone. You may also want to tape-record the session.
- After you've concluded the interview, ask your interviewer for a critique of your performance. Ask the interviewer to make as candid a judgment as he or she can as to which category you would fit into based solely on the interview: (A) offer a job; (B) don't offer a job; or (C) call back for another interview to follow up with additional questions.

After you've completed the steps outlined above, answer the following questions:

1. What did you learn from the interview?

2. Critically assess your performance as an interviewee. What was your greatest strength as an interviewee? Your greatest weakness?

3. What would you do differently during an actual interview?

4. How can you better prepare for an actual interview in the future?

Speaking *of* Success

Source: Courtesy of Geraldine Mathey

NAME: **Geraldine F. Mathey**

SCHOOL: **Thomas Nelson Community College, Hampton, Virginia**

Geraldine Mathey started—and stopped—her college education several times. Now, though, Mathey is on track to obtain a degree, and she's doing it while holding down a full-time job.

To meet this challenge, Mathey has styled her studying to meet the demands of her schedule.

"If I have a lot of reading to do, what works best for me is to do it during my lunch hour," she explained. "If I have a class later in the day, I'll use the few hours at the end of my workday to prepare for the class and review my notes."

The social science major is also a big proponent of asking questions, visiting the campus tutoring center, and meeting with faculty.

"I have no qualms about going to the instructor and asking questions," said Mathey. "I've found that instructors can offer helpful hints on studying, and some offer test review sheets," she added. "I tell other students that you can remember the information if you actually write out responses to the review topics. I believe if you write them out, there is more of a connection between hand and brain than just eye and page."

Mathey also is a proponent of TRIO, a federally funded student support program designed to motivate and support students from disadvantaged backgrounds, in which she participates. Since her school adopted the program, it has found an 86 percent retention rate for students who participate in the program and a 55 percent retention rate for those who do not, she noted.

"You have to find out what your strengths and weaknesses are," she said. "If you need help, go to your instructor, or the library, or a tutoring center. Don't hesitate to ask for help."

[RETHINK]

- Mathey is a big proponent of using college resources. How can this approach help with finding a career?

- How can knowing your strengths and weaknesses better prepare you for a job search?

Looking Back

LO 12-1 Identify your career goals and ideal job.

▶ Careful and systematic research is the key to identifying possible career options.

▶ Books, websites, and informational interviews provide useful information about careers.

▶ A career portfolio can document a person's skills, capabilities, achievements, and goals, as well as provide a place to keep notes and research findings relating to jobs. It also includes one's resume and cover letter.

LO 12-2 Describe how to a create career portfolio and its advantages.

▶ It is important to find appropriate references.

▶ The Internet not only provides substantial information about potential jobs and companies, but also can play an important role in getting a job.

LO 12-3 Discuss strategies for identifying references and interviewing well.

▶ Job interviews require a significant amount of preparation.

▶ Useful interview strategies include being punctual, dressing appropriately, using social skills effectively, asking questions, being oneself, and being honest.

▶ After an interview, follow up with the interviewer.

[KEY TERMS AND CONCEPTS]

Career portfolio (p. 305)

[RESOURCES]

ON CAMPUS

Check whether your campus has an office devoted to career planning. In addition, your college library, as well as any public library, should have books that can help you research careers and find a job.

IN PRINT

If you're planning a career, writing a resume, or getting ready to look for work, you can't go wrong with Richard Bolles' classic, *What Color Is Your Parachute? 2016: A Practical Manual for Job-Hunters and Career-Changers* (Ten Speed Press, 2016).

For tips and solid guidance on pursuing that first job just out of college, *The Career Playbook: Essential Advice for Today's Aspiring Young Professional* by James M. Citrin (Crown Business, 2015) offers solid advice on entering the professional world.

Don't Wear Flip-Flops to Your Interview: And Other Tips (Career Press, 2015) by Paul Powers presents several approaches to job hunting and interviewing, including personal experiences of successful professionals.

ON THE WEB

The following sites on the web provide opportunities to extend your learning about the material in this chapter. (Although the web addresses were accurate at the time this material was published, check the *P.O.W.E.R. Learning* Connect website or contact your instructor for any changes that may have occurred.)

▶ The "Planning Your Career" section of Mapping Your Future's website (**www.mappingyourfuture.org/PlanYourCareer/**) offers guidance on finding the right path toward pursuing a career. Also available are numerous links on finding and building a career.

▶ Welcome to Resumania (**www.resumania.com/**)—a fun but practical look at those things you shouldn't put into a resume. The term "Resumania" was coined by Robert Half, founder of the specialized staffing firm Robert Half International Inc. (RHI), to describe errors made by job seekers on resumes, applications, and cover letters.

▶ From Virginia Tech, the site https://www.career.vt.edu/Interviewing/AskQuestions.html is full of comprehensive tips and strategies on preparing for a job interview, covering everything from handshakes to behavioral interviewing.

Images in this chapter: *Pencil on stack of notebooks:* © C Squared Studios/Photodisc/Getty Images; *Four students:* © Purestock/Getty images; *Man in blue shirt with laptop:* © sidneybernstein/iStock/Getty Images Group of happy business people: ©Yuri/iStock/Getty Images.

The Case of . . .
Interviewing Superman

Trevor Fenwick would ace the interview, he was certain. He had a great personality and a winning smile, and he could talk with ease about anything and everything, whether he knew about the topic or not. His 9:00 appointment at Monsanto would be his first job interview after graduating. Armed with his new degree in engineering and his ability to talk his way into things, Trevor couldn't wait for the interview to begin.

He shook hands vigorously with the human resources assistant, read her nametag, smiled broadly, and said, "How you doing, Miss Ray? Nice suit. It makes you look thin. Let's get going. I can't wait to start working here."

His 100-watt smile drew no visible response. Ms. Ray quietly asked him why he had chosen Monsanto. Taken aback by her flat reaction to his charm, he stammered, "Uh, Monsanto's one of the biggest companies in the world, isn't it? Why shouldn't I work for the best?"

The interview went downhill from there. The more specific the question, the less useful was Trevor's store of humor and charm. When Ms. Ray asked why he thought he was a good match for Monsanto, he blurted out, "Well, this is a big company that pays well, and I'm a good worker who deserves a good salary." His final answer, to a question about his goals, was, "My goal is to work hard enough that in a year I'll have a bigger office than this."

The interview ended at 9:13 a.m.

1. What advice would you give Trevor about presenting himself at a job interview? Why wasn't his interview effective?

2. What steps should Trevor have taken to ready himself for the interview?

3. Confidence is usually a positive attribute in a job seeker. What advice would you give Trevor about properly showing confidence?

4. Should Trevor have expected the sorts of questions that the interviewer was asking? How should he have prepared for them?

5. Were Trevor's attempts to be upbeat and charming effective with Ms. Ray? How should he prepare himself to get on the good side of his next job interviewer?

A Final Word

Throughout this book you've seen how the principles of *P.O.W.E.R. Learning* can be applied to a variety of situations, ranging from reading and writing to coping with stress and getting along with others. You can use the framework in any situation where you need to organize your thinking and behavior in a systematic way. It's a tool you can call on throughout your lifetime.

College is the beginning of a journey that leads to your future. This book has been designed to help you meet the demands and challenges of college, but at the same time to prepare you for life beyond school. It also has tried to show you that it is *you* who must make things happen to fulfill your goals and aspirations.

Ultimately, however, there are certain key ingredients to success that no book can teach you and that only you can provide: integrity and honesty, intellectual curiosity, and respect and love for others. I hope this book will help you as you consider what your contribution to the world will be, and as you work to make that contribution.

Glossary

2 + 2 plan: A formal agreement between a community college and a four-year institution that permits students to transfer courses into a specific major or specialty program.

ABBCC structure: The structure of the typical research paper, consisting of *a*rgument, *b*ackground, *b*ody, *c*ounterarguments, and *c*onclusion.

Abstinence: The avoidance of sexual contact.

Academic honesty: Completing and turning in only one's own work under one's own name.

Academic program (or Major): A specialization in a particular subject area, requiring a set course of study.

Acquired immune deficiency syndrome (AIDS): A potentially lethal, sexually transmitted disease that causes the destruction of the body's immune system.

Acronym: A word or phrase formed by the first letters of a series of terms.

Acrostic: A sentence in which the first letters of the words correspond to material that is to be remembered.

Active listening: The voluntary act of focusing on what is being said, making sense of it, and thinking about it in a way that permits it to be recalled accurately.

Advance organizers: Outlines, overviews, objectives, and other clues to the meaning and organization of new material in what you are reading, which pave the way for subsequent learning.

Alcoholics: Individuals with serious alcohol abuse problems who become dependent on alcohol and continue to drink despite serious consequences.

Analogy: A comparison between concepts or objects that are alike in some respects but dissimilar in most others.

Articulation agreements: Formal arrangements with selected four-year colleges that will automatically accept certain courses or credits taken at your current institution.

Attention span: The length of time that attention is typically sustained.

Auditory/verbal learning style: A style that favors listening as the best approach to learning.

Binge drinking: Having at least four (for females) or five (for males) drinks in a single sitting.

Blended (hybrid) courses: Courses in which instruction is a combination of traditional, face-to-face, and online methods.

Blog: A web-based public diary in which a writer provides commentary, ideas, thoughts, and short essays.

Brainstorming: A technique for generating ideas by saying out loud as many ideas as can be thought of in a fixed period of time.

Browser: A program that provides a way of navigating around the information on the web.

Budget: A formal plan that accounts for expenditures and income.

Call number: A unique classification number assigned to every book (or other resource) in a library. Call numbers are used for ease of location.

Career portfolio: A dynamic record that documents your skills, capabilities, achievements, and goals, as well as providing a place to keep notes, ideas, and research findings related to careers.

Cataclysmic events: Sudden, powerful events that occur quickly and affect many people simultaneously.

Classical conditioning: A type of learning in which a neutral stimulus elicits a response after being paired with a natural stimulus.

College advisor: Also called college counselor. An individual who provides students with advice about their academic careers.

Community service: Making contributions to the society and community in which you live.

Concept mapping: A method of structuring written material by graphically grouping and connecting key ideas and themes.

Coping: The effort to control, reduce, or learn to tolerate the threats that lead to stress.

Cramming: Hurried, last-minute studying.

Critical thinking: A process involving reanalysis, questioning, and challenge of underlying assumptions.

Cultural competence: Knowledge and understanding about other races, ethnic groups, cultures, and minority groups.

Culture: The learned behaviors, beliefs, and attitudes that are characteristic of an individual society or population, and the products that people create.

cybersecurity: Measures taken to protect computers and computer systems against unauthorized access or attack.

Daily hassles: The minor irritants of life that, by themselves, produce little stress, but which can add up and produce more stress than a single larger-scale event.

Daily to-do list: A schedule showing the tasks, activities, and appointments due to occur during the day.

Date rape: Forced sex in which the rapist is a date or romantic acquaintance.

Decision making: The process of deciding among various alternatives.

Discrimination: Behavior directed toward individuals on the basis of their membership in a particular group.

Distance learning: The teaching of courses at another institution, with student participation via video technology or the web.

Double major: A course of study that fulfills all the requirements for two majors.

Educated guessing: The practice of eliminating obviously false multiple-choice answers and selecting the most likely answer from the remaining choices.

Electives: Courses that are not required.

E-mail: Electronic mail, a system of communication that permits users to send and receive messages via the Internet.

Emoticons (or smileys): Symbols used in e-mail messages that provide information on the emotion that the writer is trying to convey. Emoticons usually look like faces on their side, with facial expressions related to the intended emotion or tone.

Ethnicity: Shared national origins or cultural patterns.

Evaluation: An assessment of the match between a product or activity and the goals it was intended to meet.

Flash cards: Index cards that contain key pieces of information to be remembered.

Freewriting: A technique involving continuous, nonstop writing, without self-criticism, for a fixed period of time.

Frontmatter: The preface, introduction, and table of contents of a book.

Grade point average (GPA): Also known as *quality point average*. A numeric average in which letter grades are transformed into numbers.

Grant: An award of money that does not have to be repaid.

Growth mindset: Belief that people can increase their abilities and do better through hard work.

Hearing: The involuntary act of sensing sounds.

Impromptu talk: Unprepared presentations that require speaking on a moment's notice.

Individual response technology: This method uses a wireless handset to transmit students' answers to the instructor's computer, resulting in more classroom interactivity.

Information competency: The ability to determine what information is necessary, and then to locate, evaluate, and effectively use that information.

Instant messaging: A system that allows one to use a computer to communicate in real time with friends and instructors.

Interlibrary loan: A system by which libraries share resources, making them available to patrons of different libraries.

Internet: A vast network of interconnected computers that share information around the world.

"I" statements: Statements that cast responses in terms of oneself and one's individual interpretation.

Learning disabilities: Difficulties in processing information when listening, speaking, reading, or writing, characterized by a discrepancy between learning potential and actual academic achievement.

Learning Management System: The software that delivers a distance learning course and typically provides the course content, calendars, and tests, and tracks grades.

Learning style: One's preferred manner of acquiring, using, and thinking about knowledge.

Learning theory: A broad explanation about how one learns.

Lecture capture technology: Technology in which instructors upload in-class lectures, slides, and videos to a website, which students can later access to review the material presented in class.

Left-brain processing: Information processing primarily performed by the left hemisphere of the brain, focusing on tasks requiring verbal competence, such as speaking, reading, thinking, and reasoning; information is processed sequentially, one bit at a time.

Link: A means of "jumping" automatically from one web page to another.

Listserv: A subscription service through which members can post and receive messages via e-mail on general topics of shared interest.

Loan: Funds provided by a bank, credit union, or other agency that must be repaid after a specified period of time.

Loneliness: A subjective state in which people do not experience the level of connection with others that they desire.

Long-term goals: Aims relating to major accomplishments that take some time to achieve.

Major: A specialization in a particular subject area, requiring a set course of study.

Master calendar: A schedule showing the weeks of a longer time period, such as a college term, with all assignments and important activities noted on it.

Memory consolidation: The process by which the physical links between brain cells that represent memory become fixed and stable over time.

Meta-message: The underlying main ideas that a speaker is seeking to convey; the meaning behind the overt message.

Method of loci: A memory technique by which the elements in a list are visualized as occupying the parts of a familiar place.

Minor: A secondary specialization in a discipline different from one's major.

Mnemonics: Formal techniques used to make material more readily remembered.

Motivation: The inner power and psychological energy that directs and fuels behavior.

Online database: An index in electronic form composed of an organized body of information on a related topic.

Operant conditioning: Learning in which behavior is modified by the presence of a reinforcer.

Overlearning: Studying and rehearsing material past the point of initial mastery to the point at which recall becomes automatic.

Paraphrase: A restatement of a passage using different words.

Peg method: A memory technique by which a series of memorized words is linked by images to a list of items to be remembered.

Personal mission statement: A formal statement regarding what a person hopes to achieve during his or her lifetime.

Personal stressors: Major life events that produce stress.

Plagiarism: Taking credit for someone else's words, thoughts, or ideas.

Podcast: An audio or video recording that can be accessed on the Internet and viewed on a computer or downloaded to a mobile device.

Posttraumatic stress disorder (PTSD): A psychological disorder in which a highly stressful event has long-lasting consequences that may include reexperiencing the event in vivid flashbacks or dreams.

Power Learning: A system designed to help people achieve their goals, based on five steps: *P*repare, *O*rganize, *W*ork, *E*valuate, and *R*ethink.

Prejudice: Evaluations or judgments of members of a group that are based primarily on membership in the group and not on the particular characteristics of individuals.

Prerequisites: Requirements that must be fulfilled before a student may enroll in a course or discipline.

Principal: The stated amount of a loan.

Priorities: The tasks and activities that one needs and wants to do, rank-ordered from most important to least important.

Priority enrollment plan: A plan in which a four-year school gives preference to students from community colleges within the state when it considers which students to admit as junior-year transfers.

Problem solving: The process of generating alternatives to work on.

Procrastination: The habit of putting off and delaying tasks that need to be accomplished.

Race: Traditionally, biologically determined physical characteristics that set one group apart from others.

Read/write learning style: A style that involves a preference for written material, favoring reading over hearing and touching.

Recall: A way to request library materials from another person who has them.

Receptive learning style: The way in which we initially receive information.

Reflective feedback: A technique of verbal listening in which a listener rephrases what a speaker has said, trying to echo the speaker's meaning.

Register: To enroll formally in courses.

Registrar: The college official designated to oversee the scheduling of courses, the maintenance of grades and transcripts, and the creation and retention of other official documents.

Rehearsal: The process of practicing and learning material.

Reinforcer: A thing that increases the probability that a behavior will occur again.

Retrieval: The process of finding information stored in memory and returning it to consciousness for further use.

Right-brain processing: Information processing primarily performed by the right hemisphere of the brain, focusing on information in nonverbal domains, such as the understanding of spatial relationships and recognition of patterns and drawings, music, and emotional expression.

Scholarship: An award of money to a student based on need or merit.

Search engine: A computerized index to information on the web.

Self-actualization: A state of self-fulfillment in which people realize their highest potential in their own unique way.

Self-concept: People's view of themselves that forms over time, comprising three components: the physical self, the social self, and the personal self.

Self-efficacy: The expectation that one is capable of achieving one's goals in many different kinds of situations.

Self-esteem: The overall evaluation we give ourselves as individuals.

Self-fulfilling prophecy: A phenomenon that occurs when we hold a belief or expectation that affects our behavior, thereby increasing the likelihood that our beliefs or expectations *will* come true.

Service learning: Courses that allow a student to engage in community service activities while getting course credit for the experience.

Sexually transmitted infections (STIs): Infections acquired through sexual contact.

Short-term goals: Relatively limited steps toward the accomplishment of long-term goals.

Social support: Assistance and comfort supplied by others in times of stress.

Stacks: The shelves on which books and other materials are stored in a library.

Stereotypes: Beliefs and expectations about members of a group that are held simply because of their membership in the group.

Stress: The physical and emotional response to events that threaten or challenge us.

Study groups: Small, informal groups of students whose purpose is to help members work together and study for a test.

Study notes: Notes taken for the purpose of reviewing material.

Tactile/kinesthetic learning style: A style that involves learning by touching, manipulating objects, and doing things.

Term: The length of time for which money is lent.

Test anxiety: A temporary condition characterized by fears and concerns about test taking.

Text messaging (texting): Short messages sent from mobile phones to other phones or e-mail accounts.

Thesis: The main point of a paper, typically stating the writer's opinion about the topic of the paper.

Time log: A record of how one spends one's time.

Transcript: A college's official record of courses taken and grades received by students.

Transferring: Changing colleges.

Unique major: Specialization in a particular subject area that is geared to the student's own needs. Not offered by all colleges, and generally requires the support of faculty to oversee the process.

Values: The qualities we see as desirable and most important.

Video message services: Web services that let users communicate using video, voice, and instant messaging.

Visual/graphic learning style: A style that favors material presented visually in a diagram or picture.

Visualization: A memory technique by which images are formed to help recall material.

Voice: The unique style of a writer, expressing the writer's outlook on life and past writing experiences.

Web: A highly graphical interface between users and the Internet that permits users to transmit and receive not only text but also pictorial, video, and audio information.

Web page: A location (or site) on the web housing information from a single source and (typically) links to other pages.

Weekly timetable: A schedule showing all regular, prescheduled activities due to occur in the week, together with one-time events and commitments.

Wiki: A public document, posted on the web, that permits others to add or edit the document collectively.

Working backward: The strategy of starting at the desired solution or goal and working toward the starting point of the problem.

Zero-sum game: A situation in which when one person wins, the other person automatically loses.

Endnotes

Chapter 1

1. The American Freshman: National Norms for 2012," published by American Council on Education and University of California at Los Angeles Higher Education Research Institute.
2. G. Gottesman, *College Survival* (New York: Macmillan, 1994). p. 70.
3. Adapted from D. Lazear, *The Intelligent Curriculum: Using MI to Develop Your Students' Full Potential* (Tucson, AZ: Zephyr Press, 1999).

Chapter 2

1. National Survey of Student Engagement, *2004 Annual Report.*

Chapter 4

1. S. Tobias, *Overcoming Math Anxiety* (New York: W. W. Norton & Company, 1995).

Chapter 5

1. J. D. Bransford and M. K. Johnson, "Contextual Prerequisites for Understanding: Some Investigations of Comprehension and Recall," *Journal of Verbal Learning and Verbal Behavior* 11, 1972, p. 722.
2. P. E. Gold, L. Cahill, and G. L. Wenk, "The Low-Down on Ginkgo Biloba," *Scientific American,* April 2003, pp. 86–91.

Chapter 7

1. L. Liebovich, "Choosing Quick Hits over the Card Catalog," *The New York Times,* August 10, 2000, pp. 1, 6. Based on material from Eliot Soloway, University of Michigan, School of Education.

Chapter 8

1. Based on data from the Bureau of Labor Statistics, 2015.

Chapter 9

1. B. D. Tatum, *"Why Are All the Black Kids Sitting Together in the Cafeteria?" And Other Conversations about Race* (New York: Basic Books, 1997).
2. M. S. Malone, "Translating Diversity into High-Tech Gains," *The New York Times,* July 18, 1993, p. B2.

Chapter 10

1. E. Diener and R. Biswas-Diener, "Will Money Increase Subjective Well-Being?" *Social Indicators Research* 57, 2002, pp. 119–169.
2. The College Board, "Annual Survey of Colleges, 2009."
3. Dr. Sandy Baum and Marie O'Malley, *College on Credit: How Borrowers Perceive Their Education Debt: Results of the 2002 National Student Loan Survey* by Nellie Mae Corporation; The College Board, "Trends in Student Aid, 2008."

Chapter 11

1. L. J. Sax, A. W. Astin, W. S. Korn, and K. Mahoney, *The American Freshman: National Norms for Fall 1999* (Los Angeles: Higher Education Research Institute, UCLA, 1999).
2. R. Carlson, *Don't Sweat the Small Stuff ...and It's All Small Stuff* (New York: Hyperion. 1997).
3. M. Pereira, A. I. Kartashov, C. B. Ebbeling, L. Van Horn, M. L. Slattery, D. R. Jacobs, Jr., and D. S. Ludwig, "Fast-Food Habits, Weight Gain, and Insulin Resistance (The CARDIA Study): 15-Year Prospective Analysis," *The Lancet* 365 (2005, January 1), pp. 36–42.

Index

Mathey, Geraldine F., 324
McPherson, Fiona, 78
Meditation, 285
Meetings, notetaking and, 76
Meleo-Meyer, Florence, 297
Memory skills
    chunking, 125–126
    identifying information and,
        114–115
    memorizing key material, 121–127
    mnemonics, 124–125
    multiple senses for, 126
    notetaking and, 70–72
    overlearning, 127
    reading and, 110–112
    rehearsal, 124
    visualization, 126–127
Mental health, 291–294, 296–297
Mental organization, 10–11
Mentors, 221
Message boards, 179
Meta-message, 63
Microsoft Outlook 2013 Step by Step
    (Lambert & Cox), 56
Miller, Jordan M., 222
A Mindfulness-Based Stress Reduction
    Workbook for Anxiety (Stahl &
    Melo-Meyer), 297
Mind mapping, 72
Mistakes, 102
Mnemonics, 124, 134
Mobile devices, 169. *See also*
    Cell phones
Money matters, 250–278
    budgets, 252, 255, 260–263
    case study, 278
    credit cards, 265–268
    education, value of, 274
    Evaluate, 263
    expenditures and income, 258–260
    financial aid, applying for, 272–273
    financial aid, researching, 271–272
    financial aid packages, 273
    financial difficulties, 263–264, 264t
    financial goals, 255–257
    financial philosophy, 251–254
    funding for college, 268–271
    journal reflections, 252
    Organize, 258–260
    personal story, 275
    Prepare, 255–257
    resources for, 276–277
    Rethink, 263–264
    transferring schools and, 217
    Work, 260–262
Motivation, 12–13

Multiple-choice questions, 85–86,
    96–98
Multiple intelligences, 20–21, 24–25t
Multitasking, 240, 292
Musical intelligence, 22
Musical scores, 186
Myers-Briggs Type Indicator, 22

N

Naturalistic intelligence, 22
Netiquette, 174–176
Nonverbal communication, notetaking
    and, 64
Notebooks, 62
Notetaking, 58–80
    balancing, 68
    case study, 80
    in class, 59–68, 66f
    critical thinking and, 70
    digital annotation, 74
    Evaluate, 70
    goal setting and, 59–60
    hardcopy materials and, 74–75
    journal reflections, 61
    Organize, 60–61
    personal story, 77
    PowerPoint Presentations and, 171
    Prepare, 58–60
    problem instructors and, 68–69, 68f
    processing information from, 62–68
    resources for, 78–79
    Rethink, 70–72
    study notes, 72–73, 73f
    tools for, 60–61
    Work, 62–68
Note Taking Made Easy! (Hippie), 79
Note-Taking Made Easy (Peterson), 78

O

Obesity, 284
Occupational Outlook Handbook (DOL),
    303
Online calculators, 277
Online catalog, 186f
Online databases, 185
Online safety, 175–178
Online tests, 93, 95, 179
Open-book tests, 93
Opening Doors: Understanding College
    Reading (Cortina & Elder), 134
Operant conditioning, 26
Organize. *See* P.O.W.E.R. Learning
    Organize step

Orientation, 218
Orman, Doc, 107
Outline form, notetaking, 65–67, 66f
Overlearning, 127
Overview
    Evaluate, 13–15
    Organize, 10–11
    Prepare, 6–9
    Rethink, 15–17
    Work, 11–13

P

Parents, loans and, 270
Passwords, 177
Pavlov, Ivan, 27
Paying for College Without Going Broke
    2014 (Chany), 277
Pell grants, 270
Perceivers vs. judgers, 23
Perfectionism, 16–17
Periodicals, 185
Perkins loans, 270
Personal data, 306
Personal history, 307–308
Personal interviews, 303–305
Personality styles, 22–23, 25t, 181
Personal stories. *See* Speaking
    of Success
Personal stressors, 281
Personal styles
    academic program, 158–159
    attention span, 116
    course-taking, 180
    learning, 20–21
    listening, 63
    savings, 262
    test-taking, 87
    time management, 35, 52
Perspective, stress and, 287
Peterson, Franklynn, 78
Phillipp, Nichole Whitney, 246
Phishing, 177
Physical abuse, 244
Physical organization, 10–11
Plagiarism, 99, 192
PLUS loans, 270
Podcasts, 169
Poole, Marshall, 248
Portfolios. *See* Career portfolios
Positive thinking, 13, 285–286
Post traumatic stress disorder (PTSD),
    292–293
P.O.W.E.R. Learning Evaluate step
    career planning, 315–316